phenomenology and treatment of
PSYCHOPHYSIOLOGICAL DISORDERS

phenomenology and treatment of PSYCHOPHYSIOLOGICAL DISORDERS

Edited by

William E. Fann, M.D.
Ismet Karacan, M.D., (Med) D.Sci.
Alex D. Pokorny, M.D.
Robert L. Williams, M.D.

all of the

Department of Psychiatry
Baylor College of Medicine
Houston, Texas

S P Books Division of
SPECTRUM PUBLICATIONS, INC.
New York

SPECTRUM PUBLICATIONS, INC.
175-20 Wexford Terrace, Jamaica, N.Y. 11432

Library of Congress Cataloging in Publication Data

Main entry under title:

Phenomenology and treatment of psychophysiological
    disorders.

    Includes index.
    1. Medicine, Psychosomatic.   2. Phenomenological
psychology.   3. Neuropsychiatry.   I. Fann, William E.
[DNLM: 1. Psychosomatic medicine — Congresses. WM 90
P541 1979]
RC49.P46   616.08   81-8812
ISBN 0-89335-151-2   AACR2

Contributors

GEORGE L. ADAMS, M.D.
Professor of Psychiatry
Baylor College of Medicine
Houston, Texas

ROBERT ADER, Ph.D.
Departments of Psychiatry and Psychology
University of Rochester School of
   Medicine
Rochester, New York

PAUL E. BAER, Ph.D.
Department of Psychiatry
Baylor College of Medicine
Houston, Texas

WILLIAM H. BACHRACH, Ph.D.,
   M.D.
Department of Medicine
Baylor College of Medicine
Houston, Texas

STEPHEN A. BERMAN, M.D.
Department of Neurology
Baylor College of Medicine
Houston, Texas

KELLY D. BROWNELL, Ph.D.
Departments of Psychology and Psychiatry
University of Pennsylvania Medical School
Philadelphia, Pennsylvania

NORMAN DECKER, M.D.
Department of Psychiatry
Baylor College of Medicine
Houston, Texas

SABRI DERMAN, M.D., Ph.D.
Department of Psychiatry
Baylor College of Medicine
Houston, Texas

A. SCOTT DOWLING, M.D.
Department of Psychiatry
Case Western Reserve School of Medicine
Cleveland, Ohio

WILLIAM E. FANN, M.D.
Department of Psychiatry
Associate Professor of Pharmacology
Baylor College of Medicine
Houston, Texas

EMILE J. FARGE, M.D.
Department of Ophthalmology
Baylor College of Medicine
Houston, Texas

ARNOLD P. FRIEDMAN, M.D.
Department of Neurology
College of Medicine
University of Arizona
Tucson, Arizona

CHARLES M. GAITZ, M.D.
Department of Psychiatry
Baylor College of Medicine and
Department of Gerontology
Texas Research Institute of Mental
   Sciences
Houston, Texas

EFRAIN A. GOMEZ, M.D.
Department of Psychiatry
Baylor College of Medicine
Houston, Texas

DAVID S. JANOWSKY, M.D.
Department of Psychiatry
University of California School of
  Medicine
San Diego, California

ISMET KARACAN, M.D.(Med.) D.Sc.
Department of Psychiatry
Baylor College of Medicine
Houston, Texas

PETER KNAPP, M.D.
Department of Psychiatry
Boston University School of Medicine
Boston, Massachusetts

JAMES W. LOMAX, M.D.
Department of Psychiatry
Baylor College of Medicine
Houston, Texas

DAVID PATON, M.D.
Department of Ophthalmology
Baylor College of Medicine
Houston, Texas

ALEX D. POKORNY, M.D.
Department of Psychiatry
Baylor College of Medicine
Houston, Texas

DAVID B. ROSENFIELD, M.D.
Department of Neurology
Baylor College of Medicine
Houston, Texas

ALVIN P. SHAPIRO, M.D.
Department of Medicine
University of Pittsburgh School of
  Medicine
Pittsburgh, Pennsylvania

PONCE SANDLIN, M.D.
Department of Psychiatry
Baylor College of Medicine
Houston, Texas

ELIZABETH VENDITTI, B.A.
Department of Psychiatry
University of Pennsylvania Medical School
Philadelphia, Pennsylvania

HERBERT WEINER, M.D.
Department of Psychiatry
Albert Einstein School of Medicine
Bronx, New York

JEANINE C. WHELESS, B.A.
Biological Sciences Research Center
University of North Carolina
  School of Medicine
Chapel Hill, North Carolina

ROBERT L. WILLIAMS, M.D.
Department of Psychiatry
Baylor College of Medicine
Houston, Texas

Contents

Preface

The interrelationships between somatic and psychiatric complaints involve virtually every major organ system and every psychiatric diagnostic category. Psychiatric distress frequently finds expression in physical ailment or pain, and chronic physical illness or disability is a common exacerbant of psychiatric symptoms. The complexity of the interplay between psychological and physiological disease is profound, and many of the mechanisms involved remain undefined or imperfectly understood. Our intention in assembling this volume, the fifth in the Baylor Psychiatry Series, has been to consolidate the most recent medical and psychiatric opinion on the description and treatment of psychophysiological disorders. We have included reviews and new material on disorders long understood to be in the psychophysiological realm, such as gastrointestinal disease, pulmonary reactions, headache, and hypertension. Additionally, there are contributions on conditions less frequently, but no less clearly, recognized as psychophysiological or psychosomatic, including immune response deficits, epilepsy, stuttering, and sleep disorders. Chapters on Couvade syndrome, menstrually related mood disturbance, obesity, keratoconus, and anorexia nervosa examine the degree to which psychological and physical events interact in conditions usually considered attributable essentially to a single system. Drs. Dowling and Gaitz have written excellent reviews of developmental elements in psychophysiological events, and examine such disorders as they are specific to the very young or the very old. Treatment approaches to the variety of disorders are discussed in chapters by Dr. Decker, who describes multifaceted modalities, Dr. Lomax, who examines psychotherapeutic techniques, and in a final chapter on psychopharmacological mitigation of psychophysiological syndromes.

The editors are grateful to the staff of Baylor College of Medicine's Office of Continuing Education for their competent assistance in conducting the symposium from which this volume grew. Bruce W. Richman, Assistant Professor in Baylor's Department of Psychiatry served as managing editor, as he has in each of the previous volumes in this series. We are particularly grateful to the following pharmaceutical manufacturers, who provided partial financial support for the program and again demonstrated their genuine interest in the continuing education of physicians and other health professionals:

Boehringer Ingelheim
Hoffman LaRoche
McNeil Laboratories
Pfizer, Inc.

Sandoz Pharmaceuticals
Schering Corporation
Smith Kline & French Corp.

phenomenology and treatment of
PSYCHOPHYSIOLOGICAL DISORDERS

1

Psychological Elements of Gastrointestinal Disorders

WILLIAM H. BACHRACH

The association of symptoms with an identifiable ("organic") lesion presumed to be the result of psychological factors is called psychosomatic disease. Symptoms for which no anatomical basis can be discovered, occurring in a setting of emotional stress, are conventionally described as psychofunctional or psychophysiological.

With respect to the psychosomatic manifestations, we tend to be less concerned about identifying a precipitating emotional upset or a characteristic personality pattern or unconscious conflict because we do have reliable resources for bringing the somatic lesion under control. For achalasia we dilate the cardia; for peptic ulcer we have effective medical regimens and excellent surgical procedures. For the "functional" disorders, such as the irritable bowel syndrome, we have no uniformly successful medical or surgical measures. In these disorders, therefore, we give special attention to identifying and dealing with the psychological problems underlying the symptoms. We approach this effort with more confidence once the diagnosis is reasonably established.

Since the symptoms of psychophysiological reactions can simulate the symptoms of psychosomatic disease or disease with no psychological substrate, we rarely ever make the differential diagnosis directly. And this is reasonable. The patient with symptoms referable to the gastrointestinal system is entitled to a thorough evaluation with appropriate diagnostic measures, just as are patients with syndromes referable to other systems of the body. However, before the initial interview with the patient is over, the physician should have asked about possible psychological stresses in the patient's life, indicating that this is an important diagnostic possibility. If the diagnostic survey then rules out an "organic" cause, the patient should be reassured of the absence of serious disease and of the importance of recognizing that emotional conflicts underlie the symptoms. This approach extends to the patient an invitation to confide what it is that is bothering her or him (which, by this time, the patient is often ready to do if given permission).

Repetitive diagnostic procedures in search of organic disease are contraindicated, because they displace the focus from the basic problem and increase the patient's concern that something seriously wrong is escaping detection.

Every morning for 10 years a 52-year-old movie producer had to stop on the way from his home to his studio to vomit up his breakfast. Every year during that period he had an upper GI series and a gall bladder X ray and every year they were negative. It is not surprising. There is no known disease of the esophagus, stomach, duodenum, or biliary tract which is characterized by vomiting after breakfast every morning for ten years. To know why the man was vomiting we had to know something about the man. If we were interested we would have found out that the hypocritical conditions of his marriage were intolerable to him.

A 15-year-old girl was admitted to the hospital with a complaint of peri-umbilical and lower abdominal pain of six weeks' duration. According to the history, she had the same complaints for a period of time at age 6, age 10, and age 12; at each of those times she had a complete gastrointestinal evaluation including X rays, and on the present admission she also had a gastroscopy. On examination she was an obese little girl who had trouble describing her symptoms with any precision. None of the examinations, which took a week to complete, showed any abnormality. Thirty minutes spent finding out something about the young lady behind these complaints would have given the clue which would have spared the expense of all the hospitalizations, all the procedures, and all the irradiation.

A 17-year-old captain of his high school football team complained of nausea, early satiety, and a feeling of pressure in the upper abdomen. A clue to the diagnosis would have been forthcoming if someone had asked him one question which he was desperately wanting someone to ask. Instead, he first had to endure an upper GI series, a gall bladder series, a sonogram of the upper abdomen, and an esophagogastroduodenoscopy. Had the attention, instead of being directed at the organs, been directed at the person, it would not have taken long to discover that the young man's symptoms were a somatic expression of a serious sexual conflict.

Considering that there is an important emotional component in *most* patients presenting with symptoms referable to the digestive tract, proper evaluation and management of such patients depend upon the recognition of the emotional aspects of these symptoms, diseases and syndromes. In this chapter, I propose to outline the psychological profiles which have been discerned in various gastrointestinal conditions. These profiles will be considered to consist of first, the psychosocial aspects, which include the personality pattern, the manifest emotional reactions and the precipitating life situation; second, the psychodynamic component—i.e., the unconscious psychic conflict and the symbolic significance of the symptom or somatic disturbance; and third, the psychophysiological interaction, or the organ response to the prevailing emotional processes.

If the reader is not entirely comfortable with the term "emotion," he may take consolation in the knowledge that he is not alone in that respect. It has been said that the word emotion cannot be defined, and in fact one has to make quite a search to find a definition. The simplest, or dictionary, definition is: A state of feeling. Some of the definitions proposed by workers in this field are: "An attitude and the associated bodily changes" (1); the expression of sentiments in whose developments there has been a large measure of cultural or conventional training (2); a highly integrated conative, cognitive, and affective-somatic reaction in which not only the central nervous system but the entire organism functions as a psychological biological unit in its sensitive adaptations to the continually changing milieu (3).

The identification of the respective emotions, while not always simple, is at least assisted by some rather specific guidelines. Resentment is a feeling of indignant displeasure because of something regarded as a wrong or insult. Hostility is antagonism, especially as manifested in action. Regret is wishing that something had not happened. Anxiety is an apprehension or uneasiness, the feeling that something unfortunate is about to happen. For purposes of proper management of patients manifesting this emotion, it is important to distinguish between objective anxiety, also called physiological or appropriate anxiety, which is a reaction to a specified environment occurrence, such as the serious illness of a loved one or impending breakup of a marriage, and neurotic or inappropriate anxiety, which has no apparent basis in the individual's actual life situation.

Fear is usually understood as an emotional state which is a part of the organism's integrated behavior and serves the purpose of warning and adapting the individual to an external danger. Tension, which many consider the same as prolonged anxiety, is characterized by feeling taut, accompanied by a definite effort at control ("uptight," in the current vernacular.)

A fundamental question which recurs in any discussion of psychophysiological or psychosomatic phenomena is the relationship of the type of emotion to the somatic manifestations accompanying those emotions; that is, whether specific emotional states are generally associated with a specific pattern of abnormal gastrointestinal activity or whether the gastrointestinal reactions are the same in a given individual, regardless of the type of emotion experienced. The reader will perceive from what is to follow that the latter is in all probability nearer to the truth.

ANOREXIA

Decrease or loss of appetite on a psychological basis is ordinarily not difficult to recognize, and is usually self-limited. In rare instances a functional anorexia may be sufficiently marked to be diagnosed as anorexia nervosa. This syndrome consists of emaciation, profound loss of weight, obstipation and, in women, amenorrhea. The precipitating psychosocial causes for this condition have been described as prolonged reactions to occurrences which underlie ordinary anorexia, such as bereavements, money losses, disappointment in love, and physical strain (4), homesickness, unhappy home life, and a variety of emotional shocks (5). Patients with ordinary anorexia readily describe their personal problems, symptoms, and peculiar eating habits in a sincere and cooperative manner; insight is preserved and denial is absent. Patients with anorexia nervosa, on the other hand, persist in a stubborn determination to starve themselves, while denying that they are doing so (6).

Beumont et al. (7) recognized two types of patients with anorexia nervosa: one type (dieters) becomes emaciated solely because of dieting, food refusal, and excessive exercise, while the other type (vomiters and purgers) resorted to further means to lose weight, such as habitual vomiting and abuse of purgatives. The prognosis was considered to be better in the former group than in the latter.

Bruch (8), probably the outstanding authority on the subject, finds the personality structure of patients with anorexia nervosa to consist of three components: (i) a relentless pursuit of thinness with body image disturbances of delusional proportions; (ii) a deficit in the accurate perception of bodily sensations, manifest as lack of hunger awareness and denial of fatigue; and (iii) an underlying all-pervasive sense of ineffectiveness.

As for the psychodynamic—that is, the subconscious—level, the consensus seems to be that food is rejected because eating is equated with oral impregnation and oral incorporation of the father's phallus; the associated guilt and anxiety are avoided by not eating or by vomiting after eating. This would hardly apply to the male patient with anorexia nervosa.

The initial treatment is best undertaken by a primary physician who functions as a firm but fair parent-figure determined to correct the nutritional state by whatever measures are necessary to keep the patient from starving to death (9).

ACHALASIA

In a study of 25 patients with achalasia (10), the onset of the dysphagia was found to follow psychic trauma in all but one case, and in 19 cases symptoms were always worse when the patient was under emotional strain. The personality factors common to the group were perfectionism, lack of aggression, sensitiveness, strong feelings of inadequacy, reluctance to express their feelings, and desire to be thought of well. Precipitating emotional factors included resentment or anger, economic loss or insecurity, death of a parent, and feelings of rejection. Many of the patients were depressed.

The psychodynamics and psychophysiology of this condition have not been studied effectively to provide useful information. Cases of cardiospasm treated successfully with psychotherapy have been reported (11).

DUODENAL ULCER

Duodenal ulcer has long been considered a classic example of a psychosomatic disease. At the psychosocial level, duodenal ulcer patients have been described as hard working, conscientious, self-reliant, and serious, with a facade of independence and aggressiveness covering a sense of insecurity and inferiority. "Beneath a placid unemotional exterior there is often a seething struggle, and the battleground is the ulcer-bearing area" (12).

Numerous observations during World War II verified the relationship of emotional stress to the onset of symptoms of ulcer. Among American soldiers ulcer symptoms occurred in some on the day they appeared before their local Board, in others after the first meal was eaten at the reception center. It has been questioned whether these represented exacerbations of preexisting ulcers rather than initial onset; for example, in a study of 125 duodenal ulcer patients in an army station hospital, 90 percent had a definite history of such a diagnosis for an average period of six years preceding their induction into the army (13)

Illustrative of the effect of stress in duodenal ulcer is the difference in the reported rate of remission of ulcer patients in army hospitals when they were told that they were going to be released from service as contrasted with those who were not so advised. Also indicative of the significance of stress is the marked increase in complications of peptic ulcer during air raids in England.

A study of 33 young adults with duodenal ulcer revealed that they were all afflicted with internal strife consisting of a struggle with the environment or an object or a person when nothing could be done about it. The ulcer patient was described as being unable to get outwardly angry; he feels the anger inside, and this increase in psychic tension is connected with the onset of abdominal pain. The observations led the authors to conclude that the ulcer is a result of a sadomasochistic conflict specific for ulcer patients (14).

In an extensive survey of duodenal ulcer disease in the United Kingdom (15), the results were considered to be consistent with the hypothesis that men with a conscientious type of personality were particularly prone to develop duodenal ulcer; this was assumed to be because they set high standards for themselves and experienced anxiety in the course of trying to meet those standards.

Various theories have emerged regarding the psychodynamics of the ulcer patient. On the basis of psychoanalytic treatment of six cases of duodenal ulcer, Alexander (16) published his conclusion that the underlying problem in duodenal ulcer patients is not evident from the personality pattern or the overt reaction but is dependent upon a typical conflict situation in which strong oral receptive tendencies are rejected because of their incompatibility with the aspiration of the adult ego for independence. Garma (17) postulated what he called "the digestive bite"; that is, the repressed desire to bite the breast is transferred to the duodenum, which consequently "bites" the food in the process of digestion.

> The child's upbringing taught him to repress his wishes both to bite the breast and also later to attack other objects in situations which were frustrating to him. But as, in spite of the repression, the wishes persist, not being able now to bite with his mouth, the boy must remove this type of reaction to his stomach or intestine, which then takes up a violent attitude towards food which represents frustrating external situations.

The physiological impact of psychological reactions has been studied far more extensively in relation to duodenal ulcer than any other gastrointestinal disorder. The fact that emotions could affect the functions of the stomach was demonstrated by William Beaumont (18) in his experiments with the gastric-fistula subject, Alexis St. Martin. Subsequently, other gastric-fistula patients have been studied, with similar results.

When Alexander (16) evolved his theory of the conflict situation in peptic ulcer, he envisioned the relationship of psyche to soma as follows: If the intense wish to receive, to be loved, to depend upon others is rejected by the adult ego, then only the regressive pathway remains open; the wish to be loved becomes converted into the wish to be fed. This repressed longing mobilizes the innervations of the stomach, which serve as a chronic stimulus of the stomach functions independent of the normal organically conditioned stimulus— namely, the need of food. Such a stomach behaves all the time as if it were taking or if it were about to take food; hence the sustained hypersecretion.

One aspect of this hypothesis which was relatively new was the suggestion that emotions could *augment* gastric function: prior to that time almost all of the evidence on the effect of emotions on gastric activity indicated that the change was uniformly in the direction of inhibition.

Szasz and his associates (19) were able to produce an elevated acid secretion in an ulcer patient during feelings of intense hostility provoked by a psychiatric interview. The postulated relationship was as follows: The earliest manifestation of displeasure in the developmental history of the human being is the act of crying; this could be considered the infantile prototype of what is known and designated in the adult as anger (hostility). Crying soon assumes a very special meaning for the child, since it learns that every time it cries it gets fed. Thus, there seems little doubt that crying and its affective component of anger become emotionally equated with what they usually or invariably accomplish—namely, being fed; the result is that in the adult with peptic ulcer and probably in many normal adults also, anger produces gastric hyper-secretion and hyper-motility.

Wolf (20) summarized a long series of observations on a gastric-fistula subject named "Tom," who served as an attendant in the laboratory at Cornell University Medical College for many years. By direct observation of the gastric mucosa, simultaneous collections of gastric juice and recording of motility, it was observed that a hyperfunctioning state could be induced by situations which engendered anxiety associated with feelings of hostility and resentment; in these circumstances the mucosa became hyperemic, turgid and engorged and friable.

A rise in gastric acidity observed during examination periods in male students was closely related to the degree of conscious anxiety manifested by these subjects (21).

Sun et al. (22) determined the basal gastric secretory response of a duodenal ulcer patient in nine control studies over a period of seven months, followed by nine studies during which psychological interviews were conducted. The first of seven of these interviews served as an emotionally stressful experience for the patient, and these produced an increase in the acid output on the day of the interview. The last two studies with interviews were not followed by an increase in secretion; the interview no longer acted as a stressful stimulus because of the more mature emotional response of the patient. After several stressful interviews, an increase in gastric secretion occurred in the absence of the psychiatrist, indicating a conditioned response. These responses underwent extinction in one or two months, but reinforcement by another interview resulted in the reestablishment of the conditioned response.

In a population of 2,073 draftees being processed at an army induction camp, Mirsky (23) determined the concentration of serum pepsinogen, an index of the secretory activity of the stomach. Of the 300 who comprised the upper percent of serum pepsinogen values, 63 were selected for special study. Four of the subjects were found to have duodenal ulcer and an additional 5 developed evidence of duodenal ulcer during the course of observation. All 9 of these subjects were in the upper 15 percent of the blood pepsinogen distribution, 8 of them being in the upper 5 percent, and in all 9 significant psychological elements were identified. Of 179 men comprising a hypo-secretor group (those with the lowest 9 percent of the serum pepsinogen distribution) 57 were selected for follow-up and none of these developed ulcer disease.

To keep the picture in perspective, Mirsky wrote: "Those who insist that the development of duodenal ulcer is determined solely by 'organic' factors are as fallacious as those who claim that 'psychic' factors are the sole determinants."

GALL BLADDER DISEASE

Very little work has been done on this subject. I include it merely as an occasion to show the results of an experiment I did (24) showing spasm of the sphincter of Oddi resulting from stress (Figure 1-1).

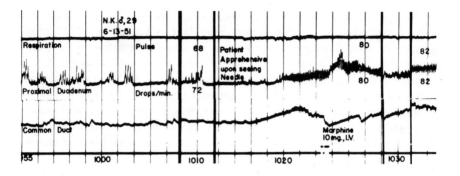

FIG. 1-1. A patient undergoing a study of common duct pressure was fortuitously subjected to an acute emotional trauma. A 29-year-old man with a T-tube in the common duct following cholecystectomy was studied in connection with a series of experiments on the effect of anticholinergic drugs on morphine-induced spasm of the choledochal sphincter. A balloon at the end of a rubber tube was introduced into the duodenum. The common duct was perfused with normal saline at a constant rate under a fixed head of pressure. Intraduodenal and intraductal pressure changes were recorded simultaneously on a multi-channel oscillograph. After a suitable control period, preparations were made for the intravenous injection of morphine. When the investigator approached with the needle-tipped syringe the patient manifested an unexpected degree of apprehension. He protested that he was mortally afraid of "shots" and begged to have the test terminated. During this interval, a spontaneous rise occurred in the intraductal pressure, similar to the pressure elevation which characteristically occurs when spasm of the sphincter is induced by morphine. Following this, a spontaneous increase in duodenal tonus occurred.

ULCERATIVE COLITIS

Attention to the psychosocial aspects of ulcerative colitis began in the early 1930s with reports (25; 26) describing patients with this disease as having an exaggerated sense of neatness, inability to dismiss the effects of an emotional episode, tendency to worry about financial matters, incompatibility or maladjustment in sex life, abnormal attachment to a parent of the opposite sex or to some close relative, and the close relationship between the emotional episode and the onset of bloody diarrhea. The frequency of the onset of the disease between the twentieth and thirtieth years of life was considered significant because it is in this decade that most individuals are called upon to assume adult responsibilities. Conflicts concerned with marriage were commonly found to be associated with attacks of ulcerative colitis. In each case the patients faced their problems in an inadequate, infantile manner.

The outstanding trait in the colitis patients, besides fearfulness, was their emotional immaturity. Of seven men interviewed, all were tied to their mothers except one, who had found a mother substitute in an older sister. None of these men was married and for the most part the onset of the colitis was associated with the conflict with the mother tie and the desire for marriage. The women, who are, more frequently, married, are apt to be housewives of a fussy type, with a marked sense of neatness. Depression is a frequent finding. These appraisals were essentially confirmed by other observers (27; 28).

In children the characteristic personality type in ulcerative colitis has been described (29) as an inability to express feelings of anger or resentment, particularly in relation to parents or figures of authority.

The psychodynamics in ulcerative colitis are often described in terms of the unconscious attitude toward the feces. Diarrhea has been interpreted as expressing a conflict between "giving" in real values or in infantile currency, whereas constipation is considered as a refusal to "give" for value received (16). The diarrhea has been explained as an attempt on the part of the patient to separate himself from the needed object, to whom he clings but whom he gives up in the diarrhea. The impotent rage of his helplessness leads the patient to a need to assert himself, to seek control over the object from which he cannot separate or detach himself emotionally; this he reenacts in the stormy diarrhea, destroying the object which he can neither control nor escape from by reducing it to feces and expelling it repeatedly and forcefully. However, White (30) observed that in every depressed colitis patient, colectomy brought relief of the depression and also a disappearance of the overt negativistic and petulant manifestations of childishness; he therefore doubted that the diarrhea of ulcerative colitis has a symbolic usefulness.

In general it is considered that colitis patients have a disorder of elimination, in contrast with the peptic ulcer patient, who has a disorder of intake. In psychiatric parlance the ulcer patient is an oral character, the colitis patient an anal character.

The reaction of the colon under conditions of emotional stress was investigated (31) in four subjects with colonic fistulas. Anger and resentment were associated with hyper-function of the colon, manifested by hyperemia, engorgement, hyper-motility, hyper-secretion of mucus and the enzyme lysozyme; under these circumstances the colonic mucosa became increasingly fragile and subject to submucosal bleeding and ulceration.

Engel (32), in one of his characteristically exhaustive reviews and thoughtful analyses, questioned the validity of the psychosomatic hypotheses that had been advanced. In his view, the pathological process in ulcerative colitis suggests that the bowel surface is responding as if to a noxious agent of microscopic or molecular size and that the bowel appears to be responding to local areas of surface irritation rather than as part of an integrated excretory act.

Information obtained (33) by the Cornell Medical Index and other assessments of emotional disturbance indicated that both ulcerative colitis and Crohn's disease patients showed a high incidence of life crises during the six months prior to the onset of the disease; more than half of the patients had been seen by a psychiatrist at least once during their lifetimes and approximately 20 percent of the patients had been in psychotherapy.

IRRITABLE BOWEL SYNDROME

This is the classical psychophysiological or psychovisceral gastrointestinal disorder. In a delightful review, Fielding (34) indicates that from the first descriptions of the disease in the early nineteenth century until the early twentieth century, the clinical descriptions concentrated on the extrusion of membranes made up of precipitated mucus; hence the term "membranous colitis," among others. The author was of the opinion that this occurred for two reasons. First, the initial descriptions of a new entity tend to emphasize the more extreme examples and, secondly, the condition at that time was most commonly caused by the abuse of purgatives and/or enemas, the latter often being given with too much water or too much pressure. "Thus, these patients had not only an irritable colon but an irritated one as well." Emotional factors were recognized by some of the observers, but it was not until well into the twentieth century that the irritable bowel syndrome came to be recognized as primarily a "neurogenic illness."

All the clinicians who have addressed the subject are agreed that the irritable colon syndrome is the most common disorder of the gastrointestinal tract; estimates of its frequency vary from 30 percent to 70 percent of all patients with digestive complaints. There is fairly good agreement, also, on the spectrum of symptoms which constitute the irritable bowel syndrome—primarily abdominal pain and symptoms related to the function of the colon. There is either constipation, characterized by delayed and difficult defecation, with the passage of scybalous or ribbonlike stools; or diarrhea, in which the defecation is frequent, especially in the morning and after meals, with a series of soft or liquid stools or sometimes an initial hard pellet emptied by straining and followed by liquid stool, or an alteration of the two types of bowel function. In any case, following defecation the patient is left unrelieved, with a painful abdomen which the patient usually describes as "gas," although there is no evidence of increased gas in the intestine. Other abdominal symptoms may be present, including postprandial distention, heartburn, flatulence, anorexia, nausea, and vomiting. Added to these bowel disturbances, and sometimes occurring without any abnormality of bowel function at all, is a whole host of symptoms which many observers include in the irritable bowel syndrome, such as headache, sighing respiration, lump in the throat, numbness and tingling of the hands, dizziness, spots before the eyes, tremor, sweating, fatigue, exhaustion, palpitation, cold hands and feet, clammy skin. All this is by way of assuming that any generalized autonomic discharge precipitated by an emotional reaction can be labeled the irritable bowel syndrome.

Descriptions of the psychosocial characteristics of patients with irritable bowel syndrome span practically the entire spectrum of life situations and emotions. According to Kirsner and Palmer (35), the syndrome occurs most frequently in people exposed to sustained anxiety and nervous tension and in persons constitutionally predisposed to overreact physiologically to the usual stresses of life.

In this country the most extensive studies of the irritable bowel syndrome are those of Almy, whose observations are summed up in a chapter in Sleisenger and Fordtran's text on gastroenterology (36). Almy found the personality of the patient to be marked by immaturity and dependence upon the opinion of others, and that he was easily discouraged by harsh words or brusque treatment, rigid, conscientious, and moralistic. His standards of performance and behavior may lead him to demand too much of himself and others and to be distressed by many of the conflicts and compromises of everyday living. The patient with spastic constipation was described as usually tense, with ill-concealed hostility and an air of rigid determination to solve his problems. The patient with functional diarrhea was usually soft-spoken, with a superficial attitude of guilt, a countercurrent of deeply buried resentment and a sense of personal inadequacy in dealing with his problems. Patients with alternating constipation and diarrhea showed a remarkable fluctuation in their moods. Thus, the irritable colon was perceived as a bodily change accompanying emotional conflict in response to environmental stress.

Psychological factors in a series of patients studied at Oxford (37) were marital difficulties, anxiety over children, sexual difficulties, financial anxieties, fear of cancer, fear of other major disease, obsessional worrying about many trivial problems, problems related to parents and to business or career. One or more psychological factors appeared to play a part either in the onset of the condition or in causing an exacerbation in four out of five patients. Psychological factors were incriminated significantly more often in women than in men.

Irritable bowel syndrome has been reported to be a symptom of, or to be accompanied by, depression (38, 39, 40, 41) and other affective disorders, primarily anxiety (40) and hysteria (41). In an internal medicine group practice (41), 72 percent of 29 consecutive patients with irritable bowel syndrome had psychiatric illness, compared with 18 percent of 33 controls; the primary physician made an accurate assessment of the psychological states in only 28 percent of the subjects.

The psychodynamics of the irritable bowel syndrome have apparently not been a subject of wide interest to psychoanalysts, considering the paucity of information available. I have indicated in the section on ulcerative colitis that the psychoanalytic theories have dwelt on the significance of constipation and diarrhea in the subconscious mind. Beyond this there is very little to be said.

The physiological consequences of the emotional state in patients with the irritable bowel syndrome have been investigated by measuring pressures in the distal colon (sigmoid and rectum), by direct inspection at sigmoidoscopy, by inflated balloons, by telemetering capsules, by water-perfused polyethylene tubes, and by tape-recording of bowel sounds. The results of these investigations are fairly uniform: colonic contractions tend to be more active, with higher pressures than in controls, and to be more sensitive to physiological (such as food intake), pharmacological, and emotionally stressful stimuli. The differences are quantitative rather than qualitative; i.e., there is no characteristic pattern of colonic motility which identifies the patient with the irritable bowel syndrome.

This concludes what is necessarily a cursory treatment of a very extensive and complex subject. The attempt has been to convey to the reader a sense of the range of observations on the role of emotions in patients with gastrointestinal problems, as an aid in assessing the factors contributing to the production of symptoms and diseases of the digestive system.

Certainly, it is beyond the province of the primary physician to probe into the psychodynamic processes underlying the disorders in his patients, but the primary physician who has the interest and is willing to take the time can deal effectively with the psychological component in most of his patients with GI disorders. Occasionally, he will find it desirable to obtain a psychiatric consultation for an opinion regarding (1) whether an important psychological element can be identified, and, if so, how the primary physician should relate to the patient to assure optimal management; and (2) whether the psychological problem is of such dimensions as to require psychotherapy.

REFERENCES

1. Grace, W.J. & Graham, D.T. Relationship of specific attitudes and emotions to certain bodily diseases. *Psychosom. Med.* 14: 243, 1952.
2. Whitehorn, J.C., Kaufman, M.R. & Thomas, J.M. *Arch. Neurol. Psych.* 33: 712, 1935.
3. Masserman, J.H. Is the hypothalamus a center of emotion? *Psychosom. Med.* 3: 103, 1941.
4. Playfair, W.S. Note on the so-called "anorexia nervosa." *Lancet* 1: 817, 1888.
5. Ryle, J.A. Anorexia nervosa. *Lancet* 2: 893, 1936.
6. Fries, H. Secondary amenorrhea, self-induced weight reduction and anorexia nervosa. *Acta Psych. Scand. Suppl.* 248, 1974.
7. Beumont, P.J.V., George, G.C., & Smart, K.E. "Dieters" and "vomiters and purgers" in anorexia nervosa. *Psychol. Med.* 6: 617, 1976.
8. Bruch, H. Psychotherapy in primary anorexia nervosa. *J. Nerv. Men. Dis.* 150: 51, 1970.
9. Berkman, J.M. Anorexia nervosa: the diagnosis and treatment of inanition resulting from functional disorders. *Ann. Int. Med.* 22: 679, 1945.
10. McMahon, J.M., Braceland, F.J., & Morersch, H.J. The psychosomatic aspects of cardiospasm. *Ann. Int. Med.* 34: 608, 1951.
11. Phillippopoulos, G.S. Three cases of cardiospasm treated successfully with psychotherapy. Catamnestic remarks. *Psychother. Psychosom.* 26: 265–69, 1975.
12. Cathcart, J.P.S. The role of emotions in the production of gastrointestinal disturbances. *Canad. M. Assoc. J.* 55: 465, 1946.
13. Zetzel, L. Peptic ulcer in army station hospitals. *Gastroent.* 3: 472, 1944.

14. Winkelstein, A. & Rothchild, L. Some clinical studies on the psychosomatic background of peptic ulcer. *Am. J. Dig. Dis.* 3: 99, 1943.
15. Doll, R., Avery, & Jones, F. Occupational factors in the etiology of gastric and duodenal ulcers. Medical Research Council Special Report No. 276, 1951. London: His Majesty's Stationery Office.
16. Alexander, F. The influence of psychologic factors upon gastrointestinal disturbances. A symposium: I. General principles, objectives and preliminary results. *Psychoan. Quart.* 3: 501, 1934.
17. Garma, A. On the pathogenesis of peptic ulcer. *Int. J. Psycho-Anal* 31: 1, 1950.
18. Beaumont, W. Experiments and observations on the gastric juice and the physiology of digestion. Plattsburgh: F.P. Allen, 1833.
19. Szasz, T.S., Levin, E., Kirsner, J.B., & Palmer, W.L. The role of hostility in the pathogenesis of peptic ulcer: Theoretical considerations with the report of a case. *Psychosom. Med.* 9: 331, 1947.
20. Wolf, S. Summary of evidence relating life situations and emotional response to peptic ulcer. *Ann. Int. Med.* 31: 637, 1949.
21. Mahl, G.F. Anxiety, HCl secretion and peptic ulcer etiology. *Psychosom. Med.* 12: 158, 1950.
22. Sun, D.C.H., Shay, H., Olin, B., & Weiss, E. Conditioned secretory response of the stomach following repeated emotional stress in a case of duodenal ulcer. *Gastroent.* 35: 155, 1958.
23. Mirsky, I.A. Physiologic, psychologic, and social determinants in the etiology of duodenal ulcer. *Am. J. Dig. Dis.* 3: 285, 1958.
24. Bachrach, W.H., Smith, J.L., & Halstad, J.A. Spasm of the choledochal sphincter accompanying sudden stress. *Gastroent.* 22: 604, 1952.
25. Sullivan, A.J. Psychogenic factors in ulcerative colitis. *Am. J. Dig. Dis.* 2: 651, 1936.
26. Sullivan, A.J. Emotion and diarrhea. *New. Eng. J. Med.* 214: 299, 1936.
27. Groen, J. Psychogenesis and psychotherapy of ulcerative colitis. *Psychosom. Med.* 9: 151, 1947.
28. Lindemann, E. Psychiatric aspects of the conservative treatment of ulcerative colitis. *Arch. Neurol. Psychiat.* 53: 322, 1945.
29. Prugh, D.G. The influence of emotional factors on the clinical course of ulcerative colitis in children. *Gastroent.* 18: 339, 1951.
30. White, B.V. The effect of ileostomy and colectomy on the personality adjustment of patients with ulcerative colitis. *New Eng. J. Med.* 244: 537, 1951.
31. Grace, W.J., Wolf, S., Wolff, H.G. Life situations, emotions and colonic function. *Gastroent.* 14: 93–108, 1950.
32. Engel, G.L. Studies of ulcerative colitis. II. The nature of the somatic processes and the adequacy of psychosomatic hypothesis. *Am. J. Med.* 16: 416, 1954.
33. McKegney, F.P., Gordon, R.O., & Levine, S.M. A psychosomatic comparison of patients with ulcerative colitis and Crohn's disease. *Psychosom. Med.* 32: 153, 1970.
34. Fielding, J.F. The irritable bowel syndrome. An historical review. *J. Irish Coll. Phys. Surg.* 6: 133, 1977.
35. Kirsner, J.B. & Palmer, W.L. The irritable colon. *Gastroent.* 34: 491, 1958.
36. Almy, T.P. Irritable bowel syndrome. In Sleisenger, M.H. & Fordtran, J.S. (Eds.), *Gastrointestinal Disease*, 2nd ed. Philadelphia: Saunders, 1978.
37. Chaudhary, N.A. & Truelove, S.C. The irritable bowel syndrome. *Quart. J. Med.* 31: 307, 1962.
38. Heffernon, E.W. & Lippincott, R.C. The gastrointestinal response to stress (the irritable colon). *Med. Clin. N. Am.* 50: 591, 1966.
39. Dorfman, W. Somatic components of depression. *Psychosom.* 8: 4, 1967.
40. Hislop, I.G. Psychological significance of the irritable colon syndrome. *Gut* 12: 452, 1971.
41. Young, S.J., Alpers, D.H., Norland, C.C., & Woodruff, R.A., Jr. Psychiatric illness and the irritable bowel syndrome. Practical implications for the primary physician. *Gastroent.* 70: 162, 1976.

2

Pulmonary Disorders and Psychosocial Stress

PETER H. KNAPP

This chapter will deal with psychophysiological disorders that affect breathing and the lungs. It will use the term "stress" to refer to a wide range of stimuli. Some of these may be imposed by the purely physical environment; for example, in a patient with emphysema and limited exercise tolerance. The vast majority, however, are social and psychological stimuli. These seldom constitute direct, unidirectional loads to which an individual responds in linear fashion (as he may, for example, to an exercise challenge or to cold). Rather, such stimuli alter the symbolic environment, influence complex intermediate systems, call upon stored maps and plans, involve mixtures of activation and inhibition and learned systems of reward and punishment, often in competition with one another. This emphasis is therefore less on external "stress" than on internal processing and resulting "strain"; the latter occurs within individuals and may reflect itself in disease.

As a start, it may help to look at health and ask what are some of the normal psychophysiological features of breathing and the lungs.

Breathing is a vital, continuous process of intake and elimination, maintaining and regulating; as well, it is maintained and regulated by metabolic factors. Carbon dioxide, affecting the respiratory center, has extensive stimulus control over respiratory rate and volume. Changes in $_pCO_2$ lead rapidly to felt distress, considerably before there is serious threat of tissue damage. Thus, it constitutes an advanced warning system, having greater impact than other regulatory factors, such as oxygen tension, acid base balance, and a number of central reflexes.

Breathing is at a crossroads between the involuntary and the voluntary nervous system. In an involuntary way it responds to many stressful stimuli; these include pain—as pointed out by Dudley (1)—and the mere anticipation of stress. Thus, breathing reflects anxiety and excitement. In addition it is voluntary, in the sense that it can be partly modulated by conscious intent, and in turn can modulate states of arousal, particularly those affecting the cardio-vascular system (e.g., breath-holding in suspense, sighing with relief, a deep breath taken to calm down; this type of respiratory maneuver calls for experimental controls—for instance, when investigating heart rate in conditioning paradigms).

The *lungs* serve breathing, and are also at a crossroads. This is similar to what we find in the upper and lower gastrointestinal tracts; namely, boundary zones between the outer world, reached by apertures of contact, and the inner world, which is for the most part perceptually silent. Sensations, both pleasurable and distressing, originating from the upper airways or outer surface of the chest become ambiguously associated with events occurring in the lungs. Some of the latter are reflexes; for example, coughing or obligatory sighing after a period of restricted lung expansion. Most of those mechanisms assist intake and elimination. The bronchial passages have a powerful eliminative capacity; they are lined with cilia, readily produce profuse secretions, and, above all, contain the mast cell. This is "the only cell type possessing a specific recognition unit, IgE, for a foreign substance and located in the tissues in general, rather than in circulation, hematogenous or lymphatic, so that the physiologic role of this cell in host defense may be to recruit proteins and cells from the circulation in the absence of appreciable local tissue injury" (2). The lungs therefore occupy another interface, with the far-reaching defensive-eliminative barrier formed by immunological systems.

This report will comment on a number of disorders involving breathing and the lungs: smoking, hyperventilation, dyspnea, chronic obstructive pulmonary disease, and, especially, bronchial asthma.

SMOKING

Inhalation of substances for purposes of gratification transcends, but also includes, pulmonary functions—and may lead to the end of those functions. Early psychoanalytic lore suggested that smoking was partially caused by "respiratory eroticism" (3). Although that may seem like an outmoded terminology, it is clear that respiratory behavior, along with oral, manual, olfactory, and visual aspects of smoking, tends to become firmly associated with the complex reinforcing properties of nicotine. These, as Jarvik (4) and others have shown, are explicable by the central effects of nicotine on limbic pleasure centers. Predominantly morphinelike, these effects are interwoven with sympathomimetic arousal, similar to that following administration of amphetamine.

Thus, tobacco inhalation has definite euphoric and energizing impact. Since this appears to last about twenty minutes after inhalation, a truly heavy smoker sustains these psychophysiological effects throughout almost his entire waking existence. By the same token, cessation of heavy smoking leads to withdrawal symptoms, in which vagotonic manifestations are mixed with depressive symptoms having psychological and possibly central nervous system components (5). Depressive tension, mixed with physiological consequences of abstinence, may be the most frequent factor undermining efforts at provoking relapse. (A recent subject spoke of marrying a woman who had three adolescent children, including a pair of identical twins; simultaneously he had given up smoking. Small wonder he stated: "There is no more pleasure in life.")

Motives for maintaining the addictive stage of heavy cigarette smoking are undoubtedly complex; one must be wary of any simple, all-embracing formulation. Another component has been reported, which may be complementary to depressive conflict; namely, the existence among certain heavy smokers of excitement-seeking and a tendency toward bravado and denial (6). When present, such personality features aid in maintaining the habit by blinding the smoker to its obvious hazards.

A similar constellation of poorly recognized danger may exist in the case of marijuana smoking. Marijuana smoke contains a variety of irritants and potential carcinogens, which have been shown to produce malignant change in hamster lung explants (7), as well as impairment of airway conductance in humans (8). Although the number of cigarettes smoked is less for the average marijuana smoker than for a heavy tobacco "addict," the manner of smoking, characterized by deep inhalations and holding the smoke in the lungs, may result in equally dangerous exposure. Further long-range studies are necessary before the risk can be adequately assessed. However, it seems likely that marijuana and hashish, like tobacco, present the problem of a substance with euphoriant quasi-addictive properties, causing potential damage to the pulmonary apparatus through which it gains entrance to the body.

Some of the many *research questions* which suggest themselves are concerned with the seriousness of the pulmonary implications and the possibility of alternative routes of administration, either as an exigency when the drug's effect is sought for palliative reasons in the case of marijuana or as a possible aid to withdrawal when dealing with heavy cigarette smokers. The precise nature of the addictive process, particularly to tobacco, needs further investigation. This is turn may add data about relationships between central nervous subsystems mediating pleasure and those mediating nonspecific arousal. We need to know more about the psychological and social factors which compel large segments of society to seek out the reinforcing effects of tobacco and enable them to screen out awareness of its lethal long-range consequences.

Finally, we need to know more about the mechanisms which permit successful intervention into the subtle processes involved in maintaining addictive smoking. Various techniques of behavior modification seem to be successful in the short run but conspicuously unsuccessful in bringing about long-term changes in smoking behavior. The mental health professions, as a whole, have not shown leadership in combating smoking. In fact there is some evidence that psychiatrists are among the medical specialists least likely to have given up the habit, possibly owing to the lack of tangible feedback they receive about its consequences, in contrast to, say, a chest surgeon or roentgenologist. No therapeutic approach, including efforts at combined group therapy and antidepressant medicine (9), has had unequivocal success over the long haul. Yet people do stop smoking, in numbers going well into the millions. Premack (10) comments on this fact and remarks further:

> The paradox between the failure inside and success outside the laboratory is important for more than a striking example of compartmentalization. How is the paradox to be resolved? Why are millions able to do by themselves outside the laboratory what apparently they cannot be trained to do inside the laboratory? The answer to that question contains, I believe, important suggestions as to how people actually control themselves, in contrast to the kinds of control mechanisms with which they are endowed by current behavior theory.

Premack goes on to suggest the inadequacy of current models, such as that of simple social "stress" as cause, or aversive control as remedy for excessive smoking. We need to study the meaning of tobacco beyond the purely pharmacological pleasure-giving qualities, and also to study the shifts in inner attitude, often sudden, related to self-esteem and self-image, which result in cessation of smoking and in lasting self-control.

Substance abuse is seldom, if ever, a matter of pure psychopharmacophysiology; rather, it involves a variety of shared attitudes and their spread through society. Research into smoking both of tobacco and marijuana must involve individual psychology and more—an examination of sociocultural factors which influence their use and also influence other, related, life-threatening behaviors, such as overeating (cf. Stunkard [11]).

HYPERVENTILATION SYNDROME

This syndrome results from the activation of breathing as part of an anxious emotional state. Overbreathing, and resultant elimination of CO_2, leads to auxiliary symptoms based on respiratory alkalosis; these are, principally, dizziness, numbness, and tingling of the extremities. They interweave with the predominantly autonomic manifestations of anxiety, such as cardiovascular changes. All of them together can lead to a state of fearfulness, bodily absorption, and phobic avoidance of relevant precipitating attitudes and conflicts.

The diagnostic status of this syndrome is confused (it is, in fact, not found in DSM III). Emphasis may be variously placed upon breathing or upon anxiety per se (as in the terms "neurocirculatory asthenia," DaCosta's or "effort" syndrome). The respiratory manifestations—indeed, the anxiety itself—may actually be masked by aggressive, violent, self-destructive, or otherwise uncontrolled behavioral manifestations.

It is important to be alert to and to dissect out the role of abnormal breathing, both as original and precipitant and as a perpetuating factor in patients with this syndrome. The role of hyperventilation can be demonstrated by having the patient rebreathe into a paper or plastic bag, elevating pCO_2, and leading to subjective relief. It is necessary to go beyond symptomatic treatment to make a characterologic diagnosis. Anxiety has diverse sources, although when it crystallizes around hyperventilation one often finds it embedded in a hysterical personality. As a pure syndrome it is infrequent; most often it occurs as a conversionlike elaboration of a wider condition. Thus, it may appear as a complication of one or another form of physiological obstructive pulmonary disease.

Hyperventilation is of *research* interest as one among a number of somatizing processes that may reflect changing sociocultural patterns of disease; also as a testing ground for studying the pathways from the brain to periphery connected with respiratory activation; and, further, as a sample symptom in which behavioral control can readily be established, so as to observe how processes of active mastery, along with suggestion, demonstrates a state of physiological dysfunction during the process of regulation.

DYSPNEA

Dyspnea is defined as "difficult, labored, uncomfortable breathing" (12). As a symptom it overlaps with, but is separate from, hyperventilation (as a sign). Most patients with hyperventilation report feeling short of breath, but not all patients who report feeling short of breath hyperventilate—as Dudley, in particular, has shown (1).

In hyperventilation the patient's focus may be on peripheral symptoms, which only indirectly reflect respiratory abnormality. Dyspnea by definition involves concern with breathing itself.

As already indicated, respiratory integrity is buffered in depth. Like other psychoadaptive sensing systems, the respiratory system has a high potential for exaggerated response to symbolic stimuli.

Put otherwise, the subjective state of dyspnea, like pain, does not necessarily correlate positively with actual signs of impairment. Just as there is a spectrum of pain proneness, shown by Engel (13) and others, individuals show a greater or lesser proneness to report dyspnea. It is elicited by a variety of stimuli—obstruction of the airways, exercise, and the physiological "stress" of intense emotional arousal. In view of this variation and its subjective components—we cannot be clear whether dyspnea represents a unitary phenomenon—whether, for example, dyspnea from severe exercise is the same as dyspnea arising from pulmonary obstruction.

Its variability was demonstrated by Dudley, who provoked dyspnea in two ways, by induction of pain, using a physical stimulus (head clamp), and by suggestion of pain, under hypnosis. The two stimuli appeared to be equally effective in calling forth dyspnea, but there appeared to be two groups of responders. Both groups reported shortness of breath. One, the larger group, showed hyperventilation, presumably designed as preparation for action. The other showed hypoventilation, which Dudley understood as part of the withdrawal-conservation response described by Engel (13).

In other studies, Dudley compared subjective ratings of distress with objective measures of respiratory impairment in a variety of subjects. He found a general lack of positive correlation. Similar findings were reported in 63 subjects, by Heim et al. (14), who examined two behavioral variables: "dyspnea proneness," reconstructed from the subject's history; and a "subjective difference score," based upon the difference between subjectively rated distress and objective respiratory impairment after minimal bronchoconstriction had been induced by Carbachol. Heim studied three groups of subjects: those with psychogenic breathing difficulties, those with asthma, and normals. Dyspnea proneness and subjective-difference score were both significantly highest in subjects with psychogenic breathing difficulties; these measures were intermediate in the asthmatics and lowest in the normal controls. Heim commented on the wide variety of personality types encountered in his subjects. In a crude sense, he felt, they were divisible into aggravators and minimizers, a kind of classification similar to that used in other studies of responses to pain.

In other words, dyspnea involves mechanical and metabolic factors, along with deeply ingrained meanings; these by themselves trigger stereotyped psychophysiological reactions, which further affect breathing.

Research may elucidate but can hardly controvert the truly psychophysiological nature of dyspneic reactions. This fact is of importance in dealing with obstructive pulmonary disease.

CHRONIC OBSTRUCTIVE PULMONARY DISEASE (COPD)

This syndrome results from a number of factors which reduce available opportunity for pulmonary gas exchange. The most common form is the most obscure—a lack of elasticity of the lungs, often, although not always, accompanied by anatomical emphysema. It leads to a series of mechanical difficulties, poor gas exchange, gradual development of hypoxemia, and, finally, carbon dioxide retention.

In such states we see a convergence of the factors mentioned so far. Probably the major etiologic agent leading to COPD is cigarette smoking. There is reason to believe that incidence of this condition is increasing in men over the age of 40.

The disorder leads to variable and increasing amounts of dyspnea. Here we see dramatically the role of psychophysiological disposition. There is a wide variation in subjective distress, and, as mentioned already, little positive correlation between its magnitude and the magnitude of measurable physiological disturbance (again documented by Dudley in [1]).

The British have an elegant terminological division of these patients into "blue bloaters," who are cyanotic and have high blood CO_2 levels, and "pink puffers," who have good skin color or are mildly flushed, breathe vigorously, and have normal CO_2 levels. Traditional views (15) have attributed the difference to lessened "sensitivity" of the respiratory center to CO_2. Some exploratory work has suggested psychological differences between these groups, hypothesizing that the cyanotic, relatively unresponsive "blue bloaters" suffer from "depression" and "giving up," in contrast to sustained compensatory efforts exhibited by their "pink puffer" counterparts. It is not certain that this hypothetical difference will be confirmed, or even that this somewhat arbitrary dichotomy will prove useful; nevertheless, it seems crucial to investigate this group of patients from the viewpoint of overall psychophysiological adaptation.

Therapeutic implications follow from what has been said so far. The need to "assess the total person" must be given more than pious lip service with these patients. Dudley, and also Agle (16) have outlined some of the detailed ingredients of an approach to the social and psychological problems which abound in such populations. First, a team effort is essential. Patients with COPD need skillful medical management to control infection and to maximize general health. Aerosol preparations of sympathomimetic and other bronchodilators and a trial of steroids are important to improve maximally the capacity of the airways. Exercise to tolerance is advised by most individuals working with such patients. Whether or not it produces true physiological benefits, it may enable an individual to cope maximally with his pulmonary disease and counteract an attitude of passive, hopeless surrender to illness.

Secondly, one must be sensitive to maladaptive psychological attitudes: These patients may be overoptimistic and minimize difficulties unrealistically, or they may, to a greater or lesser extent, surrender to their illness, exaggerate, or exploit it.

Thirdly, with these patients, one is facing all the problems of the chronically ill, ultimately dying, patient, and the resultant anxiety, avoidance, and depression and sometimes defensive anger which they evoke in those caring for them.

Research questions center around interaction between these psychosocial factors, in both patients and persons close to them, and the actual pathophysiological features of COPD. To what extent can motivation, mood, and the quality of environmental care influence medical course, and through what channels? What are the limits of technological aids for life support, especially respirators of increasing sophistication, in the face of varying stress loads, physiological and psychological? From a preventive viewpoint, can we identify potentially malignant and self-destructive trends in individuals of high risk, particularly, again, heavy smokers? Recently, Horne (17) pointed out that many of this group, but not all, get emphysema or cancer; they invite prospective investigation of factors predicting illness.

BRONCHIAL ASTHMA

Asthma is one of the disorders described by Dunbar (18) and by Alexander and his colleagues (19) in the first half of this century as psychosomatic. In fact the history of psychological speculations about asthma goes back to antiquity. Hippocrates is alleged to have said, "The asthmatic must guard against anger." It has been studied for many years by literally hundreds of investigators in the psychosomatic arena; yet it still presents puzzles and challenges. See Knapp, Mathe & Vachon (20) and Weiner (21) for comprehensive reviews of psychosomatic aspects.

Definition

Asthma is defined as reversible bronchiolar obstruction due to edema and/or hypersecretion and/or bronchospasm. It is not clear whether it constitutes a homogeneous syndrome. Weiner (21) marshals evidence to suggest that there may be subvariants of asthma, differing in etiology and pathogenesis. He points out the need in asthma, as in other putatively psychosomatic disorders, to make further distinctions—between acute and chronic forms and between predisposing, initiating, and sustaining factors. Kinsman and his colleagues (22) have offered empirical data to support the view that there are, indeed, different varieties of acute asthma.

The traditional division between extrinsic and intrinsic asthma—although boundaries are hard to establish—has withstood the test of time and may well be based upon a difference in underlying mechanisms. A further division, also having hazy boundaries, is based upon the locus of obstruction; some asthmatics have upper airway, some lower airway, obstruction. In the former, neurogenic influences may play the greater role, in the latter, hormonal and/or immunologic processes may do so.

Incidence

The incidence of asthma is hard to assess, partly because of its diagnostic variability and because of the related fact that many variants of asthma shade off into a near-normal state involving rare pulmonary episodes; for example, in persons who have hay fever or who have had respiratory distress as children, which they largely "outgrew." Despite these complicating factors, epidemiological data from different parts of the world show a rough consistency. The cumulative prevalence among children is approximately 10 percent for all allergic disorders and approximately half of that, or 5 percent, for asthma. These percentages are somewhat lower for adults. Smith (23) reports a 2–4 percent prevalence in eight widely dispersed studies of adult asthma. As we go from children to adults, other differences appear. There is a shift in sex incidence: among children, boys predominate by a ratio of 2 or 3 to 1; among adults the ratio is equal or shifted slightly toward female predominance. In any event the disorder affects large numbers of individuals; it is understandable that we must remain cautious about the role of the various factors which have been suspected as etiological.

Genetic Influence

These are generally assumed to play a role in a preponderance of cases of so-called extrinsic asthma, thought to develop in individuals before they reach the age of 14. Textbooks often state that a hereditary basis accounts for more than 50 percent of asthma cases. Yet Edfors-Lubs (24), studying more than 7,000 twin pairs in Scandinavia, found a surprisingly low concordance rate in monozygotic twins. Although it was higher than that in dizygotic pairs, concordance among identical twins was only 19 percent for bronchial asthma, 21 percent for hay fever, and 25 percent for all allergic disorders.

Immunological Influences

These appear to be abetted by genetic predisposition. The crucial immunologic aspect is ready production of the immunoglobulin, IgE, (25, 26). This becomes fixed to mast cells, situated in mucosal layers, especially of the lung (25, 2). Interaction of IgE with antigen leads to the production of a number of possible pathogenetic mediating substances. These have been thought to include serotonin and bradykinin; currently the most important intermediates appear to be histamine and slow-reacting substance of allergy (SRS-a). Histamine is released acutely by the mast cell and causes an immediate vasoactive and hypersecretory local inflammatory response. The mast cell also releases an eosinophile chemotactic factor (ECF-a), which attracts eosinphiles to the reactive site. There, these play a twofold role: they inhibit further histamine release and they contribute to a slower inflammatory destruction of accumulated products. At some point, in ways not entirely clear, SRS-a is also released. It appears to derive from mast cells and possibly other tissue sources, and to be the principal agent responsible for a long-lasting inflammatory phase; this accounts for the sustained manifestations of the allergic reaction. SRS-a, long implicated as the major chemical intermediary in immediate hypersensitivity, has recently been identified chemically from the laboratories of Austen and his colleagues (2).

The important feature, bearing on the role of psychosocial stress, is that a number of other mechanisms, closely related to the central nervous system, interact with and modulate the immunologically based hypersensitivity reaction.

The Autonomic Nervous System—Parasympathetic Activity

The parasympathetic nervous system, particularly the vagus efferents, were thought early in this century to play a prominent role in asthma and other "vagotonic" disturbances. As knowledge of allergy progressed, the role of the nervous system tended to be discredited. However, recent work by Gold and his associates (27), has produced impressive evidence that the vagus, through not only efferent but afferent bundles, plays a powerful potentiating role in experimental asthma in dogs. Gold's paradigm has used dog lungs isolated, chemically and neurogenically, right from left. An allergen introduced to one side produces a broncho-obstructive response bilaterally; this is eliminated by blocking either the descending fibers of the vagus to the opposite lung or ascending fibers from the exposed lung. The evidence thus points to transmission *to* the brain (from allergic irritation) and *from* the brain to the opposite lung as an integral part of the total "allergic" reaction.

Autonomic Nervous System—Sympathetic Activity

The sympathetic nervous system has long been known to counteract the obstructive process in asthma, whatever its ultimate etiological basis. As knowledge of the sympathetic nervous system has increased, its role has been found to be complex. The different receptor systems appear to operate in different fashion in asthma. Beta-adrenergic receptor activity, promoted by drugs such as isoproterenol, produces bronchodilatation and relief of asthma. Alpha-adrenergic stimulation, on the other hand, may well act in the opposite direction, to produce bronchoconstriction (28, 29). There is some evidence that asthmatics suffer from a relative insufficiency, possibly a "blockade," of beta-adrenergic receptors (30), or at the least failure to mobilize beta-adrenergic agonists in response to appropriate asthmatogenic stimulation.

Central Regulation of Bronchial State

A more general view traces a state of equilibrium between sympathetic and parasympathetic nervous influences, starting centrally at the limbic-hypo-thalamic level and extending into the periphery.

Prostaglandins, particularly E and $F_{2\alpha}$, give powerful reinforcement to beta adrenergic and parasympathetic activity, respectively. A final balance is observable at the intracellular level, where the second messenger systems cyclic AMP and cyclic GMP are at equilibrium. Cyclic AMP counteracts bronchoconstriction and release of inflammatory mediator substances from mast cells; cyclic GMP does the reverse.

It is apparent from what has been said that there are pathways from the brain to cells in the lung parenchyma over which neurohumeral influences may affect the inflammatory-allergic reactions involved in asthma. Considerable experimental evidence supports the view that these influences exert a marked modulating effect on asthmatic changes, some clinical evidence suggests they may even initiate such changes.

Neuropsychological Influences in Asthma: Experimental Evidence

Direct intervention at the level of the central nervous system can affect pulmonary processes. Szentivanyi and Fillip (31), and later Luparello, Stein, and Park (32), showed that lesions in the anterior hypothalamus protected rats against graded dosages of antigen to which they had been sensitized. Presumably, the lesions diminished parasympathetic tone in the lungs and thus promoted a relative sympathetic predominance.

An intriguing parallel comes from an experiment with humans by Black (33), who attempted to influence them by deep suggestion under hypnosis. He showed a highly significant shift in the dose-response curve for the Prausnitz-Küstner induced allergic skin response in four subjects selected because of their ability to enter a deep hypnotic trance.

Neuropsychological Clinical Evidence

Clinical evidence, at times difficult to evaluate, is nevertheless abundant and mixed with some ingenious clinical experiments with asthma. Two main lines can be discerned: one points toward specific emotional conflicts as precipitating and sustaining factors in asthma; the other suggests that particular kinds of learning may be involved.

Strong conflictual emotions were implicated in the early formulation of French and Alexander (34) that asthma represented a "suppressed cry for the mother." Alexander and his colleagues (35) attempted to test this view, along with similar hypotheses about six other putative psychosomatic disorders. They studied 70 patients, 10 in each diagnostic category. All of them were individuals under age 40 who had the onset of their syndrome in adult life. Extended, psychiatrically oriented interviews, lasting one to four hours, were edited by an internist to delete medical cues while retaining information about personality and situational features surrounding the first and subsequent attacks of illness. A group of psychoanalytic judges, blind to medical findings, were able to assign the typescripts to the correct psychosomatic category with a highly significant degree of success ($p < .01$ for male and $p < .001$ for female asthmatics). As a control, internist judges were asked to perform the same task. Their overall success rate, apparently based on clever "deduction-by-exclusion," using different cues than those used by the psychiatric judges, did not reach statistical significance ($p < .7$ for male and $p < .1$ for female asthmatics).

Time honored clinical observation has supported the belief that children suffering from chronic asthma, when removed from home, often improve clinically. Lamont (36), in a clinical experiment, brought children into a hospital, then exposed them to massive doses of house dust, to which they had previously shown sensitivity. Nineteen of 20 subjects failed to develop any asthmatic symptoms under this purely allergic provocation. Purcell and his colleagues (37) did an even more convincing experiment. They removed the parents from the homes of children with chronic asthma, sending them on a brief paid vacation. Skilled substitutes not only provided good care during their absence but made meticulous measurements of asthmatic status. Approximately half of the children, in statistically significant correspondence to clinical predictions, showed significant improvement in their asthma.

A number of other studies have tried to identify particular characteristics of asthmatic children, their mothers, or conflicts between them. The early concept of a "rejecting mother" yielded to that of an "engulfing" one, as postulated by Abramsom (38). A study by Block and her colleagues (39) provided evidence that clinicians working with asthma were only in partial agreement about maternal characteristics, raising the possibility of more than one subgroup of mothers and children. In another study, Block et al. (40) brought evidence that there might be an inverse relationship between the allergic potential of a child and psychopathology in the mother. The authors suggested two types of disease—one primarily biogenic, the other sociogenic. This view was reinforced by the findings of Freeman and her associates (41). Purcell, Bernstein, and Bukantz (42) had attempted also to dichotomize the population of asthmatic mothers and children, starting with the concept of "rapidly remitting" asthma, in children admitted to the Children's Asthma Research Institute, who seemed to have more neurotic components in their family backgrounds. Sources of error in such studies are underestimating the physiological complexity of asthma and, at the physiological level, overlooking the possiblity of denial. Individuals or their families may be eager to dismiss psychological contributing factors once definite allergic symptoms have become manifest. Conceivably, these tendencies could be maximal in more severely ill cases.

Jacobs and his colleagues, in two studies (6, 43), present an alternative view. They tested young adult males with hay fever and mild asthma, using selected indices of biological reactivity along with a battery of projective tests, scored blindly. Asthmatic subjects perceived their mothers retrospectively as controlling or rejecting or both; their feelings in this respect differentiated them from healthy comparison subjects. It was possible on the basis of both "allergic potential" alone and "psychological potential" alone for blind judges successfully to select individuals who showed actual manifestations of allergic disease. Jacobs's hypothesis was additive: that both psychological and biological factors are widely distributed in the allergic population and that their joint strength determines the severity of the final disorder.

As described below, intervention at a family level may be an effective therapeutic strategy in asthma; nevertheless, the exact basis for it has not yet been fully explicated.

Learning presents similar problems. The classic report by MacKenzie of an asthma-like state induced in a suggestible woman by a paper rose (44) has been followed, though only intermittently, by studies attempting confirmation and extensions, along two lines. Pure suggestion, in a well-designed series of experiments by Luparello et al. (45), led to demonstration of significant reduction in airway conductance (SGaw) in roughly 50 percent of asthmatic subjects exposed to a bogus "allergen" and tested in a whole body plethysmograph. In a subsequent experiment (46), the reaction was blocked by atropine, pointing to parasympathetic mediation.

An alternative conceptual approach has been to use a conditioning paradigm. Attempts at classical conditioning in guinea pigs by Noelpp-Eschenhagen and Noelpp (47) and by Ottenberg and Stein (48) led to equivocal results. Dekker, Pelser, and Groen (49) reported finding classical conditioned asthmatic responses in humans; however, results were sporadic, and it is not certain whether such positive findings as there were represented true conditioning or responses based on suggestion and compliance. The operant approach has provided a further avenue. Feldman (50), using biofeedback in humans, provided some evidence that airway resistance can be brought under a degree of learned voluntary control, although the extent of this and its clinical usefulness remain to be determined.

Therapeutic Approaches

These have followed the various experimental and clinical models. Asthma poses all the problems of evaluating treatment results in a chronic, remitting disease. At this point it is safe to say that no single approach, biological or psychological, has shown proven efficacy across all kinds of cases.

Acute, life-threatening asthma remains a crisis requiring emergency medical measures, including monitoring of blood gases and heroic doses of steroid medication to counteract potentially lethal inflammatory obstruction. The role of emotional factors in precipitating or exacerbating such crises remains a matter for further research.

Steroid medication has had a profound effect on the long-range management of asthma. Sustained-status asthmaticus is no longer a terrifying and uncontrollable crisis, largely because of steroids. However, their use in long-term maintenance poses many problems. Side effects—abnormal fat distribution, osteoporosis, the propensity for peptic ulceration, cataract formation, and hypertension—are distressing and potentially serious. Moreover, the underlying asthmatic process may persist, masked by medication. Thus, weaning patients from steroid is difficult, and made more so by the fact that large doses of steroids cause physiological suppression of natural pituitary adrenal stimulation, so that a state of physiological dependence develops. Withdrawal is characterized by weakness, lassitude, apathy, and, often, severe asthmatic exacerbation. Gradual reduction of exogenous steroids to a level approaching that produced by the body, aided by stretching the time between doses, as in alternate-day treatment, are aids to the weaning process.

Topical steroids, having a low absorption rate, give further aid in weaning patients. The introduction in Great Britain of Beclamethasone Diproprionate (51) was the initial step in finding these steroids, administered by inhaler, that had negligible systemic absorption. Although irritant side effects are sometimes a problem, accumulating experience with such drugs suggest that many asthmatics can be maintained on them, showing minimal evidence of side effects or adrenal suppression, and that a substantial proportion may be able to do without steroids altogether.

Psychopharmacological and psychological interventions have been reviewed more thoroughly elsewhere (52). Briefly, we may note that by and large, psychotropic drugs have not proven helpful. Some evidence has suggested that tricyclic antidepressants may benefit certain cases, as might have been hoped by virtue of their enhancement of adrenergic tone, coupled with anticholinergic activity. However, results are meager and if there exists a subclass of patients who are benefited, it has not clearly been identified.

Hypnosis, applied as a treatment modality over time, may have cumulative benefits in asthma. Falliers (53) treated 120 asthmatic patients with hypnotherapy, using 115 controlled subjects, treated with suggestion to promote body relaxation. Treatments were at weekly intervals for a year. Both groups showed improvement, the females significantly more with hypnosis. By the end of the treatment, 59 percent in the hypnotized group were better and 8 percent worse, compared to control figures of 43 percent better, 17 percent worse (p < .05). Although it is not possible to exclude a general "physician interest" effect, this nonetheless represents a start in examining an important form of treatment.

Behavior modification has been used in a number of studies. The best was that of Moore (54). In a controlled study, she compared systematic "desensitization," modeled after Wolpe, with two other treatment approaches— simple suggestion and relaxation therapy. She used 12 subjects, half of them children, in a balanced, incomplete block design, permitting comparison of each of three treatments across 8 subjects. All three forms of treatment led to some subjectively reported benefits. Significantly more improvement in peak airflow, the physiological measure used, was found in the group which received behavioral modification. However, a major share of the variance was contributed by two subjects, who received their systematic desensitization at the first treatment given and improved markedly after it. It is possible that random differences between individuals accounted for the findings. Nevertheless, the study remains a landmark of controlled investigation into therapeutic approaches in this area.

An alternative approach was that of Kahn and his associates (55), who attempted to induce asthma by exposing children to psychological stimuli and then to "countercondition" them, helping them to "learn" bronchoconstriction by selectively reinforcing increases in vital capacity and FEV_1. This procedure was repeated on an intensive schedule, then extended over six months in a series of refresher sessions. The group of children thus treated showed a reduction in frequency of asthmatic "attacks," emergency hospital visits, and amount of medication taken. These were significantly greater than reductions shown by a comparison group matched on a number of variables, although, again, we cannot be sure that the comparison subjects received the same overall amount of interest and attention.

Group therapy results were reported by Groen (56). It was combined with an extensive supportive medical and milieu range. Group therapy appeared to enhance the routine medical management, although the degree of control was insufficient to allow firm conclusions.

Family therapy has had dramatic success in the hands of Liebman, Minuchin, and Baker (57). These authors describe seven children, all chronically ill, all effectively cured by this approach. Criteria were reduction of hospitalization, of emergency-ward visits, and elimination of all medicines, including steroids. All of the children were reported to be steroid-dependent, initially. Six of them had had prior individual counseling. If the authors' striking results can be replicated in another sample of comparably ill patients, it will establish this form of treatment on an impressive basis.

Finally, it should be noted that a number of psychotherapists continue to use long-term individual psychotherapy, which is difficult to assess in the aggregate but convincing in individual difficult cases.

Research Considerations

A multitude of questions has been raised by this brief review of asthma. Reversible bronchiolar obstruction is a symptom; we need to know more about possible subtypes, which may have differing etiologic and pathogenetic mechanisms. The shifts in incidence among different age groups raise problems of possible slow-acting psychoendocrine factors which may contribute to the vicissitudes of the disease

Questions about etiology and pathogenesis call for a multifactorial approach. Genetic influences need to be studied in interaction with other etiological factors, including psychosocial influences. Edfors-Lubs's finding (24) of discordance in allergic disease in almost 75 percent of monozygotic twin pairs needs replication; and an effort to do so might throw important light on factors contributing to asthma. The modulating role of central-nervous and neuroendocrine influences upon local allergic processes—and closely related inflammatory processes (58)—needs further investigation. Suggestive evidence from clinical experiments and case studies hints that emotional factors can, in fact, initiate and sustain asthma; yet, this evidence needs to be sifted, extended, and made more rigorous.

Careful research into psychosocial therapeutic interventions is needed, using accurately specified patient groups; there is a particular opportunity and need to contrast different kinds of treatment, either in comparable populations or using a crossover design like that of Moore (54).

Finally, we must return to our opening remarks about use of the term "stress." In one sense the interference with breathing during attacks of this disorder is itself stressful. The variety of coping techniques in different groups has been a valuable area to study (22). If psychosocial factors play a more basic causal role, careful definition is needed. In asthma the pathophysiological mechanisms are not those originally identified by those writing about stress as factors designed to meet external threat and challenge. Asthma is, rather, concerned with defenses against invasion and with elimination of alien substances. Certain types of "stress response" involving, for example, mobilization of the sympathoadrenal system should ameliorate asthma, and actually do so. If emotional factors play some role, along with biological predisposition, in initiating and sustaining asthma, they must be studied in depth and differentiated with precision. We must consider a role for complex emotional patterns, related to depression as well as anxiety, and involving not only activation but inhibition. We must also consider whether complex forms of learning, affecting the involuntary nervous system, may not also be involved in the internal processing of outwardly "stressful" stimuli and in resulting psychophysiological "strain" as a part of the psychophysiology of asthma.

REFERENCES

1. Dudley, D.L. *Psychophysiology of Respiration in Health and Disease*. New York: Appleton-Century-Crofts, 1969.
2. Austen, D.F., Wasserman, S.I., & Goetzl, E.J. Mast cell derived mediators: structural & functional diversity, & regulation of expression in *Mollecular & Biological Aspects of the Acute Allergic Reaction*. (33rd Nobel Symposium). New York; Plenum, 1976.
3. Fenichel, O. *The Psychoanalytical Theory of Neurosis*. New York: Norton, 1945.
4. Jarvik, M.E. The role of nicotine in the smoking habit. In Hunt, W.A. (Ed.), *Learning Mechanisms in Smoking*. Chicago: Aldine, 1970.
5. Knapp, P.H., Bliss, C.M., & Wells, A. Addictive aspects in heavy cigarette smoking. *Am. J. Psychiat.*, 119: 966–72, 1963.
6. Jacobs, M.A. Incidence of psychosomatic predisposing factors in allergic disorders. *Psychosom. Med.* 28: 679–95, 1966.
7. Leuchtenberger, C. & Leuchtenberger, L. Cytological and cytochemical studies of the effects of fresh marihuana smoke on growth and DNA metabolism of animal and human lung cultures. In Brande, M.C. & Szara, C. (Eds.), *Pharmacology of Marihuana*. New York: Raven, 1976.
8. Tashkin, D. et al. Subacute effects of heavy marihuana smoking on pulmonary function in healthy men. *New Eng. J. Med.* 294: 125–29, 1976.
9. Jacobs, M.A., Knapp, P.H., Rosenthal, S. & Haskell, D. Psychological aspects of cigarette smoking: a clinical evaluation. *Psychosom. Med.* 32: 469–85, 1970.
10. Premack, D. Mechanisms of self-control. In Hunt, W.A. (Ed.), *Learning Mechanisms in Smoking*. Chicago: Aldine, 1970.
11. Stunkard, A.J. From explanation to action in psychosomatic medicine: the case of obesity. *Psychosom. Med.* 37(3): 195–236, 1975.
12. Comroe, J.E., Forster, R.E., & Dubois, A.B. *The Lung: Clinical Physiology & Pulmonary Function Tests*. Chicago: Year Book Medical Publishers, 1964.
13. Engel, G.L. Pain: Signs & Symptoms. MacBryde, C.M. & Blacklow, R.S. (Eds.), In *Pain Applied Physiology and Clinical Interpretation*. New York: Lippincott, 1970.
14. Heim, E., Blaser, A., & Waidelich, E. Dyspnea: psychophysiologic relationships. *Psychosom. Med.* 34(5): 405–23, 1972.
15. Howell, J.B.L. Breathlessness in pulmonary disease. In Howell, J.B.L. & Campbell, E.J.M. (Eds.), *Breathlessness*. Philadelphia: Davis, 1966.
16. Agle, D.P. & Baum, G.L. Psychological aspects of chronic obstructive pulmonary disease. *Med. Clin. N. Am.* 61: 749–758, 1977.
17. Horne, R.L. & Picard, R.S. Psychosocial risk factors for lung cancer. *Psychosom. Med.* 41(7): 503–14, 1979.
18. Dunbar, F. *Emotions and Bodily Changes*. New York: Columbia U. Press, 1938.
19. Alexander, F. *Psychosomatic Medicine: Its Principles and Applications*. New York: Norton, 1950.
20. Knapp, P.H., Mathe, A., & Vachon, L. Psychosomatic aspects of bronchial asthma: a review. In Weiss, E.B. & Segal, M.S. (Eds.), *Bronchial Asthma: Its Nature & Management*. Boston: Little, Brown, 1976.
21. Weiner, H. *Psychobiology and Human Disease*. New York: Elsevier, 1977.
22. Kinsman, R.A., Spector, S.L., Shucard, D.W., & Luparello, T.J. Observations on patterns of subjective symptomatology of acute asthma. *Psychosom. Med.* 36: 129–43, 1974.
23. Smith, J.M. Epidemiology and natural history of asthma, allergic rhinitis and atopic dermatitis. In Middleton, E., Jr., Reed, C., & Ellis, E.F., (Eds.), *Allergy: Principles and Practice*, Vol. II. St. Louis: Mosby, 1978.

24. Edfors-Lubs, M.L. Allergy in 7000 twin pairs. *Acta Allerg.* 26: 249–85, 1971.
25. Hamburger, R.N. Allergy & the immune system. *American Scientist.* 64(2): 157–64, 1976.
26. Ishizaka, K. Induction and suppression of IgE antibody responses. In Johanson, S.G.O. (Ed.), *Molecular & Biological Aspects of the Acute Allergic Response.* New York: Plenum, 1976.
27. Gold, W.M., Kessler, G.R., & Yu, D.Y.C. Role of vagus nerves in experimental asthma in allergic dogs. *J. Appl. Physiol.* 33(6): 719–25, 1972.
28. Anthracite, R.F., Vachon, L., & Knapp, P.H. Alpha-adrenergic receptors in the human lung. *Psychosom. Med.* 33: 481–89, 1971.
29. Middleton, E. Alpha adrenergic antagonists. In Middleton, E., Jr., Reed, C.E., & Ellis, E.F. (Eds.), *Allergy Principles and Practice.* St. Louis: Mosby, 1978.
30. Szentivanyi, A. The beta adrenergic theory of the atopic abnormality in bronchial asthma. *J. Allergy* 42: 204–32, 1968.
31. Szentivanyi, A. & Fillipp, G. II. Anaphylaxis and the nervous system. *J. Allergy* 16: 143, 1958.
32. Luparello, T.J., Stein, M., & Park, C.D. Effect of hypothalmic lesions on rat anaphylaxis. *Am. J. Physiol.* 207: 911–14, 1964.
33. Black, S. *Mind and Body.* London: Kimber, 1969.
34. French, T.M. & Alexander, F. Psychogenic factors in bronchial asthma. *Psychosom. Med. Mono.* 4: 2–94, 1941.
35. Alexander, F., French, T.M., & Pollock, G. *Psychosomatic Specificity. Vol. I: Experimental Study and Results.* Chicago: U. of Chicago Press, 1968.
36. Lamont, J. Psychosomatic study of asthma. *Am. J. Psychiat.* 114: 890, 1958.
37. Purcell, K., Brady, K. et al. Effect on asthma in children of experimental separation from the family. *Psychosom. Med.* 31: 144–64, 1969.
38. Abramsom, H.A. Evaluation of maternal rejection theory in allergy. *Ann. Allergy* 12: 129, 1954.
39. Black, J.H., Harvey, E., Jennings, P.H. & Simpson, E. Clinicians' conception of the asthmatogenic mother. *Arch. Gen. Psychiat.* 15: 610, 1966.
40. Block, J., Jennings, E., Harvey, E., & Simpson, M. Interaction between allergic potential and psychopathology in childhood. *Psychosom. Med.* 26: 307, 320, 1964.
41. Freeman, E.H., Feingold, B.F., Schlesinger, K., & Gorman, J.F. Psychological factors in allergy: a review. *Psychosom. Med.* 26: 543–575, 1964.
42. Purcell, K., Bernstein, L., & Bukantz, S. A preliminary comparison of rapidly remitting and persistently steroid-dependent asthmatic chilren. *Psychosom. Med.* 23: 305, 1961.
43. Jacobs, M.A., Anderson, L.S. et al. Interaction of psychologic and biologic predisposing factors in allergic disorders. *Psychosom. Med.* 29: 572–85, 1967.
44. MacKenzie, J.N. The production of "rose asthma" by an artificial rose. *Am. J. Med. Sci.* 91: 45, 1886.
45. Luparello, T., Lyons, H.A., Bleecker, E.R., & McFadden, E.R., Jr. Influence of suggestion on airway reactivity in asthmatic subjects. *Psychosomatic. Med.* 30: 819–25, 1968.
46. Luparello, T.J., Leist, N., Lourie, E.J., & Sweet, P. The interaction of psychologic stimuli and pharmacologic agents on airway reactivity in asthmatic subjects. *Psychosom. Med.* 5: 500–513, 1970.
47. Noelpp-Eschenhagen, I. & Noelpp, B. New contributions to experimental asthma. *Prog. in Allergy* 4: 361, New York: S. Karger, 1954.
48. Ottenberg, P. & Stein, M. Learned asthma in the guinea pig. *Psychosom. Med.* 20: 395, 1958.
49. Dekker, F., Pelser, H.E., & Groen, L. Conditioning as a cause of asthmatic attacks. *J. Psychosom. Res.* 2: 96, 1957.
50. Feldman, C.M. Effect of biofeedback training on respiratory resistance in children. *Psychosom. Med.* 38(1):27–34, 1976.

51. Morrow-Brown, J., Storey, G., & George, W.H.S. Beclamethasone diproprionate: a new steroid aerosol for the treatment of allergic asthma. *Brit. Med. J.* 1: 585–90, 1972.
52. Knapp, P.H. Psychotherapeutic management of bronchial asthma. In Wittkower, E.D., & Warnes, H. (Eds.), *Psychosomatic Medicine, Its Clinical Applications*. New York: Harper & Row, 1977.
53. Falliers, C.J. Treatment of asthma in a residential center—a 15-year study. *J. Allergy* 28: 513, 1970.
54. Moore, N. Behavior therapy in bronchial asthma—a controlled study. *J. Psychsom. Res.* 9: 257–277, 1967.
55. Kahn, A.V. The role of counterconditioning in the treatment of asthma. *J. Psychosom. Res.* 18(2): 89–92, 1966.
56. Groen, J. Experience with and results of group therapy with bronchial asthma. *J. Psychosom. Res.* 4: 191, 1960.
57. Liebman, R., Minuchin, S., & Baker, L. The Use of Structural Family Therapy in the Treatment of Intractible Asthma. *Am. J. Psychiat.* 131(5): 535–40, 1974.
58. Lichtenstein, L.M. The interdependence of allergic and inflammatory processes. In Johansson, S.G.O. (Ed.), *Mollecular & Biological Aspects of the Acute Allergic Reaction*. New York: Plenum, 1976.

3

Pathophysiological Aspects of Hypertension

ALVIN P. SHAPIRO

The psychophysiological aspects of hypertension comprise the set of blood-pressure responses which result from noxious stimuli of behavioral origin. Such responses may play a role in the predisposition, precipitation, and perpetuation of hypertension, and in turn their alleviation may represent a therapeutic modality in its management. However, these psychophysiological factors must be considered in the context of hypertension as a multifactorial disorder; it is a disturbance in the complex regulatory mechanisms which control the relationship between the circulating fluid volume (i.e., cardiac output) and the space in which it circulates (i.e., peripheral resistance). The system includes neural, renal, hormonal, and cardiovascular mechanisms, which in turn influence each other through multiple feedback devices to maintain normal blood pressure and oxygen delivery to peripheral sites in the body. The psychophysiological responses operate through any and all of these basic mechanisms to produce their impact.

The validity of this concept is supported by clinical experiences and by experimental studies in animals and man, but the precise and quantitative nature of the psychophysiological effect and the manner in which it integrates with other stimuli in the production of maintenance of hypertension remains elusive. Reasons include problems in quantifying the effect of behavioral stimuli, the retrospective nature of most individual case analyses, and the difficulty in preventing such stimuli, or controlling them in an experimental context. Moreover, because a stimulus has psychological impact often only because it has meaning to the specific individual, it may seem ephemeral to the observer, while acute changes observed in blood pressure fail to establish whether chronic disease can be produced. Nevertheless, although behavioral influences, in common with most other causal mechanisms in hypertension, rarely provide a single explanation for the disease, the available evidence has increasingly documented that the effects of behavioral change must be considered seriously among the variables which combine to explain the pathogenesis of this multifactorial disorder.

PATHOGENESIS

It should be understood that the primary mechanisms involved in production of an effect on blood pressure by noxious stimuli of behavioral origin is neural, and that the brain and central nervous system (CNS) are the perceptive organs in exerting their impact. Yet, it should also be clear that the CNS in turn mediates its effects through peripheral mechanisms which include the renal, hormonal, and cardiovascular pathways. Similarly, the peripheral mechanisms in turn can influence the brain and behavior so that in a very literal sense the components of reactivity involved in hypertension are not singular, but parts of a finely tuned system whose disharmonies evoke hypertensive disease. Thus, the pathophysiology of behaviorally induced hypertension must be examined in the same fashion that the pathophysiology of hypertension in general is approached. In fact, almost all of the mechanisms involved in the control of blood pressure and the development of hypertension which have been studied psychophysiologically have been shown to be responsive to noxious stimuli of behavioral origin. Such influences can be demonstrated in acute experiments and occasionally in chronic studies.

Starting at the global level of the effect of the environment on blood pressure, a number of epidemiological studies affirm that hypertension occurs with greater frequency in populations suggestively under greater behavioral stress. Thus, blacks have a higher prevalence of hypertension in this country than do whites, and studies have demonstrated that socioeconomic level among blacks may inversely correlate with this increase. Higher blood pressures have been associated with rapid cultural change in several areas of the world and with socioeconomic mobility. The argument has been made that contemporary man is faced with continuous conflict and uncertainty, which lead to cardiovascular adjustments appropriate to physical actions he might take in a primitive society, but which he no longer can utilize in present-day society. Studies of chronic behavioral stimulation in animals, ranging from noise and electric shock in rats and avoidance conditioning in monkeys to the elegant studies of social crowding in mice by Henry and his group, have demonstrated the production of elevations of blood pressure. Common to many of these situations in both animals and man, the environmental stimulus usually involves the need of the organism to adjust to a situation which has in it elements of constant threat and uncertainty, and the presence of an acquired or genetic cardiovascular or renal susceptibility.

With the brain as the perceptive organ for these environmental influences, the mechanisms by which the central nervous system transmits changes to the periphery which increase cardiac output and/or peripheral resistance are, primarily, the sympathetic nervous system and the production and release of norepinephrine. Much attention has been given to the peripheral mechanisms involved in norepinephrine metabolism within recent years, as well as to the midbrain and medullary centers which mediate adrenergic discharge. The nucleus tractus solitarius in the medullary area of the brain is the relay station to stimuli coming from the periphery by way of the baroreceptors in the carotid sinus, and passes these onto the vasomotor centers in the medulla. A variety of experiments have shown that the destruction of the nucleus solitarius leads to sustained lability of blood pressure and, in fact, in some animal models, to chronic hypertension.

Pituitary factors such as ACTH have long been known to induce peripheral changes in adrenal function after responding to stress which can affect blood pressure through increases in adrenal cortical secretions. Vasoconstrictor polypeptides such as vasopressin are released from the brain in response to stimuli and may play a role in transmitting peripheral resistance changes. Similarly, other releasing factors from the hypothalamus may be indicted in such responses, although there is a paucity of such data.

The pathophysiological mechanism of hypertension which has undergone most intensive study in the past several decades is the renin-angiotensin-aldosterone system. Among the several factors which mediate renin release from the kidneys are autonomic nervous system stimulation and norepinephrine. Peripheral renin activity levels can be shown to be raised by psychological stimulation in animals and in man, and in turn this can influence aldosterone and sodium metabolism. We have shown in studies in rats that stressors also will increase the vascular responsivity to infused angiotensin. Angiotensin has effects on behavior in terms of producing thirst and apparently represents at least a primitive control mechanism concerned with water intake. This is demonstrated clinically in patients with severe renin-dependent hypertension who may suffer from inordinate thirst to the point where it is impossible to halt their seeking of water and marked overexpansion of body fluid can develop. Moreover, there appears to be an independent renin-angiotensin system in the CNS itself which could influence thirst and vasoconstrictor receptors, and does not necessarily respond to peripheral stimulation.

The control mechanisms of the cardiovascular system, both central and peripheral, can respond directly to psychophysiological stimuli. Again, usually these effects are through autonomic nervous system mechanisms. Stressors will increase heart rate and also increase peripheral resistance by effects on beta-receptors and alpha-receptors respectively. Since blood pressure is the product of cardiac output and peripheral resistance, the relative proportion to which each of these is affected determines the peripheral outcome as reflected in blood pressure. Of considerable interest are the data from a number of investigators, that cardiovascular responses of cardiac output or peripheral resistance may be exquisitely specific to different behaviors. For instance, studies by Zanchetti and coworkers have indicated that cats prepared to fight (agonistic behavior) display vasoconstriction and diminution of cardiac output; while during defense, behavior involving movement increases in cardiac output and muscle blood flow develop. These specific patterns may arise from different centers in the brain and may interreact when the behavior involves multiple activities.

One aspect of the brain's involvement in hypertension is the indirect effect of certain overt behaviors on blood pressure. Epidemiological studies have demonstrated correlations between elevated blood pressure and salt intake. Certainly these differences in salt intake in different populations cannot simply be due to the availability of salt; they must also relate to salt-seeking behavior, which has been a fundamental part of the evolution of the vertebrate from a marine animal to a terrestrial animal. Similarly, obesity, which relates both to prevalence and mortality from hypertension, can be considered as a behavioral aberration that affects the cardiovascular system.

Past efforts concerned with behavior and hypertension have concentrated on the concept that hypertensive individuals have a specific personality pattern. This pattern has been variously described, but generally presented the hypertensive as a person with inhibited aggressive tendencies who suppressed his hostility. More recent work has suggested that these attributes of personality reflect the impact of "awareness" by the hypertensive of his pressor hyperreactivity to a variety of stimuli which cause him in turn to avoid conflictual situations and confrontations. This is an intriguing approach which requires further investigative study.

What ties these psychophysiological phenomena to the other mechanisms involved with hypertension is the fact that most theories which have evolved about the development of hypertension, whether it be essential (primary) or one of the secondary types, require an integrated multi-factorial etiology. Dr. Irving Page quite a few years ago referred to this as the "Mosaic Theory." We have argued that there are a plethora of causes of hypertension; we do not need more causes but rather an understanding of how the various mechanisms integrate with each other. For instance, it is clearly apparent that when various influences cause overexpansion of fluid and increased cardiac output, there is a diminution in "space controlling" factors (vasoconstriction), as seen, for instance, in falling levels of renin activity and norepinephrine. Similarly, when there are strong vasoconstrictive influences, volume and cardiac output may sharply decrease. Behavioral induction of hypertension probably represents a situation in which an appropriate stimulus has invoked massive activation of several of the systems, which eventually cannot be counterbalanced by checks and balances. This may lead to renal functional impairment and its consequences, or, as Falkow has described, to changes in peripheral resistance developing from increased flow through vessels, with the establishment of a permanent state of increased vasoconstriction. Thus, we need to look carefully at field theories of causation of hypertension to develop our understanding of how the system breaks down from unbalanced stimulation. This is now readily apparent in some types of hypertension. For instance, when an individual has a pheochromocytoma, the large amounts of norepinephrine which are released cannot be effectively counterbalanced. Similarly, when a patient has a renal artery lesion releasing renin autonomously or a primary aldosterone tumor causing sodium and water retention, eventually, counterbalances cannot resist these effects. Likewise, when severe emotional turmoil occurs in a genetically endowed individual who has increased peripheral reactivity or excess salt intake, hypertension may be precipitated or perpetuated.

TREATMENT

Behavioral treatment of hypertension in its simplest definition is therapy aimed at alleviating the input of noxious stimuli of psychological origin. In this sense behavioral treatment does not represent a new idea in the management of this disease. Clinicians have long recognized that relief of anxiety—whether it be by repeated measures of blood pressure in an individual who is made tense and apprehensive whenever he enters the doctor's office, by reassurance about the level of blood pressure and its meaning, by removal from an anxiety-provoking situation at home by bringing the patient into a hospital, or by psychotherapy, ranging from supportive to analytic—can at least temporarily invoke falls in levels of blood pressure. Suggestion as a "hypotensive agent" has been recognized classically by the fact that placebos can have profound effects on blood pressure levels, and has led to the development of complicated clinical pharmacological designs to test out new drugs. Thus, reassurances, psychotherapy, environmental changes, and attempts to have the patient live a more relaxed life style have been used for many years and actually antedate drugs in the treatment of high blood pressure.

In recent years, considerable interest has developed in more specific behavioral techniques which include relaxation therapies and biofeedback. These paradigms have certain advantages in that they are specific techniques which can be taught to the patient. Results to date have shown modest short-term effects, particularly with relaxation therapies. Careful analysis of results of such therapies has indicated that the antihypertensive results are similar to those which have been achieved in the past by more indirect behavioral techniques, and that further study is necessary concerning the duration and pragmatic applicability of these techniques in the overall management of the illness. They should not be considered as alternatives to appropriate drug therapy or to other nonpharmacological techniques such as weight loss and reduction of sodium intake, but as supplements to such management. It is also appropriate to point out that many of the modern-day pharmacological therapies, such as beta blocking drugs, owe much of their effect on blood pressure to blocking the end organ response to various noxious stimuli.

Behavioral techniques can be useful in solving the problem of medication compliance among hypertensives. Most patients with hypertension are asymptomatic and do not recognize the need to take daily medication for protracted periods. Educating patients about the hazards of uncontrolled blood pressure elevation is often not sufficient. Some investigators have found that specific behavioral techniques which offer "rewards" to the patient for medication compliance, particularly when added to educational efforts and measures to increase convenience, can increase compliance remarkably and lead to better control of blood pressure. Similarly, behavioral techniques can help patients to lose weight, diminish sodium intake, and stop smoking, all of which can improve blood-pressure control.

Study of the psychophysiological aspects of hypertension has become increasingly productive. The surge of knowledge about hypertension over the last few decades, although primarily concerned with understanding physiological and pharmacological mechanisms in the development and treatment of hypertension, has also led to an increased awareness of the psychophysiology of the disorder. We should continue to investigate the behavioral aspects of the disease, without encumbrance by the other theories of stress and the hypertensive personality, neither of which has value, any longer, in understanding the interrelationship of behavioral and physical factors in the etiology and management of hypertension.

REFERENCES

1. Shapiro, A.P. Stress and hypertension. In Gavras, H. & Brunner, H.R. (Eds.), *Clinical Hypertension*. New York: Dekker, in press.
2. Shapiro, A.P. Essential hypertension—why idiopathic? *Am. J. Med*. 54: 1–4, 1973.
3. Weiner, H. Psychosomatic research in essential hypertension; retrospect and prospect. In Koster, M., Musaph, H. and Visser, P. (Eds.), *Psychosomatics in Essential Hypertension*. Basel: Karger, 1970.
4. Cohen, D.H. & Obrist, P.A. Interactions between behavior and the cardiovascular system. *Cir. Res*. 37: 693, 1975.
5. Henry, J.P. & Stephens, P.M. *Stress, Health, and the Social Environment*. New York: Springer, 1977.
6. Weiner, H. Psychobiology and human disease. In *Essential Hypertension*. New York: Elsevier, 1977.
7. Shapiro, A.P., Swartz, B.E., Ferguson, D.C.E., Redmond, D.P., & Weiss, S.M. Behavioral methods in the treatment of hypertension I. Review of their clinical status. *Ann. Int. Med*. 86: 626, 1977.
8. Schwartz, G.E. Biofeedback and patterning of autonomic and central processes: CNS-cardiovascular interactions. In Schwartz, G.E. and Beatty, J. (Eds.), *Biofeedback: Theory and Research*. New York: Academic Press, 1977.

4

Psychophysiological Aspects of Headache

ARNOLD P. FRIEDMAN

Any discussion of the nature of headache brings to the forefront its psychological aspects. That emotional disturbances may cause headache is accepted, although the exact mechanism by which emotions gain access to the structures that react painfully is still undetermined. Headache of psychological origins may produce symptoms in two different ways: indirectly, as a symbolic attempt to solve a problem, or directly, as alterations of specific physiological functions. These alterations are very often the physiologic expression of an existing emotional-feeling or -tension state. The mechanisms by which functional headaches are produced include (1) changes in cranial blood vessels, (2) sustained muscle contraction of the neck and/or scalp, (3) alterations in glandular function, and (4) conversion of psychological conflict into physical symptoms, as is seen in cases of conversion hysteria. In the latter, psychic energy derived from repression is converted into a physical symptom or sign (1).

The symptoms serve as a means by which the patient discharges tensions and avoids overt expression of anxiety through psychological mechanisms. In some patients, however, all of the mechanisms already described can be observed simultaneously. Delusions and hypochondriacal states associated with disturbance of body images may also produce headache.

Headache with a psychological origin represents a symbolic attempt to solve a problem (2) and, for example, may thus be:

1. A method of handling nonspecific stress.
2. A manipulation of family members in an attempt to adapt to an almost intolerable family situation.
3. A means of coping with a threatened outburst of rage.
4. Body symptoms symbolic of body conflict.
5. A forerunner of pending major life-change situation, usually unconsciously perceived.
6. A method of dealing with an unchangeable life impasse.

7. A substitute for a major psychological illness, as a means of communicating a catastrophic life situation to oneself and the world.
8. A manifestation of a severe body-image problem.
9. An expression of resentment of authority and the temptation to rebel against it.
10. A need to inhibit sexual temptations.
11. Delusions of hypochondriacal states associated with disturbances of body image very much like the body-image problem.

In any case, the underlying emotional problems usually exist beyond the conscious awareness of the individual. The psychoneurotic (or any other) person is rarely aware of the number of times he is anxious, or of the circumstances that provoke the anxiety.

In effect, then, psychogenic headache is only one potential product of the neurotic personality. Therapeutically, one cannot hope to relieve the patient by merely abolishing the headache.

While it may seem desirable to distinguish between psychogenic headache and muscle-contraction (tension) headache when considering them as abstract entities, in actual practice, making a confident distinction is far from easy, and frequently both components are present. The pure psychogenic headache is rare, and for the most part the physician's attention can be directed to the management of muscle-contraction headache.

It should also be obvious that drug use or local organic pathology may also set into motion the same headache-producing mechanisms, particularly in the case of drug dependency, which, over a period of years, will help to continue the headache along with the other psychological dynamic situations. The headache dominates and becomes a way of life for the patient.

MIGRAINE

A common and more specific type of headache that appears to result, at least in part, from localized psychophysiological vascular reaction is migraine. For centuries it has been recognized that the arousal of emotions serves as a precipitant for an attack of migraine. Although it is tempting to establish a migraine profile and fit the patient to it, all migraine patients do not share the same personality traits. However, many patients with analogous emotional problems are not troubled with migraine. For a brief psychological characterization of a person with migraine, I would say that he has not successfully learned to handle aggressive energy, either his own or that of others, and that during his early years he was conditioned to value the approval of others more than his own. In addition, a patient with migraine is generally intense, striving, orderly, overly conscientious, meticulous in performance, exacting in his requirements of others and himself, and tends to become immersed in a morass of detail. But many patients without migraine have this same personality.

Such behavior is bound to be frustrating because it cannot be maintained with consistency. To support this kind of behavior is enervating. It can be maintained without stress only as long as energy reserves are high, as they usually are during childhood. Migraine occurs more commonly during adolescence or later, when, with increasing responsibility and decreasing energy reserve, a difficult way of life becomes harder to maintain. The migraine patient has been conditioned to use his wits to the exclusion of his feelings, with intellect assuming undue precedence; the choice of the head as a focus of pain is perhaps a natural outcome. The attack usually erupts in a setting of unconscious anger associated with sustained resentment, anxiety, and frustration in what may be thought of as a state of energy depletion.

The migraine type of vascular headache can be defined (3) as a familiar disorder characterized by periodic recurrent headache widely variable in intensity, frequency, and duration. Attacks are commonly unilateral in onset, often associated with anorexia, nausea, and vomiting. They may be preceded by or associated with neurological and mood disturbances. The headache is dramatically modified by vasoconstrictor agents. There are a variety of types of migraine in which all these characteristics are not necessarily present in each attack or in each patient (4).

On occasion, nonspecific stimuli that may not be stressful for the average person can produce an attack in the migrainous individual. Such attack-triggering factors include fatigue, bright or flickering lights, fasting or missed meals, certain chemicals in prepared foods and beverages, excessive caffeine consumption, some drugs, and exposure to less than normal atmospheric pressure.

Pathogenesis

The pain of vascular headache of the migraine type is the result of the combined effects of large-artery dilatation plus the action of pain threshold-lowering substances accumulating in the blood vessel walls and perivascular tissue (5). The prodromes of classic migraine, especially the visual and other sensory and motor phenomena, are indications of a central nervous system origin for migraine.

A possible sequence of events has been suggested by direct measurements of cerebral blood flow (6). First, a phase of vasoconstriction involving the intracranial arteries with a reduction of blood flow of sufficient degree to produce the initial symptoms, followed by the ischemic changes associated with the prodrome of the attack, and a second phase of vasodilatation, primarily of the extracranial arteries, during which the headache occurs. However, the distribution of these vascular changes does not correlate well with the clinical features of the episode of migraine.

The two phases are not always sharply separated. For example, some cortical areas show vasodilatation at a stage when vessels in other areas are still constricted (7). Furthermore, the reduction in cerebral blood flow may outlast the relatively brief aura time span; and similarly the distribution of increased cerebral blood flow may not correlate well with the locale of the headache. A recent study of cerebral vasomotor responsiveness to 5 percent CO_2 in migraine patients indicated that during the headache phase of migraine, the cerebral hemisphere on the side of the headache showed significantly greater CO_2 response than the nonheadache hemisphere. During the prodrome of migraine there was bilateral impairment of hemispheric CO_2 responsiveness (8).

Other factors include the presence of mediators of inflammation or vasoactive materials that are important to vascular permeability and are elaborated about the painful dilated arteries that characterize migraine. Studies carried out with patients suggest that the dilated migrainous arteries are hyperpermeable and are involved in a sterile local inflammatory reaction in which vasoactive substances and platelets participate. The vascular permeability may be influenced by the release of vasoactive substances from their reservoirs in the circulation or tissue sites. Present evidence implicates at least five and possibly more groups of vasoactive substances associated with arterial inflammation and increased permeability. Among the substances that have been suggested as being involved are the amines (serotonin, catecholamines, adrenaline and noradrenaline, histamine, tyramine, phenylethylamine), the polypeptides (bradykinin and angiotensin), and the free fatty acids, including the prostaglandins. The question arises in all investigations as to whether we are studying the effects or the cause of migraine.

It has been hypothesized that serotonin released from platelets in migraine first causes a vasoconstriction and is then adsorbed to the vessel wall, combining with histamine and kinins to increase the sensitivity to pain of the affected arteries. Second, the drop in plasma levels after adsorption and metabolism of the released serotonin diminishes the tonic constrictor effect that would normally tend to counteract that of any dilator substance such as histamine, bradykinin and PGE_1 (9).

Irrespective of the role of metabolic, humoral, or immunological changes in the genesis of migraine, some explanation must be found for the asymmetry of the process, because headache and focal neurological symptoms usually implicate one side more than the other. The reason for selective involvement of the vascular tree is unknown.

It is appropriate to mention that the patient who has chronic recurring or constant pain quite often develops or has a depressive reaction. It has been suggested that depression may be associated with underactivity of brain norepinephrine or brain serotonin. Patients with pain would seem to have a serotonin-type depression, if the administration of chlorimipramine, a tricyclic antidepressant, is any index. It acts primarily to block reuptake of brain serotonin, relieves depression, and reduces pain more than does amitriptyline, which has reuptaking, blocking effects on both serotonin and norepinephrine. Acceptance of this theory of increased central serotonin activity suggests that there may be possibilities for the development of analgesics that may be more appropriate for chronic use than narcotics. However, I find somewhat fragile the evidence that the lowering of one of a variety of endogenous substances that occur in other conditions as well is the sole chemical responsible for the depressive reactions associated with chronic pain.

Some patients with migraine have depressive features as part of the attack or at times depression as equivalent to a migraine attack. I call your attention to the fact that a depressed patient has mixed feelings of communication and that he shows psychological as well as physiological manifestations. For example, he may describe his depression as well as his head pain as a "hurt," an "ache," "severe pressure," or "soreness." Other overt manifestations may be malaise, weakness, sleeplessness, constipation, and appetite disturbance. These all may be tied in with his pain problem. When one scratches the depression at any depth, he may find that such patients are raging at someone or something and have internalized the rage, have had a recent loss or disappointment, or have frustrations, a sense of failure, a loss of respect or love, an unresolved sexual problem or complications, or a concealed secret.

MUSCLE-CONTRACTION HEADACHE

Muscle-contraction headache has also been termed "tension," "psychogenic," "nervous," and "rheumatic" headache. It is generally agreed that emotional factors appear to be a common precipitant for muscle-contraction headaches both in terms of the psychophysiologic translation of anxiety into physical symptoms and in terms of a symbolic communication of distress (10).

The immediate sources of pain in this type of headache appears to be sustained contraction of the muscles of the neck and scalp. This is commonly associated with an adverse reaction to life's stress. Lewis (11) demonstrated that voluntary muscle contractions of over two minutes' duration produce pain often outlasting the contraction itself. According to Hinsey (12), the pain impulse is conveyed from terminal branches in the adipose and connective tissues of the muscle to their afferent nerve fibers in the adventitia of small vessels. The mechanism of chronic muscle-contraction headaches is similar to that of chronic muscle contraction in any area of the body.

The clinical picture is similar in all of these headaches; they have no prodromes and are usually bilateral (90 percent) but may be unilateral. Most patients locate their discomfort in the back of the head and neck. However, any area of the head may be involved in any combination. The headaches may cover the head like a cap or hatband. They may be accompanied by anxiety, dizziness, and bright spots in front of the eyes. These headaches are nonpulsatile, which differs from migraine, and they vary widely in intensity and frequency. They rarely interfere with sleep. Muscle-contraction headache is not accompanied by any of the focal neurological symptoms that may occur with migraine (10).

The unconscious choice of headache as an expression of anxiety can be governed by many factors; as an example, scalp and neck muscles may be "set" according to attitudes about the environment, external or internal. Concern with climatic conditions such as exposure to the sun or to drafts may produce tension headache in some persons, or the feeling of a draft may be characteristic of a personality in which suffering gains a type of control over the environment. The individual literally uses the musculature of his head and neck to maintain his external appearance of composure while he represses his feelings.

The physician should be alerted to the common error of trying to correlate sources of tension in the patient's life situation to the onset of a specific headache. The emotional conflicting factors that contribute to the production of tension headaches are complex and are often unrelated to direct sources of tension or anxiety.

The tension headache may also be a phenomenon secondary to other types of headache or pain disorders in the head or neck. Such conditions as refractive error or eye muscle imbalance, chronic mastoid disease, cervical spondylosis, and malocclusions of the temperomandibular joint may cause a person to set the muscles in a posture that, if maintained for prolonged periods, may result in secondary pain.

TREATMENT OF THE HEADACHE PATIENT

Present-day concepts of pain have produced a number of theories—electrical, chemical, and psychological—that may influence the approach to the treatment of the headache patient. Liebeskin (13) has shown that electrical stimulation of mesencephalic periaqueduct gray matter and the region of the dorsal vagal nucleus produces analgesia by stimulation of the serotonergic system. Dietary or chemical depletion of brain serotonin levels increases sensitivity to pain. Administration of the precursors, tryptophan and 5-HTP, restores normal sensitivity. Serotonin is probably the transmitter of descending inhibitory pathways that arise in the raphe nucleus of the medulla (14).

Other neurotransmitters besides serotonin, especially dopamine, also appear important in pain biochemistry. Dopamine enhances the effect of postmorphine analgesia and brain-stem stimulation and may be the transmitter that serves to promote ascending inhibitory pathways to the brain-stem reticular formation.

The recent discovery of opiate receptors and endogenous opiatelike compounds, the endorphins, in the central nervous system and pituitary gland has refocused attention on the anatomical and physiological substrates of pain and pain modulation (15). The endorphins are a class of endogenous brain constituents that bind to opiate receptors. They have potent opiate properties and are attached to the specific brain receptors for morphine. Active work is now being done to elucidate their role in stress, pain modulation, and narcotic addiction and to determine the possibility of developing nonaddictive analgesics from these compounds.

It must be understood that in treatment of head pain there are three parallel centers interacting and modulating sensory input: the neo-spinal-thalamic projection, which is discriminative; the reticular limbic structures, from which a motivation drive triggers the organism into action; and the neocortical centers, in which attention, suggestion, and anxiety play a part. This histological principle suggests that the ultimate of total pain relief from a given form of therapy will not be achieved for all patients. Headache is not a simple one-to-one relationship of stimulus and sensation. If the drug is given for headache, we are evaluating the original pain sensation and its mechanism, the associated anxiety in the patient, and a secondary increase in dysfunction, which includes the additional pain sensation accompanying anxiety.

Pharmacological Approaches

Pharmacological approaches to the treatment of headache have been based not only on treating the symptom of headache but also on treating the underlying cause and associated symptoms. There have been few agents developed in recent years solely for the treatment of head pain.

The various antiheadache agents introduced cover a broad spectrum of pharmacological action and include the analgesic agents, psychopharmacological agents such as antianxiety, antidepressive, and antipsychotic drugs, agents that modify vasoactive substances and those that block receptor sites, such as the beta-adrenergic blockers, and a variety of miscellaneous drugs such as anticonvulsant and anti-inflammatory agents, as well as hormones and antihistamines. These appear and reappear as recommended treatment for headache, as they have throughout the years. More headaches are treated with ordinary analgesics—i.e., drugs that decrease pain without causing loss of consciousness—than with any other group of drugs. No new nonnarcotic analgesic has been developed that is better than acetylsalicylic acid (aspirin). Aspirin and aspirinlike drugs in adequate amounts inhibit the biosynthesis of prostaglandins in tissues of all species so far studied. There is evidence that establishes this biochemical action as the basic mode of the therapeutic action of aspirinlike drugs as anti-inflammatory, analgesic, and antipyretic compounds. It may also account for the shared side effects, including the hypersensitivity to aspirinlike drugs, shown by some allergic patients.

The principal pharmacologic agents suggested for the treatment of migraine include the following:

1. Those producing vasoconstriction: e.g., ergotamine tartrate, serotonin, norepinephrine, and other sympathomimetic amines.
2. Those stimulating the action of serotonin on receptor sites: e.g., methysergide (Sansert), cyproheptadine (Periactin), and Pizotifen (BC 105).
3. Those blocking beta-adrenergic receptors on blood vessels and thereby preventing vasodilatation: e.g., propranolol hydrochloride (Inderal).
4. Those preventing the depletion of serotonin and possibly other vasoactive amines (catecholamines and histamines) by interfering with the action of their deactivating enzymes: e.g. monoamine oxidase inhibitors.
5. Those acting by inhibiting the uptake of norepinephrine and serotonin, including the tricyclic antidepressants such as imipramine hydrochloride (Tofranil) and amitriptyline hydrochloride (Elavil).
6. Those having a direct stimulating effect on arterial alpha-receptors, e.g., clonidine (Catapres).
7. A miscellaneous group, including tranquilizers, sedatives, anticonvulsants, muscle relaxants, heparin, and lithium carbonate.

For attacks of severe, persistent muscle-contraction headaches, the nonaddictive analgesics alone are seldom effective. Acetylsalicylic acid is the most practical and useful analgesic for head pain of low intensity. The pain threshold can be raised and anxiety reduced by use of a nonnarcotic analgesic sedative or tranquilizer-drug combination.

Psychotherapeutic Approach

The most effective prescription for chronic headache is dynamic psychotherapy, which allows recognition of conflict and modification of the underlying pathological personality structure. Psychotherapy may cover a wide area, from supportive (including relaxation therapy) to long-term treatment. In general the physician's skill and the patient-physician relationship determines the success or failure of the therapy. Therefore, effective management pivots on competent counseling by the physician or, in some cases, psychotherapy by a psychologist or psychiatrist.

Other Approaches

Physical therapy, including gentle massage, hot packs, cervical traction, and cervical collars, should be considered in the treatment of muscle-contraction headache. Injections of local anesthetics into trigger areas of spastic muscles can bring dramatic but usually temporary relief. Correcting faulty posture may prevent recurrence, but this requires a great deal of time and effort. Biofeedback and other autogenic techniques are now under consideration.

As our understanding of the influence of chemical agents on the behavior of the individual increases, we may be entering a new era, in which our present concepts of the pathogenesis and treatment of headache will be markedly altered. However, our knowledge of the direct effect of certain chemical agents on the brain chemistry has not reached the stage to permit substituting chemical agents for the treatment of the total patient by the dual approach of psychotherapy and pharmacotherapy.

In closing, it might be noted that the ills of the people are rarely caught on the printed page. The physician-writer, with the neatness of his manual, is not always related to the world of medicine, where he must consider at all times the person behind the distress, maintain a constant concern for the kind of person he is treating, and draw on his own personal experience with that symptom.

REFERENCES

1. Kolb, L.C. Psychiatric and psychogenic factors in headache. In Friedman, A.P. & Merrit, H.H (Eds.), *Headache: Diagnosis and Treatment*. Philadelphia: Davis, 1959.
2. Frazier, S.H. Psychotherapy of headache. In Friedman, A.P. (Ed.), *Research and Clinical Studies in Headache*, Vol. 30. Basel: Karger, 1972.
3. Ad hoc committee on classification of headache. Classification of headache. *Arch. Neurol.* 6: 173–176, 1962.
4. Friedman, A.P. The infinite variety of migraine. In Smith, R. (Ed.), *Background to Migraine*, Vol. 1. London: Heinemann Medical, 1970.
5. Dalessio, D.J. Mechanisms of headache. In Friedman, A.P. (Ed.), *Headache and Related Pain Syndromes*. Philadelphia: Saunders, in press.
6. Marshall, J. The regulation of cerebral blood flow—its relationship to migraine. *Arch. Neurobiol.* 37 (suppl.): 15–25, 1974.
7. Edmeads, J. Cerebral blood flow in migraine headache. *Headache* 17: 148–52, 1977.
8. Sakai, F. & Meyer, J.S. Abnormal cerebrovascular reactivity in patients with migraine and cluster headache. *Headache* 19: 251–66, 1979.
9. Lance, J.W. Migraine. In Matthews, W.G. & Glaser, G.H. (Eds.), *Recent Advances in Clinical Neurology*. Edinburgh: Churchill Livingstone, 1978.

10. Friedman, A.P. Characteristics of tension headache. *Psychosom. Med.* 20: 457–61, 1979.
11. Lewis, T. *Pain.* New York: Macmillan, 1942.
12. Hinsey, J.C. Observation on the inervation of blood vessels in skeletal muscle. *J. Comp. Neurol.* 47: 23, 1928.
13. Liebeskin, J.C. Pain modulation by central nervous system stimulation. In Bonica, J.J. (Eds.), *Advances in Pain Research and Therapy,* Proceedings of the First World Congress on Pain, Florence. New York: Raven, 1976.
14. Sternbach, R.A., Janowsky, D.S., Huey, L.Y., & Segal, D.S. Effects of altering brain serotonin activity on human chronic pain. In Bonica, J.J. (Eds.), *Advances in Pain Research and Therapy,* Proceedings of the First World Congress on Pain, Florence. New York: Raven Press, 1976.
15. Basbaum, A.I., Clanton, C.H., & Fields, H.L. Opiate and stimulus-produced analgesia: function anatomy of a medullospinal pathway. *Proc. Natl. Acad. Sci. USA* 73: 4,685–88, 1976.

5

The Etiology
and Treatment of Obesity

KELLY D. BROWNELL
ELIZABETH M. VENDITTI

Obesity is one of the most common, yet most puzzling, disorders of modern times. Cultural views of excess weight range from high regard to abhorrence. The prevalence of obesity within many societies has changed dramatically over time. Even within the United States, the prevalence of obesity varies widely among cultural and ethnic subgroups. The scientific community maintains that obesity is a complex phenomenon with multiple origins, yet the public view of the obese person is a rather simple one of a weak-willed individual who is gratified only by eating to excess.

Obesity has been a major concern for centuries (1). In 399 B.C. Socrates issued this warning to overweight persons:

> Beware of those foods that tempt you to eat when you are not hungry and those liquors that tempt you to drink when you are not thirsty.

In 1825, Jean Brillat-Savarin, the French gourmet, offered his cure for this tenacious problem (2):

> Any cure for obesity must begin with the three following and absolute precepts: discretion in eating, moderation in sleeping, and exercise on foot or on horseback.

William Beaumont described the plight of the obese person in 1883 (3):

> In the present state of civilized society with the provocation of the culinary art, and the incentive of highly seasoned foods, brandy and wine, the temptation to excess in the indulgences of the table are rather too strong to be resisted by poor human nature.

Fortunately, science has gone beyond attributing obesity to "poor human nature." Great strides have occurred in the assessment of the physiology of adiposity and in the study of treatment methods. There are many new frontiers in this exciting area. The search encompasses questions as basic as "What makes a person eat, and what stops eating once it begins?" The information exists among the disciplines of physiology, biology, metabolism, nutrition, psychology, sociology, anthropology, and psychiatry. We will attempt to bring some order to this diverse collection of information.

THE PREVALENCE AND HAZARDS OF OBESITY

Obesity is the number-one nutrition problem in the United States (4). Thirty percent of men and 40 percent of women between the ages of 40 and 19 are at least 20 percent overweight (5). The prevalence is even higher with advancing age (6), with decreasing socioeconomic status (7), and a variety of ethnic groups (8). The prevalence of obesity is high even in children. Between 10 and 15 percent of young children are obese (9, 10); this increases to 30 percent by adolescence (11, 12). Parents and physicians hoping that an obese child will "grow out of it" are hoping for an event which is unlikely indeed. Eighty percent of overweight children become overweight adults (13). Stunkard and Burt (14) estimated that if childhood-onset obese persons have not slimmed down by the end of adolescence, the odds against their doing so as an adult are 28 to 1. It is clear that obesity affects a large percentage of the American population. What are the consequences?

The Medical Hazards of Obesity

Obesity is associated with a number of serious disorders (15). Insulin insensitivity and diabetes mellitus are more common among obese persons than among thin persons (16, 17, 18). Pulmonary function is more likely to be impaired in obese persons (19, 20, 21), and renal problems have been noted in massively obese persons (15, 22). Obesity is also associated with surgical risk (23), greater risk with anesthesia (24), and complications during pregnancy (25).

The most important medical complication of obesity is its association with coronary heart disease (26, 27). Gordon and Kannel (28) have used the results from the Framingham Study to conclude that obesity plays an important role in heart disease, probably through its influence on blood lipids, blood pressure, and carbohydrate intolerance. Kannel et al. (29) have shown that relative weight is positively correlated with elevated low density lipoprotein (LDL) cholesterol. Hypertension is more common among obese persons than among thin persons (30, 31). Some researchers claim that obesity is not a coronary risk factor independent of its effect on blood pressure and on blood lipids (32), but other studies indicate that such an independent effect does exist (27). Gordon and Kannel (28) have noted: "Obesity is probably the most common metabolic disorder affecting mankind. It is a serious condition adversely affecting several organ systems, causing decades of disability and contributing to premature death."

There are many medical benefits of weight reduction. These include improvement in glucose tolerance (33), decreased blood pressure (30, 34) and decreased cholesterol and triglycerides (35, 36). Alexander and Peterson (37) studied the cardiovascular effects of weight loss in nine grossly obese patients. Table 5-1 shows that every parameter of cardiovascular function improved after weight loss. Gordon and Kannel (38) estimate that if everyone were at optimal weight, there would be 25 percent less coronary heart disease and 35 percent fewer episodes of congestive failure and brain infarctions. Recent data from the Framingham study (27) indicate that "because it reversibly promotes atherogenic traits like LDL, low HDL, diabetes and hypertension, correction of overweight is probably the most important hygienic measure (aside from avoidance of cigarettes) available for the control of cardiovascular disease."

TABLE 5-1
Effects of Weight Loss on Measures of Cardiovascular Function in 9 Grossly Obese Patients. Adapted from Alexander and Peterson (37); reproduced by permission.

Measure	Before	After
Weight (kg)	112 to 218	53 kg loss
Heart rate (min^{-1})	73 ± 10	68 ± 8
Stroke volume (ml)	107 ± 15	92 ± 17
Left ventricular stroke work (g-m)	150 ± 29	110 ± 29
Left ventricular work (kg-m/min)	11.1 ± 3.9	7.4 ± 2.0
VO_2 (ml/min)	360 ± 82	247 ± 43
Cardiac output (1/min)	7.9 ± 1.8	6.2 ± 1.2
Systemic arterial pressure (mmHg)	102 ± 16	87 ± 12
Blood volume (1)	7.8 ± 1.5	6.1 ± 1.4

The Psychological Hazards of Obesity

The psychological difficulties of obesity have only recently been studied. Not all obese persons suffer long-term consequences from their excess weight, but the psychological perils of obesity for many people can be far-ranging, disabling, and permanent (39, 40).

The most common psychological concomitant of obesity is body-image disparagement. Body image refers to a person's picture of his or her physical appearance, and to the associated feelings and judgments. Body-image disturbance in the obese is characterized by a feeling that one's body is grotesque and detestable, and that others view it with contempt and hostility (40). This is particularly true of persons who have been overweight since childhood. This disturbance can lead to intense self-consciousness and to feelings that others are uniformly negative in their view of overweight people. Consequently, obese persons with negative body images tend to be withdrawn, shy, and socially immature (40). These reactions are similar to those of persons suffering from deformities of the face, breasts, and genitals.

Preoccupation with weight is common among obese persons. The obese person may view all people in terms of body weight, to the exclusion of more important attributes. He or she may feel envy for thinner persons and contempt for fatter persons (40). This obsession lingers even in persons who have dieted successfully and have maintained normal body weight for many years (14). The preoccupation with weight can influence both intellectual and physical performance. Some persons may attribute academic and professional setbacks to their obesity, thus placing little importance on personal performance. Obese persons often avoid interactions that would call attention to their physical appearance (e.g., shopping for clothes with others). Dining in public may also be avoided because the obese person may feel his or her eating is the subject of constant scrutiny.

The social consequences of obesity can be devastating (41). Obesity is generally devalued in industrialized countries (40), and this bias can breed insecurity. Monello and Mayer (42) studied obese high-school girls at a summer camp and found that the girls showed passiveness, obsessive concern with self-image, expectation of rejection, and progressive withdrawal—all similar to traits shown by members of minority groups who are victims of prejudice.

The social bias against obesity is surprising in both its magnitude and its early development. In one study, boys ages 6 to 10 assigned characteristics to silhouettes of fat, thin, and muscular boys (43). Responses to the muscular silhouette were uniformly positive, whereas the fat body type evoked objectionable labels including lazy, sloppy, cheat, forgetful, naughty, dirty, ugly, and stupid. Two other studies had children and adults rate six line drawings depicting a normal child, a child with a brace on one leg and crutches, a child sitting in a wheelchair, with a blanket covering both legs, a child with one hand missing, a child with a facial disfigurement, and a grossly overweight child (44, 45). The overweight child was consistently ranked as least likable, irrespective of the rater's sex, age, race, socioeconomic status, or disability. Obese persons suffer not only from the social stigma of their excess weight, but also, unlike persons with other physical disabilities, they are blamed for their condition. The terms used to characterize obese persons (self-indulgent, gluttonous, and so on) connote responsibility.

The most important psychological hazard of obesity may lie in the attempt to lose weight. The obese person is under unrelenting pressure from family, friends, acquaintances, and society in general to lose weight. The value of thinness is internalized at an early age, and most obese persons embark upon a career of repeated diets. The average patient in our clinics has been on 10 or more formalized diet programs, and has undertaken countless informal attempts to "cut back." This desire to reduce is so powerful that ordinarily rational people can be seduced into buying miracle devices, creams, pills, and diet books.

Dieting is clearly related to untoward emotional symptoms (46). In one retrospective study of 100 obese persons, 54 percent experienced emotional symptoms at least once, 21 percent experienced nervousness, 21 percent weakness, 8 percent irritability, 5 percent fatigue, and 4 percent nausea (47). In another report, 50 percent of obese persons experienced the onset or intensification of depression when dieting (48). Stunkard concluded: "Most forms of dieting carry with them a high likelihood of emotional disturbance" (49). This is one reason why repeated bouts of weight loss followed by weight gain may be more dangerous than static obesity (50). Fortunately, some recent forms of treatment, most notably behavior therapy, have minimized the untoward consequences of dieting.

ETIOLOGY AND CONTRIBUTING FACTORS

The development of obesity is quite complicated. Even the basic mechanisms of hunger and satiety are surprisingly complex. There are at least 25 different ways to experimentally induce obesity in animals, and there may be at least as many contributing factors in humans. The causes for obesity in an individual may even change over time. Thorough discussion of the multiple causes of obesity can be obtained elsewhere (15, 51). We will, however, outline some of the most recent developments in research on the behavioral, biological, social, and psychological determinants of obesity.

Behavioral Determinants—Eating versus Exercise

Body weight is a function of the balance between energy intake and energy expenditure. Weight gain can result from increased intake, decreased expenditure, or both. The treatment of obesity has traditionally involved a reduction in food intake. In fact, when obese persons attempt to lose weight, a restriction in consumption is nearly always the primary concern. This is a natural consequence of the widely held belief that obese persons eat far more than normal-weight persons, and that weight loss will occur if the obese can be taught to eat "normal amounts." Food consumption is typically assigned a more important role in the development and treatment of obesity than is energy expenditure. Is this justified?

Wooley et al. (52) addressed the issue of whether obese persons eat excessively, and noted, "The belief that obese people 'overeat' is so widespread that one wonders if this conviction will give way to the actual data on this question." More than 20 studies have been published on food intake in obese and lean subjects; the studies are consistent in showing that the intake of heavier subjects is less than or equal to that of the thinner subjects (52, 53). There are methodological problems with many of the studies; most have been done with adults and have concentrated on eating outside the home. However, the consistency of their findings is striking.

The role of energy expenditure in the development of obesity has been studied by comparing the physical activity of obese and normal-weight persons. Rose and Mayer (54) mechanically recorded physical movements in overweight and normal-weight infants, and found the overweight infant to be less active. Studies using parental report or self-report of activity have shown obese adolescents to be less active than their thin peers (55, 56). Bullen, Reed, and Mayer (57) reported relative inactivity in obese adolescent girls, using motion pictures taken during several sporting activities. Aside from the motion-picture study, the studies showing inactivity in obese children have relied on subjective measures of activity. Four studies using more objective measures (pedometers or heart-rate monitoring) showed no difference between obese and nonobese children (58, 59, 60, 61).

Waxman and Stunkard (62) carried out the most extensive comparison of obese and nonobese children. Caloric intake and energy expenditure were measured directly for four boys during meals and play at home and in school. The activity levels of the boys were converted to caloric expenditure by obtaining oxygen consumption measures in the laboratory. The results were surprising. The obese boys consumed more calories than did their nonobese brothers at supper, and far more calories than their nonobese peers at school. The obese boys ate faster than their controls in both settings. Time-sampled measures of activity showed that the obese boys were far less active than their controls inside the home, slightly less active outside the home, and equally active at school. However, when these values were converted to energy expenditure, using the oxygen consumption information, the obese boys expended more calories per unit of activity than did their controls. Consequently, there was no difference in caloric expenditure between the obese and nonobese boys inside the home, while the obese boys actually expended more calories outside the home and in school. From this study and from those listed above, it appears that obese children are at least as active as nonobese children. The picture may be different in adults.

Obese adults appear to be less active than nonobese adults, as measured by self-report (63, 64), pedometers (65), a device that discriminates sitting from standing (66), and the spontaneous use of stairs in lieu of escalators in public places (67, 68). No study of adults has as yet converted these measures of activity into measures of caloric expenditure.

Energy intake and energy expenditure may play different roles in the genesis, maintenance, and treatment of obesity. Obese children appear to consume more than normal-weight children, although more research is needed in this important area. The obese children, however, are as active, if not more active, than their thin peers. In adults, obese persons appear to eat no more than normal-weight persons, but appear to be less active. This suggests that physical inactivity may be more a consequence than a cause of obesity, and that it may play a role in the maintenance of excess weight (69). The reasons for differences in patterns between children and adults are not clear. In addition, the degree to which these factors indicate the most fruitful means of treatment has not been established.

Biological Factors

The biology of obesity encompasses studies in many areas. These include the physiology of adiposity, the metabolic relationship between energy intake and output, and the basic study of hunger and satiety. These studies have generated many possible explanations for the development of obesity. We will outline two of the most prominent theories, the set-point theory and the adipose cellularity theory. These represent some of the most interesting developments in the field, but are by no means the only working theories on the subject.

The Set-Point Theory

Keesey (70) noted that complex organisms maintain remarkable stability in their internal environment. Using an engineering term, each physiological system could have a "set-point" regulator that controls input and output to maintain regulatory balance. There is some evidence that humans have such a set-point for body weight and that, in the presence of weight changes, psychological and metabolic changes occur to defend the suitable body weight (71). Suitable body weight is determined by many factors, most notably genetics, prenatal conditions, early feeding experiences, and hypothalamic development (15). The set-point may vary among individuals so that obesity may be the ideal physiological state for some persons. The remarkable failure of most obese persons to lose weight and to maintain the loss may reflect the tenacity to which the body adheres to a certain weight.

Many studies have demonstrated that laboratory animals will adjust food intake and activity to compensate for changes in body weight produced by forced feeding or food restriction (72, 73). Lesions of the lateral hypothalamus and the ventromedial hypothalamus respectively, will cause hypophagia and hyperphagia in animals; these changes are accompanied by reliable changes in body weight. These animals will subsequently defend a new body weight, as if a new set-point had been established. Mitchel and Keesey (74) showed this in lateral hypothalamically lesioned rats whose weights were lowered via food restriction below the already reduced levels (Figure 5-1). Humans also tend to regulate body weight around a defined point, in the face of experimental starvation (75) or excessive feeding (76).

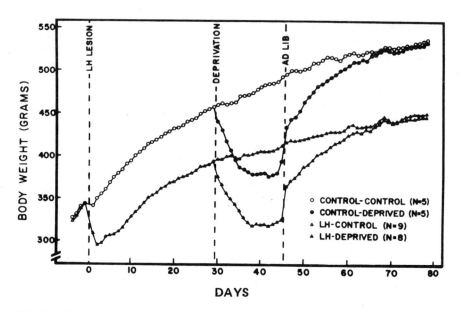

FIG. 5-1.   Recovery of body weight by control and lateral hypothalamically lesioned rats, following
a period of food restriction. The body weights of the control-deprived and the LH-deprived groups
were first reduced to 80% of the value maintained by nondeprived control and LH-lesioned animals,
respectively. Both deprived groups were then returned to an libitum feeding schedule. From Mitchel
and Keesey, (74); reproduced by permission.

One possible mechanism for the defense of body weight is a change in
metabolic efficiency (the ratio of energy intake to changes in body weight).
During high metabolic efficiency, the body converts a large percentage of
available energy to body weight. During low efficiency, the body loses some
available energy and is less efficient at converting the energy to body weight. This
is most likely to occur through changes in basal metabolism. If basal metabolism
slows, the body is expending less of its available energy and therefore is more
efficient at increasing body weight. If basal metabolism increases, the body
"wastes" energy, and less is converted to body weight.

Basal metabolism is responsible for a large percentage of total energy
expenditure (15, 52, 53). Small changes in metabolic rate could produce
significant changes in body weight. If metabolic rate is related to a set-point,
basal metabolism would be expected to decline as weight decreases. There is
evidence of this in both humans and animals. Caloric restriction produces a 15
percent to 30 percent decrease in basal metabolic rate in both obese and lean
persons (77, 78, 79, 80). The consequence of this decrease is clear—weight
reduction creates adaptive changes in energy expenditure, which can limit
further weight loss. Apfelbaum et al. (81) calculated that an individual will lose

approximately 40 grams per day of body fat if daily intake is reduced from 2,000 to 1,500 calories. The rate of weight loss will decrease to 20 grams per day by the end of the second month, then will decrease to 10 grams per day by the third month, and then will stop completely.

Garrow (53) reported that with each episode of caloric restriction, recovery of metabolic rate to baseline levels takes longer, and that the rate falls more rapidly with each return to caloric restriction. Hamilton (82) found that increased length of starvation in animals leads to smaller intakes at refeeding, but that the weight gain during refeeding is the same as during previous refeedings at higher intakes. Another study found that animals starved to 80 percent of normal body weight showed an 18-fold increase in metabolic efficiency during refeeding, compared to normal-weight animals not restricted (83). Bray (77) measured oxygen consumption and body weight in six obese patients whose daily caloric consumption was reduced from 3,500 to 450 calories. Though both body weight and oxygen consumption declined for the 24 days of observation, the 17 percent decline in oxygen consumption was far greater than the 3 percent decline in body weight (Figure 5-2).

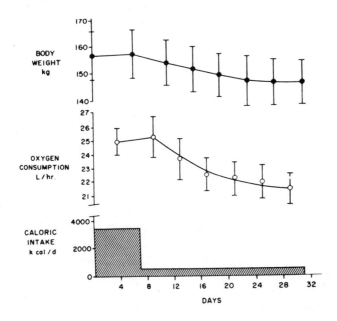

FIG. 5-2. Changes in body weight and oxygen consumption in 6 obese patients during caloric restriction. After 7 days on a 3,500-calorie diet, the intake was restricted to 450 calories and maintained for an additional 24 days. By the end of this period, the decline in oxygen consumption was approximately 17% of the prerestriction values, while body weight had declined less than 3%. From Bray (77); reproduced by permission.

These findings suggest that animals and humans adapt to changes in body weight to encourage movement back to the original weight. When weight falls below the hypothesized set-point, there is a decrease in the rate of energy expenditure. This reduces the number of calories needed to maintain body weight, so that normal levels of intake are sufficient to promote rapid weight gain (70). Wirtshafter and Davis (84) have proposed an alternative model for this phenomenon that does not include a set-point. Nevertheless, a set-point does seem to exist even though its controlling mechanisms are not understood clearly (70).

Adipose Cellularity

Adipose tissue is fundamental in determining body weight (85). Changes in the adipose depot can influence body weight through cellular multiplication (hyperplasia) or through cellular enlargement (hypertrophy) (86, 87, 88). In adults with juvenile-onset obesity (prior to age 12), fat cell *size* typically does not differ from that of normal-weight adults, whereas fat cell *number* can be increased by as much as fivefold (88). Persons with adult-onset obesity are likely to have a normal number of adipocytes but an enlarged cell size (88, 89). It was concluded, therefore, that weight gain during adult years results from cellular hypertrophy, and that weight reduction results from decreased cell size—not number (88).

Weight loss in a hyperplastically obese person could create lipid-depleted adipose cells if body weight declined while fat cell number remained constant. The body would then respond as if in starvation to replenish the large number of adipose cells with essential constituents. The implication is that persons with juvenile-onset obesity will resist weight reduction in order to maintain a minimum level of fat in the adipose cells (90). Several studies have evaluated the association between age at onset of obesity and weight loss, and the evidence is consistent; juvenile-onset obese persons do not differ in their response to treatment from adult-onset obese persons (91, 92, 93, 94, 95, 96). The lack of a relationship between age at onset and success at weight reduction does not rule out the possbliity of a relationship between cellularity and weight reduction (97). Age at onset may not relate strongly enough to cellularity, thus making age at onset a poor predictor (88, 90). Sjöström (85) concluded that the formation of fat cells *can* occur after adolescence.

Björntorp and his colleagues (98) obtained remarkable results by studying hyperplastic and hypertrophic obese women during weight reduction. Fat-cell size and number were measured prior to treatment and at the point where each subject stopped losing weight. When weight loss ended, fat-cell size for hyperplastic and hypertrophic subjects had reached the size of fat cells for controls, but fat-cell number remained unchanged (Figure 5-3). Thus, the hypertrophic subjects had a normal amount of body fat, whereas the hyperplastic

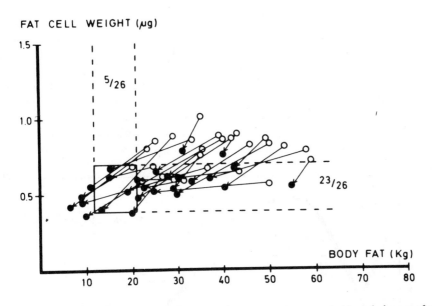

FIG. 5-3.   Body fat and average fat-cell size in obese women (open symbols), and changes after failure to reduce in body weight on an energy-reduced diet (arrows and filled symbols). Rectangle denotes mean ± SD of values of controls. Values are corrected for age effects on body fat and cell size. Not the consistent fat-cell weight at which patients failed to decrease body weight. From Björntorp et al. (98); reproduced by permission.

subjects remained obese. This suggests that fat-cell number may determine response to treatment and may set an upper limit on weight reduction. Weight loss in hyperplastically obese persons may cease before "ideal" body weight is attained. Adipose cellularity may be a major determinant of obesity and an important predictor of success at weight reduction.

Social Factors

Social factors constitute some of the most influential determinants of obesity (8, 99, 100). The first study to demonstrate the magnitude of this effect was the Midtown Study, a comprehensive survey of the epidemiology of mental illness in Manhattan (101). Several studies on obesity patterns from this large population have provided a clear view of the impact of the social environment on obesity (7, 102).

There is a strong inverse relationship between socioeconomic status and the prevalence of obesity, especially in women (7). In the Midtown study, 30 percent of women of lower socioeconomic status were obese, compared to 16 percent of middle-status women and 5 percent of the upper-status group. When only the very highest- and lowest-status subjects were considered, the results were even more striking; fewer than 2 percent of the highest-status subjects were obese, compared to 37 percent of the lowest-status subjects. The results for men were similar, but not quite as dramatic; the prevalence of obesity in men was 32 percent in the lower-status subjects and 16 percent in the higher-status subjects.

Stunkard (8) has developed a qualitative model for the relationship between affluence and the prevalence of obesity and thinness (Figure 5-4). The constraint on obesity in the very lowest level of affluence is the availability of food. With increasing affluence, social factors take effect. The prevalence of obesity reaches a peak in the lower range of affluence and then decreases as affluence increases.

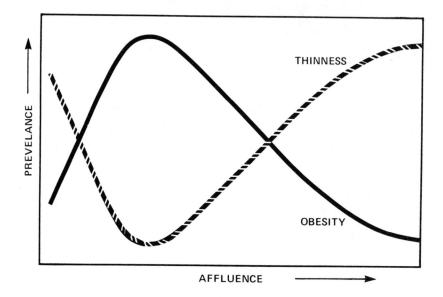

FIG. 5-4. Schematic representation of the relationship between affluence and obesity. From Stunkard (8); reproduced by permission.

The Midtown Study (7) permitted causal inferences about the influence of socioeconomic status on obesity by determining not only the status of the subjects at the time of the study, but also the status of the subjects' parents when the subjects were eight years old. Even though a subject's obesity could influence his or her own social class, it is unlikely that this would influence the social class of the parents (8). These associations were almost as strong as those between the subjects' own social class and obesity. For example, 7 percent of the children of upper-class parents were obese, compared to 5 percent of the *members* of the upper class; 26 percent of the children of lower-class parents were obese, compared to 30 percent of *members* of the lower class (7).

The strong relationship between the social environment and obesity extends to other variables and to persons living in countries other than the United States. The Midtown study revealed that obesity is more prevalent among persons who are downwardly mobile than in those who are upwardly mobile, that obesity becomes less prevalent as the number of generations in the U.S. increases, and that the prevalence varies widely among ethnic and religious groups (7). Two studies from England show results that are consistent with those from the U.S. (102, 103). Stunkard has concluded that social factors are among the most important, if not *the* most important, influence on the prevalence of obesity (100).

Psychological and Environmental Factors—An Interaction

The psychology of obesity is a popular topic for speculation and for unsubstantiated claims. Books and articles have been written on the subject, yet surprisingly little is known about the contribution of psychological factors to obesity. Obese and normal-weight persons cannot be distinguished in terms of childhood experiences, rearing practices, or family constellation. Despite numerous attempts, investigators have not been able to find consistent psychological patterns that differ in obese and nonobese persons (8). It is possible, of course, that psychological factors are primary determinants of obesity, but there is little evidence of this in the existing literature.

There has been increasing interest in the interaction between psychological factors and the environmental control of eating. This began in 1964, when Stunkard and Koch reported high correlations between gastric contractions and reported hunger for normal-weight subjects but not for overweight subjects (105). Gastric motility may not be a useful measure of hunger (106, 107), but the implication of the original study—that the obese differ from the nonobese in response to internal and external cues—had a strong impact on both research and treatment in obesity. Schacter (108) used these findings to argue that obese persons are highly responsive to external eating cues. Several ingenious experiments supported this notion (109, 110, 111), and Schacter and Rodin (112) proposed heightened external responsiveness as an etiological factor in obesity. This theory spurred the development of two experimental paradigms for studying psychological and environmental factors in eating—externality and restrained eating.

Externality

External influences on eating include time, sight of food, environmental factors, and the taste of food (113). Schacter's hypothesis, that the obese are extraordinarily sensitive to these factors, has been the single most important laboratory finding to be used in clinical practice. One major part of behavioral treatment is stimulus control (structuring the eating environment to minimize contact with food cues) (8, 41, 114, 115, 116). A description of the research in this area will help demonstrate the importance of psychological and environmental factors.

One of the first factors studied was *time*. Rodin (117) found that obese subjects showed greater changes in eating in response to the time they *thought* had passed while they were engaged in various tasks. Schachter and Gross (110) pointed out that east-west travelers face eating times that are dissonant with the scheduled times at the point of departure, thus allowing a test of whether obese persons are more responsive to the body's need for energy or to the scheduled eating times at the location of arrival. Accordingly, Goldman et al. (118) studied personnel of Air France and discovered a consistent relationship between degree of overweight and difficulty adjusting to differences in physiological state and local meal times.

The prominence of visual food cues has also been studied in detail. Nisbett (119) allowed obese and nonobese subjects access to an unlimited number of sandwiches while manipulating the number of sandwiches in sight. Obese subjects ate almost one sandwich more when three were in sight than when one was in sight, whereas nonobese subjects did not differ in the two situations. In another study, obese persons ate twice as much when cashews were brightly lighted than when they were dimly lighted; obese subjects actually ate less than normal-weight subjects when the cashews were dimly lighted (120). In contrast Meyers et al. (121) manipulated the accessibility of high- and low-calorie desserts in a cafeteria and found that obese and nonobese subjects were equally responsive to changes in the salience of these cues.

Taste may be the most important external determinant of eating (113). Palatability of food influences the intake of people in all weight categories, although the obese may be especially responsive in this regard. Studies consistently show that obese persons eat significantly more of highly palatable foods and significantly less of unpalatable foods than do nonobese persons (117, 119, 122, 123). Wooley and Wooley (124) have noted that these studies have not been replicated, yet the findings are consistent enough to suggest that palatability of food influences eating more in obese than in nonobese persons.

Many of the studies on externality suffer from methodological problems, and many are based on untested assumptions (97, 125). It is possible that overweight persons show increased responsiveness to food stimuli, but it is more likely that extraordinary sensitivity can be found in persons in all weight categories (113). This issue is further complicated by findings that animals can show increased responsiveness to food cues, that obese animals can differ from nonobese animals in this regard, and that increased responsiveness may have physiological consequences that may influence subsequent responsiveness (97, 112, 126). There is probably a subgroup of the obese population that displays this heightened sensitivity. This may or may not contribute to their obesity, and modification of this sensitivity may or may not facilitate weight reduction (97). More research is needed in this area, because only the success of behavioral treatments can be used to infer the importance of these cues.

Restrained Eating

The set-point theory suggested that suppression of body weight below the set-point creates physiological and psychological changes which promote increased food intake and decreased expenditure (71). This influence might exert itself through increased responsiveness to food cues. Deviation from the set-point, rather than body weight itself, would determine sensitivity to food cues (71, 127).

Herman and Mack (128) expanded upon externality theory and proposed that persons below their set-point are "restrained eaters"; i.e., by definition they must restrain the tendency to overeat, to return to their natural weight. This resistance to physiological signals (restraint) is manifested by attempts at dieting. These authors administered a restraint scale to subjects who were given zero, one, or two milk shakes before having free access to ice cream (128). Subjects not dieting (unrestrained eaters) showed a consistent decrease in eating in response to the size of the preload, whereas restrained eaters consumed *more* as the size of the preload increased. Polivy (129) then manipulated the perceived size of the preload and found that restrained eaters consumed more when they thought they had received a large preload than when they thought they had received a small preload. Several subsequent studies have confirmed these findings (130).

It is counterintuitive that restrained eaters increase consumption after a large preload, because these persons have the strongest desire to limit intake. Herman suggested that the ingestion of a large preload was inconsistent with short-term dieting, thus creating disinhibition for later eating (130, 131, 132). Such an event might lead a restrained eater to say, "I've already blown my diet for today; I might as well have all I want." Ruderman and Wilson (133) noted several problems with the work on restrained eating, and conducted a well-controlled test with both obese and normal-weight subjects. Their data, along with data from two studies they reanalyzed (132, 134), showed that restraint is a powerful predictor of food consumption, but that restraint is more predictive with normal-weight than with obese subjects.

Restrained eating is a measurable and useful construct for use in obesity research (97). Unlike almost all psychological factors associated with dieting, restraint can be quantified and can be related to problems that may be associated with difficulty losing weight. The studies on restraint also show how psychological and physiological factors can interact to influence eating.

TREATMENT APPROACHES

There are hundreds of treatments for obesity. One need only look at popular magazines, newspapers, or on the shelves of bookstores and supermarkets to find "guaranteed" cures. These treatments range from the moderately feasible to the utterly bizarre. In 1978 Brownell (50) did a survey of four women's magazines (*Cosmopolitan, Glamour, Mademoiselle, Redbook*). There was an average of three articles on weight reduction in each magazine, and an average of six advertisements for weight-loss devices, pills, and diet plans. One advertisement was common to three of the four magazines. This was from Slim Skins, a sweatsuit type of device to be attached to a vacuum cleaner. From Women's Day (April 1978):

> All new—the most phenomenal slenderizer ever conceived. Guaranteed to reduce your waist, abdomen, hips and thighs a total of 9 to 15 inches in just 3 days or your money refunded! Using this newly discovered method of slenderizing the Slim Skins combines with your own vacuum cleaner to create a super new inch reducer that is infinitely more effective than any reducing method known.

That these miracle cures are commercially successful is indisputable; full-page advertisements in leading magazines are not cheap. One wonders why obese persons purchase such incredible devices, particularly when the obese are the first to say that such devices are worthless. Stunkard and Brownell (135) have addressed this question:

> Why is there such a booming market for weight reduction methods? The answer seems clear: millions are plagued by excess weight. Many attempt to reduce by methods that are largely ineffective. Confronted by failure, they move to another approach and then another, creating a lucrative market for those who promise what cannot be delivered. The fact that so many overweight people are attracted to such questionable measures is testimony to how desperately they want to lose weight and how difficult it is for them to do so. Millions more have given up even trying.

It can be inferred that professionally administered treatments are either ineffective or are reaching a small portion of those wishing to lose weight. What is the status of professional and nonprofessional treatments?

In 1958 Stunkard (136) noted that the results from most treatments for obesity were quite discouraging: "Most obese persons will not enter treatment for obesity. Of those who enter treatment, most will not lose weight, and of those who do lose weight, most will regain it." This dismal verdict could still be applied to most treatments, including traditional doctor's-office treatment of diet and drugs. There are, however, several new forms of treatment that offer new promise in the treatment of this forbidding disorder. We will present each of these, along with suggestions for use in clinical practice.

Behavioral Treatments

Initial Studies

In 1967 Stuart (137) pioneered an approach that initiated more than a decade of research on the behavioral treatment of obesity. Figure 5-5 presents the weight losses from 4 of Stuart's patients. Of the original 10 patients, 8 remained in treatment for one year. Three subjects lost more than 40 pounds (18.2 kg), and 6 lost more than 30 pounds (13.6 kg). The treatment was no more intensive than many treatments showing far poorer results, and there was no evidence of "symptom substitution." In fact most of the subjects reported an increased range of social activities and improved marital relationships. Even though Stuart's findings were from uncontrolled case studies, the weight losses were impressive enough to gain the attention of both researchers and clinicians.

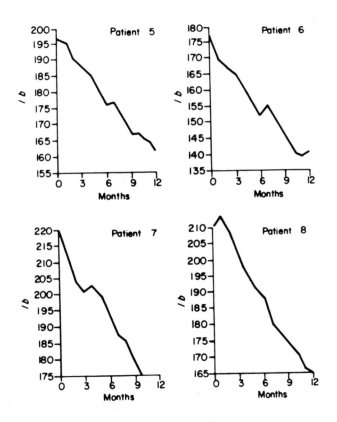

FIG. 5-5.   Weight changes in pounds for 4 of Stuart's 10 patients receiving behavior therapy. From Stuart (137); reproduced by permission.

The next logical step was to compare Stuart's behavioral program to no treatment and to alternative treatments. Harris (138) randomly assigned 24 overweight subjects to behavioral groups or to a no-treatment control group. After 10 weeks of treatment and a 16-week follow-up period, the behavioral group lost significantly more weight than the control group. This study demonstrated that group behavior-therapy could be used for the treatment of obesity. Wollersheim (139) then compared behavior therapy to no therapy and to two alternative treatments: a nonspecific group treatment that focused on unconscious motives and personality factors underlying obesity, and a social pressure treatment based on a commercial self-help group approach. Subjects in the behavioral group lost more weight than subjects in the other three conditions.

Wollersheim's study (139) controlled for the expectations of the patients but could not control for therapist bias. Penick et al. (140) controlled for therapist bias by comparing behavioral groups led by novice therapists with control groups conducted by seasoned psychotherapists with extensive experience in nonbehavioral treatments for obesity. After weekly sessions for three months, the behavioral groups lost more weight than the control group.

It began to appear that behavior therapy was an effective treatment for obesity and that the strength of the procedures outweighed even the personal characteristics of the therapist. This raised the possibility that the program could be self-administered. In 1974 Hagen (141) compared Wollersheim's behavioral program (group treatment with a therapist) to a "bibliotherapy" program, in which a ten-lesson manual was mailed to subjects in weekly installments. For each lesson, subjects mailed homework assignments to a therapist who corrected and returned them. After 10 sessions over three months, both groups averaged 12 pounds (5.5 kg) lost, prompting Hagen to conclude that bibliotherapy is effective for weight reduction. Ferstl et al. (142) and Hanson et al. (143) conducted similar studies and also found no difference between these two treatments. However, Fernan (144) and Brownell et al. (145) found that group therapy was more effective than bibliotherapy, and, further, that bibliotherapy produced negligible weight losses. Current behavioral treatments are probably not very effective when self-administered, and the initial enthusiasm for bibliotherapy resulted in comparing it to a standard program that was only modestly effective.

Methods for Improving Maintenance

By the mid-1970's more than 75 articles had been published on behavior therapy for obesity. The results were encouraging enough to suggest that behavior therapy was the treatment of choice for mild to moderate obesity (8, 146). However, few studies were longer than three months, and in most reports there was a pattern of weight gain after treatment ended. Several theorists argued that initial behavior changes and the maintenance of that change are governed by different processes (147, 148). This led to the development of specific procedures to promote maintenance of weight loss.

Wilson was among the first to design and evaluate methods for improving maintenance (149, 150). One such method was to schedule "booster" sessions after the termination of treatment so that patients could receive training and reinforcement during the time when they were most likely to falter. Kingsley and Wilson (151) used four booster sessions during the one-year maintenance phase that followed their eight-week treatment program. The booster sessions improved maintenance for subjects receiving group therapy but not for those receiving individual treatment. Ashby and Wilson (152) and Wilson and Brownell (153) then found that booster sessions did not improve maintenance. Craighead, Stunkard, and O'Brien (154) recently completed the most rigorous test of booster sessions. Even though booster sessions were statistically superior to no boosters, the additional weight losses were not clinically significant. It appears that booster sessions, as they are presently used, do not promote maintenance of weight loss to the extent that the extra treatment justifies the cost.

Several recent reviews have shown that the long-term efficacy of behavior therapy is encouraging but far from impressive (155, 156). The basic behavioral approach is promising, but new directions must be taken in its application. Two such directions are the modification of the social environment and the combination of behavior therapy with other therapies.

Modifying the Social Environment

Eating and dieting do not occur in a social vacuum. Afflicted by a disorder as visible and distressing as obesity, the dieter can be very responsive to influence from other persons in the immediate social environment. Many social interactions occur within the family, the work environment, fraternal organizations, religious groups, self-help programs, and the community. Self-help groups will be discussed later in this chapter, and descriptions of community programs are available elsewhere (100, 157). Of the remaining social systems, the family and the work environment have received the most research attention. These two areas offer new promise in encouraging behavior change.

Family Interventions. The family is the source of numerous social interactions involving food—from purchase to consumption. Family members may play an important role in aiding or hindering the dieter. Stuart and Davis (114) recorded mealtime interactions between overweight women and their husbands and found that the husbands were more likely than the wives to bring up food as the topic of conversation and to offer food to the spouse. Husbands were 12 times more likely to criticize their wives' eating behavior than to praise it, leading Stuart to conclude that husbands "are not only not contributors to their wives' efforts to lose weight, but they may actually exert a negative influence." Mahoney and Mahoney (158) treated obese subjects in a behavioral program and calculated a social-support index based on attendance and therapist reports of family cooperation. The index was positively correlated with weight loss during treatment and follow-up.

The first study to systematically manipulate the influence of family intervention was performed by Wilson and Brownell (153). All subjects received a standard behavioral program (114); half of the subjects attended sessions alone, while the other half attended sessions with a family member. The family members were taught behavioral principles, were instructed to cease criticizing the subject's eating behavior, and were encouraged to help the subject restructure the conditions and consequences of eating. After an 8-week treatment phase and a 6-month follow-up, there were not significant differences in weight losses between the two conditions. Wilson and Brownell suggested that the lack of structure for the family members' behavior contributed to the lack of success for the family intervention.

Brownell et al. (93) then conducted a highly structured couples intervention. With the couple as the focal point of treatment, subjects and spouses were instructed in a variety of techniques including mutual monitoring of food-related behaviors, stimulus control, modeling, and reinforcement. Subjects and spouses had their own treatment manuals with corresponding lessons. The program stressed mutual efforts and that behavior change was required from both partners.

This couples condition was compared to two other conditions. In one condition, subjects had "cooperative" spouses, who were willing to take part in the program but did not actually participate; and in the other condition, subjects had "noncooperative" spouses, who were unwilling to participate. Treatment sessions were held once weekly for 10 weeks, followed by monthly follow-up meetings for 6 months. At the end of treatment, the couples group lost an average of 20 pounds (9.1 kg), the "cooperative spouse-subject alone" condition lost 15 pounds (6.8 kg), and the "noncooperative spouse" condition lost 12 pounds (5.5 kg) (Figure 5-6). These weight losses did not differ statistically, but at the 6-month follow-up the couples group had lost 30 pounds (16.6 kg)—significantly more than the other two conditions, 19 and 15 pounds (8.6 and 6.8 kg) respectively. These results were striking because the weight losses were nearly triple those reported in most studies of behavior therapy, and because one-third of the total weight loss in the couples condition occurred *after* weekly treatment sessions ended.

Within the past several years, more well-controlled studies have appeared on social-support interventions using spouses, other family members, or peers. Some of these studies report increased weight losses with this approach (159,

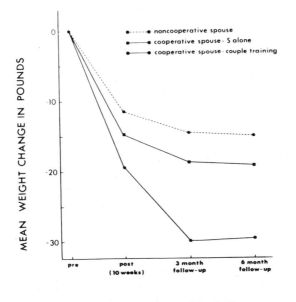

TIME OF ASSESSMENT

FIG. 5-6. Mean weight changes in pounds during treatment and follow-up for three conditions of spouse intervention. From Brownell et al. (93); reproduced by permission.

160, 161, 162, 163), but others do not (165). The distinguishing characteristic among these studies appears to be the degree to which the spouses have been involved in treatment. The studies in which the spouses have been trained in specific behavioral techniques have found this approach to be useful; studies in which spouses were spectators in the treatment process did not find this positive effect. Direct training of both subjects and spouses—with the emphasis on mutual behavior change—appears to be effective.

Work-Site Treatment.   Millions of people spend many hours each day at the work place. There are several advantages to mobilizing the naturally occurring social forces in this environment. Large numbers of people can be reached, time away from work can be kept to a minimum, the employer may be willing to support such a program, and, most important, the social support system in this setting may encourage adherence to behavior-change programs. The employers and fellow employees may strongly encourage attendance, and treatment efficacy itself may be enhanced by improved morale. The potential benefits for the employer include decreased absenteeism, improved productivity and morale, and reduced medical costs.

Stunkard and Brownell (166) conducted the first controlled clinical trial of work-site treatment for obesity. The program was done with the employees of

Bloomingdale's and Gimbel's retail department stores in New York, and followed a successful work-site program for hypertension by Alderman (167). The study tested work-site vs. medical-site treatment, nonprofessional vs. professional group leaders, and four weekly vs. the traditional once weekly treatment. Patients met for a 16-week behavioral program and were assigned to one of four treatment conditions: i) Professional Therapist-Work Site-Weekly Treatment; ii) Professional Therapist-Medical Site-Weekly Treatment, iii) Lay Therapist-Work Site-Weekly Treatment; iv) Lay Therapist-Work Site-Four Weekly Treatments. Two measures of success were used—attrition and weight loss. Attrition rates were lower in the groups led by lay therapists (50 percent and 31 percent) than in groups led by the professional therapist (82 percent and 75 percent), and those treated four times per week showed a lower attrition than those given conventional once-weekly treatments (85 percent, 75 percent, 50 percent). There were no significant differences in weight losses between the conditions after treatment or a six-month follow-up.

This first study showed that work-site treatment is feasible (166). Attrition compared favorably to the other broad-scale administration of treatment for obesity, self-help groups, but was still higher than anticipated. This suggests that simply treating people at the work site does not guarantee success. Rather, this social system must be investigated more fully before its potential can be realized.

Combining Behavior Therapy With Other Treatments

Several forms of treatment are notable for producing large weight losses. Two such methods are fasting and pharmacotherapy. These have not enjoyed widespread use because of troublesome complications and because of the almost universal relapse that follows treatment. Combining behavior therapy with other approaches may be useful if the habit change produced by the behavioral procedures aids in the maintenance of weight loss produced by other procedures.

Behavior Therapy and Pharmacotherapy

Pharmacological approaches to weight reduction have been in disrepute because of short-lived weight losses and the abuse potential of many drugs, particularly amphetamines. Craighead, Stunkard, and O'Brien (154) brought new hope to this area, with a recent study using behavior therapy and fenfluramine (a sympathomimetic amine). Subjects were assigned to four treatment conditions: i) Routine doctor's-office treatment with fenfluramine, ii) Behavior therapy in groups; iii) Fenfluramine with Rogerian nondirective therapy in groups; iv) Fenfluramine combined with group behavior-therapy. After 25 weekly sessions, the average weight losses for the four conditions were 6.4, 10.9, 13.6, and 14.5 kg, respectively. These data suggested that medication can lead to substantial weight loss if used in the context of group therapy. Adding behavior therapy improved weight loss somewhat, and the drug (with or without behavior therapy) was more effective than behavior therapy alone. However, the picture changed during the follow-up. At a one-year assessment, the doctor's office subjects had received other treatment. The losses for the three remaining conditions were 9.1, 6.4, and 4.6 kg respectively. Subjects receiving behavior therapy alone regained little weight, whereas subjects receiving the drug rebounded rapidly. Surprisingly, subjects receiving the combined treatments relapsed as rapidly as subjects receiving only the drug.

The results of the Craighead et al. study (154) are important for several reasons. First, the study had the largest sample and the most complex follow-up of any study of weight reduction: 119 subjects completed the study, and 98 percent of the subjects were actually weighed one year after treatment. Second, the magnitude of weight loss was higher than in most studies. Third, behavior therapy was effective at long-term weight loss when used alone, but it was not effective in preventing the relapse that occurred with medication. A recent study by Brightwell and Naylor (168) also showed that these two therapies can be combined. The problem of maintaining weight loss is the most immediate challenge for researchers in this area.

Behavior Therapy and Diet

The most innovative and promising dietary treatment for obesity is the protein-sparing modified fast (PSMF) (169). This program involves an outpatient fasting regimen supplemented with a protein formula or small amounts of high-protein foods. This exogenous protein "spares" the body's protein that is lost during complete fasting (170, 171). Weight losses from the PSMF are generally high (15–50 kg), and there has been great public interest in widely distributed liquid protein products. With the news of many deaths from the commercial products, interest has waned. However, the PSMF appears to be relatively safe when administered under tightly controlled conditions and when specially designed protein formulas are used (169).

Bistrian (169) has presented guidelines for the administration of the PSMF, and has reported impressive results from a program involving the PSMF and behavior therapy. Lindner and Blackburn (172) combined behavior therapy with the PSMF with 167 patients in two clinics. Loss of body protein was minimized by providing 1.4 grams of protein per kg of lean body mass. Patients were instructed in behavioral procedures during an intensive two-week period, followed by a prolonged phase of fasting and increased physical activity. During a termination phase, patients returned to a balanced diet which restricted only concentrated carbohydrates; behavior-therapy sessions were also held. The mean weight loss after one year was 40 pounds (18.2 kg), and a majority of patients were said to have maintained their weight losses. This study was done without adequate controls, but the magnitude of weight loss suggests that this approach merits further testing.

The Current Status of Behavior Therapy

Behavior therapy has become a popular treatment for obesity. The largest self-help organization for obesity—Weight Watchers—has incorporated behavioral procedures into its standard program. Behavior-therapy clinics have been established in many cities, and self-help books for weight reduction have been published by many of the top researchers in the field. Research has shown that behavior therapy is more effective than most alternative treatments. Just how effective is it?

Several reviews and reports from large-scale programs document the effectiveness of behavior therapy. Jeffrey, Wing, and Stunkard (96) reviewed 21 controlled studies of behavior therapy published prior to 1976 and found that average weight loss after 8–12-week treatment periods was 11.5 pounds (5.2 kg). The same authors reported the progress of 125 patients who completed a 12–20-week program at the Stanford Eating Disorders Clinic; average weight loss was 11.04 pounds (5 kg). Brownell, Heckerman, and Westlake (92) studied 98 subjects in a 10-week behavioral program and found an average weight loss of 11.01 pounds (5 kg). The consistency of these findings is striking, considering that patient populations, therapists, fees for treatment, and other factors varied among the programs. It can be concluded that behavior therapy produces weight losses of 10–13 pounds (1–2 pounds per week) during a treatment period that may range between 8 and 20 weeks (8, 41, 52, 96, 125, 146, 156, 173). For a person who may be 50 percent above ideal weight, such a loss may not be medically, psychologically, or cosmetically significant. The true test of any therapy is its ability to sustain an adequate rate of weight loss over the long term and to maintain that loss once ideal weight is attained.

Stunkard and Penick (155) have reviewed each of the behavior therapy studies with a follow-up of one year or longer. For the ten studies with a one-year follow-up, mean weight losses ranged from zero to 27.7 pounds (12.6 kg). The only study with a 5-year follow-up found that behavior-therapy subjects averaged an 11.7-pound (5.3-kg) loss, but subjects receiving traditional treatment had virtually identical weight losses (155). Stunkard and Penick concluded that weight losses from behavior therapy are only modestly maintained, but that its comparative effectiveness cannot be determined because long-term data on other treatments are not available.

Behavior therapy has not been given an adequate test for long-term maintenance of weight loss (155, 156). It is unreasonable to expect that a 10-week program can cure a longstanding problem having so many biological, psychological, behavioral, and social consequences. Behavior therapists have concentrated their efforts on the induction of weight loss and, with a few notable exceptions, have not applied their technology to the maintenance of weight loss. This area is a new frontier for research on obesity (155).

It is important to distinguish behavior therapy from the procedures commonly used in "behavioral" programs. We have focused on the *procedures* most commonly used in behavioral programs. However, behavior therapy is not a group of procedures, but a system for conceptualizing the acquisition, generalization, and maintenance of behavior (147, 148). The principles of behavior therapy have been described in great detail (147, 148) and can be applied to any behavior.

The primary concern in the treatment of obesity is the problem of nonadherence. Regardless of the treatment approach, adherence to the prescribed regimen is crucial for success. The principles of behavior therapy may be useful for improving adherence. The programs that have combined the behavioral treatment package with other treatments have yielded encouraging results. However, the *principles* of behavior therapy have not been used systematically with other treatments. This may be the most important contribution behavior therapy can make in the treatment of obesity. Other treatments may be effective if applied conscientiously. Behavior therapy may help improve adherence and thereby increase the effectiveness of any treatment.

Self-Help Treatments

Persons afflicted with a problem often join one another for mutual assistance. The most widely known self-help group is Alcoholics Anonymous (AA), but similar groups exist to help with many problems. This tendency toward self-help is very strong among obese persons. More than one million obese Americans take part each week in nonmedical group efforts at weight reduction (135). Stuart (174) has argued that self-help groups offer an attractive, available, and cost-effective form of treatment, and that the peer support in such groups may be more powerful than professional consultation. The few studies on self-help treatments show some promise, but there are still some unresolved problems involved in this approach.

TOPS (Take Off Pounds Sensibly) has been the most closely studied self-help program. Founded in 1948 by an overweight housewife from Milwaukee, this nonprofit organization has grown to over 350,000 members in 12,000 chapters; the members are predominantly female. Weekly meetings begin with official "weigh-ins" followed by an announcement of each member's weight change from the previous week. Weight losses are applauded and weight gains elicit group responses ranging from silence or sympathy to jeers of disapproval. The meetings are then devoted to group discussions of dieting, and successive steps in weight reduction are rewarded with charms and other small tokens. Attaining goal weight is rewarded in a graduation ceremony, and members are allowed membership in KOPS (Keep Off Pounds Sensibly).

A survey of the records of 21 TOPS chapters in 1968 showed mean weight losses of 15 pounds (6.8 kg), with a standard deviation of 15 pounds (6.8 kg), and a survey of the same chapters two years later showed a mean weight loss of 14 pounds (6.5 kg), with a standard deviation of 17 pounds (7.7 kg) (175). These weight losses seem impressive, even though the high standard deviations indicate large variability among subjects. However, these results must be interpreted with caution because of the high rates of attrition from these programs. The drop-out rate for the TOPS chapters mentioned earlier was 47 percent at one year and 70 percent at two years (175). In another study of TOPS, records were kept by professional personnel, and the attrition rate at one year was 67 percent (176).

Attrition appears to be the major problem confronting self-help groups (135). The attrition rate of TOPS, which falls between 40 percent and 70 percent, is the *best* among the self-help groups for which data have been collected. Ashwell (177) has assembled the attrition rates for self-help groups from the United Kingdom and Australia, and Stunkard and Brownell (135) have added data from several U.S. self-help groups (Figure 5-7). The curve labeled X/USA describes attrition from an unidentified self-help group in the U.S. This study was done by Nash (178) and was the most intensive yet undertaken on self-help groups. When Nash carried out this study, in the mid-1970s, members joining this group had joined three times previously.

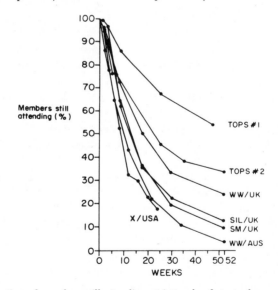

FIG. 5-7. Proportion of members still attending at intervals of up to 1 year after first joining self-help groups. Groups are from the United Kingdom, the United States, and Australia. The groups are Take Off Pounds Sensibly (TOPS), Weight Watchers (WW), Silhouette Slimming Clubs (SIL), Slimming Magazine Slimming Clubs (SM), and an unidentified group (X). TOPS data are from an initial study of the organization (175) (TOPS No. 1), and from a later study of the same group (176). Adapted from Ashwell (177), printed in Stunkard and Brownell (135); reproduced by permission.

Weight Watchers is the largest of the self-help groups. Their format owes much to TOPS, with its inclusion of weekly weigh-ins and group support. Two measures have been added. A structured, palatable, satisfying, and nutritionally balanced diet has been offered, and paid lecturers conduct the group meetings. These lecturers are usually highly effective speakers and have been selected from successful program graduates. The structured Weight Watchers program is a popular approach and it may be the most effective. Little research has been done on Weight Watchers, so the effectiveness of the program cannot be determined. Stuart (174) is conducting a major research effort involving this organization, and new information should be available soon. Stuart has introduced behavior modification "modules" into the Weight Watchers program. These may improve the program, judging from the first controlled study of behavior therapy within a self-help group (176).

Levitz and Stunkard (176) carried out a large-scale clinical trial to test the combination of self-help group methods with behavior therapy. Four treatment conditions were instituted in each of four TOPS chapters: 1) Behavioral modification with a professional therapist; 2) Behavior modification with a TOPS chapter leader; 3) Nutrition education with a TOPS leader; 4) The standard TOPS program. TOPS effectiveness was enhanced by the behavioral techniques, resulting in lowered attrition and greater weight loss, both during the three months of active treatment and at a nine-month follow-up. At this follow-up, only 38 percent and 41 percent had dropped out of the two behavior-modification conditions, compared with 55 percent and 67 percent for the nutrition-education and standard TOPS groups. The subjects receiving behavior modification also maintained their weight losses better than the subjects in the other conditions.

Self-help may be a valuable treatment for obesity. From the available evidence, weight losses are small and attrition is very high. As with other forms of treatment, lack of adherence is a serious problem. Combining the behavioral program with self-help treatment may boost effectiveness. A comprehensive behavioral analysis of the social, psychological, and behavioral factors which govern adherence in self-help programs is needed. Behavioral principles may then be helpful in using this unique social system to encourage adherence to a dietary regimen.

Surgical Treatments

Surgical treatments were developed in response to the lack of safe and effective methods for massively obese persons. The increased morbidity and mortality for grossly overweight persons, along with the failure of conservative methods for weight reduction, prompted experimentation with several surgical procedures (15). Jejunoileal (intestinal) bypass was developed first, and more than fifty thousand operations have been performed. The long-term complications of intestinal bypass have begun to appear only in recent years because the procedure is relatively new. Gastric bypass procedures were then proposed as an alternative to intestinal bypass. The indications for these two approaches are similar, but the outcomes are quite different.

Jejunoileal or gastric bypass procedures are indicated only in certain cases (15, 179). Patients must be at least 110 pounds (50 kg) above ideal weight, and some clinics operate only on patients weighing more than 300 pounds (140 kg). Some patients with complications such as hypertension, diabetes mellitus, serious orthopedic problems, and pulmonary alveolar hypoventilation (Pickwickian syndrome) may qualify at lower weights because these problems usually improve with weight reduction (180). The patient's obesity must be refractory despite repeated attempts to reduce with more traditional methods. Most patients are between age 20 and 50. Patients must be aware of the radical nature of the surgery, must be conscious of the possibility of revision, and must not become pregnant for 6 to 12 months after surgery (180). The high mortality rate among patients treated at hospitals performing few of these operations (181) argues for treatment at medical centers with adequate facilities and personnel (180).

Jejunoileal Bypass

Two variations of the intestinal bypass have been used (15). In the end-to-side (Payne) operation (182), the distal segment of the jejunum is attached to the side of the ileum near the ileocecal valve. The end-to-end (Scott) operation (183) involves the anastomosis of the distal end of the jejunum to the end of the ileum; the defunctionalized bowel drains into the colon with an ileocolonic anastomosis. The rationale for these procedures was to impair the absorption of nutrients, by the radical shortening of the small bowel. This malabsorption would be sufficient to control obesity and would take place even in the presence of large food intake. Mills and Stunkard (184) discovered that decreased food intake occurs after intestinal bypass, so two mechanisms (malabsorption and decreased intake) interact to produce weight loss (180).

Intestinal bypass patients typically lose 90 to 130 pounds (40.9 to 59 kg) during the first year after surgery (15, 179). Body weight stabilizes between 12 and 36 months after surgery, and the rate of weight loss is related to the length of the anastomosed intestine, initial body weight, and the type of surgery (180). Most of the early weight loss is fat, and, although some lean tissue is also lost, lean body mass returns to normal within one year or more after surgery (180).

The complications for jejunoileal bypass are considerable. These involve not only the surgical complications, but the complications of an altered anatomy. The overall mortality is approximately 3 percent. Surgical complications include pulmonary embolism, serious wound infection, gastrointestinal hemorrhage, renal failure, and pancreatitis (180). Severe diarrhea accompanies all cases; patients may have as many as 20 stools per day in the early postoperative period. This decreases as time passes, but persistent diarrhea may induce patients to voluntarily restrict food intake, thus partially explaining the weight loss (184). Malnutrition, serious liver disease, bacterial overgrowth, renal failure, and arthritis are other frequent complications. The mortality rate for this surgery exceeds that for any other treatment for obesity, and the complications argue for a cautious stance.

Gastric Bypass

Mason's gastric bypass procedure involves the creation of a small gastric pouch by separating the proximal and distal portions of the stomach with a continuous row of staples (185). A portion of the small intestine is then anastomosed to the gastric pouch to establish a new food pathway. This operation has been performed on approximately 3,000 patients, nearly half of whom have been treated by Mason, at the University of Iowa. Weight losses average 0.9 to 2 pounds (0.4 to 0.8 kg) per week. The small pouch and the delay in gastric emptying produce a sensation of fullness and satiety after small meals, and patients generally report normal hunger and satiety patterns after surgery (185).

Several studies have compared jejunoileal and gastric bypass procedures. Hemrick et al. (186) reported a high frequency of metabolic complications following intestinal bypass and few complications with gastric bypass. Alden compared hospital charts from 100 intestinal bypass patients and 100 gastric bypass patients (187). Weight losses were similar for both groups (88 pounds [40 kg]), and the gastric bypass patients did not report the complications reported by the intestinal bypass patients (hemorrhoids, diarrhea, fatigue, lethargy). Griffen et al. (188) randomly assigned obese patients to either jejunoileal or gastric bypass surgery. This prospective study found that jejunoileal bypass patients average 127 pounds (57.9 kg) lost and gastric bypass patients averaged 112 pounds (51 kg) lost. Surgical and metabolic complications were less frequent in the gastric bypass patients.

Surgical treatment is indicated only as a last resort and only for massively obese persons (15). Morbidity and mortality are higher for surgery than for other forms of treatment, but the increased health and psychological hazards of massive obesity suggest that surgery is a viable and important treatment in some cases. Gastric bypass appears to be preferable to jejunoileal bypass because of similar weight losses and a dramatic reduction in complications.

CONCLUSIONS

Obesity is a serious disorder with many physical and psychological complications. It has genetic, social, environmental, nutritional, metabolic, and emotional determinants. Most obese persons find their condition so distressing that dieting and body weight become constant obsessions. The obese person is faced with a choice between resignation to a condition for which society has little sympathy, or a career of dieting, which may be associated with its own problems.

The etiology of obesity can be defined in very few individuals. Research with animals indicates that biological and metabolic factors play a major role in the regulation of body weight. The same is probably true of humans. Specifying etiological factors in humans is complicated by the enormous variation in human eating patterns and the degree to which humans are responsive to social and psychological factors. In addition, body weight is determined not only by energy intake but by energy expenditure as well. The interaction between these two systems is complex, and the extent to which individuals can control these systems is unclear. One thing is certain: characterizing the obese person as a weak-willed, gluttonous individual with little self-respect is an oversimplification which ignores mounting evidence that body-weight regulation has powerful physiological determinants.

Traditional medical treatment of obesity with diet and drugs has met with little success. New hope developed with the advent of behavior therapy, and many well-controlled studies appeared, using this approach. Behavior therapy is the treatment of choice for mild to moderate obesity, but the results from treatment with the "behavioral package" have not been impressive. This suggests that behavioral principles, rather than behavioral procedures, should be applied to the problem of obesity. Behavior therapy is particularly promising when combined with other treatments, notably pharmacotherapy, dietary management, and family interventions. Self-help organizations offer great potential because of the low cost of treatment, but high attrition in self-help groups is a major problem. Surgical treatments, particularly gastric bypass surgery, lead to large weight losses, but are to be used only as a last resort for massively obese persons.

REFERENCES

1. Jordan, H.A. In defense of body weight. *J. Amer. Diet. Assoc.* 62: 17–21, 1973.
2. Brillat-Savarin, J.S. *The Physiology of Taste* (transl. from French by Fisher, M.F.K.). New York: Knopf, 1971.
3. Beaumont, W. *Experiments and observations on the gastric juice and the physiology of digestion. New York: Dover, 1959.*
4. *United States Senate Select Subcommittee on Nutrition and Human Needs. Proceedings from hearings. Washington, D.C.: US Government Printing Office, 1977.*
5. *Metropolitan Life Insurance Company. Frequency of overweight and underweight. Stat. Bull.* 41: 4–7, 1960.
6. Build and Blood Pressure Study. Chicago: Society of Actuaries, 1959.
7. Goldblatt, P.B., Moore, M.E., & Stunkard, A.J. Social factors in obesity. *JAMA* 192: 1,039–44, 1965.

8. Stunkard, A.J. From explanation to action in psychosomatic medicine: The case of obesity. *Psychosom. Med.* 37: 195–236, 1975.

9. Hathaway, M.I. & Sargent, D.W. Overweight in children. *J. Amer. Diet. Assoc.* 40: 511–15, 1962.

10. Huenemann, R.L., Hampton, M.C., Behnke, M., et al. *Teenage Nutrition and Physique.* Springfield, Ill: Thomas, 1974.

11. Colley, J.R.T. Obesity in school children. *Brit. J. Soc. Prev. Med.* 28: 221–25, 1974.

12. Garn, S.M. & Clark, D.C. Trends in fatness and the origins of obesity. *Pediat.* 57: 443–56, 1976.

13. Abraham, S. & Nordsieck, M. Relationship of excess weight in children and adults. *Pub. Health Rep.* 75: 263–73, 1960.

14. Stunkard, A.J. & Burt, V. Obesity and the body image. II. Age at onset of disturbances in the body image. *Am. J. Psychiat.* 123: 1443–47, 1967.

15. Bray, G.A. *The Obese Patient.* Philadelphia: Saunders, 1976.

16. Drash, G. Relationship between diabetes mellitus and obesity in the child. *Metabol.* 22: 337–44, 1973.

17. Gordon, T., Castelli, W.P., Hjortland, M.C. Diabetes, blood lipids and the role of obesity in coronary heart disease risk for women. *Ann. Int. Med.* 87: 393–97, 1977.

18. Rimm, A.A., Werner, L.H., Bernstein, R. Disease and obesity in 73,532 women. *Obes. Bariat. Med.* 1: 77–84, 1972.

19. Barrera, F., Reidenberg, M.M., & Winters, W.L. Pulmonary function in the obese patient. *Am. J. Med. Sci.* 254: 784–796, 1967.

20. MacGregor, M.I., Block, A.J., & Ball, W.C., Jr. Topics in clinical medicine: Serious complications and sudden death in the Pickwickian Syndrome. *Bull. J. Hopkins Hosp.* 126: 279–95, 1970.

21. Lourenco, R.V. Diaphragm activity in obesity. *J. Clin. Invest.* 48: 1609–14, 1969.

22. Weisinger, J.R., Kempson, R.L., Eldridge, R.L. The nephrotic syndrome: A complication of massive obesity. *Ann. Int. Med.* 81: 440–47, 1974.

23. Prem, K.A., Mensheha, N.M., & McKelvey, J.L. Operative treatment of adenocarcinoma of the endometrium in obese women. *Am. J. Ob. Gyn.* 92: 16–22, 1965.

24. Warner, W.A. The obese patient and anesthesia. *JAMA* 205: 102–103, 1968.

25. Peckham, C.H. & Christianson, R.E. The relationship between prepregnancy weight and certain obstetric factors. *Am. J. Ob. Gyn.* 111: 1–7, 1971.

26. Dyer, A.R., Stamler, J., Berkson, D.M. Relationship of relative weight and body mass index to 14-year mortality in the Chicago Peoples Gas Company Study. *J. Chr. Dis.* 28: 109–23, 1975.

27. Kannel, W.B. & Gordon, T. Physiological and medical concomitants of obesity: The Framingham study. In Bray, G.A. (Ed.), *Obesity in America.* Washington, DC: US D.H.E.W. NIH Publication No. 79-359, 1979.

28. Gordon, T. & Kannel, W.B. The effects of overweight on cardiovascular disease. *Geriat.* 28: 80–88, 1973.

29. Kannel, W.B., Gordon, T., & Castelli, W.P. Obesity, lipids, and glucose intolerance: The Framingham Study. *Am. J. Clin. Nutr.* 32: 1,238–45, 1979.

30. Chiang, B.N., Perlman, L.V., & Epstein, F.H. Overweight and hypertension: A review. *Circ.* 39: 403–21, 1969.

31. Kannel, W.B., Brand, N., Skinner, J.J., Jr. Relation of adiposity to blood pressure and development of hypertension: Framingham Study. *Ann. Int. Med.* 67: 48–59, 1967.

32. Mann, G.V. The influence of obesity on health. *New Eng. J. Med.* 291: 178–85, 1974.

33. Olefsy, J., Reaven, G.M., & Farquhar, J.W. Effects of weight reduction on obesity: Studies of lipid and carbohydrate metabolism in normal and hyperlipoproteinemic subjects. *J. Clin. Invest.* 53: 64–76, 1974.

34. Heyden, S., Walker, L., & Hames, C.G. Decrease of serum cholesterol level and blood pressure in the community: Seven to nine years of observation in the Evans County Study. *Arch. Int. Med.* 128: 982–86, 1971.
35. Oscai, L.B., Patterson, J.A., Bogard, D.L. Normalization of serum triglycerides and lipoprotein electrophoretic patterns by exercise. *Am. J. Card.* 30: 775–80, 1972.
36. Reaven, G.M., Lerner, R.L., Stern, M.P. Role of insulin in hypertriglyceridemia. *J. Clin. Invest.* 46: 1,756–67, 1967.
37. Alexander, J.K. & Peterson, K.L. Cardiovascular effects of weight reduction. *Circ.* 45: 310–18, 1972.
38. Gordon, T. & Kannel, W.B. Obesity and cardiovascular disease: The Framingham study. *Clin. Endocrin. Metab.* 5: 367–75, 1976.
39. Dwyer, J. & Mayer, J. The dismal condition: Problems faced by obese adolescent girls in American society. In Bray, G. (Ed.), *Obesity in perspective.* Bethesda: US DHEW, NIH Publication No. 75-708, 1975.
40. Stunkard, A.J. & Mendelson, M. Obesity and body image: I. Characteristics of disturbances in the body image of some obese persons. *Am. J. Psychiat.* 123: 1,296–1,300, 1967.
41. Brownell, K.B. & Stunkard, A.J. Behavioral treatment of obesity in children. *Am. J. Dis. Child.* 132: 403–12, 1978.
42. Monello, L.F. & Mayer, J. Obese adolescent girls: An unrecognized minority group. *Am. J. Clin. Nutr.* 13: 35–40, 1963.
43. Staffieri, J.R. A study of social stereotype of body image in children. *J. Pers. Soc. Psych.* 7: 101–04, 1967.
44. Richardson, S.A., Hastorf, A.H., Goodman, N. Cultural uniformity in reaction to physical disabilities. *Am. Soc. Rev.* 26: 241–47, 1961.
45. Maddox, G.L., Back, K.W., & Liederman, V.R. Overweight as social deviance and disability. *J. Health Soc. Behav.* 9: 287–98, 1968.
46. Stunkard, A.J. & Rush, A.J. Dieting and depression reexamined: A critical review of reports of untoward responses during weight reduction for obesity. *Ann. Int. Med.* 81: 526–33, 1974.
47. Stunkard, A.J. The dieting depression: Incidence and clinical characteristics of untoward responses to weight reduction regimens. *Am. J. Med.* 23: 77–86, 1957.
48. Silverstone, J.P. & Lascelles, B.D. Dieting and depression. *Brit. J. Psychiat.* 112: 513–19, 1966.
49. Stunkard, A.J. *The Pain of Obesity.* Palo Alto: Bull, 1976.
50. Brownell, K.D. The psychological and medical sequelae of nonprescription weight reduction programs. Paper presented at the annual meeting of the American Psychological Association, Toronto, August 1978.
51. Stunkard, A.J. (Ed.). *Obesity.* Philadelphia: Saunders, in press.
52. Wooley, S.C., Wooley, O.W., & Dyrenforth, S.R. Theoretical, practical, and social issues in behavioral treatments of obesity. *J. Appl. Behav. Anal.* 12: 3–26, 1979.
53. Garrow, J. *Energy Balance and Obesity in Man.* New York: Elsevier, 1974.
54. Rose, H.E. & Mayer, J. Activity, caloric intake, and the energy balance of infants. *Pediat.* 41: 18–29, 1968.
55. Johnson, M.L., Burke, M.S., & Mayer, J. Relative importance of inactivity and overeating in the energy balance of obese high school girls. *Am. J. Clin. Nutr.* 4: 37–44, 1956.
56. Stephanic, P.A., Heald, F.P., & Mayer, J. Caloric intake in relation to energy output of obese and nonobese adolescent boys. *Am. J. Clin. Nutr.* 7: 55–62, 1959.
57. Bullen, B.A., Reed, R.B., & Mayer, J. Physical activity of obese and nonobese adolescent girls appraised by motion picture sampling. *Am. J. Clin. Nutr.* 14: 211–33, 1964.
58. Bradfield, R., Paulos, J., & Grossman, H. Energy expenditure and heart rate of obese high school girls. *Am. J. Clin. Nutr.* 24: 1,482–86, 1971.

59. Maxfield, E. & Konishi, F. Patterns of food intake and physical activity in obesity. *J. Am. Diet. Assoc.* 49: 406–408, 1966.

60. Stunkard, A.J. & Pestka, J. The physical activity of obese girls. *Am. J. Dis. Child.* 103: 812–17, 1962.

61. Wilkinson, P., Parklin, J., Pearloom, G. Energy intake and physical activity in obese children. *Brit. Med. J.* 1: 756, 1977.

62. Waxman, M. & Stunkard, A.J. Caloric intake and expenditure of obese children. *J. Pediat.*, in press.

63. Mayer, J., Roy, P., & Mitra, K.P. Relation between caloric intake, body weight, and physical work: Studies in an industrial male population in West Bengal. *Am. J. Clin. Nutr.* 4: 169–75, 1956.

64. Rand, C. & Stunkard, A.J. Obesity and psychoanalysis. *Am. J. Psychiat.* 135: 547–51, 1974.

65. Chirico, A. & Stunkard, A.J. Physical activity and human obesity. *New Eng. J. Med.* 263: 935–40, 1960.

66. Bloom, W.L. & Eidex, M.F. Inactivity as a major factor in adult obesity. *Metabol.* 16: 679–84, 1967.

67. Brownell, K.D., Stunkard, A.J., & Albaum, J.M. Evaluation and modification of exercise patterns in the natural environment. *Am. J. Psychiat.*, in press.

68. Meyers, A.W., Stunkard, A.J., Coll, M. Obesity and activity choice. *Behav. Mod.*, in press.

69. Brownell, K.D. & Stunkard, A.J. Exercise in the development and control of obesity. In Stunkard, A.J. (Ed.), *Obesity*. Philadelphia: Saunders, in press.

70. Keesey, R.E. Set-points and body weight regulation. *Psych. Clin. N. Am.* 1: 523–44, 1978.

71. Nisbett, R.E. Hunger, obesity, and the ventromedial hypothalamus. *Psych. Rev.* 79: 433–53, 1972.

72. Adolph, E.F. Urges to eat and drink in rats. *Am. J. Physiol.* 151: 110–25, 1947.

73. Brooks, C.McC. & Lambert, E.F. A study of the effect of limitation of food intake and the method of feeding on the rate of weight gain during hypothalamic obesity in the albino rat. *Am. J. Physiol.* 147: 695–707, 1946.

74. Mitchel, J.S. & Keesey, R.E. Defense of a lowered weight maintenance level by lateral hypothalamically lesioned rats: evidence from a restriction-refeeding regimen. *Physiol. Behav.* 18: 1,121–25, 1977.

75. Keys, A., Brozek, J., Henschel, A. *The Biology of Human Starvation*, Vols. 1 & 2. Minneapolis: U. of Minnesota Press, 1950.

76. Sims, E.A.H. & Horton, E.S. Endocrine and metabolic adaptation to obesity and starvation. *Am. J. Clin. Nutr.* 21: 1,455–70, 1968.

77. Bray, G.A. Effect of caloric restriction on energy expenditure in obese patients. *Lancet* 2: 397–98, 1969.

78. Buskirk, E.R., Thompson, R.H., Lutwak, L. Energy balance of obese patients during weight reduction: influence of diet restriction and exercise. *Ann. NY. Acad. Sci.* 110: 918–40, 1963.

79. Drennick, E.J. & Dennin, H.F. Energy expenditure in fasting men. *J. Lab. Clin. Med.* 81: 420–21, 1973.

80. Grande, F., Anderson, J.T., & Keys, A. Changes in basal metabolism rate in man in semistarvation and refeeding. *J. Appl. Physiol.* 12: 230–38, 1958.

81. Apfelbaum, M., Bostsarron, J., & Lacatis, D. Effect of caloric restriction and excessive caloric intake on energy expenditure. *Am. J. Clin. Nutr.* 24: 1,405–09, 1971.

82. Hamilton, C.L. Problems of refeeding after starvation in the rat. *Ann. NY Acad. Sci.* 157: 1,004–17, 1969.

83. Boyle, P.C., Storlien, H., & Keesey, R.E. Increased efficiency of food utilization following weight loss. *Physiol. Behav.* 21: 261–64, 1978.

84. Wirtshafter, D. & Davis, J.D. Set-points, settling points, and the control of body weight. *Physiol. Behav.* 19: 75–78, 1977.

85. Sjöström, L. The contribution of fat cells to the determination on body weight. *Psych. Clin. N Am.* 1: 493, 522, 1978.

86. Björntorp, P. & Sjöström, L. Number and size of adipose tissue fat cells in relation to metabolism in human obesity. *Metabol.* 20: 703, 713, 1971.

87. Bray, G.A. Measurement of subcutaneous fat cells from obese patients. *Ann. Int. Med.* 73: 565–69, 1970.

88. Hirsch, J. & Knittle, J.L. Cellularity of obese and nonobese human adipose tissue. *Fed. Proc.* 29: 1,516–21, 1970.

89. Salans, L.B., Horton, E.S., & Sims, E.A.H. Experimental obesity in man: cellular character of the adipose tissue. *J. Clin. Invest.* 50: 1,005–11, 1971.

90. Grinker, J. Behavioral and metabolic consequences of weight reduction. *J. Am. Diet. Assoc.* 62: 30–34, 1973.

91. Ashwell, M. The relationship of the age of onset of obesity to the success of its treatment in the adult. *Brit. Med. J.* 34: 201–204, 1975.

92. Brownell, K.D., Heckerman, C.L., & Westlake, R.J. The behavioral control of obesity. A descriptive analysis of a large-scale program. *J. Clin. Psych.*, in press.

93. Brownell, K.D., Heckerman, C.L., Westlake, R.J. The effect of couples training and partner cooperativeness in the behavioral treatment of obesity. *Behav. Res. Ther.* 16: 323–33, 1978.

94. Ferguson, J.M. A clinical program for the behavioral control of obesity. In Williams, B.J., Martin, S., & Foreyt, J.P. (Eds.), *Obesity: Behavioral Approaches to Dietary Management*. New York: Brunner/Mazel, 1976.

95. Mahoney, B.K., Rogers, T., Straw, M.K. *Human obesity: Assessment and Treatment*. Englewood Cliffs: Prentice-Hall, in press.

96. Jeffrey, R.W., Wing, R.R., & Stunkard, A.J. Behavioral treatment of obesity: the state of the art in 1976. *Behav. Ther.* 9: 189–99, 1978.

97. Brownell, K.D. Assessment in the treatment of eating disorders. In Barlow, D.H. (Ed.), *Assessment of Adult Disorders*. New York: Guilford, in press.

98. Björntorp, P., Carlgren, G., Isaksson, B. Effect of an energy-reduced dietary regimen in relation to adipose tissue cellularity in obese women. *Am. J. Clin. Nutr.* 28: 445–52, 1975.

99. Mayer, J. *Overweight: Causes, Cost, and Control.* Englewood Cliffs: Prentice-Hall, 1968.

100. Stunkard, A.J. The social environment and the control of obesity. In Stunkard, A.J. (Ed.), *Obesity*. Philadelphia: Saunders, in press.

101. Srole, L., Langer, T.S., Michael, S.T. *Mental Health in the Metropolis: The Midtown Manhattan Study.* New York: McGraw-Hill, 1962.

102. Moore, M.E., Stunkard, A.J., & Srole, L. Obesity, social class and mental illness. *JAMA* 181: 962–66, 1962.

103. Silverstone, J.T., Gordon, R.P., & Stunkard, A.J. Social factors in obesity in London. *Practitioner*, 202: 682–88, 1969.

104. Baird, I.M., Silverstone, J.T., & Grimshaw, J.J. The prevalence of obesity in a London borough. *Practitioner.* 212: 706–14, 1974.

105. Stunkard, A.J. & Koch, C. The interpretation of gastric motility. I. Apparent bias in the reports of hunger by obese persons. *Arch. Gen. Psychiat.* 11: 74–82, 1964.

106. Janowitz, H.D. Role of the gastrointestinal tract in the regulation of food intake. In Code, C.F. (Ed.), *Handbook of Physiology. I. Alimentary canal.* Washington, D.C.: American Physiological Society, 1967.

107. Stunkard, A.J. & Fox, S. The relationship of gastric motility and hunger: a summary of the evidence. *Psychosom. Med.* 33: 123–34, 1971.

108. Schachter, S. Obesity and eating. *Science.* 161: 751–56, 1968.

109. Schacter, S., Goldman, R., & Gordon, A. Effects of fear, food deprivation and obesity on eating. *J. Pers. Soc. Psych.* 10: 91–97, 1968.

110. Schachter, S. & Gross, L. Manipulated time and eating behavior. *J. Pers. Soc. Psych.* 10: 98–106, 1968.
111. Rodin, J. & Slochower, J. Externality in the nonobese: The effects of environmental responsiveness on weight. *J. Pers. Soc. Psych.* 29: 557–65, 1976.
112. Schachter, S. & Rodin, J. *Obese Humans and Rats.* Washington, D.C.: Erlbaum/Halsted, 1974.
113. Rodin, J. Environmental factors in obesity. *Psych. Clin. N. Am.* 1: 581–92, 1978.
114. Stuart, R.B. & Davis, B. *Slim Chance in a Fat World: Behavioral Control of Obesity.* Champaign, Ill: Research Press, 1972.
115. Mahoney, M.J. & Mahoney, K. *Permanent Weight Control: A Total Solution to the Dieter's Dilemma.* New York: Norton, 1976.
116. Brownell, K.D. *The Partnership Diet Program.* New York: Rawson, Wade, in press.
117. Rodin, J. The effects of obesity and set-point on taste responsiveness and intake in humans. *J. Comp. Physiol. Psych.* 89: 1,003–09, 1975.
118. Goldman, D., Jaffa, M., & Schachter, S. Yom Kippur, Air France, dormitory food and eating behavior of obese and normal persons. *J. Pers. Soc. Psych.* 10: 117–23, 1968.
119. Nisbett, R.E. Taste, deprivation and weight determinants of eating behavior. *J. Pers. Soc. Psych.* 10: 107–16, 1968.
120. Ross, L. Effects of manipulating the salience of food upon consumption by obese and normal eaters. In Schachter, S. & Rodin, J. (Eds.), *Obese Humans and Rats.* Washington, D.C.: Erlbaum/Halstad, 1974.
121. Meyers, A.W., Stunkard, A.J., & Coll, M. Food accessibility and food choice: a test of Schachter's externality hypothesis. *Arch. Gen. Psychiat.*, in press.
122. Price, J.M. & Grinker, J. Effects of degree of obesity, food deprivation and palatability on eating behavior of humans. *J. Comp. Physiol. Psych.* 85: 265–71, 1973.
123. Decke, E. Effects of taste on the eating behavior of obese and normal persons. In Schachter, S. (Ed.), *Emotion, Obesity, and Crime.* New York: Academic Press, 1971.
124. Wooley, O. & Wooley, S.C. The experimental psychology of obesity. In Silversteon, T. & Fincham, J. (Eds.), *Obesity: Pathogenesis and Management.* Lancaster, England: Medical and Technical Publishing, 1975.
125. Wilson, G.T. Methodological considerations in treatment outcome research on obesity. *J. Consult. Clin. Psych.* 46: 687–702, 1978.
126. Powley, T. The ventromedial hypothalamic syndrome, satiety, and a cephalic phase hypothesis. *Psychol. Rev.* 84: 89–96, 1977.
127. Mrosovsky, N. & Powley, T.L. Set-points for body weight and fat. *Behav. Biol.* 20: 205–23, 1977.
128. Herman, C.P. & Mack, D. Restrained and unrestrained eating. *J. Pers.* 43: 647–60, 1975.
129. Polivy, J. Perception of calories and regulation of intake in restrained and unrestrained subjects. *Addic. Behav.* 1: 237–43, 1976.
130. Herman, C.P. Restrained eating. *Psych. Clin. N. Am.* 1: 593–607, 1978.
131. Herman, C.P. & Polivy, J. Anxiety, restraint and eating behavior. *J. Abn. Psych.* 84: 666–72, 1975.
132. Hibscher, J.A. & Herman, C.P. Obesity, dieting, and the expression of "obese" characteristics. *J. Comp. Physiol. Psych.* 91: 374–80, 1977.
133. Ruderman, A.J. & Wilson, G.T. Weight, restraint, cognitions, and counterregulation. *Behav. Res. Ther.*, in press.
134. Spencer, J. & Fremouw, W. Binge eating as a function of restraint and weight classification. Unpublished manuscript, West Virginia University, 1979.
135. Stunkard, A.J. & Brownell, K.D. Behavior therapy and self-help programs for obesity. In Munro, J.F. (Ed.), *The Treatment of Obesity.* London: MTP Press, 1979.

136. Stunkard, A.J. The management of obesity. NY J. Med. 58: 79–87, 1958.

137. Stuart, R.B. Behavioral control of overeating. Behav. Res. Ther. 5: 357–65, 1967.

138. Harris, M.G. Self-directed program for weight control: a pilot study. J. Abn. Psych. 74: 263–70, 1969.

139. Wollersheim, J.P. Effectiveness of group therapy based on learning principles in the treatment of overweight women. J. Abn. Psych. 76: 462–74, 1970.

140. Penick, S.B., Filion, R., Fox, S. Behavior modification in the treatment of obesity. Psychosom. Med. 33: 49–55, 1971.

141. Hagen, R.L. Group therapy versus bibliotherapy in weight reduction. Behav. Ther. 5: 222–34, 1974.

142. Ferstl, R., Jokusch, V. & Brengelman, J.C. Die verhaltenstherapeutische Behandlung des Ubergewichts. Int. J. Health Ed. 18: 119–36, 1975.

143. Hanson, R.W., Bordon, B.L., Hall, S.M. Use of programmed instruction in teaching self-management skills to overweight adults. Behav. Ther. 7: 366–73, 1976.

144. Fernan, W.S. The role of experimenter contact in behavioral bibliotherapy of obesity. Unpublished manuscript, Pennsylvania State University, 1973.

145. Brownell, K.B., Heckerman, C.L., & Westlake, R.J. Therapist and group contact as variables in the behavioral treatment of obesity. J. Consul. Clin. Psych. 46: 593–94, 1978.

146. Stunkard, A.J. & Mahoney, M.J. Behavioral treatment of eating disorders. In Leitenberg, H. (Ed.), The Handbook of Behavior Modification. Englewood Cliffs: Prentice-Hall, 1976.

147. Bandura, A. Principles of Behavior Modification. New York: Holt, 1969.

148. Kazdin, A.E. & Wilson, G.T. Evaluation of Behavior Therapy: Issues, Evidence, and Research Strategies. Cambridge: Ballinger, 1978.

149. O'Leary, K.D. & Wilson, G.T. Behavior Therapy: Application and Outcome. Englewood Cliffs: Prentice-Hall, 1975.

150. Franks, C.M. & Wilson, G.T. (Eds.). Annual Review of Behavior Therapy: Theory and Practice, vol. 3: 1975. New York: Brunner/Mazel, 1975.

151. Kingsley, R.G. & Wilson, F.T. Behavior therapy for obesity: a comparative investigation of long-term efficacy. J. Consult. Clin. Psych. 45: 288–98, 1977.

152. Ashby, W.A. & Wilson, F.T. Behavior therapy for obesity: booster sessions and long-term maintenance of weight loss. Behav. Res. Ther. 15: 451–64, 1977.

153. Wilson, F.T. & Brownell, K.D. Behavior therapy for obesity: including family members in the treatment process. Behav. Ther. 9: 943–45, 1978.

154. Craighead, L.W., Stunkard, A.J., & O'Brien, R. New treatments for obesity. Paper presented at the annual meeting of the American Psychological Association, Toronto, August 1978.

155. Stunkard, A.I. & Penick, S.B. Behavior modification in the treatment of obesity: the problem of maintaining weight loss. Arch. Gen. Psychiat. 36: 801–806, 1979.

156. Wilson, G.T. Behavior modification and the treatment of obesity. In Stunkard, A.J. (Ed.), Obesity. Philadelphia: Saunders, in press.

157. Farquhar, J.W., Macoby, N., Wood, P.D. Community education for cardiovascular health. Lancet 1: 1,192–95, 1977.

158. Mahoney, M.J. & Mahoney, K. Treatment of obesity: a clinical exploration. In Williams, B.J., Martin, S., Foreyt, J.P. (Eds.), Obesity: Behavioral Approaches To Dietary Management. New York: Brunner/Mazel, 1976.

159. Rosenthal, B. Involvement of spouses in the treatment of obesity. Unpublished dissertation, University of Connecticut, 1975.

160. Fremouw, W.J. & Zitter, R.E. Individual and couple behavioral contracting for weight reduction and maintenance. Behav. Ther., in press.

161. Saccone, A.J. & Israel, A.C. Effects of experimenter versus significant other-controlled reinforcement and choice of target behavior on weight loss. Behav. Ther. 9: 271–78, 1978.

162. Israel, A.C. & Saccone, A.J. Follow-up effects of choice of mediator and target of reinforcement on weight loss. *Behav. Ther.* 10: 260–65, 1979.

163. Pearce, J.W., LeBow, M.D., & Orchard, J. The role of spouse involvement in the behavioral treatment of obese women. Paper presented at the annual meeting of the Canadian Psychological Association, Quebec, 1979.

164. Zitter, R.E. & Fremouw, W.J. Individual versus partner consequation for weight loss. *Behav. Ther.* 9: 808–13, 1978.

165. O'Neil, P.M., Currey, H.S., Hirsch, A.A. Effects of sex of subject and spouse involvement on weight loss in a behavioral treatment program: a retrospective investigation. *Addic. Behav.* 4: 167–78, 1979.

166. Stunkard, A.J. & Brownell, K.D. Work site treatment for obesity. *Am. J. Psychiat.*, in press.

167. Alderman, M.H. & Schoenbaum, E.E. Detection and treatment of hypertension at the work site. *N. Eng. J. Med.* 293: 65–68, 1975.

168. Brightwell, D.R. & Naylor, C.S. Effects of a combined behavioral and pharmacological program on weight loss. *Int. J. Obes.* 3: 141–48, 1979.

169. Bistrian, B.R. Clinical use of a protein-sparing modified fast. *JAMA* 21: 2,299–2,302, 1978.

170. Genuth, S.M., Castro, J.H., & Vertes, V. Weight reduction in obesity by outpatient semistarvation. *JAMA*, 230: 987–91, 1974.

171. Bistrian, B.R., Winterer, J., Blackburn, G.L. Effect of a protein-sparing diet and brief fast on nitrogen metabolism in mildly obese subjects. *J. Lab. Clin. Med.* 89: 1,030–35, 1977.

172. Lindner, P.G. & Blackburn, G.L. An interdisciplinary approach to obesity, utilizing fasting modified by protein-sparing theory. *Obes. Bariat. Med.* 5: 198–216, 1976.

173. Leon, G.R. Current directions in the treatment of obesity. *Psych. Bull.* 83: 557–78, 1976.

174. Stuart, R.B. Self-help for self-management. In Stuart, R.B. (Ed.), *Behavioral Self-Management.* New York: Brunner/Mazel, 1977.

175. Garb, A.R. & Stunkard, A.J. Effectiveness of a self-help group in obesity control. *Arch. Int. Med.* 134: 716–20, 1974.

176. Levitz, L.S. & Stunkard, A.J. A therapeutic coalition for obesity: behavior modification and patient self-help. *Am. J. Psychiat.* 131: 423–27, 1974.

177. Ashwell, M. Commercial weight loss groups. In Bray, G. (Ed.), *Recent Advances In Obesity Research, II.* London: Newman, in press.

178. Nash, J.D. Curbing drop-out from treatment for obesity. Unpublished dissertation, Stanford University, 1977.

179. Bray, G.A. & Benfield, J.R. Intestinal bypass surgery for obese patients: a summary and perspective. *Am. J. Clin. Nutr.* 30: 121–27, 1977.

180. Bray, G.A. Intestinal bypass surgery for obese patients: behavioral and metabolic considerations. *Psych. Clin. N. Am.* 1: 673–89, 1978.

181. Iber, F.L. & Cooper, N. Jejunoileal bypass for the treatment of massive obesity: prevalence, morbidity, and short- and long-term consequences. *Am. J. Clin. Nutr.* 30: 4–15, 1977.

182. Payne, J.E. & DeWind, L.T. Surgical treatment of obesity. *Am. J. Surg.* 118: 141–47, 1969.

183. Scott, H.W., Jr., & Law, D.H. Clinical appraisal of jejunoileal shunt in patients with morbid obesity. *Am. J. Surg.* 117: 246–53, 1969.

184. Mills, M.J. & Stunkard, A.J. Behavioral changes following surgery for obesity. *Am. J. Psychiat.* 133: 527–31, 1976.

185. Mason, E.E. & Ito, C. Gastric bypass in obesity. *Surg. Clin. N. Am.* 47: 1,345–51, 1967.

186. Hermrick, A.S., Jewell, W.R., & Hardin, C.A.L. Gastric bypass for morbid obesity: results and implications. *Surgery*, 80: 498, 1976.

187. Alden, J.F. Gastric and jejunoileal bypass: a comparison in the treatment of morbid obesity. *Arch. Surg.* 112: 799–806, 1977.

188. Griffen, W.O., Young, V.L., & Stevenson, C.C. Prospective comparison of gastric and jejunoileal bypass procedures for morbid obesity. *Ann. Surg.* 186: 500–509, 1977.

6

The Effects of "Stress" and Conditioning on Immune Responses

ROBERT ADER

This chapter does not deal with psychophysiological disorders. I am nevertheless gratified by this volume's contents and its implicit acknowledgment that the relationship between psychological and physiological factors is fundamental to an analysis of the phenomenology and treatment of disease, not just certain diseases that the layman and, too frequently, the professional have come to label as "psychosomatic." As a result of the psychosomatic research of today, it is becoming clear that there is probably no major organ system or homeostatic defense mechanism that is subject to the impact of an interaction between psychological and physiological events. However, to paraphrase further the stated rationale for this volume, the complexity of the mechanisms underlying this interaction are, for the most part, undefined or imperfectly understood. It is these latter issues that I will address, even if I can provide no clarification. On the contrary, I wish to further increase the breadth of the approach to an understanding of psychophysiologic relationships by discussing a new field which has, for the most part, remained undefined and is poorly understood—namely, the interrelationship between behavioral and immune processes. In contrast to the commonly held notion—or at least the belief, in the common approaches to immunologic research—that the immune system is an autonomous defense system, I submit that, like any other physiologic system functioning in the interests of homeostasis, the immune system is sensitive to the influence of central nervous system processes. As such, the immune system can stand as a potential mediator of psychophysiological disorders.

All one need do is browse through the table of contents or the index of textbooks in immunology to confirm that little or no attention is given to the central nervous system or to environmental factors which, operating through the nervous system, could be acting to influence immune function. We can, perhaps, attribute this limited perspective to the complexity of immune function itself and to the difficulties encountered in studying and defining a relatively new and rapidly growing discipline. Quite understandably, the strategy of immunologic research is modeled after the successful approach adopted by Koch, Pasteur, and a following generation of scientists who designed and conducted their studies in such a way as to purposely reduce or eliminate "extraneous" factors that might influence the phenomena being studied. As Dubos (1) has so eloquently argued, though, such an approach reduces or eliminates the myriad factors which, in reality, do influence the behaving individual in his adaptation to the real world. Such a model, therefore, is incomplete; the issues involved have recently been elaborated elsewhere (2, 3, 4) and need not be repeated here. In his James Ewing Lecture before the Society of Surgical Oncology, Theodore Miller (5) acknowledged that "trying to convince the members of this society that cancer has a psychodynamic basis would be like trying to convert a bunch of lions to a life of vegetarianism." I do not believe that my task is quite that difficult, so let me proceed to outline some of the diverse data which directly or indirectly implicate the central nervous system in the regulation of immune responses.

That host factors are of critical importance in determining physiologic responsivity, disease susceptibility, or, if you will, the maintenance of homeostasis, is almost intuitively evident. Indeed, the diversity of material covered in this volume testifies to the range of disorders that may be defined or influenced by the psychophysiologic interactions involved. Immunologically mediated disorders are not yet represented. As a result of the evolving research in this area, however, they are likely to be represented in the future. Immunology has, to be sure, attended to some characteristics of the host. These have included the species and strain of animals selected for study, genetic factors that make certain species particularly suitable for study or that actually define the phenomenon being investigated, and variables such as age, sex, nutritional status, and circadian rhythmicity. For the most part, these variables have been taken into consideration for methodologic reasons rather than as acknowledgment of host factors that might modify immune responses and that warrant systematic variation and study in their own right. It may be that, while the potential impact of central nervous system processes is recognized, such processes are de-emphasized in order to conduct straightforward experiments or to avoid further complicating an already complicated phenomenon. At this stage in the development of immunology, such a pragmatic strategy may seem appropriate. Nevertheless, it is inadequate for a complete understanding of the immune system as an adaptive defense mechanism acting in concert with other adaptive processes to maintain the integrity of the whole organism.

That the immune system represents a homeostatic defense mechanism that is integrated with other homeostatic processes is not a speculative hypothesis. There are several quite disparate lines of evidence based on data from different disciplines and studies at different biobehavioral levels of organization that support the proposition that the central nervous system is capable of exerting some regulatory influence on immunologic reactivity (6). First, and most indirectly, there is a great deal of research documenting the effects of "stress" on susceptibility to immunologically mediated disease processes. More directly, there are also studies delineating the effects of "stress" on various *in vitro* and *in vivo* parameters of immunologic competence per se. This material has been reviewed on several occasions (7, 8, 9, 10, 11, 12), and new, detailed reviews, together with recent data, are in preparation (6). Another line of evidence consists of recent studies on the impact of conditioning in modifying immunologic reactivity (13, 14, 15, 16, 17). As extensions of the literature on the learning of visceral and autonomic responses (18, 19) and the conditioning of pharmacologic effects (e.g., 20), these studies suggest that conditioning can influence at least some immune responses. Such research was actually initiated in the Soviet Union more than 50 years ago and is reviewed elsewhere (21). As a behaviorist, I will, for the purpose of this presentation, provide a brief overview of these data, emphasizing the new work on conditioning. There is, however, further evidence of a central nervous system involvement in immune processes, which may be derived from the parallel ontogenetic development of neuroendocrine and immune function (22); the relationship between hormones and immune processes (23, 24, 25); the effects of a variety of pharmacologic agents (26), including, for example, cholinergic substances (27) and psychotomimetic drugs such as marijuana (28) on immune responses; and the circadian rhythmicity in immunologic phenomena (29, 30). In addition, there are now several reports of the effects of lesioning or electrical stimulation of specific areas within the hypothalamus on humoral and cell-mediated immune responses (31, 32, 33). These contributions, too, are described in a forthcoming compendium of research in psychoneuroimmunology (6).

"STRESS" EFFECTS

Disease Susceptibility

Studies of the effects of "stress" on neoplastic processes constitute one source of data with respect to experimentally induced disease processes that may involve immunologic mechanisms. Fox (34) has provided an extensive review and analysis of the available data on humans. LaBarba (9) and Riley (35) have reviewed the animal research that shows that a variety of experimental conditions—including the manipulation of early life experiences, changes in the psychosocial environment of laboratory animals, and any number of stressful stimulus conditions—can influence cancer susceptibility. Presumably, experiential events including the capacity to cope with "stressful" circumstances (36) induce psychophysiologic changes within the organism. In interaction with the changes induced by the superimposed pathogen, these result in alterations in susceptibility to mammary tumors, transplanted tumors, and experimentally induced as well as spontaneously occurring forms of leukemia.

Viral disease represents another example. In general, it would appear that "stress" increases susceptibility to a variety of infectious agents. The results, however, are not uniform or simple, and the effects are frequently small and sometimes equivocal. Moreover, it is not entirely clear that all the behavioral manipulations imposed can be subsumed under the single rubric of "stress." Rasmussen et al. (37), for example, subjected mice to a daily avoidance-conditioning regimen (animals could avoid electric foot-shock by jumping over a barrier in response to a conditioned stimulus). Mortality from herpes simplex virus inoculation increased from 44 percent in controls to 56 percent in mice stimulated for two weeks, and to 74 percent in mice stimulated for four weeks before being inoculated with the virus. Physical restraint of the same duration (plus food and water deprivation) per day yielded the same results. Johnson et al. (38) used the same avoidance conditioning situation before inoculating mice with Coxsackie B virus. "Stressed" animals showed significantly more weight loss than controls. Further, all the animals that died came from the "stressed" group, and these mice also showed the greatest amounts of virus present in various organs.

Similar results were obtained by Friedman et al. (39), in a study in which an attempt was made to control for the direct physical effects of the electric shock used in avoidance-conditioning paradigms. Adult mice were subjected to a periodic schedule of a light followed by electric shock. Other groups experienced either the light or the shock stimulus alone, on the same periodic schedule, or remained unmanipulated. Stimulation was introduced three days before inoculation with Coxsackie B virus and continued for four days after inoculation. Control mice experienced the same environmental conditions but were not inoculated with the virus. Neither the "stressful" stimulation nor the inoculum alone was sufficient to cause any weight change. Mice inoculated with Coxsackie virus *and* not subjected to the periodic presentation of light-shock stimulation, however, showed a significant reduction in body weight, and all the animals that died came from this light-shock group.

Rasmussen et al. (40) inoculated mice with polyoma virus at birth. Some time after being weaned, the animals were subjected to an avoidance-conditioning paradigm plus high-intensity sound stimulation. In this instance, the stressful stimulation did not influence disease susceptibility. The negative results were attributed to the delay between virus inoculation and the initiation of "stress." When the environmental stimulation was introduced immediately after inoculation with the virus (at 2–3 weeks of age), the stimulated mice were more susceptible than controls (41). Additional evidence of the critical nature of the temporal relationship between "stress" and susceptibility to viral infection, and the potential influence of variables such as the nature of the "stress" and the route of inoculation, comes from studies on susceptibility to vesicular stomatitis virus in mice (42, 43).

The response to parasitic infection may also be affected by exposing animals to stressful environmental circumstances. Weinmann and Rothman (44), for example, observed a depressed resistance to *Hymenolepsis nana*, a tapeworm, when intense fighting occurred among male mice. Hamilton (45) also observed an increased susceptibility to *H. nana*, reflected by the rate of reinfection, which increased in proportion to the frequency with which immunized mice were subjected to "predator-induced stress"; i.e., exposure to a cat.

Despite the apparent uniformity in the data cited above, stressful stimulation does not always increase susceptibility to infectious disease. There are instances in which no differences in susceptibility have been observed, and other instances in which "stress" decreased susceptibility. Subjecting mice to light and/or electric shock stimulation as described above had no effect on the response to encephalomyocarditis virus, but increased resistance to *P. berghei*, a rodent malaria (46). Monkeys exposed to avoidance conditioning have been shown to have an increased resistance to poliomyelitis (47), and the physical restraint of rats (but not immersion in a cold bath) suppresses development of experimental allergic encephalomyelitis (48).

Experimental manipulation of the social interactions among animals provides an especially compelling illustration of the multiple effects of "stress" on responses to infectious disease. Group housing or manipulations that are effective in increasing or altering the social interactions among animals have been found to increase resistance to encephalomyocarditis virus (49) and *E. coli* (50), while increasing susceptibility to trichinosis (51), malaria (52), and a Salmonella infection (53). In a related example, Amkraut et al. (54) found that the "stress" of crowding increased susceptibility to adjuvant-induced arthritis in the rat, while Rogers et al. (55) observed an increased resistance to a collagen-induced arthritis in rats "stressed" by exposure to a cat. Comparable data could be cited in the case of neoplastic (9, 35) and other pathophysiologic processes (56, 57).

These are some of the data which, in documenting the effects of environmental manipulations on susceptibility and responses to infectious disease, suggest that experiential influences and behavioral responses may affect the immune system. These studies tell us little about the underlying mechanisms that may be involved; they do, however, provide an important message with respect to the concepts and strategies that have to be adopted if one is to pursue this line of research. It seems clear that the effects of "stress" on susceptibility to infectious disease depend upon several factors (e.g., age, sex, and species of animal), including the experientially determined psychophysiological state of the organism upon which the potentially pathogenic stimulation is superimposed; that is, it is influenced by a variety of factors interacting within the host. Susceptibility will also be determined by the nature and intensity of both the stressful stimulation and the challenge to the host. It is also clear that the several forms of stimulation used and referred to as being stressful do not necessarily have the same effects. Therefore, to refer to responses to electric shock, avoidance conditioning, restraint, "overcrowding," and the like, as responses to stressors, contributes little to our understanding of the mechanisms that could be mediating the altered susceptibility to disease. As I have argued before (56), such a generalization may even impede progress in this field, because of its implicit assumption of an equivalence of stimuli, fostering the search for simple, single-cause explanations. Whatever stimulation is imposed, and however it may be interpreted by the experimenter, the effects of such stimulation are not likely to be either uniformly beneficial or detrimental to the organism. Whether experimentally imposed stimulation effects an increase or decrease in susceptibility to disease depends upon the nature of the disease process under study. That is, the adaptive significance of the psychophysiological response to some change in environmental circumstances depends upon the pathogenic stimulus to which the organism may be exposed. Therefore, until we are prepared to determine which of the myriad physiologic (and immunologic) changes that accompany the response and adaptation to environmental stimuli are relevant in relation to the response elicited by potentially pathogenic stimuli, we will be unable to predict or control the effects of behavioral factors on disease susceptibility.

Immunological Reactivity

A more direct source of data relating to behavior and immune function consists of studies in which the effects of "stress" have been detected within the immune system. Technological advances in immunology now permit relatively sensitive *in vitro* assays that can be applied to the analysis of psychoimmunologic phenomena. Gisler et al. (58), for example, found that spleen cell suspensions obtained after mice were exposed to acceleration in a centrifuge or ether anesthesia caused a suppression of *in vitro* immunologic reactivity. The onset and degree of suppression varied among the several mouse strains tested and the procedures used. Data obtained in a subsequent study (59) suggested that such "stress" effects could be reproduced by treatment with ACTH. Solomon (personal communication), however, reports that neither he nor Gisler could suppress *in vivo* responses by such hormone administration.

Increases as well as decreases in lymphocyte response have been observed in "stressed" animals (60, 61). In the study by Monjan and Collector (61), mice were subjected to loud noise for one to three hours daily. Initially, lymphocyte cytotoxicity and the response of splenic lymphocytes to mitogenic stimulation were depressed; after approximately one month of daily stimulation, however, there was an increase in responsivity. The biphasic response to environmental stimulation attests, again, to the critical effect of the time at which samples are obtained, in attempting to describe immunologic responses.

"Stress"-induced changes in cellular immunity have also been observed *in vivo*. Guinea pigs show increased reactivity in response to a topically applied chemical irritant, as a result of electric shock stimulation (62, 63). A delayed hypersensitivity reaction, however, was reduced in mice subjected to high temperature (64). Reduced responsivity was also reported by Wistar and Hildeman (65), who observed prolonged survival of a skin allograft in mice subjected to an avoidance-conditioning regimen. Amkraut et al. (66) observed changes in a graft-versus-host response in mice placed on a limited feeding schedule. When limited feeding was introduced before, and continued after, induction of a graft-versus-host response, the response was suppressed. Limited feeding confined to the period before the injection of donor cells had no effect. Experiments conducted in adrenalectomizeda or ACTH-treated hosts indicated that the effects of restricted feeding could not be ascribed to changes in corticosteroid levels.

Adrenal changes do seem to be involved in the response to anaphylactic shock. Mice subjected to daily avoidance conditioning showed a less severe shock reaction and a lower mortality than unstimulated controls (67, 68). A "stress"-induced resistance to anaphylaxis was not observed in adrenalectomized animals, but resistance was restored in adrenalectomized mice treated with hydrocortisone. Adrenalectomy can increase resistance to analphylactic shock, but the hypothesis that adrenal activity alone can account for the protective effects of acute and/or chronic "stress" is not entirely clear. Based on the literature indicating that "crowded" mice show the higher adrenocortical steroid levels, Treadwell and Rasmussen (68) examined the anaphylactic response in group- and individually-housed animals. Under the smaller of two challenge doses, the "incidental stress of isolation" resulted in increased resistance to anaphylaxis.

Although the effects are frequently small and by no means uniform, there are now studies documenting the effects of experiential manipulations on the production of antibody in response to immunogenic stimulation. Yamada et al. (43), for example, were able to demonstrate the effects of an avoidance-conditioning regimen on the response to inoculation with vesicular stomatitis virus, but were unable to detect differences in antibody response. Hill et al. (69) exposed monkeys to a variety of stimuli (noise, light, loss of support) and were able to observe an attenuated antibody response to bovine serum albumin. Vessey (70) found less precipitating antibody in response to beef serum in mice that were changed from individual to group housing conditions. Edwards and

Dean (53) also observed a reduced humoral reactivity in mice housed in high relative to low density groups in response to an injection of typhoid-paratyphoid vaccine. In contrast, Glenn and Becker (71) observed that group-caged mice previously immunized with bovine serum albumin had higher levels of precipitating antibody in response to a booster injection of antigen than did individually caged animals.

Solomon (72) noted a reduced primary and secondary response to flagellin, a bacterial antigen, when group housing was introduced before, and continued after immunization. Group housing was the only one of the four "stressors" used, that influenced antibody responses. Generalizing from their published and unpublished work, Solomon et al. (73) conclude that "stress" is immunosuppressive when imposed before and immediately after inoculation with flagellin, but "stress" imposed several days after inoculation is ineffective. Futhermore, "stress" effects are observable only in response to relatively small doses of antigen; large doses of flagellin or sheep erythrocytes, for example, appear to be insensitive to the subtle effects of environmental factors.

Another example of the effects of experiential factors on humoral immunity is the observation that the immunologic competence of the adult may be influenced by experiences that occur during early development (74). Rats that were handled daily during the period from birth through weaning were subsequently found to have a more pronounced primary and secondary antibody response to inoculation with flagellin than unstimulated controls.

Experiential factors are capable of influencing immunologic reactivity. Like the data on disease susceptibility cited earlier, the effects depend upon the quality and quantity of the environmental stimulation, the immunogenic stimulus, a variety of host factors, and the parameters of immunologic reactivity that are measured. In general, the effects of experiential factors on immune responses are small and, superficially, at least, inconsistent, but this may reflect more upon our incomplete understanding of the mechanisms involved than upon the phenomenon itself.

Conditioning Effects

Very recent data implicating the central nervous system in the regulation of immune responses comes from studies of conditioning. The hypothesis that conditioning procedures could be used to suppress an immune response was derived from the serendipitous observation of mortality among animals being observed in a taste-aversion learning situation (75).

Briefly, a single trial on which a novel, distinctively flavored drinking solution is paired with an injection of a toxic agent will result in an aversion to that drinking solution when it is subsequently presented. In one study, we varied the volume of a saccharin solution, the conditioned stimulus (CS), that was paired with a constant dose of cyclophosphamide, the unconditioned stimulus (US). The magnitude of the initial aversion to saccharin and resistance to extinction was directly related to the volume of saccharin consumed on the single conditioning trial. During the course of extinction trials, however, some of the rats died, and mortality rate also tended to vary directly with the amount of saccharin originally consumed. As it happens, cyclophosphamide, the US in this study, is a potent cytotoxic drug that suppresses immunologic responses. Therefore, in order to account for this observation, it was hypothesized that pairing a neutral stimulus with an immunosuppressive drug could result in the conditioning of immunosuppressive response. If conditioned rats were repeatedly reexposed to such a CS and thereby immunologically impaired, they might have become susceptible to the superimposition of any latent pathogens that might have existed in the environment.

These speculations were translated into a study specifically designed to examine conditioned immunosuppression (13). The experimental protocol is described in Table 6-1. Details of our initial experiment were as follows:

Individually caged rats were gradually adapted to consuming their daily allotment of fluid during a single 15-minute drinking period that occurred at the same time each day. This regimen was imposed throughout the period of observation. On the day of conditioning, conditioned animals received a 0.1 percent saccharin chloride solution of tap water during their 15-minute drinking period, followed by an ip injection of 50 mg/kg cyclophosphamide (CY). Nonconditioned rats were, as usual, provided with plain tap water and similarly injected with CY. A placebo group received plain water and was injected with an equal volume of vehicle. Three days after conditioning, all animals were injected ip with sheep erythrocytes (SRBC). Thirty minutes later, one subgroup of

TABLE 6-1
Experimental Protocol

Group	Day 0 Drnk. Sol'n.	Inj.	Sub-grp.	Day 3 Antgn.	Drnk. Sol'n.	Inj.	Day 6 Drnk. Sol'n.	Inj.	Day 9
Conditioned	SAC +	CY	US	SRBC +	H_2O +	CY	H_2O +	−	Sample
				SRBC +	H_2O +	−	H_2O +	CY	Sample
			CSo	SRBC +	H_2O +	Sal	H_2O +	−	Sample
				SRBC +	H_2O +	−	H_2O +	Sal	Sample
			CS1	SRBC +	SAC +	Sal	H_2O +	−	Sample
				SRBC +	H_2O +	−	SAC +	Sal	Sample
			CS2	SRBC +	SAC +	Sal	SAC +	−	Sample
Nonconditioned	H_2O +	CY	NC	SRBC +	SAC +	Sal	H_2O +	−	Sample
				SRBC +	H_2O +	−	SAC +	Sal	Sample
Placebo	H_2O +	Plac.	P	SRBC +	H_2O +	−	H_2O +	−	Sample

conditioned animals (Group CS) received a single drinking bottle containing the saccharin solution for 15 minutes and was then injected with saline. To control for the effects of conditioning per se, a second subgroup of conditioned animals (Group CSo) was given only plain water (i.e., no reexposure to the CS) and was injected with saline. A third conditioned group (Group US) received plain water followed by an injection of CY, to define the unconditioned immunosuppressive effects of CY. Following injection of the antigen, nonconditioned animals (Group NC) were provided with the saccharin drinking solution and injected with saline like Group CS, while placebo-treated rats (Group P) received plain water and remained unmanipulated. In some studies, these groups were treated in an identical manner on a second occasion following antigenic stimulation. In this initial experiment, independent groups were treated on the day that they received SRBC (Day 0), 3 days after the antigen, or on Day 0 and Day 3. On intervening days, animals were provided with plain water during their regularly scheduled drinking period. Six days after injection of SRBC, all animals were killed and blood samples were obtained for the assay of hemagglutinating antibody.

The results of our initial study are shown in Fig. 6-1. Conditioned animals reexposed to saccharin on the day that they received SRBC or 3 days after receiving the antigen did not differ. These groups were collapsed into a single group that received one CS presentation (Group CS_1). The comparable control groups did not differ either, and were similarly combined. The relationship among the several groups was exactly as predicted. Placebo-treated animals showed the highest antibody titers, and CY treatment coincidental with antigenic stimulation suppressed the immune response. Nonconditioned animals exposed to saccharin (Group NC), and the subgroup of conditioned animals that were not reexposed to saccharin (Group SCo), did not differ, but these groups had lower titers than Group P. This probably reflects the residual effects of CY administered on the day of conditioning (16). It is, then, the NC and CSo groups that represent the appropriate control conditions against which one must evaluate the effects of conditioning. The critical experimental groups, conditioned animals reexposed to the CS on either one or two occasions after inoculation with SRBC, displayed an attenuated antibody response; the titer in Group CS was significantly lower than the titers seen in both the NC and CSo groups. Our initial findings, then, reinforce the notion that the pairing of saccharin, a neutral stimulus, with an immunosuppressive drug enabled saccharin to elicit a conditioned immunosuppressive response.

These basic results on conditioned suppression of the antibody response to SRBC have been independently replicated by Rogers et al. (14), Wayner et al. (15), and King (76). Moreover, the absolute antibody titers and the degree of attenuation effected by conditioning are remarkably similar in these studies.

Several additional studies have been conducted in an attempt to circumvent

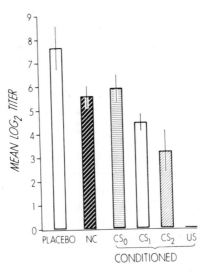

FIG. 6-1.   Mean (± SE) hemagglutination titers obtained 6 days after ip injection of SRBC. NC = nonconditioned animals provided with saccharin on the day of antigenic stimulation or 3 days after SRBC; CSo = conditioned animals that were not reexposed to saccharin following antigen; CS_1 = conditioned animals reexposed to saccharin on the day of antigen treatment or 3 days later; CS_2 = conditioned animals reexposed to saccharin on the day of antigen treatment *and* 3 days later; US = conditioned animals injected with CY following treatment with SRBC. From Ader and Cohen (13); reproduced by permission.

some of the problems identified as potential sources of interference with the conditioning effect, to increase the magnitude of the effect, and to define the parameters of the conditioning paradigm that may be optimal for observing conditioning effects. For example, we have eliminated ip injections of saline for the control groups, based on the evidence that an ip injection itself, can function as a CS (e.g., 77, 78, 79, 80). Also, it has been shown that the *water* consumption of animals conditioned to a taste aversion to saccharin is reduced by the mere presence of a saccharin solution in their room (81). Therefore, we now house different groups in separate colony rooms. The relevance of these seemingly trivial variables suggests that our original control groups were being reexposed to some part of the original complex of stimuli that constituted the CS.

  We have defined the dose-related residual effects of CY (16) and, accordingly, increased the interval between conditioning and the introduction of antigenic stimulation. We have used a different CS solution and a different immunosuppressive drug, and we have varied the concentration of CY and the concentration of SRBC. In all these experiments, we have observed a conditioned suppression of the antibody response. However, there have been experiments in which the conditioned animals reexposed to the CS have differed significantly from both control groups, instances in which Group CS has differed significantly from only one of the two control groups, and instances in which titers in Group CS were insignificantly lower than those in control animals. The magnitude of the conditioned response has remained on the order of approximately 25 percent. Thus, the compelling feature of the conditioning data has been the consistency rather than the magnitude of the effect.

In addition to using SRBC, a T-cell dependent antigen, Wayner et al. (15) conducted an experiment with *Brucella abortus*, A T-cell independent antigen. This experiment did not yield significant conditioning effects. Since the data are based on a single dose of antigen and a single sample obtained following that dose of antigen, this study must be viewed as preliminary. Besides, there are other data indicating that the effects of conditioning can be generalized to a T-cell independent system (17). Conditioned mice reexposed to the CS at the time of treatment with trinitrophenyl-lipopolysaccharide showed a significant attenuation of the antibody response.

Antibody titer, as a reflection of immunologic responsivity, is the result of a complex chain of events which, at any of several levels, might be influenced by neuroendocrine changes effected by conditioning. Since high levels of adrenocortical steroids can be immunosuppressive, it could be hypothesized that the depressed antibody response found in conditioned animals is a direct reflection of a nonspecific "stress" response induced by the conditioning procedures or, more likely, a conditioned elevation in steroid level (82). Studies specifically directed to this issue, however, indicate that this is probably not the case. In one experiment designed to control for the effects of reduced fluid intake in conditioned animals that avoid consuming saccharin on the test day (when antigen is introduced), a two-bottle preference test was used. Under this procedure, there is still a reduction in saccharin consumption, but there is no reduction in the total volume of fluid consumed; under these conditions, there is also no rise in steroid level (83); and under these conditions, we still observed a conditioned suppression of antibody titer. In the study by Ader and Cohen (13), there was a second experiment, in which LiCl, instead of CY, was used as the US in the conditioning paradigm. Like Cy, LiCl has noxious gastrointestinal effects that are sufficient to induce a taste aversion, and it is an effective CS for inducing and conditioning an elevation in corticosterone level (82). However, LiCl is not immunosuppressive and did not induce a conditioned attenuation of antibody titer.

The possibility that there might be some synergistic relation between an elevated corticosteroid level and the residual immunosuppressive effects of CY, led to two additional experiments (16). In them, an additional group of conditioned animals was treated with LiCl or with corticosterone instead of being reexposed to the CS solution on the day that the antigen was introduced. As in previous studies, reexposure to the CS caused a significant attenuation of antibody titer, but neither LiCl nor corticosterone was effective in suppressing the immune response. These results, then, fail to support the hypothesis that the attenuation in antibody titer observed in conditioned animals is mediated simply by an elevation in corticosteroid level.

As I indicated earlier, studies on the conditioning of immunobiological responses were initiated in the Soviet Union 50 years ago. An historical account of this work is being prepared (21), not because it represents sophisticated research or definitive findings, but for its historical interest and the ideas it may stimulate. Like our own studies, the results are compelling because of the consistency rather than the magnitude of the effects observed. However, we are in a better position to undertake such studies today than we were several years ago, and the effort would appear to be justified. The data that are already available with respect to "stress," neuroendocrine influences, and, now, conditioning, call into serious question the assumption that the immune system is an autonomous defense mechanism. On the contrary, it would appear that there is an intimate and virtually unexplored relationship between the central nervous system and immunologic processes, and that this relationship may be amenable to analysis using behavioral techniques. It may be anticipated that interdisciplinary research in psychoneuroimmunology will serve to broaden our perspective with respect to the phenomenology and eventual treatment of psychophysiological disorders.

REFERENCES

1. Dubos, R. *Mirage of health*. New York: Harper, 1959.
2. Ader, R. Animal models in the study of brain, behavior and bodily disease. *Res. Publ. Ass. Res. Nerv. Ment. Dis*, 1975, in press.
3. Engel, G. The need for a new medical model: a challenge for biomedicine. *Science* 196: 129–36, 1977.
4. Weiner, H. The illusion of simplicity: the medical model revisited. *Am. J. Psychiat.* (Suppl.)135: 27–33, 1978.
5. Miller, T.R. Psychophysiologic aspects of cancer. *Cancer* 39: 413–18, 1977.
6. Ader, R. (Ed.). *Psychoneuroimmunology*. New York: Academic Press, in press.
7. Friedman, S.B. & Glasgow, L.A. Psychologic factors and resistance to infectious disease. *Ped. Clin. N. Am.* 13: 315–35, 1966.
8. Bahnson, C.B. (Ed.). Second conference on psychophysiological aspects of cancer. *Ann. NY Acad. Sci.* 164: 307–634, 1969.
9. LaBarba, R.C. Experiential and environmental factors in cancer. *Psychosom. Med.* 32: 259–76, 1970.
10. Solomon, G.F. Pathophysiological aspects of rheumatoid arthritis and auto-immune disease. In Hill, O.W. (Ed.), *Modern Trends in Psychosomatic Medicine*, vol. 2. London: Butterworths, 1970.

11. Amkraut, A. & Solomon, G.F. From the symbolic stimulus to the pathophysiologic response: immune mechanisms. *Int. J. Psychiat. Med.* 5: 541–63, 1974.
12. Rogers, M.P., Dubey, D., & Reich, P. The influence of the psyche and the brain on immunity and disease susceptibility. *Psychosom. Med.* 41: 147–64, 1979.
13. Ader, R. & Cohen, N. Behaviorally conditioned immunosuppression. *Psychosom. Med.* 37: 333–40, 1975.
14. Rogers, M.P., Reich, P., Strom, T.B., & Carpenter, C.B. Behaviorally conditioned immunosuppression: replication of a recent study. *Psychosom. Med.* 38: 447–51, 1976.
15. Wayner, E.A., Flannery, G.R., & Singer, G. Effects of taste aversion conditioning on the primary antibody response to sheep red blood cells and *Brucella abortus* in the albino rat. *Physiol. Behav.* 21: 995–1,000, 1978.
16. Ader, R., Cohen, N., & Grota, L.J. Adrenal involvement in conditioned immunosuppression. *Int. J. Immunopharmac.* 1: 141–45, 1979.
17. Cohen, N., Ader, R., Green, N., & Bovbjerg, D. Conditioned suppression of a thymus independent antibody response. *Psychosom. Med.* 41: 000–000, 1979.
18. Miller, N.E. Learning of visceral and glandular responses. *Science* 163: 434–45, 1969.
19. DiCara, L.V. Learning in the autonomic nervous system. *Scient. Amer.* 222: 31–39, 1970.
20. Siegel, S. Learning and psychopharmacology. In Jarvik, M.E. (Ed.), *Psychopharmacology in the Practice of Medicine.* New York: Appleton-Century-Crofts, 1977.
21. Ader, R. An historical account of conditioned immunobiologic responses. In Ader, R. (Ed.), *Psychoneuroimmunology.* New York: Academic Press, in press.
22. Pierpaoli, W., Fabris, N., & Sorkin, E. Developmental hormones and immunological maturation. In Wolstenholme, G.E. & Knight, J. (Eds.), *Hormones and the immune response.* London: Churchill, 1970.
23. Ahlqvist, J. Endocrine influences on lymphatic organs, immune responses, inflammation and autoimmunity. *Acta Endocrinol.* 83 (Suppl. 206), 1976.
24. Besedovsky, H. & Sorkin, E. Network of immunoendocrine interactions. *Clin. Exp. Immunol.* 27: 1–12, 1977.
25. Wolestenholme, G.E. & Knight, J. (Eds.). *Hormones and the Immune Response.* London: Churchill, 1970.
26. Pierpaoli, W. & Maestroni, G.J.M. Pharmacological control of the immune response by blockade of the early hormonal changes following antigen injection. *Cell. Immunol.* 31: 355–63, 1977.
27. Goldberg, N.D., Haddox, M.K., Dunham, E., Lopez, C., & Hadden, J.W. The Yin Yang hypothesis of biological control: opposing influences of cyclic GMP and cyclic AMP in the regulation of cell proliferation and other biological processes. In Clarkson, B. & Baserga, R. (Eds.), *Control of Proliferation in Animal Cells.* New York: Cold Spring Harbor Biological Association, 1974.
28. Munson, A.E., Levy, J.A., Harris, L.S., & Dewey, W.L. Effects of Δ^9-tetrahydrocannabinol on the immune system. In Braude, M.C. & Szara ,S. (Eds.), *The Pharmacology of Marihuana.* New York: Raven, 187–197, 1976.
29. Halberg, F. Chronoimmunology. In Ader, R. (Ed.), *Psychoneuroimmunology.* New York: Academic Press, in press.
30. Haus, E., Fernandes, G., Kuhl, J.F.W., Yunis, E.J., Lee, J.D., & Halberg, F. Murine circadian susceptibility rhythm to cyclophosphamide. *Chronobiologia* 1: 270–77, 1974.
31. Jankovic, B.D. & Isakovic, K. Neuroendocrine correlates of immune response: I. Effects of brain lesions on antibody production, arthus reactivity and delayed hypersensitivity in the rat. *Int. Arch. Allergy* 45: 360–72, 1973.
32. Stein, M., Schiavi, R.C., & Camerino, M. Influence of brain and behavior on the immune system. *Science* 191: 435–40, 1976.

33. Korneva, E.A., Klimenko, V.M., & Schinek, A.K. *Neurohumoral Basis of Immune Homeostasis*. Leningrad: Nauka, 1978.
34. Fox, B.H. Psychosocial factors and the immune system in human neoplasia. In Ader, R. (Ed.), *Psychoneuroimmunology*. New York: Academic Press, in press.
35. Riley, V. Psychosocial factors in neoplasia: studies in animals. In Ader, R. (Ed.), *Psychoneuroimmunology*. New York: Academic Press, in press.
36. Sklar, L.S. & Anisman, H. Stress and coping factors influence tumor growth. *Science* 205: 513–15, 1979.
37. Rasmussen, A.F., Jr., Marsh, J.T., & Brill, N.Q. Increased susceptibility to herpes simplex in mice subjected to avoidance-learning stress or restraint. *Proc. Soc. Exp. Biol. Med.* 96: 183–89, 1957.
38. Johnson, T., Lavender, J.F., & Marsh, J.T. The influence of avoidance learning stress on resistance to Coxsackie virus in mice. *Fed. Proc.* 18: 575, 1959.
39. Friedman, S.B., Ader, R., & Glasgow, L.A. Effects of psychological stress in adult mice inoculated with Coxsackie B viruses. *Psychosom. Med.* 27: 361–68, 1965.
40. Rasmussen, A.F., Jr., Hildemann, W.H., & Sellers, M. Malignancy of polyoma virus infection in mice in relation to stress. *J. Nat. Cancer Inst.* 30: 101–112, 1963.
41. Chang, S. & Rasmussen, A.F., Jr. Stress-induced suppression of interferon production in virus-infected mice. *Nature* 205: 623–24, 1965.
42. Jensen, M.M. & Rasmussen, A.F., Jr. Stress and susceptibility to viral infections. II. Sound stress and susceptibility to vesicular stomatitis virus. *J. Immunol.* 90: 21–23, 1963.
43. Yamada, A., Jensen, M.M., & Rasmussen, A.F., Jr. Stress and susceptibility to viral infections. III. Antibody response and viral retention during avoidance learning stress. *Proc. Soc. Exp. Biol. Med.* 116: 677–80, 1964.
44. Weinmann, C.J. & Rothman, A.H. Effects of stress upon acquired immunity to the dwarf tapeworm *Hymenolepsis nana*. *Exp. Parasitol.* 21: 61–67, 1967.
45. Hamilton, D.R. Immunosuppressive effects of predator-induced stress in mice with acquired immunity to *Hymenolepsis nana*. *J. Psychosom. Res.* 18: 143–53, 1974.
46. Friedman, S.B., Ader, R., & Grota, L.J. Protective effect of noxious stimulation in mice infected with rodent malaria. *Psychosom. Med.* 35: 535–37, 1973.
47. Marsh, J.T., Lavender, J.F., Chang, S., & Rasmussen, A.F., Jr. Poliomyelitis in monkeys: decreased susceptibility after avoidance stress. *Science* 140: 1,415–16, 1963.
48. Levine, S., Strebel, R., Wenk, E.J., & Harman, P.J. Suppression of experimental allergic encephalomyelitis by stress. *Proc. Soc. Exp. Biol. Med.* 109: 294–98, 1962.
49. Friedman, S.B., Glasgow, L.A., Ader, R. Psychosocial factors modifying host resistance to experimental infections. *Ann. NY Acad. Sci.* 164: 381–92, 1969.
50. Gross, W.B. & Siegel, H.S. The effect of social stress on resistance to infection with *Escherichia coli* or *Mycoplasma gallisepticum*. *Poult. Sci.* 44: 98–1,001, 1965.
51. Davis, D.E. & Read, C.P. Effect of behavior on development of resistance in trichinosis. *Proc. Soc. Exp. Biol. Med.* 99: 269–72, 1958.
52. Plaut, S.M., Ader, R., Friedman, S.B., & Ritterson, A.L. Social factors and resistance to malaria in the mouse: effects of group vs. individual housing on resistance to *Plasmodium berghei* infection. *Psychosom. Med.* 31: 536–52, 1969.
53. Edwards, E.A. & Dean, L.M. Effects of crowding of mice on humoral antibody formation and protection to lethal antigenic challenge. *Psychosom. Med.* 39: 19–24, 1977.
54. Amkraut, A.A., Solomon, G.F., & Kraemer, H.C. Stress, early experience and adjuvant-induced arthritis in the rat. *Psychosom. Med.* 33: 203–14, 1971.
55. Rogers, M.P., Trentham, D., McCune, J., Ginsberg, B., Reich, P., & David, J. Abrogation of Type II collagen-induced arthritis in rats by psychological stress. *Clin. Res.* (Abstr.), 1979.
56. Ader, R. The effects of early life experiences on developmental processes and susceptibility to

disease in animals. In Hill, J.P. (Ed.), *Minnesota Symposia on Child Psychology*. Minneapolis: U. of Minnesota Press, 1970.

57. Ader, R. Experimentally induced gastric lesions: Results and implications of studies in animals. *Adv. Psychosom. Med.* 6: 1–39, 1971.

58. Gisler, R.H., Bussard, A.E., Mazie, J.C., & Hess, R. Hormonal regulation of the immune response. I. Induction of an immune respónse *in vitro* with lymphoid cells from mice exposed to acute systemic stress. *Cell. Immunol.* 2: 634–45, 1971.

59. Gisler, R.H. & Schenkel-Hulliger, L. Hormonal regulation of the immune response. II. Influence of pituitary and adrenal activity on immune responsiveness *in vitro*. *Cell. Immunol.* 2: 646–57, 1971.

60. Folch, H. & Waksman, B.H. The splenic suppressor cell: activity of thymus-dependent adherent cells: changes with age and stress. *J. Immunol.* 113: 127–39, 1974.

61. Monjan, A.A. & Collector, M.I. Stress-induced modulation of the immune response. *Science* 196: 307–308, 1976.

62. Guy, W.B. Neurogenic factors in contact dermatitis. *Arch. Dermatol. Syphil.* 66: 1–8, 1952.

63. Mettrop, P.J.G. & Visser, P. Exteroceptive stimulation as a contigent factor in the induction and elicitation of delayed-type hypersensitivity reactions to 1-chloro-,2-4, dinitrobenzene in guinea pigs. *Psychophys.* 5: 385–88, 1969.

64. Pitkin, D.H. Effect of physiological stress on the delayed hypersensitivity reaction. *Proc. Soc. Exp. Biol. Med.* 120: 350–51, 1965.

65. Wistar, R., Jr. & Hildemann, W.H. Effect of stress on skin transplantation immunity in mice. *Science* 131: 159–60, 1960.

66. Amkraut, A.A., Solomon, G.F., Kasper, P., & Purdue, P. Stress and hormonal intervention in the graft-versus-host response. In Jankovic, B.D. & Isakovic, K. (Eds.), *Microenvironmental aspects of immunity*. New York: Plenum, 1973.

67. Rasmussen, A.F., Jr., Spencer, E.S. & Marsh, J.T. Decrease in susceptibility of mice to passive anaphylaxis following avoidance-learning stress. *Proc. Soc. Exp. Biol. Med.* 100: 878–79, 1959.

68. Treadwell, P.E. & Rasmussen, A.F., Jr. Role of the adrenals in stress-induced resistance to anaphylactic shock. *J. Immunol.* 87: 492–97, 1961.

69. Hill, C.W., Greer, W.E., & Felsenfeld, O. Psychological stress, early response to foreign protein, and blood cortisol in vervets. *Psychosom. Med.* 29: 279–83, 1967.

70. Vessey, S.H. Effects of grouping on levels of circulating antibodies in mice. *Proc. Soc. Exp. Biol. Med.* 115: 252–55, 1964.

71. Glenn, W.G. & Becker, R.E. Individual versus group housing in mice: immunological response to time-phased injections. *Physiol. Zool.* 42: 411–16, 1969.

72. Solomon, G.F. Stress and antibody response in rats. *Int. Arch. Allergy* 35: 97–104, 1969.

73. Solomon, G.F., Amkraut, A.A., & Kasper, P. Immunity, emotions and stress. *Ann. Clin. Res.* 6: 313–22, 1974.

74. Solomon, G.F., Levine, S., & Kraft, J.K. Early experience and immunity. *Nature* 220: 821–22, 1968.

75. Ader, R. Letter to the editor. *Psychosom. Med.* 36: 183–84, 1974.

76. King, M. Personal communication, 1979.

77. Dolin, A.O., Krylov, V.N., Luk'ianenko, V.I., & Flerov, B.A. New experimental data on the conditioned reflex production and suppression of immune and allergic reactions. *Zh vyssh nervn Deiatel* 10: 832–41, 1960.

78. Hutton, R.A., Woods, S.C., Makous, W.L. Conditioned hyperglycemia: pseudoconditioning controls. *J. Comp. Physiol. Psychol.* 71: 198–201, 1970.

79. Pavlov, I.P. *Lectures on conditioned reflexes*. New York: Liveright, 1928.

80. Siegel, S. Conditioned insulin effects. *J. Comp. Physiol. Psychol.* 89: 189–99, 1975.
81. Ader, R. A note of the role of olfaction in taste aversion learning. *Bull. Psychon. Soc.* 10: 402–04, 1977.
82. Ader, R. Conditioned adrenocortical steroid elevations in the rat. *J. Comp. Physiol. Psychol.* 90: 1,156–63, 1976.
83. Smotherman, W.P., Hennessy, J.W., & Levine, S. Plasma corticosterone levels during recovery from LiCl produced taste aversion. *Behav. Biol.* 16: 401–12, 1976.

7

Menstrual and Premenstrual Mood Disorders

DAVID S. JANOWSKY

INTRODUCTION

Throughout recorded history, the phenomenon of menstruation has been a cause of concern to both men and women, and society has developed many rituals and customs to deal with this concern. For example, in the Old Testament, Leviticus XV states, "When a woman has a discharge of blood which is her regular discharge from her body, she shall be in her impurity for seven days, and whoever touches her shall be unclean until that evening." Stephens (1), in a publication concerning the cross-cultural study of menstrual taboos, refers to such taboos as "beliefs or superstitions about dangers inherent in menstruation, and the avoidance customs rationalized by these beliefs." He states that a dominant belief in many societies with menstrual taboos is that menstruating women are directly or indirectly dangerous to men. The reason for such customs as menstrual huts, menstrual cooking taboos, and menstrual sexual taboos is ostensibly to protect men from such women, which may be a reflection of male castration anxiety. However, since a wide range of indices demonstrate impaired behavior in menstruating women, it may be that menstrual taboos may also be based on more than male intrapsychic castration anxiety, and that such taboos may be a society's way of dealing with negative behavioral changes in women and between men and women (2).

There is evidence that cyclic behavioral changes, including affective changes, occur in subhuman species. Evidence from studies of animals suggests that ovarian hormone-linked behavioral phenomena are ubiquitous among mammals, and that such cyclic behavioral changes in primates may parallel those human behavioral changes which have led to menstrual taboos. First of all, there is evidence that, at least in captivity, rhesus macaques show approximately 30-day menstrual cycles. Also, Lancaster (3) states that females of almost all species of primates observed in the field are reported to have cyclic irritability which is correlated with the female fertility cycle. This is substantiated in

DeVore's book on primate behavior (4). Rowell (5) reports: "Immediately after menstruation, a female rhesus macaque becomes more aggressive to other females, begins to approach the males, and sometimes copulates. Her confidence reaches a fairly high level in a few days, and the time she spends with the male, and the frequency with which she mates, continues to increase slowly until a few days before the next menstruation. Then, quite suddenly, she begins to get attacked and leaves the male."

More recently, evidence has been offered showing that in rhesus macaques, aggressive behavior toward females increases during the premenstrual-menstrual phases of their cycles. In captive female rhesus macaques, counts of bites from fighting showed a dramatic increase occurring in the premenstrual-menstrual phases of their cycle (6).

Some authors have suggested that cyclic primate behavioral changes in sexual and aggressive interactions may have important survival value. By showing increased irritability and negative affect during the menstrual cycle, early humans, and possibly subhuman primates, might have focused sexual activity on those females in a colony or society who were sexually and emotionally receptive and, most important, were ovulating. As a parallel phenomena in human societies, institutionalization of menstrual sanctions may represent societies' ways of limiting sexual intercourse to women who are more likely to conceive, and of protecting women from the kind of attack which occurs in lower primates (2, 7).

PSYCHIATRIC IMPLICATIONS OF THE MENSTRUAL CYCLE

For many years, the general medical literature has discussed the physiologic and pathologic aspects of the human menstrual cycle. However, consideration in the psychiatric literature has been relatively rare. The term "premenstrual tension" was first introduced by Frank, in 1931, to designate the cyclic irritability, anxiety, depression, and edema experienced by some women during the premenstrual period. Reports on the incidence of the syndrome have varied from 25 to 100 percent of women, depending on the definitions used (8). Dalton, in a classic monograph, lists depression, irritability, lethargy, alcoholic excess, nymphomania, feelings of unreality, sleep disturbances, epilepsy, vertigo, syncope, paresthesia, nausea, vomiting, constipation, bloating, edema, colicky pain, enuresis, urinary retention, increased capillary fragility, glaucoma, migraine headaches, relapses of meningiomas, schizophrenic reactions and relapses, increased susceptibility to infection, suicide attempts, admissions to surgical and medical wards, increased crime rates, work morbidity, manic reactions, and dermatological disease as some of the cyclically recurring phenomena of the premenstrual and menstrual phases. More recently, she has noted that more children are battered by their mothers during the premenstrual-menstrual phases, and more are taken to emergency rooms for medical illnesses (9).

Specifically, Dalton reports that of 156 newly convicted prisoners, 28 percent committed crimes while menstruating and 22 percent while in the premenstrual period. Fifty-six percent of thefts occurred menstrually and premenstrually. Of 94 disorderly prisoners, 35 percent were menstruating. Significantly, the "premenstrual syndrome" was present in 27 percent of 156 prisoners, and this subgroup had an even higher incidence of crime during the premenstrual and menstrual periods (9).

In one study, Dalton divided a 28-day month into seven 4 day periods. She then measured the time of hospital admission of 276 female acute psychiatric patients. According to normal probability, 14 percent of the admissions would have been expected to enter the hospital during any 4 day period. Instead, 28 percent entered during the 4 days of menstruation, and 17 percent entered during the 4 days prior to menstruation. Of 36 attempted suicides, 38 percent occurred during menstruation, 22 percent occurred during the 4 days including ovulation, and 14 percent occurred during the premenstrual period. Of 185 admitted for depression, 33 percent were menstruating and 4 percent were premenstrual. Of 114 diagnosed schizophrenic, 26 percent were menstruating and 21 percent were premenstrual (10).

Similarly, in a study I conducted with my colleagues in 1967, data were gathered on 90 consecutive female admissions to an acute psychiatric inpatient service (11). Since these admissions were unplanned, it was assumed that each patient was admitted at the height of her emotional upset. Women who were amenorrheic, due to pregnancy, menopause, prior hysterectomy, or other causes, were excluded from the group. Of the 90 women screened, 44 qualified as experiencing regular or irregular menstrual function and were included as subjects.

We found that a significantly greater number of admissions occurred during the menstrual and premenstrual phases of the patient's cycles than at other times. Admission peaks occurred 2 and 3 days prior to onset of menstruation and on the second, third, and fourth days of menstruation. During the 10 days before and the 5 days after the onset of menstruation, 35 admissions occurred, as compared to 9 admissions during the remaining 15 days. Individual cycle lengths varied from 15 to 40 days, with a mean of 27.5 days.

The subject group contained a wide range of psychiatric diagnoses, and each of the predominant diagnostic groups (depressive, schizophrenic, and situational reactions) showed premenstrual-menstrual increases in admission rates. The subgroup of patients who were admitted following a suicide attempt showed a similar trend. These data differ from those of Dalton in that we obtained relatively higher admission rates during the premenstrual phase. Also, our mid-cycle admissions were only minimally elevated. Our increased premenstrual admission rates may be explained by the fact that, unlike Dalton, we did not exclude from the study women with cycles longer than 28 days.

With respect to suicidal behavior, Ribero (12) reported that of 22 Hindu women who committed suicide by pouring kerosene over themselves and igniting it, 19 were menstruating. MacKinnon and MacKinnon (13) reported that of 23 women autopsied after they committed suicide, 20 had ovaries which were pathologically in the middle and late luteal phases of the reproductive cycle. Others have similarly found increases in suicide attempts and calls to suicide-prevention centers during the premenstrual-menstrual phases of the menstrual cycle.

With respect to specific cases, my colleagues and I previously reported data on a patient with a repetitive history of premenstrual suicidal activity who was studied psychiatrically and biochemically for a period of 67 consecutive days (14). The patient, a 24-year-old divorced mother of two, had exhibited premenstrual suicidal activity since menarche, at age 12. She complained of recurrent premenstrual irritability and lability, depression, feelings of hopelessness and unreality, suicidal ideation, and onset dysmenorrhea. She had attempted suicide premenstrually about a dozen times, and never at any other time during the cycle. She described herself as cheerful and able to work and socialize during the first two weeks of her menstrual cycle. During the second two weeks, her symptoms would begin and progress, remitting with the onset of menstruation. She had been entirely free of symptoms only during her two pregnancies. She generally had regular 26- to 28-day menstrual cycles, with menstruation lasting 3 to 5 days. During the 67-day period of observation, the results of the Nurses' Behavioral Rating Form subscales, BPRS, and Clyde Mood Scale scores generally paralleled each other, with mid-cycle and mid-luteal peaks in behavioral disturbances indicated by all these methods of evaluation. More normal behavior occurred during the menstrual and follicular phases. Clinically, during a typical menstrual-follicular day, the patient exhibited much charm and friendliness. She was sheepishly apologetic for her previous behavior and was ingratiating to the staff, especially her doctors. She treated staff members as equals, exhibited an entertaining and empathetic sense of humor, was filled with energy to accomplish goals, and was cooperative in giving urine specimens. She was coquettish, seductive, and very well groomed. She exhibited a realistic approach in evaluating her problems, and was quite rational. She exhibited superficial insight into her problems and helped other patients. She was anxious to communicate with nursing and physician staff members. She showed no anger toward men and sought relationships with them.

During the ovulatory or mid-luteal phases, she was exceedingly angry, manipulative, testing, irritable, depressed, assaultive, disparaging toward the staff in terms of their credentials and intelligence, belligerent, uncooperative, and disheveled. She displayed a generally paranoid attitude and cried frequently. She ruminated about her estranged children. She complained that she felt unreal and pinched herself to prove she was alive. She made numerous suicidal gestures and threatened to leave the hospital. At times she became hypomanic, hyperactive, and unapproachable. Occasionally, she capitulated and begged for help, bemoaning her miserable condition. She expressed the opinion that no one could help her. Her affect was extremely labile and inappropriate in degree.

Similarly, Lederer (15) discussed recurrent premenstrual emotional upsets manifested by kleptomania in a 17-year-old woman, and Verghese (16) refers to a periodic manic psychosis occurring about the menstrual period. Krasowska (17) described a syndrome occurring regularly in the second half of the menstrual cycle, characterized by depression, agitation, confusion, anxiety, emotional outbursts, delusions, and hallucinations, which remitted with the onset of menstruation; and Ota and Mukai (18) described patients with mania, catatonia, and schizophrenia who repeatedly became ill during the premenstrual and menstrual phases of the cycle.

CYCLIC CHANGES IN EMOTIONALITY IN NORMALS

In addition to evidence that increased premenstrual-menstrual psychiatric and other behavioral upsets of a serious nature can and do occur, there is evidence that a majority of women experience an intensification of irritability, depression, and anxiety during the premenstrual and early menstrual phases of their menstrual cycles. Reports from retrospective surveys in which women filled out questionnaires have demonstrated evidence of premenstrual tension in between 25 and 100 percent of women, depending on the definitions used. Thus, for example, Steiglitz and Kimble reported an incidence of premenstrual-menstrual emotional instability in 68 percent of 67 women tested; and Gorney and I, in unpublished data, found that up to 90 percent of women claim to undergo some degree of premenstrual or menstrual hopelessness, depression, or irritability (8).

Although retrospective studies have demonstrated a very high incidence of increased emotional symptoms during the premenstrual-menstrual phases of the cycle, prospective studies have revealed less dramatic findings. Indeed, several prospective studies in which women reported their moods on a daily to weekly basis, over one or more menstrual periods, reported no significant cyclic fluctuations in mood (19). In one study (20), it was demonstrated that if women were fooled into thinking their menstrual period was not about to occur, even though it was, they would report fewer premenstrual physical symptoms, although negative affect would still be equal to that reported in those who thought, correctly, that they were about to have a menstrual period. However, many other prospective studies have been supportive of the existence of premenstrual-menstrual upsets. Although methodologies have varied, these studies have reported cyclic premenstrual-menstrual fluctuations in moods in normals, as measured by a variety of means (21).

My colleagues and I measured self-rated negative affect in 11 normal college-age volunteers on a metabolic ward at the NIMH, controlling for caloric and sodium intake and activity (22). As a group, the volunteers' negative affect score increased 11 days prior to the onset of menses, peaked the day before the onset of menses, and subsequently decreased on the second day of menstrual flow.

There appears to be a relationship between the phenomenon of mild to moderate premenstrual-menstrual emotional upsets and/or psychiatric upsets and psychiatric illness in general. Several studies have suggested that the degree of premenstrual tension is correlated with "generalized neuroticism," as measured by the Maudsley personality inventory (23). More recently, several studies have suggested that episodes of premenstrual-menstrual affective changes such as anxiety, depression, and irritability may predict later episodes of psychiatric illness—especially bona fide affective disorders (24, 25). Similarly, Dalton previously described a link between premenstrual tension, postpartum "blues" and postpartum psychosis (9).

In addition to the demonstration of a link between severe psychiatric illness, as well as minor psychiatric upsets, and the menstrual cycle, a number of reports have alleged that intellectual performance and cognitive variables decrease during the premenstrual-menstrual phases of the cycle. However, more recent studies, which have generally been quite well controlled, suggest that very few, if any, decreases in intellectual ability and/or performance occur, related to the menstrual cycle (26).

ETIOLOGIC CONSIDERATIONS

With respect to etiology, speculations, as will be discussed below, have ranged from the psychoanalytic to the biochemical. To date, none of the proposed hypotheses is altogether satisfactory.

Psychodynamic Hypotheses

From a psychodynamic perspective, the clinical, behavioral, and psychological findings occurring in severe premenstrual tension may reflect intense conflicts concerning the womanly role, described by Benedek and other psychoanalysts as characteristic of premenstrual tension sufferers. Helene Deutsch (27) and other psychoanalysts indicate that the perception of menstrual flow intensifies a woman's preexisting conscious and unconscious conflicts about pregnancy, having a child, castration fears, uncleanliness, lack of control of bodily function, aggression, penis envy, and masturbation. In the presence of a vulnerable ego structure, neurotic, psychotic, or characterological reactions may occur. In most women, the compensation for the hypothesized deprivations of femaleness is the process of pregnancy and the bearing of a child (2); hence the common psychoanalytic observation that a menstrual period is experienced as a "lost child." In a more general sense, Dalton has pointed out that external stress in a patient's life at a given time is linked to the increased premenstrual tension during that time period (9).

Biological Hypotheses

Biological hypotheses of the etiology of premenstrual tension have implicated water and sodium retention, estrogen, progesterone, prolactin, the renin-angiotensin-aldosterone system, adrenal corticosteroids, central catecholamines, central serotonin, and central acetylcholine in the etiology of the premenstrual tension syndrome. These hypotheses will be discussed next.

The Ovarian Hormone Hypothesis

The hypothesis that the affective changes and more severe psychiatric illnesses linked to the menstrual cycle are caused by changes in ovarian hormones is widely accepted. As reviewed elsewhere (28, 29, 30), considerable evidence supports an ovarian hypothesis of premenstrual-menstrual emotional disorders. There is evidence of many behavioral-ovarian hormone correlations. With respect to sexual activity, exogenous progesterone, administered to castrated estrogen-pretreated rhesus monkeys, causes a reduction in sexual activity. Likewise, diminished sexual activity in humans and intact primates occurs during the luteal phase of the cycle, correlating with peak blood and urine progesterone levels.

Dysphoric emotional symptoms often begin in the luteal phase of the menstrual cycle, as progesterone levels rise, and intensify as these levels later fall in the premenstrual-menstrual phase. Similarly, dysphoria occurs in the third trimester of pregnancy, when progesterone is elevated, and increases postpartum, as progesterone levels fall.

In contrast to progesterone, exogenous estrogen, administered to castrated female rhesus monkeys, restores attempts to initiate sexual encounters and increases male mounting attempts and ejaculatory potential. Furthermore, human and primate sexual activity correlates with peak blood and urinary estrogen levels. Increased psychiatric symptoms and negative affect occur during the luteal phase, when estrogen levels are high, and further intensify as these levels fall. However, these symptoms do not consistently increase at mid-cycle, when estrogen is most elevated. Interestingly, the premenstrual fall in estrogen levels may not reflect central-nervous-system estrogen activity, since estrogen is selectively bound and concentrated in the hypothalamus. Of further interest is the fact that a premenstrual-tensionlike syndrome has been reported to occur when high doses of estrogen are administered.

Although much of the information presented in the foregoing implies a direct effect of progesterone and estrogen on the female central nervous system, leading to increases and decreases in female receptivity or emotionality, respectively, evidence exists that these hormones also may alter female "attractiveness." Local application of estrogen to the vaginal wall of rhesus monkeys induces sexual excitation in the male partner without increasing the female's sexual interest. Evidence exists that this effect occurs through the induction of vaginally emitted olfactory cues. Furthermore, progesterone, given to a female rhesus monkey, appears to decrease male sexual interest while also increasing female sexual refusals.

In lower mammals, the ability of ovarian steroids to regulate behavior is more clear-cut. In intact animals, where cyclic periods of heat occur, sexual excitation and activity are correlated with elevations of a combination of estrogen and progesterone.

Castration abolishes the cyclic heat response in mammals. Estradiol induces mating activity in a variety of castrated female animals, and estradiol implants in the anterior hypothalamus of female cats and rats cause increased mating and running behavior. Exogenous progesterone decreases mating activity in estrogen-primed rabbits and causes sedative effects in many mammals. In contrast to higher mammals, rats primed with low doses of estrogen show augmented sexual activation when progesterone is also administered.

Greene and Dalton (31) believed the symptoms of premenstrual tension were owing to a relatively high estrogen/progesterone ratio. They substantiated this hypothesis by noting that intramuscular progesterone alleviates the premenstrual syndrome (a finding recently challenged in controlled studies), and by citing evidence that the premenstrual tension syndrome was able to be reproduced in castrates, with large doses of estrogen. Other researchers have shown an increase in symptoms in some patients, following administration of estrogenic oral contraceptives (32).

Several more recent studies have biochemically supported the aforementioned hypothesis, finding relatively low progesterone levels in at least some sufferers of premenstrual tension, although other investigators have not replicated this finding (29, 30, 33).

Several other facts, however, make it difficult to completely implicate estrogen and progesterone in the ovarian hormone-linked emotional disorders. As reviewed before (14, 9, 22), estrogen and progesterone are usually falling or have fallen at the maximum peak in the luteal phase. In a related study,

Hamburg was able to induce a depression in a subject, upon withdrawal of exogenously administered progesterone. Thus, the role of ovarian hormones at least should be considered with respect to withdrawal phenomena, rather than as a direct effect. Similarly, the well-known transient increase in emotional lability (weepiness, depression, and so on) and the increased incidence of psychiatric illness in the postpartum period occur at times of estrogen-progesterone withdrawal. Furthermore, Greene and Dalton found 16 percent of their 87 sufferers of premenstrual tension attributing onset of symptoms to the menopause or following the menopause, a time when estrogen and progesterone secretion is relatively low. Dalton reports that many premenstrual tension sufferers show increases in symptoms after menopause or after oophorectomy-hysterectomy (surgical castration). Thus, it is possible that the premenstrual-menstrual emotional disorders may have nothing directly to do with changes in ovarian hormones (9).

Mineralocorticoid Hypotheses

A major and rather enduring hormonal hypothesis concerning the etiology of premenstrual tension suggests that adrenal steroids may be causative. Evidence exists that the adrenal cortex plays a role in the regulation of sexual and emotional behavior. Sexual activity in women is often not decreased following menopause or oophorectomy, when ovarian hormone levels are low, but does decrease when both the ovaries and adrenal glands are removed (9, 28). Also, androgens stimulate sexuality in women (14, 22, 28). Administration of testosterone to female rhesus monkeys increases sexual receptivity, but does not appear to activate an increase in male sexual interest. Furthermore, there is evidence that endogenous adrenal androgens are necessary for full receptivity in female rhesus monkeys, since adrenal cortical suppression by dexamethazone decreases receptivity in estrogen-treated castrated females. This effect is reversed by administrations of small amounts of testosterone, but not reversed by administration of cortisol.

With regard to the premenstrual tension syndrome, as mentioned above, symptoms of an emotional and physical nature often begin or intensify following menopause or oophorectomy, suggesting extraovarian etiologic focus (9, 22, 28).

Cortisol has been postulated as causative of the premenstrual-menstrual cyclic disorders (8). However, there is no evidence from the pattern of fluctuations in serum cortisol levels during the menstrual cycle to indicate such a behavioral-endocrine link. Similarly, adrenal androgens have been postulated as etiologic, but similar arguments concerning their fluctuations make their role unlikely.

Dalton (9) refers to E. B. Pellanda's hypothesis that the symptoms of premenstrual-menstrual emotional upsets occur whenever there is an increase in mineralocorticoids and glucocorticoids in relation to ovarian steroids, and Dalton postulates that aldosterone, a mineralocorticoid whose sodium-retaining properties are antagonized by progesterone, may be the hormonal cause.

In contrast to adrenal glucocorticoids such as cortisol and hydrocortisone, mineralocorticoids, including aldosterone and possibly corticosterone, fluctuate more, in parallel with the cyclic emotional fluctuations. Thus, Reich (34) reported slight mid-cycle elevation of urinary aldosterone excretion, followed by a luteal rise which peaked during the premenstrual phase of the cycle, falling just before or soon after the onset of menses; and Gray et al. (35) noted increased aldosterone secretory rates in the luteal phase of the cycle. In our own study of the previously mentioned 24-year-old woman with severe premenstrual tension, we found a luteal biphasic peak of urinary increased aldosterone levels during menstrual cycles. Of importance is the observation that in some patients, aldosterone remains elevated above follicular phase levels after estrogen and progesterone levels have fallen in the late luteal-early menstrual phases of the cycle (28, 34, 35, 36, 37, 38). In some studies, abnormal aldosterone elevations have been reported to occur in patients with the premenstrual tension syndrome (14, 39), although other studies have not substantiated this (40, 41). As in the mid-cycle and premenstrual phases of the menstrual cycle, aldosterone secretion is increased in late pregnancy and following ingestion of oral contraceptives (14, 22).

It is likely that underlying the aforementioned elevations in aldosterone secretion and excretion are increases on the aldosterone-stimulating renin-angiotensin system, which is elevated during oral contraceptive ingestion, late pregnancy, and the luteal phase of the menstrual cycle (36, 37).

Supportive evidence for a role for mineralocorticoids in the etiology of the cyclic emotional upsets comes from a series of reports which have noted a relationship between the phases of the menstrual cycle and changes in weight and/or sudden retention (22). Generally, these studies have demonstrated mid-cycle and premenstrual-menstrual weight gains associated with sodium retention. Usually, these studies did not systematically evaluate mood.

A few studies of cyclic weight and sodium changes have utilized metabolic balance techniques and have been well controlled. Bruce and Russell (42) studied 10 women with a history of premenstrual tension, keeping their subjects on a fixed caloric, water, sodium, and potassium intake on a metabolic ward. They demonstrated small ovulatory and premenstrual increases in weight, associated with water and sodium retention. Thorn et al. reported that of two obese and four normal subjects on a fixed intake of sodium, food, and water, half gained weight and retained sodium in the premenstrum and during ovulation (43), and Landau and Lugibihl noted premenstrual sodium retention in four women studied on a metabolic unit (44).

In 1969, my colleagues and I were unable to find controlled studies in which mood, weight, and sodium retention were simultaneously measured on a daily basis. For this reason, we evaluated changes in mood, weight, and urinary potassium/sodium (K/Na) ratio over a total of 15 menstrual cycles in 11 women in order to investigate whether these changes indeed did correlate in the same patients (22).

We measured the urinary K/Na ratio, since there is evidence that when dietary factors are controlled, this variable may in part reflect aldosterone and other mineralocorticoid effects. Our data indicated that increases in negative affect, weight, and K/Na ratio follow similar patterns in normal women when studied longitudinally. The changes in negative affect were consistent with the findings of others, who have evaluated the cyclic emotional fluctuations, and reported luteal, premenstrual, and early menstrual increases in negative affect, such as decreased good humor and increased anxiety, hostility, and aggressiveness. Similarly, our data were consistent with that of others in defining a small but definite progressive increase in weight during the luteal and premenstrual phases. Our data differed from some reports showing a large ovulatory weight increase, in that we noted a relatively small mid-cycle weight gain.

Our data indicated that a statistically significant increase in urinary K/Na ratio occurred in the premenstrual phase of the cycle. The shift in K/Na ratio, with its implied increase in sodium retention, may in part underlie the weight changes described in our study. Furthermore, it appears at least possible that the K/Na ratio changes noted may reflect changes in circulating aldosterone or other mineralocorticoids, since the K/Na ratio has been found to increase when aldosterone is administered and since the curve of the K/Na ratio noted in this study strikingly parallels the aldosterone excretion curve noted by Reich (34).

However, there is little evidence that the aldosterone changes noted during the menstrual cycle are directly causative of the cycle emotional upsets, since other diseases with increased aldosterone levels are not necessarily associated with mental upsets. Thus, it is reasonable to hypothesize that a substance which fluctuates in parallel with aldosterone causes the cyclic behavioral changes. As reviewed in previous papers, (14, 22), angiotensin may be a reasonable candidate to be this substance, since, like aldosterone, angiotensin is activated during the luteal phase of the menstrual cycle, after progesterone administration, and during pregnancy—all times when psychic upsets may be increased. Angiotensin is probably the endogenous stimulant which regulates aldosterone secretion, and it is probably activated by renin, possibly in response to elevated exogenous or endogenous progesterone levels.

Angiotensin exerts effects on animal behavior, central neurotransmitters, and autonomic function. It causes increased drinking behavior when given by vertebral artery infusion or intraventricularly, a probable cholinergic effect antagonized by atropine. It counteracts the anesthetic effects of amobarbitol and decreases exploratory activity in mice when given intraventricularly. Furthermore, a central hypertensive effect has been reported which appears to have cholinergic and adrenergic components.

Also, Ganten et al. demonstrated that a reninlike enzyme exists in the brain and noted that this enzyme's activity is increased by progesterone. These investigators state that all components necessary to form angiotensin II are present in the brain. However, in spite of this above information, supportive of implicating the renin-angiotensin-aldosterone system in the cyclic emotional upsets, some data do not support a renin-angiotensin-aldosterone hypothesis of premenstrual tension. There is evidence from some studies that aldosterone is not particularly elevated in sufferers of premenstrual tension, compared to normals, although other studies, including our own, do show such an increase. In addition, Steiner and Carroll (21) have noted that the renin-angiotensin-aldosterone system, which is progesterone-dependent, is not elevated during the luteal phase of anovulatory women. They refer to Adamopoulos et al.'s observation that premenstrual emotional symptoms can occur in anovulatory cycles (45). Lastly, the late luteal (premenstrual) increase in serum aldosterone is not an absolutely consistent feature, although it has been noted in a number of cases (21). However, in support of a role for the renin-angiotensin-aldosterone system in the premenstrual tension syndrome, spironolactone, at least in one well-controlled study, was effective in decreasing symptoms of premenstrual tension, and spironolactone is an aldosterone antagonist (40). Furthermore, other mineralocorticoids, such as corticosterone (which is elevated in the luteal phase) could be etiologic (38).

The Prolactin Hypothesis

Like estrogen and progesterone, the pituitary hormone, prolactin, has been proposed as causative of the premenstrual tension syndrome (46, 47, 48). It appears likely that prolactin shows a fluctuation in levels through the menstrual cycle, with peaks occurring at ovulation and later in the mid- and late luteal phase. Furthermore, prolactin has sodium- and potassium-relating abilities. Most importantly, a number of studies have suggested that bromocriptine, a dopamine agonist which decreases prolactin, may ameliorate premenstrual tension syndrome, as well as premenstrual weight gain and breast enlargement (47). This implicates prolactin in the etiology of premenstrual tension. However, at least one well-controlled study has shown prolactin only equal to placebo in its efficacy in treating premenstrual tension, and others have shown no efficacy (47, 48). Furthermore, it is possible that the primary effects of bromocriptine, if it is effective, may rest in its dopaminergic effects, rather that its antiprolactin effects. Lastly, at least one study suggests that prolactin does not increase in the luteal phases in anovulatory woman, and Coppen et al. (23) have noted that premenstrual tension continues to occur during anovulatory cycles, although their observations are limited to a very small number of subjects.

Finally, negating a prolactin hypothesis is the fact that elevators of prolactin from other causes, such as from dopamine blocking agents and pituitary tumors, do not seem to lead to psychologic upsets.

The Monoamine Hypothesis

As reviewed elsewhere (28), studies suggest that serotonin, norepinephrine, and dopamine may be involved in the etiology of premenstrual tension, as they may be in the etiology of affective and other psychiatric disorders, and that such changes may be linked to cyclic changes in various neuroendocrines and endocrines.

Animal studies indicate that ovarian hormones and monoamines show overlapping behavioral effects. Like certain antidepressants, estrogen induces running behavior in rats, and, like reserpine, progesterone induces sedation and anesthesia in rats and other mammals.

Brain monoamines and sex steroids show overlapping effects in the regulation of sexual behavior in rats. Reserpine and tetrabenazine, both monoamine depletors, may be substituted for progesterone in activating sexual behavior in estrogen-primed castrated female rats. In contrast, tricyclic antidepressant drugs and MAO inhibitors decrease sexual activation in estrogen-progesterone-primed castrated female rats, especially when brain serotonin is selectively increased. Furthermore, selective depletion of rat-brain serotonin induces sexual excitation, especially when brain catecholamines such as dopamine and norepinephrine are simultaneously elevated.

Although it is possible that the parallel or overlapping effects of the ovarian steroids and various monoamine-altering drugs on animal behavior are owed to independent effects on a common receptor, there is much evidence to indicate that such cyclically fluctuating hormones such as estrogen, progesterone, and angiotensin directly affect monoamine activity levels.

Ovarian hormones and monoamines also exhibit overlapping functions in regulating ovulation. Elevation of brain serotonin blocks superovulation in immature rats, and decreased norepinephrine levels inhibit physiological estrus as determined by vaginal smears. Norepinephrine administration into the third ventricle in large doses induces ovulation. Reserpine administration inhibits ovulation in the rat, and this effect is antagonized by the administration of MAO inhibitors or dopamine. Reserpine induces pseudopregnancy in rats when given systematically and following local hypothalamic administration, and this effect is also prevented by treatment with MAO inhibitors. Dopamine appears to exhibit a very important role in the regulation of gonadotropin secretion. Small doses of dopamine, incubated *in vitro* in the presence of pituitary and hypothalamic tissue, induce the release of LH and FSH. Kamberi and others have recently found that administration of small doses of dopamine or relatively high doses of norepinephrine or epinephrine significantly increase blood LH levels, while serotonin causes an opposite effect.

With respect to actual changes in monoamines, hypothalamic norepinephrine is minimal at estrus, increases during diestrus; and becomes maximal at proestrus; and at least one report notes that exogenous estrogen decreases hypothalamic norepinephrine in intact female rats. Also, castration produces increased norepinephrine turnover rates.

Enzymes which participate in the breakdown of monoamines are influenced by the ovarian hormones. In the rat midbrain, COMT, an enzyme involved in catecholamine metabolism, decreases during estrus. Also, COMT activity is inhibited *in vitro* by estrogen, progesterone, and deoxycorticosterone. In contrast, monoamine oxidase activity is increased during estrus and proestrus. In humans, increased endometrial monoamine oxidase occurs in the late luteal phase of the menstrual cycle and in direct proportion to the progestin content of oral contraceptives. Conversely, Belmaker et al. have noted a decrease in platelet monoamine oxidase premenstrually. Plasma dopamine hydroxylase, the enzyme which converts dopamine to norepinephrine, is lowest in the premenstrual-menstrual phases of the cycle. During a premenstrual-menstrual phase of the cycle, sensitivity to tyramine, a measure of noradrenergic receptor sensitivity or increased presynaptic norepinephrine activity, increases.

The effects of estrogen, progesterone, and angiotensin on monoamine activity have also been more directly demonstrated in a number of *in-vitro* studies using neurophysiological preparations. Angiotensin has been found to accelerate the biosynthesis of norepinephrine by rat-heart atrium and to inhibit the uptake and reuptake of tritiated norepinephrine by brain-stem slices and perfused rat-brain ventricles. Also, endogenous rat-brain norepinephrine is lowered by intraventricular angiotensin administration. Estrogen, progesterone, and deoxycorticosterone enhance the contractile effect of norepinephrine and epinephrine on aortic strips, and my colleagues and I have shown that estrogen decreases by more than 25 percent the amount of labeled preequilibrated tritiated norepinephrine released by electrically stimulated rat-brain slices.

In addition, the uptake and passive release of various monoamines from nerve endings can be studied *in vitro*, using isolated nerve endings (synaptosomes). My colleagues and I reported that progesterone and estradiol block the uptake of labeled norepinephrine by synaptosomes, and that the passive efflux of preequilibrated norepinephrine from synaptosomes is slightly slowed by estradiol and increased by progesterone. Estradiol and progesterone inhibit the uptake of tritiated dopamine and norepinephrine by synaptosomes. Hydrocortisone causes minimal inhibition of norepinephrine uptake and no significant effects on dopamine uptake. Progesterone (1×10^{-4}M) increases the rate of passive efflux of labeled dopamine and norepinephrine from synaptosomes, and estradiol $(1x10^{-5}M)$ does not affect dopamine efflux. Angiotensin amide $(1x10^{-4}M$ to $1x10^{-5}M)$ also blocks the uptake of tritiated norepinephrine, but does not affect the passive efflux of preequilibrated tritiated norepinephrine.

Thus, there is evidence that alterations in monoamines may be linked to ovarian hormone/adrenal hormone fluctuations on the one hand and mood changes on the other. On this basis, a serotonin hypothesis and a catecholamine (norepinephrine/dopamine) hypothesis of premenstrual tension have evolved.

With respect to serotonin, oral contraceptives cause a functional decrease in pyridoxine, a coenzyme crucial in the regulation of serotonin and nicotinic acid formation. Shunting of the serotonin precursor, tryptophan, toward the formation of nicotinic acid, and possibly away from the formation of serotonin, occurs in the presence of oral contraceptives. Estrogen, in contrast, decreases the formation of nicotinic acid and related metabolites (28).

On the basis of the foregoing information, a number of workers have speculated that the depressed effect caused by oral contraceptives and premenstrual dysphoria may be owed to a decreased production of serotonin. Vitamin B6 (pyridoxine), which is thought to reverse this progesterone/progestin effect, was originally considered useful in treatment of premenstrual tension, a finding not confirmed in a later well-controlled study (21).

With respect to the role of catecholamines in the cyclic emotional fluctuations, there is little direct evidence substantiating this. Antidepressant drugs, which generally do increase catecholamine activity, have been reported to improve the cyclic emotional disorders, and some reports of increases in premenstrual fallopian tube and urinary norepinephrine activity exist.

ACETYLCHOLINE HYPOTHESIS

Some evidence exists that cholinergic mechanisms may be etiologic in the premenstrual-menstrual emotional upsets. As reviewed elsewhere (22), angiotensin increases brain acetylcholine content in rats and mice and causes an increase in the output of acetylcholine from the parietal cortex of cats. It causes an increase in the secretion of antidiuretic hormone, which appears to be cholinergically mediated and itself is water retaining. Consistent with these observations, it has been noted that the uterine hyperemia which precedes menstruation is a result of increased acetylcholine activity, and neostigmine, a cholinesterase inhibitor, can induce menstruation in nonpregnant women who have delayed menstruation, presumably by increasing uterine acetylcholine activity. Furthermore, a variety of ovarian hormones and other steroids can increase acetylcholine activity in physiologic preparations, and can increase sensitivity to acetylcholine in muscle preparations. In support of the possibility that depression may represent a relative predominance of central cholinergic activity, John Davis, my colleagues, and I recently demonstrated that physostigmine, a centrally acting cholinomimetic drug, alleviates manic symptoms and causes withdrawal, lethargy, dysphoria, psychomotor retardation, and, in some cases, depression in normals, remitted patients, schizophrenics, and manics (49). Possibly, then, the premenstrual-menstrual emotional upsets in part represent a relative predominance of central cholinergic activity, caused by angiotensin or a variety of endogenous steroid compounds. Finally, there is some evidence that a proprietary combination drug containing an ergot, a barbiturate, and an anticholinergic agent can alleviate premenstrual tension better than placebo can (50). If this finding is valid, and if the effects are due to the anticholinergic agent, this would support the role of acetylcholine in the ovarian-linked emotional disorders.

TREATMENTS AS ETIOLOGIC CLUES

As inferred earlier, in the treatment of premenstrual-menstrual emotional upsets may lie clues as to the etiology of the cyclic upsets. Unfortunately, at least for mild to moderate premenstrual-menstrual psychic upsets, most treatments, including diuretics, oral contraceptives, minor tranquilizers, antidepressants, oral progestin-progesterone, aldosterone antagonists, dopamine agonists (bromocriptine), serotonergic drugs (Vitamin B6), lithium, a combination drug with an anticholinergic compound, and even psychotherapy have proved initially efficacious.

However, where scrutiny in well-controlled studies has occurred, these treatments have shown decreasing usefulness. Ultimately, it is obvious that the premenstrual-menstrual disorders are extraordinarily fluctuating in intensity from month to month, probably in part owing to differing levels of external stress. Furthermore, the symptoms are extraordinarily well relieved by placebo and/or interpersonal support. Thus, usually the treatment proves efficacious but not particularly better than placebo. Indeed, this appears to have been the fate of such enthusiastically heralded compounds as the thiazide diuretics, pyridoxine (Vitamin B6), and lithium, although in each of these cases, even the results of controlled studies tend to be conflicting.

Oral Contraceptives

The results of treatment with the estrogen-progestin combined oral contraceptives appear somewhat positive. Several controlled studies suggest that these compounds are helpful for some women, and for other women make symptoms worse (51). Several studies, one of which was controlled, have suggested improvement or deterioration as an interaction between the symptoms of premenstrual tension vs. the estrogen/progestin ratio of the oral contraceptives, with irritability most alleviated by progestagen-dominated oral contraceptives. We have speculated that when oral contraceptives do work to alleviate the premenstrual-menstrual disorders, they may do so by preventing fluctuations in the renin-angiotensin-aldosterone system (22).

Progesterone

Greene and Dalton (31), Dalton (9), and others have been strong advocates of the use of intramuscular progesterone in the treatment of the premenstrual-menstrual cyclic emotional and physical disorders. Such a treatment would be compatible with a progesterone withdrawal, a low progesterone, or a high mineralocorticoid-relatively low progesterone hypothesis of premenstrual tension. However, most studies utilizing progesterone have not been well controlled. One study which was well controlled found progesterone no better than placebo (33).

Bromocriptine

Considerable initial enthusiasm existed for the use of bromocriptine in the treatment of premenstrual-menstrual upsets. Bromocriptine depresses prolactin activity and serves as a dopamine agonist, thus implicating both of these chemicals etiologically. However, more recent controlled studies of bromocriptine's efficacy show it no better than an effective placebo, except in treating mastodynia (47, 48).

Anticholinergic Agents

Anticholinergic agents are often a part of many proprietary treatments for premenstrual tension, and specifically are part of a drug called bellergal, consisting of a combination of ergotamine, belladonna alkaloids, and phenobarbitone. In a well-controlled study, this drug was found to improve the physical and emotional symptoms of premenstrual tension, thus suggesting a cholinergic etiology (50).

Diuretics

Early hypotheses as to the etiology of premenstrual tension postulated that increased sodium and water retention may lead to cerebral edema and secondary neurologic findings, including emotional instability. However, although one well-controlled study suggests their efficacy, thiazide diuretics generally show little more efficacy than placebo in relieving the emotional aspects of premenstrual tension syndrome, although they do relieve the physical effects such as bloating and weight gain (21).

Lithium Carbonate

Lithium carbonate was initially considered useful in the treatment of premenstrual-menstrual emotional upsets. If this were in fact substantiated, it would suggest a linkage between monoamines or sodium balance and the cyclic fluctuations, since lithium affects both of these systems and is efficacious in the treatment of affective disorders. Unfortunately, well-controlled trials of lithium in the treatment of premenstrual tension show it to be no better than placebo and possibly worse, at least in most cases (21, 52, 53).

Pyridoxine

As was already mentioned, pyridoxine was initially believed useful in alleviating premenstrual tension and in reversing a progesterone-induced shunting of the serotonin precursor, tryptophan, away from the formation of serotonin. Unfortunately, controlled trials of pyridoxine's effects on premenstrual tension have been less enthusiastic (21).

Spironolactone

As discussed earlier, spironolactone, an aldosterone antagonist, has been shown more effective than placebo in decreasing physical and psychologic symptoms of premenstrual tension. Further studies will determine whether this single observation is indeed valid, and can be thus used to support a renin-angiotensin-aldosterone hypothesis of premenstrual tension (40).

CONCLUSIONS

The information presented in this chapter has indicated that changes in human and primate emotional behavior are in part correlated with, and possibly regulated by, fluctuations in the menstrual cycle. At present, not enough information exists to precisely define which neurohormone, hormone, or combination of hormones is actually causative of menstrual-cycle linked behavioral changes, since there is no single or simple correlation with a given hormone's behavioral effects, presence, or pattern of excretion. However, in general, stable hormone levels, such as occur in the follicular phase of the menstrual cycle, are associated with periods of relative emotional stability. In contrast, elevated or rapidly falling levels of desoxycorticosterone, estrogen, progesterone, aldosterone, and angiotensin, and a potential myriad of undiscovered or unstudied compounds such as occur in third-trimester and postpartum phases of pregnancy, during or after progestin ingestion, and in the late luteal and premenstrual-menstrual phase of the cycle, seem to be associated with emotional instability.

A central hypothesis of this chapter has been that hormones which fluctuate in the menstrual cycle alter neurotransmitters in the brain, and that it is through this mechanism that cyclic emotional, and possibly sexual, changes occur. In regard to this point, it is important to note that the serotonin, catecholamine, and the acetylcholine hypotheses of mental illness in general remain unproven, awaiting further direct studies. However, if one of the neurotransmitter hypotheses is valid, it is still uncertain how specific neurotransmitters or combinations of neurotransmitters actually affect emotions. Similarly, although much evidence exists indicating that neurotransmitters are affected by the hormones previously considered, the actual occurrence of these changes in women under physiological conditions is uncertain, since it is largely based upon indirect evidence. Lastly, although the direction of this review has been to imply that circulating hormones or neurohormones alter neurotransmitters, thus leading to cyclic emotional changes, it is at least as possible that circadian fluctuations in neurotransmitters cause ovarian and adrenal changes which lead to temporal correlates of disturbed behavioral changes, but which are in no way etiologic of these changes. Indeed, the neurotransmitter changes themselves may be primary in regulating mood and hormonal fluctuations. However, more likely is the possibility that the hormonal, neurotransmitter, and behavioral changes are mutually interactive, regulating one another in a variety of systems.

In any case, although a number of unanswered questions, alternate possibilities, and conflicting facts and paradoxes do exist, it seems reasonable to conclude that the proposed etiological relationship of endocrine-related neurotransmitter alterations to menstrual-cycle-linked emotional and sexual behavioral changes remains a hypothetical possibility, worthy of continued investigation. Furthermore, since the cyclic emotional upsets are of ubiquitous and serious psychiatric significance, their continued study represents a very important direction for psychiatric research.

REFERENCES

1. Stephens, W.N. A cross-cultural study of menstrual taboos. *Genet. Psychol. Monogr.* 64: 385–416, 1961.
2. Gorney, R., Janowsky, D.S., & Kelley, B. The curse—vicissitudes and variations of the female fertility cycle: Part II, evolutionary aspects. *Psychosom.* 7: 283–87, 1966.
3. Lancaster, J. Personal communication, 1965.

4. DeVore, I. (Ed.). *Primate Behavior.* New York: Holt, 1965.
5. Rowell, T.E. Behavior and female reproductive cycle in rhesus macaques. *J. Reprod. Fertil.* 6: 193–203, 1963.
6. Sassenrath, E.N., Rowell, T.E., & Hendrickx, A.G. Perimenstrual aggression in groups of female rhesus monkeys. *J. Reprod. Fertil.* 34: 509–11, 1973.
7. Morriss, G.M. & Keverne, E.B. Premenstrual tension. *Lancet* 2: 1,317–18, 1974.
8. Janowsky, D.S., Gorney, R., & Kelley, B. The curse—vicissitudes and variations of the female fertility cycle: Part I, Psychiatric aspects. *Psychosom.* 7: 242–46, 1966.
9. Dalton, K. *The premenstrual syndrome.* London: Heineman Medical, 1964.
10. Dalton, K. Menstruation and acute psychiatric illnesses. *Brit. Med. J.* 1: 148–49, 1959.
11. Janowsky, D.S., Gorney, R., Castelnuovo-Tedesco, P. Premenstrual-menstrual increases in psychiatric hospital admission rates. *Amer. J. Gyn.* 103: 189, 1969.
12. Ribero, A.L. Menstruation and crime. *Brit. J. Med.* 1: 640, 1962.
13. MacKinnon, P.C.B. & MacKinnon, I.L. Hazards of the menstrual cycle. *Brit. Med. J.* 1: 555, 1956.
14. Janowsky, D.S., Gorney, R., & Mandell, A.J. The menstrual cycle: psychiatric and adrenocortical hormone correlates. *Arch. Gen. Psychiat.* 17: 459, 1967.
15. Lederer, J. Premenstrual kleptomania in a case of hypothyroidism and hyperfolliculinism. *Ann. Edoc.* 24: 460–65, 1963.
16. Verghese, A. The syndrome of premenstrual psychosis. *Indian. J. Psychiat.* 5: 160–63, 1963.
17. Krasowska, J. Psychotic syndromes of premenstrual tension in puberty. *Ann. Med. Psychol.* 118: 849–76, 1960.
18. Ota, J. & Mukai, T. Studies on the relationship between psychotic symptoms and sexual cycle. *Folia Psychiat. Neural. Jap.* 8: 207–17, 1954.
19. Parlee, M.B. The premenstrual syndrome. *Psychol. Bull.* 80: 454–65, 1973.
20. Ruble, D.N. Premenstrual symptoms: a reinterpretation. *Science* 197: 291–92, 1977.
21. Steiner, M. & Carroll, B.J. The psychobiology of premenstrual dysphoria: review of theories and treatments. *Psychoneuroend.* 2: 321–35, 1977.
22. Janowsky, D.S., Berens, S.C., & Davis, J.M. Correlations between mood, weight and electrolytes during the menstrual cycle: a renin-angiotensin-aldosterone hypothesis of premenstrual tension. *Psychosom. Med.* 35(2): 143–53, 1973.
23. Coppen, A. & Kessel, N. Menstrual disorders and personality. *Acta Psychother.* 11: 174–80, 1963.
24. McClure, J.N., Jr., Reich, T., and Wetzel, R.D. Premenstrual symptoms as an indicator of bipolar affective disorder. *Br. J. Psychiat.* 119: 527–28, 1971.
25. Wetzel, J.N., Reich, T., McClure, J.N., Jr. Premenstrual affective syndrome and affective disorder. *Br. J. Psychiat.* 127: 219–21, 1975.
26. Sommer, B. The effect of menstruation on cognitive and perceptual-motor behavior: a review. *Psychosom. Med.* 35: 515–34, 1973.
27. Deutsch, H. *The Psychology of Women,* vols. 1 & 2. London: Grune & Stratton, 1945.
28. Janowsky, D.S., Fann, W.E., & Davis, J.M. Monoamines and ovarian hormone-linked sexual and emotional changes: a review. *Arch. Sex. Behav.* 1: 205–18, 1971.
29. Backstrom, T. & Carstensen, H. Estrogen and progesterone in plasma in relation to premenstrual tension. *J. Steroid Biochem.* 5: 257–60, 1974.
30. Backstrom, T. and Mattsson, B. Correlation of symptoms in pre-menstrual tension to estrogen and progesterone concentrations in blood plasma. *Neuropsychobiol.* 1: 80–86, 1975.
31. Greene, R. & Dalton, K. The premenstrual syndrome. *Brit. Med. J.* 1: 1,007–13, 1953.
32. Morton, J.H. Premenstrual tension. *Am. J. Obstet. Gyn.* 60: 343–52, 1950.
33. Smith, S.L. Mood and the menstrual cycle. In Sachar, E.J. (Ed.), *Topics in Psychoendocrinology.* New York: Raven Press, 1975.

34. Reich, M. The variations in urinary aldosterone levels of normal females during the menstrual cycle. *Aust. Ann. Med.* 11: 41–49, 1962.
35. Gray, M.J., Strausfeld, K.S., Wantanabe, M. Aldosterone secretory rates in the normal menstrual cycle. *J. Clin. Endocr. Metab.* 28: 1269–75, 1968.
36. Strausfeld, K. Variations in aldosterone secretory rates during the menstrual cycle. *Obstet. Gyn.* 23: 631, 1964.
37. Katz, F.H. & Romfh, P. Plasma aldosterone and renin activity during the menstrual cycle. *J. Clin. Endocr. Metab.* 34: 819–21, 1972.
38. Schwartz, U.D. & Abraham, G.E. Corticosterone and aldosterone levels during the menstrual cycle. *Obstet. Gyn.* 45: 339–42, 1975.
39. Perrini, N. & Piliego, N. The increase of aldosterone in the premenstrual syndrome. *Minerva Med.* 50: 2,897–99, 1959.
40. O'Brien, P.M., Craven, D., Selby, C. Treatment of premenstrual syndrome by spironolactone. *Br. J. Ob. Gyn.* 86: 142–47, 1979.
41. Munday, M., Brush, M.G., & Taylor, R.W. Progesterone and aldosterone levels in the premenstrual tension syndrome. *J. Endocr.* 73: 21, 1977.
42. Bruce, J. & Russel, G.F.M. Premenstrual tension. A study of weight changes and balances of water, sodium and potassium. *Lancet* 2: 267–71, 1962.
43. Thorn, G.W., Nelson, K.R., & Thorn, D.W. A study of the mechanism of edema associated with menstruation. *Endocr.* 22: 155–63, 1938.
44. Landau, R.I. & Lugibihl, K. Catabolic and natriuretic effects of progesterone in man. *Recent Prog. Horm. Res.* 17: 249–92, 1961.
45. Adamopoulos, D.A., Loraine, J.A., Lunn, S.F. Endocrine profiles in premenstrual tension. *Clin. Endocr.* 1: 283–92, 1972.
46. Halbreich, U., Ben-David, M., Assael, M. Serum-prolactin in women with premenstrual syndrome. *Lancet* 2: 654–56, 1976.
47. Graham, J.J., Harding, P.E., Wise, P.H. Prolactin suppression in the treatment of premenstrual syndrome. *Med. J. Aust.* 2: 18–20, 1978.
48. Andersen, A.N., Larsen, J.F., Streenstrup, R. Effect of bromocriptine of the premenstrual syndrome. A double-blind clinical trial. *Br. J. Obstet. Gyn.* 84: 370–74, 1977.
49. Janowsky, D.S., El-Yousef, M.K., Davis, J.M., & Sekerke, H.J. A cholinergic-adrenergic hypothesis of mania and depression. *Lancet* 1: 632–35, 1972.
50. Robinson, K., Huntington, K.M., & Wallace, M.G. Treatment of the premenstrual syndrome. *Br. J. Obstet. Gyn.* 84: 784–88, 1977.
51. Gullberg, J. Mood changes and menstrual symptoms with different gestagen/estrogen combinations. *Acta Psychiat. Scand.* (Suppl.) 236: 1–86, 1972.
52. Singer, K., Cheng, R., & Schou, M. A controlled evaluation of lithium in the premenstrual tension syndrome. *Brit. J. Psychiat.* 124: 50–51, 1974.
53. Mattsson, B. & von Schoultz, B. A comparison between lithium, placebo and a diuretic in premenstrual tension. *Acta Psychiat. Scand.* (Suppl.) 255: 75–85, 1974.

Phenomenology and Treatment of Psychophysiological Disorders

8

The Couvade Syndrome: Its Psychophysiological, Neurotic, and Psychotic Manifestations

EFRAIN A. GOMEZ
PONCE SANDLIN
GEORGE L. ADAMS

INTRODUCTION

The psychosomatic and other emotional problems of fatherhood are probably more frequent than the relatively small number of publications on the subject would indicate. Couvade is the name given a process or custom in which a husband develops symptoms of pregnancy during his wife's parturient and puerperal periods. Much neglected in the psychiatric literature, most references to couvade are limited to the psychophysiological reactions seen in expectant fathers. The purpose of this paper is to explore the complexities of couvade and to demonstrate its occurrence not only as a psychophysiologic reaction but as a neurotic and psychotic disorder as well.

The practice of couvade has been noted since antiquity, in such diverse places as Africa, China, Japan, and India. Diodorus Siculus described the custom on the island of Corsica as early as 60 B.C. (1). Later, it was observed on Cyprus, in Spain, and among the Indians of North and South America. Initially studied by anthropologists and ethnologists, the custom of couvade was divided into two forms: the pseudo-maternal and the dietetic (2). In the pseudo-maternal form of couvade, the expectant father at or about the time of delivery retires to bed and simulates childbirth in order to receive attention usually given to the parturient woman. The dietetic form consists of dietary restrictions by the father, who pretends to be weak and ailing, following labor. These sham rituals are still practiced today in certain primitive cultures.

Tyler (3) attempted to explain couvade as an adoption ceremony marking the transition from matrilineal to patrilineal descent, with intent to insure the legitimacy of the child. A more generally accepted anthropological opinion is that couvade is one of the many examples of sympathetic magic which account for numerous superstitions; for example, the idea of insertion of evil into a person is basic to the concept of witchcraft (4, 5). The expectant father must prevent anything malevolent from being transmitted to the child. Therefore, he feigns pregnancy to divert evil to himself, while the mother and child go unharmed.

In the nineteenth century, couvade was reported among the Basque of the Pyrenees and in the Bearn region of France, where it probably received its name from the French verb *couver*, meaning to brood or to hatch. Subsequently, the custom came to the attention of physicians and psychoanalysts, and was described as the Couvade Syndrome as custom, ritual, and mores were being redefined in psychopathological terms in more civilized cultures. (It should be noted, however, that the custom still exists in its original form in certain cultures.) In his psychoanalytic explanation of couvade, Theodore Reik (6) emphasized the role of hostility and ambivalence. In his view, the pseudo-maternal form of couvade represents a reaction formation against hostile feelings toward the wife. In the case of the dietetic couvade, he explains the ritual as a defensive maneuver to protect the newborn from the father's hostile feelings.

Other analytic interpretations of couvade stress the importance of bisexuality. Bisexual strivings have been dealt with in myths and rituals throughout man's history. Initiation rites such as circumcision are related to bisexual conflicts and are attempts to accept and integrate socially prescribed sexual roles. The ambivalence characteristic of these rituals has its roots in pregenital fixations and is related to envy of one sex regarding the sexual organs of the other (7).

The masculine envy of the woman's childbearing capacities has been ascribed to some crucial historical determinants such as the feminine identifications and productivity of mother earth in agrarian cultures (8). Hunting cultures, antedating agrarian ones, emphasized masculine strivings (9). The mythologies of these cultures have been interpreted in terms of the conflict between these two trends. In the creation myths, the "primordial androgynous giant" represents the construct of a bisexual being, who as a male becomes separated from, or gives origin to, his female half while retaining urges for subsequent reunion. In colloquial Spanish, one refers to one's spouse as one's beloved half.

In this century, the medical and psychiatric literature has paid more attention to the emotional problems of expectant mothers than to those of expectant fathers. When signs and symptoms of pregnancy have been described in expectant fathers, they have been psychophysiologic in nature, such as morning sickness, nausea, vomiting, diarrhea, constipation, aberrations of appetite, backache, toothache. If these symptoms could not be otherwise explained or ignored, this was then called the Couvade Syndrome in civilized societies. The authors believe that this is only one manifestation of intrapsychic conflict in expectant fathers and that the syndrome may occur not only as a psychophysiological reaction, but also as psychoneurotic and psychotic disorders.

COUVADE AS A PSYCHOPHYSIOLOGICAL REACTION

In this form of couvade, probably the most common and easiest to recognize, the expectant father usually develops gastrointestinal symptoms including morning sickness, increased appetite (eating for two), and cravings for certain foods. Although these symptoms may appear at any time during the wife's pregnancy, they are more common during the first trimester. They may last until the child is born or in some cases continue after birth. Many cases do not come to medical or psychiatric attention either because the symptomatology is mild and transient, or because, in civilized cultures, such symptoms in men threaten their masculine image and lead to the stigma of being considered effeminate. Most of these cases of Couvade Syndrome resolve without difficulty, but there may be recurrences with future pregnancies. Severe cases with pernicious and intractable vomiting are admitted to medical services and treated as cases of malnutrition or dehydration.

Trethowan and Colon (22) were the first authors to collect a large number of cases. They found significant differences when they compared 327 husbands of pregnant women with 220 men whose wives were not expecting and had not been pregnant during the previous year. The expectant fathers were more afflicted with gastrointestinal symptoms, changes of appetite, and toothache than the control group. It is important to note that the association of physical symptoms and anxiety is not complete. Almost one third of those with physical symptoms denied feeling anxious, whereas expectant fathers without symptoms admitted being anxious. These authors define the Couvade Syndrome as follows: "Couvade by definition only occurs in men during their wives' pregnancies or at the time of parturition. Following childbirth, and sometimes possibly even before, they disappear, though may recur in chronological relationship to future pregnancies. Each subject, therefore, being free of couvade symptoms in between times, can be regarded as his own control."

Trethowan (10) reported on Dickens' personal communication of the incidence of pica and cravings and other perversions of appetite in 50 percent of husbands of pregnant women. In all instances, the symptoms appeared in chronological relationship to pregnancy. Curtis (11) observed the occurrence of morning sickness, disturbances of appetite, and epigastric discomfort in 22 out of 55 expectant fathers. He found that the majority of his subjects were unaware of any connection between fatherhood and their symptoms. Wilson (25) makes reference to reported cases of military men during World War II who suffered from couvade symptoms upon learning of their wife's state of pregnancy. Some of them developed constipation, diarrhea, and even abdominal bloating about the time their wives were expected to begin labor. While it is chiefly husbands who are affected, occasionally other male relatives may be victims of this curious disorder (13).

Case 1

A 51-year-old Mexican-American tile-setter who fathered 6 children was referred by a primary-care physician from whom he had demanded "male hormones" for impotence. The patient was annoyed by the psychiatric referral, denying any history of emotional or mental problems and attributing his impotence to physical reasons. However, during the initial interview, he revealed that the impotence had started following his wife's last pregnancy. He was married to a Mexican-American woman whom he had abandoned every time she became pregnant. The children ranged in age from 5 months to 13 years. The fourth pregnancy had coincided with the death of the patient's mother. His wife was in the first trimester of her fifth pregnancy when he developed morning sickness and breast tenderness. He felt repugnance to certain smells, such as burning cigarettes and cheese. His wife, who was with him during the interview, added, "We both craved pickles and banana splits." They both developed chloasma gravidarum, and he was teased by his peers. Sexual desire for his wife was nonexistent. He avoided the sight of children with skin sores or those dressed in dirty clothes and felt nauseous at the sight of pregnant women. During the fifth and sixth pregnancies, most of his symptoms disappeared after the first trimester. At no time did he consider himself sick or sufficiently anxious to seek medical attention.

An examination of his background showed that his mother had abandoned the family for another man when the patient was 5 years old. The patient and his older brother had been brought up by a paternal aunt, who mistreated them and openly preferred her own children to them. The patient said that both his parents suffered from diabetes, and he had read that diabetes causes impotence. His physical examination and laboratory reports were within normal limits. The patient was offered psychiatric treatment and accepted but did not return for his appointments. A telephone call to follow up on the patient revealed that he had found a general practitioner who had started him on hormones.

This case is an example of the psychophysiologic manifestations of couvade. These cases usually do not come to the attention of the psychiatrist unless the patient is referred by a primary-care physician, but even after referral, the patients are rarely motivated to seek psychiatric treatment. The precipitating events in this man's case are his wife's pregnancy, the death of his mother, and the decline of his masculine powers. Dynamically, one has to consider the role of ambivalence and reactivation of early feminine identifications. Although the patient did not experience symptoms of pregnancy during his wife's first four pregnancies, he felt extreme ambivalence about her and about having children. He abandoned her every time she became pregnant. The psychophysiologic symptoms of couvade appeared in his wife's fifth and sixth pregnancies and after the death of his mother, who had abandoned him when he was five. The couvade seems to express in the language of the body the patient's repressed feminine wishes, his longing for anaclitic dependence, and his ambivalent feelings toward the wife and mother. Through couvade, the patient identifies with the image of the pregnant mother and the unborn child at the same time, thus solving his problem of dependence and the feelings of hostility for his abandonment by the mother. His impotence can be viewed as an attempt to reconcile his dependent and hostile feelings. By becoming impotent, he can stay with her and punish her by leaving her sexless and childless. His hope to recapture the masculine powers which had protected him from conflict in the past is demonstrated by his demand for male hormones.

When conflicts are expressed not in emotional but in somatic terms, psychiatric treatment is hampered. Appropriate at this time is MacLean's reference to the Papez-MacLean theory [14]. In considering the limbic system as the center of emotions, Papez and MacLean referred to the rich connections between the limbic system and the autonomic nervous system, in contrast with the poorly demonstrable connections between the neocortex and the hypothalamus. MacLean called the limbic system the "visceral brain" to distinguish it from the neocortex, which he called the "word brain" and added, "It should be remarked that one of the striking observations regarding the patient with psychosomatic illness is his apparent intellectual inability to verbalize his emotional feelings." Other authors have referred to the same phenomenon as "alexithymia." Sifneos [15], in a controlled study, was able to validate a group of characteristics in psychosomatic patients. Among the characteristics he listed were poverty of fantasy life, constricted affect, inability to talk about feelings, and lack of the capacity for introspection. He found that 25 psychosomatic patients had twice as many of these characteristics as did 25 control subjects.

Emotional feelings sometimes are not expressed in words but in the language of the body. In line with this trend of thought, Eylon [16] found a significant association between birth events and appendectomies. Groddeck [17] interpreted an attack of appendicitis as a pregnancy fantasy in a man. According to him, the wish to bear a child was expressed through many somatic symptoms. Inman, a British ophthalmologist, was interested in a belief in several cultures about the efficacy of a gold wedding ring as a cure for styes. The wedding ring symbolizes marriage, and marriage implies procreation. Inman (18) found that his patients with disorders of the eyelid glands such as styes and tarsal cysts had an increased incidence of thoughts and fantasies about births.

COUVADE AS A NEUROTIC DISORDER

The neurotic manifestations of couvade are more difficult to recognize, since the varied symptomatology may prompt a diagnosis of depressive, anxiety, or hysterical, neurosis. Rather than psychophysiologic responses to the wife's pregnancy appearing in the husband, the intrapsychic conflict is more subtle in its presentation. Freud alluded to pregnancy fantasies in the male in the case of Little Hans (19). He also referred to this topic in the history of the Wolf-man (20). Zilboorg (21), without recognizing the implications of couvade, wrote about depressive reactions related to fatherhood. He concentrated on the feelings of rivalry between father and child for the mother's affection. He also brought into focus unconscious incest fantasies arising when a man fathers a child with a woman who represents a mother image. He saw postpartum depression in men as a defense against complete identification with their own fathers.

The wish for a child in men has not been neglected in the psychoanalytic literature. Boehm (22) called it "parturition envy." He emphasized the attitude of the boy toward his mother in the negative Oedipus complex, stating that the negative Oedipus was not just hate toward the mother but envy of her capacity to bear children. Klein (23) maintained that the frustration of a boy's wish for a child made him feel inferior to the mother, and consequently he overcompensated for his disadvantage by stressing masculine strivings. Brunswick (24), writing about the two great wishes of childhood—the wish for a penis and the wish for a baby—found that the wish for a baby arises very early, is asexual, and is based on a primitive identification of the child of either sex with the mother. That earliest period of exclusive attachment to the mother before the father appears as a rival is the pre-Oedipal phase of psychosexual development. Lampl de Groot extended this notion by stating, "The passive feminine relation to the father in the case of the male child, is a second edition of his primitive love relation to the mother . . . and contributes to pathologic trends which may later disturb his normal sexuality" (25). Jarvis emphasized another important issue: "We have been accustomed to considering childhood, adolescence, and climaterium as points of flux in the dynamic relations of the psyche. I suggest that pregnancy is also one of these crucial times for the male as well as for the female" (26). Cavenar and Butts suggested that in men with childbirth neuroses, the issue of sibling rivalry has to be considered as an important psychodynamic factor (27).

Case 2

Mr. B., a 24-year-old Anglo male, was referred for psychiatric outpatient treatment because of symptoms of anxiety and depression following the birth of a second daughter. The symptoms started shortly after his wife and new baby returned from the hospital. The patient came to the first interview accompanied by his mother, who had lived with her son and his wife from the beginning of their marriage. The mother stated that the reason for seeking psychiatric treatment had to do with suicidal ideas expressed by her son. The patient complained of lack of interest and pleasure in his daily activities, anorexia, insomnia, and decreased energy. He could not stand the sight of the baby or to hear it cry. He blamed himself for his emotional problems and for bringing children into this "miserable world," saying that he had to pay for this.

Background information revealed that at age 15, he had lost his father and had been forced to assume responsibilities such as working on the farm and caring for his mother, his younger sister, and another girl adopted by his mother. Following the marriage of his sister, his mother pressured him to marry his adopted sister when he was 20 years old. The patient described his mother as a very possessive woman who suffered from fits of depression. He resented his mother's habit of calling on her alcoholic brother (the patient's uncle) to help solve family problems. He felt hurt because this indicated that his mother did not trust him, and his uncle's intrusion was considered insulting and demeaning. His own father was described as kind and hard-working but distant.

The patient's marriage and the birth of his first child did not bring with them any significant problems, but when he learned that his wife was pregnant for the second time, he intensely wished for a boy. After the delivery, when informed that he was the father of another baby girl, he refused to see the baby and subsequently developed symptoms as described.

In this case, the contributory factors leading to depressive manifestations of couvade are the death of the patient's father during adolescence, the fatherlike responsibilities the young man had to assume prematurely, his marriage to a young woman who was like a sister to him, and his uncle's undermining his self-esteem. The precipitating event was related to the birth of a baby girl, when he had intensely wished for a boy. All these factors combined to produce a condition similar to a postpartum depression. Dynamically, the lack of strong identification with father or a father figure, plus the frustration of not having a male child, made him feel inferior and reactivated ambivalent identification with his mother, who had always suffered from fits of depression. His symptoms of depression may also be viewed as punishment for incest fantasies, since his wife symbolized aspects of his mother and sister, and since his father's early death forced him to assume his father's responsibilities prematurely, thus reinforcing the fantasy. Also, by becoming depressed in the puerperium, he rendered himself helpless about feelings of hostility and ambivalence directed against his wife and child.

COUVADE AS A PSYCHOTIC DISORDER

Freud, describing the analysis of the Schreber case, explained that "much more material remains to be gathered from the symbolic content of the fantasies and delusions of this gifted paranoic" (28). Most of the literature that followed Freud's analysis was concerned with confirming the mechanisms of projection in paranoia and stressing the importance of latent homosexuality, not only in paranoia, but also in jealousy, alcoholism, and drug addiction. Freud used the inverted Oedipus situation to explain Schreber's pregnancy fantasies: "Nothing sounds so repugnant and incredible . . . as a little boy's feminine attitude to the father and the fantasy of pregnancy derived from it" (29). Macalpine and Hunter (30) called attention to the fact that somatic delusions had been neglected by Freud and some of his followers. The emphasis on genital, homosexual, and neurotic aspects had led to the neglect of psychotic mechanisms such as the eruption of archaic procreation fantasies into consciousness. In reexamining Schreber's autobiography, they viewed Schreber's psychosis as a reactivation of pregenital procreation fantasies. Schreber's absolute ambisexuality represented to them the "balanced imbalance" of sex regularly found in schizophrenics. In *The Ego and the Id*, Freud states:

> A boy has not merely an ambivalent attitude towards his father and affectionate object relation towards his mother, but at the same time he also behaves like a girl and displays an affectionate feminine attitude to his father and corresponding hostility and jealousy towards his mother. It is this complicating element introduced by bisexuality that makes it so difficult to obtain a clear view of the facts in connection with the earliest object-choices and identifications, and still more difficult to describe them intelligibly. It may even be that the ambivalence displayed in the relation to the parents should be attributed entirely to bisexuality (31).

Jacobson used the wish for a child in boys as her central theme in writing a detailed paper in which the main emphasis is on pregenital material (32). Reik, in his paper on couvade, quotes the case of a male hebephrenic treated by Abraham who had suffered from a fictitious pregnancy at the age of 15 (6). Evans (33) reported the analysis of a man who had simulated pregnancy during the course of psychoanalytic treatment. Interestingly enough, this male patient had previously suffered couvade symptoms during his wife's first pregnancy. Evans viewed the simulated pregnancy as a primitive identification with his mother and her unique capacity to have babies. Towne and Afterman (34) reported 18 men with schizophrenic disorders in association with a birth in the family. They stressed the lack of parental affection and the effect of traumatic experiences in infancy. Knight (35) reported the case of a merchant marine who developed pregnancy symptoms including abdominal distention. Physical examination and laboratory reports were negative. His physicians thought that the symptoms were suggestive of liver disease, but the patient had the delusion of being pregnant, believing that he was going to give birth to children who would be resistant to atomic radiation. He was diagnosed as schizophrenic, paranoid type. Wainwright (36) presented 10 cases who required hospitalization after becoming fathers. In some of the cases, the increased responsibility of fatherhood triggered latent homosexual conflicts. In one case, the fear of identification with the father was the causative factor. In the rest, a marked dependence on the wife was the most significant dynamic factor leading to psychosis and subsequent psychiatric hospitalization. Cavenar and Weddington (37) reported three cases demonstrating significant emotional difficulties surrounding fatherhood. The factor common to all three was abdominal pain for which no physical cause could be found. Their disorders superficially appeared to be a variant of the relatively benign psychophysiologic form of couvade. However, each patient was ultimately hospitalized because of a serious psychiatric disturbances.

Case 3

An unemployed 26-year-old black father of three children, with a history of previous psychiatric hospitalization, was readmitted because he showed signs and symptoms of psychosis. The present illness had begun, following arguments and fights with his wife. He had become increasingly disturbed because she had insisted on suckling their new baby. When he was not fighting with his wife, he actively avoided her and the baby. Shortly before his hospitalization, he started to complain of a nagging pain on his left side, for which no physical reason was found. He insisted on going to the street to preach the Word of the Lord because "the end of the world was in sight" and the beginning of a new era was imminent. When he tried to take his two other children with him, saying that the Lord was commanding him to do so, his wife called the police, and the patient was hospitalized.

In the hospital, he was found to be hallucinating and delusional, and displayed bizarre behavior such as demanding to be number nine in line while waiting for his daily showers or for his tray of food. He masturbated with complete disregard of the presence of others. Sometimes he was found using the female bathrooms, claiming that he had to sit because he had an "itch in his crotch." He continued to complain about the pain in his side, saying that the tumor was growing, that it was going to burst and crack his ribs, and that the new era would then begin.

Relevant background information showed that the patient was the first of nine children. His father had died when the patient was 12. Following his death, the patient did poorly in school and engaged in antisocial behavior, refusing to help his ailing mother. He moved to New York City at age 18, and was married at age 20 to an older woman. He worked as a groundskeeper in a cemetery until the death of his mother, at which time he returned to South Carolina to her funeral and had his first nervous breakdown. He was hospitalized at a state hospital in South Carolina for several months. Details of his first hospitalization are unknown.

The diagnosis of paranoid schizophrenia was based on presenting symptomatology and family history of mental illness. His maternal grandmother died in a state hospital, and a younger brother was also hospitalized with the diagnosis of schizophrenia. The patient was treated with antipsychotics, supportive and milieu therapy. He recovered in eight weeks and was discharged as improved.

The dynamic sequence of this case can be viewed as follows: The patient displayed behavioral disturbances and personality changes in adolescence, after the death of his father; a period of relative quiescence followed, during which he married an older woman and worked as a groundskeeper; the death of his mother precipitated his first breakdown, of which little is known. His unemployment, the birth of a second child, and the insistence of his wife on nursing the baby precipitated his second breakdown. His psychotic productions illustrated his regression to pregenital ambivalent fixations and the eruption of procreation fantasies. The state of complete confusion about his sexual identity is characteristic of schizophrenics. This confusion is seen in the patient's behavior, in the use of the female and the male bathrooms, and in his public masturbatory activities. The masturbation enabled him to enact in a solitary activity the role of man and woman in the sexual act. His insistence on being number nine can be viewed as symbolic of his pregnancy fantasies. It is also an allusion to his mother's reproductive capacities (she had nine children) and to his own lack of productivity (unemployment). The left-sided growing tumor, ready to burst, crushing his ribs, can be seen as the somatic expression of the act of birth in the symbolic language of the unconscious. It is interesting to note that myths and legends of the creation of man and woman use the same language—for instance, Eve was created from one of Adam's ribs.

CONCLUSION

The concept and manifestations of couvade have been viewed historically, from the first recorded appearance in diverse cultures of antiquity to modern times. This ancient custom, which began with cultural acceptance and with the symbolic and ritualistic intent of protecting and enhancing the well-being of the child, is still practiced today in certain primitive societies. Couvade, however, is, in more sophisticated cultures, a complex phenomenon with medical and psychological manifestations which therefore encompass a wide range of psychiatric manifestations. Intrapsychic conflict around the issue of a wife's pregnancy may be demonstrated by the expectant father not only with psychophysiological reactions but with signs and symptoms of a psychoneurotic disorder or with an illness of psychotic proportions.

Parenthood for the father involves reactivations of early identifications with the mother, father, and significant others, as well as issues of hostility, ambivalence, and bisexuality. The conflict between regression toward narcissism versus preservation of object choices and cathexes constitutes a latent residue in the adult life of expectant fathers (38). The father's maturity is tested and influenced not only by the desire to recapture his own infantile narcissism via the newborn, but by further introjections and identifications based on the reality of having children and the acceptance of a changing relationship with his wife. Unsuccessful resolution of this conflict negates further emotional development on the part of the father and sets the stage for the manifestations of couvade. If a man's psychosexual development has been successful, fatherhood will bring compensations for unfulfilled feminine wishes through healthy identifications with wife and children.

The psychodynamic aspects of couvade are easier to explain than its genetics. Thus, it is more difficult to explain why, given a similar psychodynamic constellation, some patients develop psychophysiological reactions, others neurotic conditions, and still others psychotic disorders. Temperament, heredity, environment, and the like are probably important considerations. But psychological and sociocultural factors are necessary in the explanation of couvade. In certain cultures, a male's identifications with motherhood, childbearing, and child-rearing are egosyntonic and do not produce serious psychopathology. By and large in our society, these identifications are conflict-laden and egodystonic; therefore, their manifestations are often subtle, deceiving, and difficult to diagnose. For this reason, the information on incidence and prevalence of couvade is scarce and unreliable. One suspects that the figures are much higher than the literature would indicate, especially in light of the mild and transient nature of most forms of the psychophysiologic type plus the male reluctance to seek attention for such symptoms. Then, too, the neurotic and psychotic forms are frequently not recognized in regard to the couvade connection.

Reid (39), after examining the major research in this field, suggests that fathers-to-be are in need of more and better preparation for approaching parenthood. Free and easy communication with their wives is necessary. Munroe et al.'s psychological analysis of a cross-cultural survey of data from 22 societies supports the hypothesis that the level of male salience experienced in childhood is a significant determinant of whether or not a man will practice couvade as an adult (40).

To summarize, in cultures in which male identifications with motherhood are relatively conflict-free, couvade is not a serious problem, or it is expressed in culturally accepted rituals rather than as symptoms of illness indicating psychopathology. In cultures in which male identification with motherhood is fraught with conflict and anxiety, the conflict is manifested in individual cases of psychophysiologic, neurotic, or psychotic couvade, depending on temperament, constitution, and personality structure of each individual.

REFERENCES

1. Licht, H. *Sexual Life in Ancient Greece*. London: Routledge, 1935.
2. Trethowan, W. & Colon, M. The couvade syndrome. *Brit. J. Psychiat.* 3: 57–66, 1965.
3. Tylor, E.B. *Researches into the Early History of Mankind and the Development of Civilization*. London: Murray, 1865.
4. Malinowski, B. *Sex and Repression in Savage Society*. London: Kegan Paul, 1937.
5. Frazer, J.G. *Totemism and Exogamy*, vol. 4. London: 1910.
6. Reik, T. *Ritual*. London: Hogarth, 1931.
7. Bettelheim, B. *Symbolic Wounds*. New York: Free Press, 1954.
8. Fromm, E. Sex and character. *Psychiat.* 6: 21–31, 1934.
9. Campbell, J. *The Masks of God: Primitive Mythology*. New York: Viking, 1959.
10. Trethowan, W.H. The couvade syndrome: some further observation. *J. Psychosom. Res.* 12: 107–15, 1968.
11. Curtis, J.L. A psychiatric study of 55 expectant fathers. *US Armed Forces Med. J.* 6: 937, 1955.
12. Wilson, L.G. The couvade syndrome. *Am. Family Phys.* 15: 157–60, 1977.

13. Freeman, T. Pregnancy as a precipitant of mental illness in men. *Brit. J. Med. Psychol.* 24: 49, 1951.
14. MacLean, P.D. Psychosomatic disease and the "visceral brain." *Psychosom. Med.* 11: 338–53, 1949.
15. Sifneos, P. The prevalence of "alexithymic" characteristics in psychosomatic patients. *Psychoth. and Psychosom.* 22: 255–62, 1973.
16. Eylon, Y. Birth events, appendicitis, and appendectomy. *Brit. J. Med. Psychol.* 40: 317–32, 1967.
17. Groddeck, G.W. *The Book of the It.* New York: Random, 1961.
18. Inman, W.S. The couvade in modern England. *Brit. J. Med. Psychol.* 19: 37–55, 1941.
19. Freud, S. Analysis of a phobia in a five-year-old boy. *Collected Papers*, vol. 3. London: Hogarth, 1949.
20. Freud, S. From the history of an infantile neurosis. *Collected Papers*, vol. 3. London: Hogarth, 1949.
21. Zilboorg, G. Depressive reactions related to parenthood. *Am. J. Psychiat.* 87: 927–62, 1931.
22. Boehm, F. The femininity complex in man. *Int. J. Psychoanal.* 11: 456–69, 1930.
23. Klein, M. *Contributions to Psychoanalysis.* London: Hogarth, 1948.
24. Brunswick, R.M. The Pre-oedipal phase of libido development. *Psychoanal. Quart.* 9: 293–319, 1940.
25. Lampl de Groot, J. The pre-oedipal phase in the development of the male child. *The Psychoanalytic Study of the Child*, vol. 2. New York: International Universities Press, 1946.
26. Jarvis, W. Some effects of pregnancy and childbirth on men. *J. Am. Psychoanal. Assoc.* 10: 689–700, 1962.
27. Cavenar, J.O. & Butts, N.T. Fatherhood and emotional illness. *Am. J. Psychiat.* 134: 429–31, 1977.
28. Freud, S. Psychoanalytic notes upon an autobiographical account of a case of paranoia. *Collected Papers*, Vol. 3. New York: Basic, 1959.
29. Freud, S. A neurosis of demoniacal possession in the seventeenth century. *Collected Papers*, vol. 4. London: Hogarth, 1949.
30. Macalpine, I. & Hunter, R.A. The Schreber case: a contribution to schizophrenia, hypochondria, and psychosomatic symptom-formation. *Psychoanal. Quart.* 22: 328–71, 1953.
31. Freud, S. *The Ego and the Id.* New York: Norton, 1962.
32. Jacobson, E. Development of a wish for a child in boys. *The Psychoanalytic Study of the Child.* New York: International Universities Press, 1950.
33. Evans, W. Simulated pregnancy in a male. *Psychoanaly. Quart.* 20: 265–78, 1951.
34. Towne, R.D. & Afterman, J. Psychosis in males related to parenthood. *Bull. Menninger Clin.* 19: 19–26, 1955.
35. Knight, J.A. False pregnancy in a male. *Psychosom. Med.* 22: 260–66, 1960.
36. Wainwright, W. Fatherhood as a precipitant of mental illness. *Am. J. Psychiat.* 123: 40–44, 1966.
37. Cavenar, J.O. & Weddington, W.W. Abdominal pain in expectant fathers. *Psychosom.* 19: 761–68, 1978.
38. Jaffe, D.S. The masculine envy of woman's procreative functions. *J. Am. Psychoanal. Assoc.* 16: 521–48, 1968.
39. Reid, K.E. Fatherhood and emotional stress: the couvade syndrome. *W. Mich. U. School of Soc. Work J.* 2: 3–14, 1975.
40. Munroe, R.L., Unroe, R.H., & Whiting, J.W. The couvade: a psychological analysis. *Ethos* 1:30–74, 1973.

9

The Problem
of Anorexia Nervosa:
Psychobiological Considerations

HERBERT WEINER

INTRODUCTION

This chapter will address the many questions about primary anorexia nervosa (AN) that remain unanswered, with particular attention given to certain factual aspects of the syndrome that are well-established but unexplained. I shall refrain from mentioning the observations that have been made by psychiatric and psychoanalytic clinicians (1). These observations have led to concepts about the nature of the remorseless self-starvation, or the excessive control over eating, that are an important but not the invariant feature of the behavior of some patients with AN. Therefore, these concepts can only account for some aspects of the syndrome, and do not explain the fact that the syndrome begins with amenorrhea in about half the patients.

We have no satisfactory explanation of this onset of AN, and despite extensive investigations in the past 15 years, we know little about the predisposing factors for, or initiation of, primary AN. One reason for our ignorance may be that primary AN is not a homogeneous disease entity. We are already aware that subforms of primary AN exist: A small but indeterminate number of patients with AN have a specific chromosomal abnormality—Turner's syndrome (2). Rarely, a hypothalamic tumor will manifest itself as AN. Additionally, one might speculate that two other subforms of AN exist as defined by their modes of onset: One subform begins with self-starvation, another with amenorrhea.

Less speculative are certain facts about AN which also suggest a heterogeneous illness: We do not understand why the age of onset of the illness has a double peak—one at about 12 years of age, and the other at 18–20 years of age (3). The context in which AN begins is also variable; the impact of peer or professional pressures to be thin is one such context. In other patients, AN begins after a separation from another person, following a sexual temptation or experience, or as a defiant protest against the demands of another person. Obviously, many future AN patients diet for cosmetic reasons. Other young women develop AN after they stop taking an oral contraceptive (4). Occasionally, pseudocyesis antecedes AN (5).

We still do not really understand how these variable-onset conditions could possibly produce a disturbance in two major biological functions—eating and reproduction. One reason for our failure to understand AN is that, despite extensive and intensive research about many different aspects of AN, we are not able with any degree of certainty to ascribe the rich pathophysiology of the syndrome to any one central predisposing or initiating factor. Many of the changes in the physiology of the disorder could be laid at the door of semistarvation, weight loss, malnutrition, a chronic illness state (the low T_3 syndrome); or the motoric hyperactivity, sleep, or mood disturbances that are such obvious manifestations of AN.

Another impediment to our understanding of AN is that we have little normative data about eating, sleep, and activity in adolescence, with which to compare the behaviors of AN patients. In fact, our understanding of adolescence is mainly phrased in psychological, not behavioral, terms.

I would suggest that our understanding of the AN syndrome would be advanced by obtaining such behavioral information. We might then begin to have answers to the following puzzles:

1) We do not understand why the incidence of AN has measurably increased (6, 7).

2) We do not understand why the incidence of AN is class-related. It occurs with a fivefold frequency in the higher economic strata of society (8, 9).

3) We do not understand why the incidence of AN occurs predominantly in young women.

4) We do not understand AN because our facts about the natural history of AN are based on a limited sample (7): only about 30 percent of all patients come to the attention of behavioral scientists.

5) We do not understand the sleep disturbance that occurs in AN patients.

6) We do not understand why AN patients are physically active before, during, and after their illness (10).

Because we still know little about the natural habits of adolescents—especially, adolescent girls—we cannot understand why some dieting adolescent girls go on to develop AN. About 10 percent of 14-year-old girls, and 40 percent of 18-year-old girls, diet for various reasons. About 2.7 percent of dieting girls develop amenorrhea, and about 1.2 percent lose very significant amounts of weight (10 kg). Of those who lose that amount of weight, one half develop the

AN syndrome (11). However, our understanding of the AN syndrome is aided by the finding that adolescent girls who diet for cosmetic reasons first become amenorrheic, later develop a mounting concern about their (assumed excessive) weight and about eating, and still later stop eating altogether (11).

This sequence may be one way in which AN develops. Another sequence also occurs: AN patients concerned with their weight do remorselessly inhibit their eating. The complexity of their eating manifests itself in two ways. Some are not hungry before eating. Hunger manifests itself again after they gain weight. Others are nauseated after a standard diet that is high in carbohydrate content. The nausea also disappears after they gain weight (12).

These data suggest that the state of hunger or nausea (which may additionally inhibit eating) is a consequence of weight loss and is not an antecedent cause of the inhibition of eating.

In fact, about one half of all AN patients have no desire to eat—the issue of control of eating and food intake is not evident; in the other half, it is *the* predominant concern. This second group has a major disturbance in the control of eating: it fears a loss of control. Those in this category wish to be thin. Yet their voluntary control of food intake frequently and repetitively breaks down. They binge, often at night. They vomit or purge themselves after eating (9, 12).

Students of AN have mainly emphasized the issue of control over food intake. But food-related behavior consists of more than simply eating. Both man and animals forage for food, select, store, prepare, and eat it. In some AN patients, these food-related activities are also disturbed. AN patients tend to store and prepare food, and some are highly selective in what they will eat. Other anorectics are preoccupied with one or another aspect of these behaviors, but they finally eschew eating.

PATHOPHYSIOLOGY OF ANOREXIA NERVOSA

Many of the behavioral aspects of AN remain unexplained for the reasons that I have enumerated. The very extensive pathophysiology of AN has similarly resisted explanation (Table 9-1). Once AN has begun, and by the time many or all of the pathophysiological changes have taken place, we are no longer able to ascertain what factors or mechanisms initiate the syndrome. In fact, the pathophysiology of AN has most usually been ascribed to weight loss, semistarvation, or protein calorie malnutrition. For example, elevated morning levels of growth hormone (hGH) have been correlated with a diminished nutritional intake (especially with the low-protein content of the diet) but not with weight loss (13, 14, 15, 16, 17). In addition, the thermoregulatory

TABLE 9-1
Summary of Some Pathophysiological Findings in Anorexia Nervosa

I.	***Hypothalamic-Pituitary-Gonadal Axis***	
	A. LH and FSH levels	↓
	B. 24-hour LH and FSH patterns. Age-Inappropriate	+
	C. Serum estrogen levels	↓
	D. Serum testosterone levels	↓
	E. Ratio: $\dfrac{\text{Etiocholanolone}}{\text{androsterone}}$	↑
	F. Responses of LH and FSH to LHRH	↓ or N
II.	***Hypothalamic-Pituitary-Adrenal Axis***	
	A. Urinary 17-OH corticosteroid levels	↓
	B. Half-life plasma cortisol	↑
	C. Metabolic clearance rate of cortisol	↑
	D. Cortisol binding capacity	N
	E. Cortisol production rate/Kg. body weight	↑
	F. Urinary free cortisol	↑
	G. Dexamethasone suppression	↓
	H. Response to ACTH	N or ↑
III.	***Hypothalamic-Pituitary-Thyroid Axis***	
	A. Free T_4 levels	N
	B. Mean T_4 and T_3 levels	↓
	C. Serum reverse T_3 and 3, 3' T_2	↑
	D. T.R.H. effect on T_3	↑
	E. T.S.H. levels	N or ↑
	F. T.R.H. effect on T.S.H.	↑ or Delayed
IV.	***Other Pituitary Hormones***	
	A. Human growth hormone (hGH) levels	N or ↑
	B. hGH response to hypo- or hyperglycemia	N or Paradoxical
	C. hGH response to apomorphine	↓
	D. Prolactin levels	N
	E. Prolactin response to L-DOPA and chlorpromazine	N
	F. Antidiuretic hormone levels	N
	G. Ability to excrete water load	↓
V.	***Other Disturbances***	
	A. Body temperature	↓
	B. Excessive response to hypothermia and hyperthermia	+
	C. Sleep disturbance	+
	D. Eating disturbances (various)	+
	E. Motor activity	↑
	F. Various disturbances	
	1. Circulation	
	2. Skin	
	3. Blood and bone marrow	
	4. Blood constituents	

disturbances described by Vigersky and Loriaux (18) in anorexia nervosa have been ascribed directly to the degree of weight loss (percent below ideal body weight). However, the correlation is not absolute, and the degree of weight loss accounts for about 30–35 percent of the variance in thermoregulation. (Many other examples of the relationship of protein-calorie malnutrition, weight loss, and loss of body fat to the pathophysiology of anorexia nervosa will be mentioned later in this chapter.)

Our own work has been directed toward the elucidation of some of the variables that might account for the wide range of pathophysiological disturbances enumerated earlier (19, 20, 21). My coworkers and I believe that many of the controversial findings are in part based on spot, or mean, levels of hormones, some of which are known to be pulsed into the bloodstream and also show circadian patterns.

Our studies show that the circadian patterns of luteinizing hormone (LH) and, to a lesser extent, of follicle stimulating hormone (FSH), secretion in every patient with anorexia nervosa are age-inappropriate (21). These circadian patterns are believed to be "programmed" by unknown hypothalamic mechanisms.

The age-inappropriate circadian patterns of LH and FSH are not found in other forms of amenorrhea such as uncomplicated Turner's or the Stein-Levinthal syndromes, amenorrhea-galactorrhea, or the menopause in women.

Many of the pathophysiological changes in anorexia nervosa point to a functional hypothalamic disturbance (22, 23). Perhaps the most interesting and significant evidence for such a disturbance is that ethinyl estradiol fails to have the usual positive feedback of raising LH levels in underweight patients with anorexia nervosa, yet the negative feedback effects of this hormone with depression of LH levels is seen in such patients. When 8 of these 12 patients regained weight, the positive feedback effects of administered estradiol on LH were again observed (24). Persistent abnormalities of the response of LH to clomiphene citrate have also been observed in weight-recovered patients with anorexia nervosa (25).

These data provide evidence that weight recovery is not necessarily followed by a renormalization of the hypothalamic-pituitary-gonadal axis in anorexia nervosa. Nonetheless, urinary or basal serum LH levels tend to increase with weight recovery in *some* but not all patients with anorexia nervosa (26, 27, 28, 29, 30, 31, 32). When we have studied the circadian patterns of LH during and after weight recovery, no consistent trend is found (19). In other words, weight recovery alone does not itself assure the maturation of the LH pattern to an age-appropriate one.

Several other pieces of evidence militate against a simple relationship of ideal weight to normal levels or patterns of LH. First, in 19 dieting women who did not have anorexia nervosa but who developed secondary amenorrhea due to simple weight loss of 19.5 ± 10.1 percent below ideal body weight, LH levels were the same as in normal, age-matched controls. FSH levels were lower than in these normal women but greater than in patients with anorexia nervosa (33).

Second, in patients with uncomplicated Turner's syndrome, LH and FSH levels are strongly and inversely correlated with body weight and fat; that is, the highest levels of LH occur in the lightest girls with the least percentage of body fat (34).

Finally, in preliminary studies, we have found that binge-eating young adult women of *normal* weight have age-inappropriate circadian patterns of LH (35).

Therefore, the argument that low LH and FSH levels are wholly a function of the percent of body weight or fat lost in anorexia nervosa is oversimplified. In fact, Brown and his coworkers (13) have accounted for only 22 percent of the variance in LH levels in anorexia nervosa on the basis of weight loss. (They found no relationship between resting LH levels and the amount of caloric intake.) No explanation exists at present to account for the rest if the factors that produce low levels of the gonadotropins and age-inappropriate circadian patterns in anorexia nervosa.

In order to determine other reasons for the depression of gonadotropin levels in these patients, the gonadotropin releasing hormone (LHRH) has been given to them. The levels might be depressed either because the pituitary gland fails to produce or release the gonadotropins or because the hypothalamic stimulus to their release is deficient or absent. Many recent studies have been carried out to test the effect of LHRH on the release of LH and FSH in patients with anorexia nervosa. The results of these studies have produced conflicting results; they show that the response of LH and FSH to the stimulus of LHRH may be normal (20, 22, 36, 37); inconsistent—that is, some patients do, and others do not, respond (38, 39, 40); absent or blunted (32, 41, 42, 43); quantitatively normal, but the time course of the increments of LH and FSH responses is delayed (44, 45); or present, but only after repeated injections (46, 47, 48, 49).

A number of investigators have found that in some patients the responses of LH and FSH to LHRH are inverted; that is, the increase of LH is relatively small or absent, and the FSH response is disproportionately large (29, 32, 43, 46, 47, 49, 50, 51). This disproportion in the responses of the two gonadotropins is not invariably observed. Nevertheless, it has been claimed (48) that the inversion of the response of LH and FSH is characteristic of those seen in prepubertal children (52, 53, 54).

Presumably, the adult response patterns of LH and FSH to LHRH appear at puberty; they are believed to be related to increases in body weight. Some investigators claim that in anorexia nervosa, normal gonadotropin responses to LHRH are related to the patient's weight. In very emaciated patients, the responses of LH and FSH are absent, minimal, or inverted; in those whose body weight is about 25 percent below ideal, the FSH response to LHRH is either normal or exaggerated and the LH response is diminished, compared to control subjects of normal weight, or to weight-recovered patients. When about 10 percent below ideal weight, patients may have normal or even exaggerated LH and FSH responses (13, 39, 32, 42, 43, 48, 55, 56, 57, 58). However, other investigators have not been able to confirm this clear-cut relationship between the quantitative gonadotropin response to LHRH and body weight (20, 22, 37, 39, 40 ,45).

In some instances, it is possible to calculate that up to 50 percent of the variance in response to LHRH is accounted for by weight loss alone (42). Therefore, one must conclude that additional (unknown) factors are responsible for these variable results.

Another reason for giving LHRH might be to test the hypothesis that the age-inappropriate patterns of LH and FSH in anorexia nervosa patients are analogous, if not homologous, to the prepubertal or pubertal patterns of normal girls. However, no agreement has been reached as to whether LHRH releases LH and FSH before, or during, puberty and thereafter.

Roth et al. (54) found that LH (but not FSH) release is minimal in prepubertal children when they are given LHRH in various doses up to 100 μm. On the other hand, Job et al. (53) found that LHRH does produce a significant rise in LH in prepubertal children, but that its increase is not as great relative to the rise in FSH levels; nor does it compare in magnitude with that seen after puberty (52).

Therefore, one cannot argue with conviction that the absence of a response of LH to LHRH in a postpubertal girl with anorexia nervosa is indicative of a state analogous to a normal prepubertal girl.

The controversy in this area of investigation has resisted explanation. Some disenchantment with the LHRH test in clinical practice is discernible in the literature. The anticipation that this stimuluation test would provide a tool for differentiating the functional amenorrheas from those produced by structural lesions of the pituitary gland has not been realized; response of LH to LHRH occurs despite structural lesions of the pituitary gland brought on by a variety of etiologies. The concept that LHRH injection is a test of the pituitary "reserve" for LH and FSH is also a tenuous one.

However, one conclusion seems to have emerged: The responsiveness of LH and FSH to LHRH reflects their basal levels; the lower the initial levels of the gonadotropins, regardless of cause, the less is the responsiveness of the releasing hormone (46, 49, 59, 60).

Malnutrition, starvation, surgery, and a variety of chronic illnesses (61, 62, 63, 64, 65, 66, 67) are associated with the low triiodothyronine (T_3) syndrome (68, 69, 70). Indeed, in anorexia nervosa, this syndrome is present, and has been held responsible for some of the metabolic changes seen in that illness. Boyar and Bradlow (71) showed that the mean ratio of androsterone to etiocholanolone is depressed because of a diminution of activity of the enzyme 5 alpha-reductase. Administration of T_3 restored the ratio to normal. Boyar and his colleagues (72) have also found that the prolonged half-life and the diminished metabolic clearance rate of cortisol, and the increase in tetrahydrocortisol to tetrahydrocortisone ratio, could all be normalized by the administration of T_3 to patients with anorexia nervosa.

Therefore, these alterations in cortisol metabolism may account for the decreased urinary levels of 17-OH corticosteroids and the increased mean levels of plasma cortisol that many investigators have found (73, 74, 75, 76, 77).

But, on the other hand, a number of investigators have observed disruption of the circadian rhythm of plasma cortisol (17, 21, 72, 77), the increase in cortisol production rates (72, 76) and the failure to suppress cortisol production by dexamethasone (15, 27, 76, 78).

In our most recent studies (76), we have found that (1) cortisol production rates (C.P.R.) in 19 AN women, when compared with 7 normal, age matched controls, were significantly increased ($p < .001$) relative to body mass, and to body surface area ($p < .02$). (2) Plasma cortisol concentration was greater than in 13 controls ($p < .001$). (3) Urinary free cortisol excretion in AN was 3 times greater ($p < .01$) than in the controls; this finding is not owing to the fact that patients with AN are excreting more urine.

These changes cannot be ascribed to weight loss alone because usually there is a linear regression of C.P.R. on weight; C.P.R. is elevated in obese patients but C.P.R. body surface area (3) is not. In other words, the elevated C.P.R. in AN patients who have lost weight is in the direction opposite that of the usual regression line between body surface areas and C.P.R. In addition, the C.P.R. generally falls with weight loss in obese patients and rises in malnourished subjects when they gain weight, (79, 80, 81, 82). These data indicate that the increase of C.P.R. in anorexia nervosa is related in an unusual manner to weight loss.

The increased C.P.R. might, however, be related to malnutrition. Many changes in adrenal function are also observed in uncomplicated malnutrition, but others are not, as Table 9-2 indicates. Therefore, the elevation of C.P.R. relative to body weight and size in patients with anorexia nervosa suggests activation of the hypothalamic-pituitary adrenal axis for reasons that remain unknown.

CONCLUSIONS

This chapter has concerned itself with the impediments to our understanding of factors that predispose to, initiate, and sustain anorexia nervosa. Despite an

TABLE 9-2
Cortisol Production & Metabolism in Anorexia Nervosa and Protein-Calorie Malnutrition

	Anorexia Nervosa	Uncomplicated Malnutrition
Urinary 17-OH Corticosteroids	↓[3, 11, 15]	↓[6, 14]
½-life Cortisol	↑[4]	↑[1, 14]
Mean Levels Plasma Cortisol	↑[3, 4, 5, 16]	↑[1, 12, 13, 14]
Response to ACTH	N or ↑[7, 10, 17]	N[1, 12, 14]
Dexamethasone Suppression	↓[2, 7, 8, 16]	↓[1, 14]
Cortisol Binding Capacity	N[4]	↓[13]
Cortisol Production Rate/Kg. body wt.	↑[16]	N[1, 14]
Urinary Free Cortisol (UFC)	↑[16]	N[9, 14]
UFC/creatinine clearance ratio	↑↑[16]	↑[14]

explosion of information about this disorder, we are still a long way from understanding it. Although we have a rather complete account of the rich and varied pathophysiology of AN, we do not understand the antecedent factors that bring it about. Clearly, many of the behavioral, psychological, and physiological manifestations of AN are secondary to some manifestation of the illness, such as semistarvation, malnutrition, weight loss, and the loss of body fat. But others are not, as I have tried to highlight in this paper. Many of the pathophysiological manifestations of AN—for example, the disturbances of thermoregulation, the age-inappropriate circadian patterns of LH and FSH, the increase in cortisol production, or the sleep disturbance—point to a functional disorder of hypothalamic function. Yet we do not know whether such a functional disorder is primary in AN or merely secondary to weight loss. At least in some patients with AN, the disorder seems to antecede significant weight loss, because the disorder manifests itself first with amenorrhea. But this last statement is partly speculative.

In any case, our understanding of AN would be advanced if patients at risk for AN were studied prior to, or at the inception of, the illness.

REFERENCES

1. Bruch, H. *Eating and Eating Disorders: Obesity, Anorexia Nervosa and the Person Within*. New York: Basic, 1973.
2. Kron, L., Katz, J.L., Gorzynski, G. Anorexia nervosa and gonadal dysgenesis: further evidence of a relationship. *Arch. Gen. Psychiat.* 34: 332–35, 1977.
3. Askevold, F. Personal communication.
4. Fries, H. & Nillius, S.J. Dieting anorexia nervosa and amenorrhea after oral contraceptive treatment. *Acta Psych. Scand.* 49: 669–79, 1973.
5. Katz, J.L. & Weiner, H. Unpublished observations.
6. Duddle, M. An increase of anorexia nervosa in a university population. *Brit. J. Psychiat.* 123: 711–12, 1973.

7. Theander, S. Anorexia nervosa, a psychiatric investigation of 94 female patients. *Acta Psych. Scand.* 214: 1–190, 1970.

8. Crisp, A.H., Palmer, R.L., & Kalucy, R. How common is anorexia nervosa? A prevalence study. *Brit. J. Psychiat.* 128: 549–54, 1976.

9. Halmi, K.A., Goldberg, S.C., & Eckert, E. Pretreatment evaluation in anorexia nervosa. In Vigersky, R. (Ed.), *Anorexia Nervosa*. New York: Raven, 1977.

10. Kron, L., Katz, J.L., Gorzynski, G. Hyperactivity in anorexia nervosa: a fundamental clinical feature. *Compr. Psychiat.* 19: 433–40, 1978.

11. Nylander, I. The feelings of being fat and dieting in a school population: epidemiological interview investigation. *Acta Sociomed. Scand.* 3: 17–45, 1971.

12. Folstein, M.F., Wakeling, A., & DeSouza, V. Analogue scale measurement of the symptoms of patients suffering from anorexia nervosa. In Vigersky, R. (Ed.), *Anorexia Nervosa*. New York: Raven, 1977.

13. Brown, G.M., Garfinkel, P.E., Jeuniewic, N. Endocrine profiles in anorexia nervosa. In Vigersky, R. (Ed.), *Anorexia Nervosa*. New York: Raven, 1977.

14. Casper, R.C., Davis, J.M., & Pandey, G.N. The effect of the nutritional status and weight changes on hypothalamic function tests in anorexia nervosa. In Vigersky, R. (Ed.), *Anorexia Nervosa*. New York: Raven, 1977.

15. Frankel, R.J. & Jenkins, J.S. Hypothalamic-pituitary function in anorexia nervosa. *Acta Endocrinol.* (KbH) 78: 209–21, 1975.

16. Garfinkel, P.E., Brown, G.M., Stancer, H.C. Hypothalamic-pituitary function in anorexia nervosa. *Arch. Gen. Psychiat.* 32: 739–44, 1975.

17. Landon, J., Greenwood, G.D., Stamp, T.C.B. The plasma sugar, free fatty acid, cortisol and growth hormone response to insulin and the comparison of this procedure with other tests of pituitary and adrenal function. II. In patients with hypothalamic or pituitary dysfunction or anorexia nervosa. *J. Clin. Invest.* 45: 437–49, 1966.

18. Vigersky, R.A. & Loriaux, D.L. Anorexia nervosa as a model hypothalamic dysfunction. In Vigersky, R. (Ed.), *Anorexia Nervosa*. New York: Raven, 1977.

19. Katz, J.L., Boyar, R.M., & Roffwarg, H. Weight and circadian LH secretory pattern in anorexia nervosa. *Psychosom. Med.* 40: 549–67, 1978.

20. Katz, J.L., Boyar, R.M., Hellman, L. LHRH responsiveness in anorexia nervosa: intactness despite prepubertal circadian LH pattern. *Psychosom. Med.* 39: 241–51, 1977.

21. Katz, J.L., Boyar, R.M., Weiner, H. Toward an elucidation of the psychoendocrinology of anorexia nervosa. In Sachar, E. (Ed.), *Hormones, Behavior and Psychopathology*. New York: Raven, 1976.

22. Mecklenburg, R.S., Loriaux, D.L., Thompson, R.H. Hypothalamic dysfunction in patients with anorexia. *Medicine* 53: 147–59, 1974.

23. Vigersky, R. (Ed.). *Anorexia Nervosa*. New York: Raven, 1977.

24. Wakeling, A., De Souza, V., & Beardwood, C.J. Effects of administered estrogen on luteinizing hormone release in subjects with anorexia nervosa in acute and recovery stages. In Vigersky, R. (Ed.), *Anorexia Nervosa*. New York: Raven, 1977.

25. Wakeling, A., Marshall, J.C., Beardwood, C.J. The effects of clomiphene citrate on the hypothalamic-pituitary-gonadal axis in anorexia nervosa. *Psychosom. Med.* 6: 371–80, 1977.

26. Beumont, P.J.V., George, G.C., Pimstone, B.L. Body weight and the pituitary response to hypothalamic releasing hormones in patients with anorexia nervosa. *J. Clin. Endocrinol. Metab.* 43: 487–96, 1976.

27. Danowski, T.S., Livstone, E., Gonzales, A.R. Fractional and partial hypopituitarism in anorexia nervosa. *Hormones* 3: 105–18, 1972.

28. Hurd, H.P., Palumbo, P.J., & Charib, H. Hypothalamic-endocrine dysfunction in anorexia nervosa. *Mayo Clin. Proc.* 52: 711–16, 1977.

29. Palmer, R.L., Crisp, A.H., MacKinnon, P.C.B. Pituitary sensitivity to 50 μg LH/FSH/RH in subjects with anorexia nervosa in acute and recovery stages. *Brit. Med. J.* 1: 179–82, 1975.

30. Russell, G.F.M. Metabolic aspects of anorexia nervosa. *Proc. R. Soc. Med.* 58: 811–14, 1965.

31. Russell, G.F.M. Psychological and nutritional factors in disturbances of menstrual function and ovulation. *Postgrad. Med. J.* 48: 10–13, 1972.

32. Sherman, B.M., Halmi, K.A., & Zamudio, R. LH and FSH response to gonadotropic-releasing hormone in anorexia nervosa: effect of nutritional rehabilitation. *J. Clin. Endocrinol. Med.* 41: 135–42, 1975.

33. Vigersky, R.A., Andersen, A.E., Thompson, R.H. Hypothalamic dysfunction in secondary amenorrhea associated with simple weight loss. *New Eng. J. Med.* 297: 1,141–45, 1977.

34. Boyar, R.M., Ramsey, J., Chipman, P. Regulation of gonadotropin secretion in Turner's syndrome. *New Eng. J. Med.* 298: 1,328–31, 1978.

35. Walsh, B.T., Katz, J.L., Weiner, H. Unpublished observations.

36. Espinosa-Campos, J., Robles, C., Gual, C. Hypothalamic, pituitary, and ovarian function assessment in a patient with anorexia nervosa. *Fertil. Steril.* 25(5): 453–57, 1974.

37. Wiegelman, W. & Solbach, H.G. Effects of LH-RH on plasma levels of LH and FSH in anorexia nervosa. *Horm. Metab. Res.* 4: 404, 1972.

38. Crosignani, P.G., Reschini, E., D'Alberton, A. Variability of gonadotropin response to luteinizing hormone-releasing hormone in amenorrheic women. *Am. J. Ob. Gyn.* 120: 376–84, 1974.

39. Mortimer, C.H., Besser, G.M., McNeilly, A.S. Luteinizing hormone and follicle stimulating hormone-releasing hormone test in patients with hypothalamic-pituitary-gonadal dysfunction. *Brit. Med. J.* 4: 73–7, 1973.

40. Travaglini, P., Beck-Peccoz, P., Ferrari, C. Some aspects of hypothalamic-pituitary function in patients with anorexia nervosa. 81: 252–62, 1976.

41. Jequier, A.M., O'Shea, A., & Jacobs, H.S. Functional and post-oral contraceptive amenorrhea: response to luteinizing hormone releasing hormone (LH-RH). *Brit. J. Ob. Gyn.* 82: 333–36, 1975.

42. Warren, M.P. Weight loss and responsiveness to LH-RH. In Vigersky, R. (Ed.), *Anorexia Nervosa*. New York: Raven, 1977.

43. Warren, M.P., Jewelewicz, R., Dyrenfurth, R. The significance of weight loss in the evaluation of pituitary response to LH-RH on women with secondary amenorrhea. *J. Clin. Endocrinol. Metab.* 40: 601–11, 1975.

44. Vigersky, R.A., Loriaux, D.L., Andersen, A.E. Delayed pituitary hormone response to LRF and TRF in patients with anorexia nervosa and with secondary amenorrhea associa with simple weight loss. *J. Clin. Endocrinol. Metab.* 43: 893–900, 1967.

45. Vigersky, R.A., & Loriaux, D.L. Anorexia nervosa as a model hypothalamic dysfunction. In Vigersky, R. (Ed.), *Anorexia Nervosa*. New York: Raven, 1977.

46. Nillius, S.J. & Wide, L. Gonadotropin-releasing hormone treatment for induction of follicular maturation and ovulation in amenorrheic women with anorexia nervosa. *Brit. Med. J.* 3: 405–408, 1975.

47. Nillius, S.J., Fries, H., & Wide, L. Successful induction of follicular maturation and ovulation by prolonged treatment with LH-releasing hormone in women with anorexia nervosa. *Am. J. Ob. Gyn.* 122: 921–28, 1975.

48. Nillius, S.J. & Wide, L. The pituitary responsiveness to acute and chronic administrations of gonadotropic-releasing hormone in acute and recovery stages of anorexia nervosa. In Vigersky, R. (Ed.), *Anorexia Nervosa*. New York: Raven, 1977.

49. Yoshimoto, Y., Moridera, K., & Imura, H. Restoration of normal pituitary gonadotropic reserve by administration of luteinizing-hormone-releasing hormone in patients with hypogonadotropic hypogonadism. *New Eng. J. Med.* 292: 242–45, 1975.

50. Franchimont, P., Demoulin, A., & Bourgignon, J.P. Clinical use of LH-RH test as a diagnostic tool. *Horm. Res.* 6: 177–91, 1975.
51. Vandekerckhove, A., Dhont, M., & Van Eyck, J. Diagnostic value of the LH-releasing hormone stimulation tests in functional amenorrhea. *Acta Endocrinol.* (KbH) 78: 625–33, 1975.
52. Franchimont, P., Becker, H., Ernould, C. The effect of hypothalamic luteinizing hormone releasing hormone (LH-RH) on plasma gonadotropin levels in normal subjects. *Clin. Endocrinol. Clin. Endocrinol.* 3: 27–39, 1974.
53. Job, J.C., Garnier, P.E., Chaussain, J.L. Evaluation of serum gonadotropins (LH and FSH) after releasing hormone (LH-RH) injection in normal children and in patients with disorders of puberty. *J. Clin. Endocrinol. Metab.* 35: 473–76, 1972.
54. Roth, J.C., Kelch, R.P., Kaplan, S.L. FSH and LH response to luteinizing hormone-releasing factor in prepubertal and pubertal children, adult males and patients with hypogonadotropic and hypergonadotropic hypogonadism. *J. Clin. Endocrinol. Metab.* 35: 926–30, 1972.
55. Akande, E.O., Carr, P.J., Dutton, A. Effect of synthetic gonadotropin-releasing hormone in secondary amenorrhea. *Lancet* 2: 112–16, 1972.
56. Beumont, P.J.V., George, G.C., Pimstone, B.L. Body weight and the pituitary response to hypothalamic releasing hormones in patients with anorexia nervosa. *J. Clin. Endocrinol. Metab.* 43: 487–96, 1976.
57. Jeuniewic, N., Brown, G.M., Garfinkel, P.E. Hypothalamic function as related to body weight and body fat in anorexia nervosa. *Psychosom. Med.* 40: 187–98, 1978.
58. Taymor, M.L., Thompson, I.E., Berger, M.J. Luteinizing hormone-releasing hormone (LH-RH) as a diagnostic and research tool in gynecologic endocrinology. *Am. J. Obstet. Gyn.* 120: 721–32, 1974.
59. Mortimer, R.H., Fleischer, N., Lev-Gur, M. Correlation between integrated LH and FSH levels and the response to luteinizing hormone releasing factor (LRF). *J. Clin. Endocrinol. Metab.* 43: 1,240–49, 1976.
60. Nillius, S.J. & Wide, L. The LH-releasing hormone test in 31 women with secondary amenorrhoea. *Brit. J. Ob. Gyn.* 79: 874–82, 1972.
61. Bermudez, F., Surks, M.I., & Oppenheimer, J.H. High incidence of decreased serum triiodothyronine concentration in patients with nonthyroidal disease. *J. Clin. Endocrinol. Metab.* 41: 27–40, 1975.
62. Carter, J.N., Eastman, C.J., Corcoran, J.M. Effect of severe, chronic illness on thyroid function. *Lancet* 2: 971–74, 1974.
63. Chopra, I.J. & Smith, S.R. Circulating thyroid hormones and thyrotropin in adult patients with protein calorie malnutrition. *J. Clin. Endocrin. Metab.* 40: 221–27, 1975.
64. Chopra, I.J., Chopra, U., Smith, S.R. Reciprocal changes in serum concentrations of 3, 3', 5'-triiodo-thyronine (reverse T_3) and 3, 3' 5-triiodothyronine (T_3) in systemic illness. *J. Clin. Endocrin. Metab.* 41: 1,043–49, 1975.
65. Nomura, S. & Pittman, C.S. Hypothyroidism in liver patients due to failure of the peripheral conversion of thyroxine (T_4) to triiodothyronine. *J. Clin. Invest.* 53: 57a, 1974.
66. Portnay, G.I., O'Brien, J.T., Bush, J. The effect of starvation on the concentration and binding of thyroxine and triiodothyronine in serum and the response to TRH. *J. Clin. Endocrinol. Metab.* 39: 191–94, 1974.
67. Reichlin, S., Bollinger, J., Nejad, I. Tissue thyroid concentration of rat and man determined by radioimmunoassay: biologic significance. *Mt. Sinai J. Med.* (NY) 40: 502–10, 1973.
68. Miyai, K., Yamamoto, T., Azukizawa, M. Serum thyroid hormones and thyrotropin in anorexia nervosa. *J. Clin. Endocrinol. Metab.* 40: 334–38, 1975.

69. Moshang, T., Jr., Parks, J.S., Baker, L. Low serum triiodothyronine in patients with anorexia nervosa. *J. Clin. Endocrinol. Metab.* 40: 470–73, 1975.

70. Moshang, T., Jr. & Utiger, R.D. Low triiodothyronine euthyroidism in anorexia nervosa. In Vigersky, R. (Ed.), *Anorexia Nervosa*. New York: Raven Press, 1977.

71. Boyar, R.M., Bradlow, H.L. Studies of testosterone metabolism in anorexia nervosa. In Vigersky, R. (Ed.), *Anorexia Nervosa*. New York: Raven, 1977.

72. Boyar, R.M., Hellman, L.D., Roffwarg, H.P. Cortisol secretion and metabolism in anorexia nervosa. *New Eng. J. Med.* 296: 190–93, 1977.

73. Bliss, E.L. & Migeon, C.J. Endocrinology of anorexia nervosa. *J. Clin. Endocrinol. Metab.* 17: 766–76, 1957.

74. Perloff, W.H., Lasche, E.M., Nodine, J.H. The starvation state and functional hypopituitarism. *JAMA* 155: 1,307–13, 1954.

75. Thorn, G.W., Forsham, P.H., Frawley, F.G. The clinical usefulness of ACTH and cortisone. *New Eng. J. Med.* 242: 783–93, 1950.

76. Walsh, B.T., Katz, J.L., Levin, J. Adrenal activity in anorexia nervosa. *Psychosom. Med.* 40: 499–506, 1978.

77. Warren, M.P. & Vande Wiele, R.L. Clinical and metabolic features of anorexia nervosa. *Am. J. Ob. Gyn.* 117: 435–49, 1973.

78. Bethge, H., Nagel, A.M., Solbach, H.G. Zentrale Regulationsstörung der Nebennierenrinden-funktion bei der anorexia nervosa. *Materia Medica Nordmark* 22: 204–14, 1970.

79. Alleyne, C.A.O. & Young, V.H. Adrenocortical function in children with severe protein-calorie malnutrition. *Clin. Sci.* 33: 189–200, 1967.

80. Garces, L.Y., Kenny, F.M., Drash, A. Cortisol secretion rate during fasting of obese adolescent subjects. *J. Clin. Endocrin. Metab.* 28: 1,843–47, 1968.

81. Jackson, I.M.D. & Mowat, J.I. Hypothalamic-pituitary-adrenal function in obesity and the cortisol secretion rate following prolonged starvation. *Acta Endocrinol.* (KbH) 63: 415–22, 1970.

82. Smith, S.R., Bledsoe, T., & Chhetri, M.K. Cortisol metabolism and the pituitary-adrenal axis in adults with protein-calorie malnutrition. *J. Clin. Endocrin. Metab.* 40: 43–52, 1975.

10

Neurobehavior and Temporal-Lobe Epilepsy

STEPHEN A. BERMAN
DAVID B. ROSENFIELD

Epileptic seizures refer to an intermittent paroxysmal derangement of central-nervous-system functioning due to abnormal neuronal discharge. The Epilepsy Foundation of America states that four million Americans are afflicted with this problem (1). This high prevalence makes it likely that many psychiatrists will encounter epileptic patients. It is therefore important to know about epilepsy, even were there no relationship between epilepsy and psychiatric disorders, other than the chance coexistence of both problems in the same patient. For at least a century, however, the study of epilepsy has continued to raise important controversial questions about the psychiatric functioning of epileptics. These questions are particularly pertinent to the variety of seizures upon which this review will focus: temporal-lobe or psychomotor seizures. Such questions may provide insight into the underlying nature of psychological processes of all individuals.

A practical classification of seizures is the international classification of epileptic seizures devised by Gastaut (Table 10-1) (2). In this classification scheme, what had previously been called focal seizures are now called partial seizures with elementary symptoms. Grand mal seizures are listed as "generalized seizures tonic/clonic." Petit mal is "generalized seizures-absences." Temporal-lobe or psychomotor seizures are classified as "partial seizures with complex symptoms."

Some basic neuroanatomy will facilitate an understanding of seizure types. Figure 10-1 is a simplified illustration of the brain. Abnormal discharge in the motor region corresponding to the arm would result in jerking of the arm. This would be classified as a partial seizure with elementary symptoms. In this particular case, the symptoms would be a motor symptom confined to the arm. Consciousness would not be lost in the situation because it is necessary for the hemispheres to be involved bilaterally or for the deep midline structures to be affected in order for consciousness to be impaired.

TABLE 10-1
International Classification of Epileptic Seizures

I. *Partial Seizures* (seizures beginning locally)
    A. Partial seizures with elementary symptoms (generally without impairment of consciousness)
        1. motor symptoms (includes Jacksonian seizures)
        2. special sensory or somatosensory symptoms
        3. autonomic symptoms
        4. compound forms
    B. Partial seizures with complex symptoms (generally with impairment of consciousness)
           (Temporal lobe or Psychomotor seizures)
        1. impairment of consciousness only
        2. cognitive symptomatology
        3. affective symptomatology
        4. "psychosensory" symptomatology
        5. "psychomotor" symptomatology (automatisms)
        6. compound forms
    C. Partial seizures secondarily generalized

II. *Generalized Seizures* (bilaterally symmetrical and without local onset)
    A. Absences (petit mal)
    B. Bilateral massive epileptic myoclonus
    C. Infantile spasms
    D. Clonic seizures
    E. Tonic seizures
    F. Tonic-clonic seizures (grand mal)
    G. Atonic seizures
    H. Akinetic seizures

III. *Unilateral Seizures* (predominantly)

IV. *Unclassified Epileptic Seizures*

Abnormal cortical discharges may produce a generalized seizure. If the motor areas were involved, it is likely that tonic/clonic activity would result, a "grand mal." If bilateral synchronous frontal activity were the type of abnormal discharge present, an absence—i.e., "a petit mal"—would be the result.

Let us now consider the temporal lobe and other closely related structures. There are many well-defined areas in the temporal lobe. The medial and lateral surface are numbered in Figure 10-1 according to the method of Brodman (3). This numbering system provides a convenient reference point for stimulation and ablation studies, although it is now considered somewhat obsolete with respect to cyto-architectural features of the brain.

Functional localization techniques do not prove that the function so localized resides specifically in the designated area. They merely indicate that

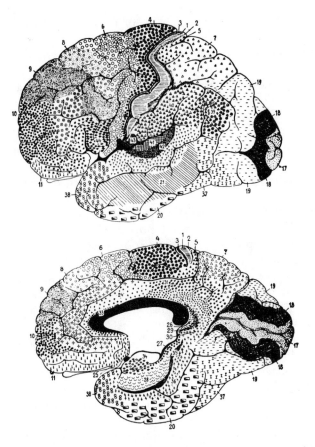

FIG. 10-1. The medial and lateral brain surfaces are numbered according to Brodman's system. From Ranson, S.W. & Clark, S.L. *The Anatomy of the Nervous System.* p. 238. Philadelphia: Saunders, 1953; reproduced by permission.

stimulation, ablation, or some type of interaction with the designated area produces a particular type of change in a given function. With that reservation in mind, it is commonly believed that the area of the brain designated Area 41 is a primary auditory area, whereas Area 42 is concerned mainly with sound identification and recognition. Area 22 is the posterior part of the superior temporal gyrus. The posterior third of Area 22 is Wernicke's area, a language comprehension center (in the dominant hemisphere). The posterior portion of Area 22 may relate to further aspects of word understanding and may also be involved in the comprehension of music (4). The foreward extension of the superior temporal gyrus, comprising the temporal pole, is Area 38. This is essentially an association area where integration of information may occur, although the specific function is not well understood. Some believe that personality integration and self-awareness is mediated in this area (4).

Area 21, the middle temporal gyrus, primarily receives occipital-lobe input. Visual information is integrated or processed further in this area. There is some evidence that visual memory is mediated here; stimulation in this area, particularly the part of the area most posterior and thus closest to the temporal lobe, often results in perceiving visual imagery (4, 5). Area 20, the inferior temporal gyrus, has sparse connections with other parts of the brain, although overall integrative functions and general orientation may be mediated in this area (4).

Area 28, which is only visible on the medial surface, comprises the uncus and the entorhinal area. This is a secondary olfactory area, essentially an olfactory association area, and is important in mediating olfactory memories (4). Area 27, the presubicular area, is comprised of the para-hippocampal convolution, also called the para-hippocampal gyrus or, sometimes, simply the hippocampal gyrus. This is part of the limbic system, most of which is not readily describable in terms of Brodman nomenclature since many deep subcortical nuclei as well as specific tracts are involved. Many aspects of memory and emotion are mediated by the limbic system, a system which is closely related to the temporal lobe. (The limbic system will be described more extensively later.) Area 34, a further part of the entorhinal area, is believed to be absent in man. Area 34 is a closely related area sometimes called the perirhinal area and is probably also related to the sense of smell, although interpretation of somatic sensation may also be involved.

The occipital temporal gyrus, Area 37, is a transitional area between the temporal and occipital cortex. It receives many visual afferents. It is important in the interpretation and psychic integration of visual information. Here, too, stimulation often provokes visual imagery (4, 5).

Areas 39 and 40 border the temporal lobe. Area 39, the angular gyrus, integrates afferents from occipital, parietal, and temporal areas and is important in interpretation of speech and in word recognition. Area 40, the supramarginal gyrus, receives many somesthetic and auditory afferents. It is instrumental in facilitating the understanding of sensory impulses and is also related to aspects of speech organization.

The portion of the temporal lobe which comprises the insula area is not well displayed on the standard diagrams. Stimulation experiments have demonstrated that the insula is related to peristalsis and, perhaps, other aspects of autonomic function. Gastric and abdominal sensations, as well as taste sensation, may be induced by stimulating particular insula areas.

Deep to the temporal lobe, and closely related to it, is the limbic system. It can be noted from Figure 10-2 that this area consists of numerous deep nuclear structures connected by curving C-shaped arcs of fiber tracts which form circuits. Papez (6) was the first to note the possible significance of the anatomic relationships of the limbic system and to theorize that aspects of emotion, behavior, visceral reactions, and, possibly, memory, may be mediated by these structures. He contended that "reverberating circuits" could be established within the limbic system which would influence such activity. The major circuit extends from the hippocampal formation, which, as previously noted, is actually part of the temporal lobe, to the fimbria of the fornix, to the fornix proper, through a C-shaped arc, to reach the mammilary bodies, and even through the mamillo-thalmic tract to the anterior nucleus of the thalmus. From there it travels through the cingulate gyrus, back to the hippocampal or para-

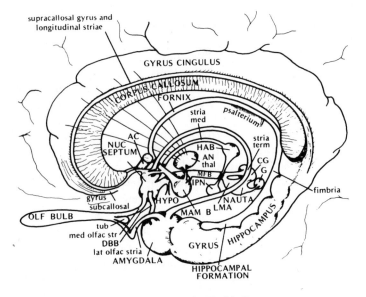

FIG. 10-2. A Schematic Diagram of the Limbic System.
Stimulation of the hippocampus produces behavior which is usually interpreted as alerting, defensive, bewildered, or anxious. Sometimes it appears that the stimulated animal is experiencing hallucinations. Stimulation of the amygdala gives similar results, except that there appears to be portions of it which specifically provoke rage, whereas stimulation of other portions causes placidity. Bilateral destruction of the hippocampus, anterior gyrus, or fornices produces short-term memory loss. Finally, bilateral removal of the amygdala and overlying hippocampal cortex produces docility, decreased fearfulness, and increased oral and sexual activity (Kluver-Bucey Syndrome). From Pincus, J.H. & Tucker, G.J. *Behavioral Neurology,*p. 45. New York: Oxford Press, 1974; reproduced by permission.

hippocampal gyrus, and then to the hippocampal formation again, completing the circuit.

Bilateral damage to this circuit can cause profound deficits in memory, particularly recent memory, and a comprised ability to acquire new information (7). In studies employing surgical lesions, the lesions frequently involved not only Papez circuit but also nearby structures as well (8).

Stimulation of the hippocampus in animals causes behavior similar to states of anxiety and bewilderment, along with alerting and defensive reactions which may be related to hallucinations. Stimulation of the amygdala can produce similar states of anxiety and bewilderment. Stimulation of certain portions of the amygdala produces rage; stimulation of other portions produces placidity. Bilateral amygdalectomy induces a permanent state of placidity in animals. Conversely, lesions in the ventral medial nucleus of the hypothalamus or in certain of the septal nuclei, cause fierce and savage behavior. In addition to placidity, the bilateral removal of the amygdala with some overlying hippocampal cortex produces decreased fear reactions, increased oral behavior, and an increase in sexual activity (9).

The foregoing anatomical discussion illustrates general types of temporal-lobe function and the associated limbic areas. This region of the brain deals with integration and interpretation of sensory stimuli, including understanding of language. Emotional reactivity, memory, and certain visceral functions are mediated in these areas. Just as a seizure discharge in the motor cortex can cause abnormal motion, a seizure discharge in the temporal lobe and/or related limbic areas can cause disturbances in sensory function, language interpretation, visceral and autonomic control, as well as disturbances in memory and emotionality. Focal seizures affecting the temporal lobe and the related limbic areas can produce complex patterns of behavior.

Temporal-lobe, psychomotor, or—as they are described in more recent terminology—partial complex seizures most commonly arise from deep temporal structures such as the amygdala, hippocampus, para-hippocampal gyrus, uncus, or other related areas of the limbic system. The clinical features of these seizures are in accord with their functional anatomy. These seizure phenomena may be divided into four groups: subjective sensory or an emotive phenomenon, automatic behavior (automatism), autonomic changes, and tonic and/or clonic motor manifestations.

The subjective phenomena and autonomic disturbances often occur as an aura at the beginning of the seizure (9), although they can persist into ictal phenomena. Any sensory modality may be represented: parasthesias, pain, heat, or cold, in localized areas or generally throughout the body. Since temporal lobes do not embrace modality-specific areas for pain or temperature, it may be that one of the areas related to the association of bodily sensation and awareness (such as Area 20) is involved in such cases; or, alternatively, feelings of pain and temperature may reflect spread of excitation to somesthetic parietal areas. Visual hallucinations are a common symptom. These may consist of shapes and colors or may be more complex, consisting of formed objects. Alternatively, illusions, distortions, or misinterpretations of vision may occur.

The middle temporal gyrus may also be involved in these phenomena. The more complex hallucinations and illusions may arise from the anterior parts of Area 21, whereas the simple unformed hallucinations may involve the more posterior parts of Area 21 as well as Area 37, which lie close to the occipital lobe. Indeed, the visual-association areas of the occipital lobe, particularly Area 19, may be involved. Similarly, both simple and complex auditory hallucinations may be explained by excitation of the primary auditory area 41 as well as the auditory association areas 42 and 22. Vertiginous feelings probably arise from closely related areas.

Olfactory hallucinations may evolve from the medial temporal area (Area 36), parts of the nearby limbic cortex (Area 28), as well as the nearby olfactory portions of the medial frontal lobe (Area 25). Gustatory phenomena and pharyngeal and visceral sensations in autonomic dysfunction can be explained by involvement of the deep insular regions, particularly areas 50 and 53. Finally, the more complex objective symptoms, such as feelings of fear and strangeness and feelings of *déjà vu* and *jamais vu*, may be related to activity of the limbic system deep in the temporal lobe as well as related medial temporal cortical areas (e.g., medial surface of Area 20) (10, 11, 12).

Stereotyped automatic movements such as lip smacking and licking, repetitive movements of extremities such as buttoning and unbuttoning, mumbling, stereotyped utterances, pacing, turning, and laughter or crying may be associated with complex partial seizure. These activities may first appear normal, although upon more prolonged inspection, they are usually seen as inappropriate. Similar behavior has been elicited in man and animals by stimulation of the insular cortex (5).

Finally, tonic and/or clonic motor manifestations occur at least some of the time in many patients experiencing complex partial seizures. These activities probably result from spread of excitation to motor areas. At times, sustained postures closely resembling catatonic states may occur.

The issue of violent behavior as a manifestation of a psychomotor seizure is often raised. This question is not settled, but it can be stated that violent acts as a specific ictal phenomenon are extremely rare. Rodin (13) studied 57 patients with known complex partial seizures. Extensive photography of these patients during documented seizures failed to delineate any violent behavior. Most neurologists contend that if violence occurs during an ictal period, it is of the nondirected type such as pushing or hitting an attendant who attempts to restrain the patient during a seizure. We do not believe that a directed, complicated act such as robbing a bank is a specific ictal manifestation. The question of violent propensities in the interictal period is considered later.

Many signs and symptoms observed during a partial complex seizure are similar to manifestations of functional psychiatric illnesses. In particular, hallucinations are suggestive of schizophrenia. The subjective experiences may be suggestive of hysterical complaints. Rarely, long periods of automatic behavior may mimic a fugue state. Thus, problems in differential diagnosis may confront the clinician, especially in acute situations in which the past history is unknown (10, 11, 12).

No single rule can be applied to every situation. However, the differentiation of a psychomotor seizure from an acute psychotic episode or from a hysterical reaction can usually be made (11, 12). There are several guidelines.

1) The evolution of the events in question should be carefully observed and evaluated. This is not always possible, but the events can often be reconstructed. A well-defined beginning of a subjective aura that precedes automatisms and hallucinations, followed by a well-delineated end, is characteristic of psychomotor seizures. Focal tonic/clonic motor activity, if it occurs, substantiates the diagnosis. A postictal dullness is common. Of course, not every psychomotor seizure is so characteristic.

2) The EEG is helpful. However, many complex partial seizures involve deep temporal-lobe activity which is difficult to assess with traditional scalp electrode EEG monitoring. Also, the brief period of the EEG monitoring may not coincide with the occurrence of an infrequent seizure. Although some patients have characteristic interictal spikes, the absence of interictal spikes proves nothing. Conversely, some (normal) people who have never experienced ictal phenomena have spikes in their EEG tracings. Thus, the best demonstration of epileptic behavior is the appearance of that behavior simultaneous with characteristic EEG abnormalities.

Several diagnostic maneuvers can increase the likelihood of observing epileptiform activity on an EEG. Nasopharyngeal and transcutaneous sphenoidal electrodes lie closer to the mesial temporal area than do the ordinary scalp electrodes. Thus, they may reflect activity that would otherwise be missed. Activating procedures such as sleep deprivation and hyperventilation are also helpful.

A more potent method of activation employs metrazole and/or bemegride (11). A "positive test" for the presence of seizures is the simultaneous appearance and disappearance of the behavior in question, in tandem with specific EEG abnormalities. A result suggestive of the absence of a seizure disorder is reproduction of the behavior in question, coincident with negative EEG findings, particularly if sphenoidal or nasopharyngeal electrodes have been used. Evocation of a temporal EEG focus without behavioral accompaniment favors the existence of a complex partial seizure disorder.

3) One should assess the patient's personality structure. Although this may not be possible in the acute situation, one may be considerably aided by a knowledge of the patient's usual affect, social relationships, and defense mechanisms. For example, if observation and interview of a patient known to have presented with hallucinations revealed a personality structure characterized by autistic thinking, ambivalence, inappropriate affect, and loose associations, one would suspect that a schizophrenic process might also explain the hallucinations.

Implicit in this reference to personality is the supposition that the psychomotor seizure has a definite beginning and end, is relatively brief compared to most psychiatric disorders, and that the personality structure of the psychomotor epileptic is essentially normal. The first two of these suppositions are usually true. Most ictal phenomena last minutes, occasionally hours. Although temporal-lobe status is not unknown (12), it is rare, and reports of its lasting more than a few days are open to question. In such cases, EEG monitoring is likely to provide the diagnosis. A purely psychiatric disorder usually implies a personality disturbance over a longer time (14). A brief reactive psychosis may last several hours to one week (which would still be long for a seizure) and often has a demonstrable catastrophic antecedent (14). It is the assumption that the inter-ictal personality is normal which has been called into question (see below).

4) Additional differentiating points are confusion during the episode and impaired memory of the ictal event, both of which suggest seizure. These may be less helpful guidelines because it may be difficult to tell whether an acutely decompensated schizophrenic is confused. Likewise, it is not clear whether schizophrenics in remission can give a good account of their psychotic activity.

5) Finally, a trial of therapy is sometimes beneficial. If a patient's schizophreniform activity were due to temporal-lobe status, intravenous diazepam therapy might quickly relieve the behavioral abnormalities (12). Conversely, rapid neuroleptization (e.g., haloperidol) is frequently effective in removing acute schizophrenic signs and symptoms but may have no effect on (except perhaps to aggravate) a true behavior disorder.

There is considerable controversy regarding the personality of epileptics, and in particular, temporal lobe epileptics. The following survey of the literature provides some tentative conclusions, practical aids in understanding epileptic behavior, and a framework which may permit better understanding of current research.

In past centuries, epilepsy was associated with magic and witchcraft. By the 19th and early 20th centuries, these views were largely abandoned by the medical profession, although the opinions which replaced them were scarcely more favorable. Epileptics were held to be unintelligent, sexually perverse, and criminally inclined (1).

It is tempting to associate such ideas with the earlier beliefs in witchcraft and simply dismiss them as prejudicial mistakes of the past. To do so, however, would ignore some important lessons about how scientific evidence is gathered and evaluated, and would make us less able to understand the current controversies about the personality structure of the temporal-lobe epileptic. A perusal of the literature on epilepsy in the late 1800s and early 1900s demonstrates that the opinions then were buttressed by an impressive number of studies. Although these studies did not employ the sophisticated neuropsychiatric tests available today, they did survey symptoms, occupational status, social adjustment, and psychiatric characteristics of a large number of patients. These studies showed that epileptics had low intelligence, a high prevalence of criminal behavior, and high rates of psychosis. Two defects are evident in these studies (1, 10).

First, they were drawn from populations of institutions which housed the most serious cases, who could not care for themselves. Thus, it is not surprising that the patients turned out to be less than intelligent and less socially adaptable than normal. Second, different etiologies of seizures were not separated. An individual with seizures due to a large brain tumor or to severe head injury may have cognitive deficits simply as a result of physical brain destruction.

It is not easy to eliminate such problems from large studies, even today. Large numbers of patients are generally available only at institutions, and most institutions select for various types of patients in ways that are difficult to control. Selectivity may depend not only upon institutional standards but also upon referral patterns. In addition, it is not always easy to be certain on the basis of a review of the charts of an institutionalized individual that the patient did not have a structural or metabolic disease that was overlooked.

The influence of confounding factors affecting validity of studies has never been completely resolved, but the artifacts of patient selection and classification were rectified, and the notion that epileptics were grossly intellectually defective was abandoned by the 1930s or 1940s. In its place rose the more sophisticated concept of the epileptic personality, which entailed more subtle deficits.

Stauder (15) demonstrated that epileptics had tendencies toward perseveration, retardation, "stickiness," circumstantial thinking, poverty of intellectual content, explosiveness, and irritability. The Rorschach test was one of the instruments utilized in this assessment. This study, employing Rorschach testing, suffered from many of the defects in the earlier studies. However, it was one of the first studies to use psychological testing instruments to isolate certain aspects of personality which are altered in epilepsy. In addition, Stauder anticipated an important point by studying the same psychological parameters in normals who had been given high doses of phenobarbital; they had psychological aberrations similar to those of the epileptics.

Later studies employing the Rorschach test (16, 17, 18, 19, 20, 21) found that epileptics exhibited an abnormal but by no means unique pattern. Similarly, Mignone et al. (22) observed that epileptics had an abnormal pattern of response on the MMPI, but did not have any particular differentiation pattern.

Further attempts to delineate an epileptic personality generated an impressive roster of personality traits, recently enumerated by Stevens (10):

> adhesive, aggressive, apathetic, antagonistic, ambitious, bigoted, brutal, circumstantial, depressed, dissatisfied, dyscontrolled, dysphoric, garrulous, hyposexual, hypersexual, hyperactive, hypergraphic, hostile, inadequate, impulsive, importunate, irritable, litigious, meticulous, moody, monotonous, narrow-minded, obstinate, paranoid, pedantic, peevish, perseverative, rage-prone, retarded, religious, slow, sly, sensitive, schizoid, shallow, sticky, stubborn, suspicious, temperamental, troublesome, unctuous, unstable, unpredictable, vain, vague, vicious, withdrawn, and willful.

The faults of the older studies reasserted themselves in the newer works on the epileptic personality. Stevens (23) and Lennox (24) questioned not only aspects of patient selection but also stressed the effect that environmental and social influences might have in the development and expression of the epileptic's personality. Other writers (25, 26, 27, 28) have further stressed the influence of the social milieu, the reaction of parents and friends to the patient's illness, and other aspects of the psychosocial environment. The extent to which drug therapy may play an important role in personality problems is another unknown.

Such objections forced a reexamination of the concept of the "epileptic personality." Several studies using the Rorschach test (29, 30, 31) and the MMPI (32, 33, 34) failed to confirm a difference between epileptics and normals. These criticisms gradually led to the thesis that it was the personality structure of the *temporal-lobe epileptic* that was truly different from normal (35, 36, 37). In addition to the focus upon temporal-lobe epilepsy, the topic of aggression and criminality in epileptics became increasingly prominent. The prominence of this topic may have been owing to the rise of prison psychology as a separate discipline and to the increasing use of epilepsy as a defense in criminal trials.

Bitemporal "flat-top waves" (now called *theta* waves) were observed in many patients with psychomotor epilepsy and behavior disorders (35, 36). However, many patients with these waves did not have epileptic phenomena. Instead, they had hysteria, psychopathic personality disorders, or psychosis. Investigators theorized that perhaps these psychological findings were the "psychic equivalent" of temporal-lobe epilepsy (36).

These findings were pursued. The Gibbs group (35, 36, 37) made an attempt to obtain nonbiased data by using the University of Illinois hospitals and clinics and related institutions. They analyzed data from forty thousand patients, most of whom were not primarily psychiatric patients. Twelve percent exhibited personality disorders, 2.5 percent paranoid tendencies, and 0.2 percent were considered schizophrenic (37). These findings substantiate a large number of uncontrolled reports (38, 39, 40, 41). Various European investigators have also observed personality differences in temporal-lobe epileptics (42, 43, 44, 45).

The exact nature of the presumed typical temporal-lobe personality is not well delineated in all reports, nor is it always the same in every report. Nevertheless, common themes repeatedly emerge (46, 47, 48): (1) There is reduced sexual arousal, reduced responsiveness, and, often, hypersexuality in the immediate postictal period. (2) In children, "episodic rages and hyperkinesis" are claimed to occur concomitant with the first seizures. (3) In adults, there occurs "viscosity," a deepening of the emotional response, in which everything is taken very seriously and there is an overemphasis on right and wrong (which often includes hyperreligiosity). There is also a loss of sense of humor and a slow, verbose or pedantic manner of speech. (4) Impulsive and/or irritable behavior with rage attacks alternating with unusually good-natured behavior. (5) With increasing age, episodic rages diminish and depressive attacks become more common. (6) A psychosis which is similar to, or identical with, schizophrenia may supervene, usually many years after the patient has had temporal-lobe seizures. The viscosity and depression usually become fixed personality traits, once developed (46), whereas the schizophreniform psychosis seems to have an inverse relationship with the frequency of the actual seizures (46, 49, 50).

These concepts are fairly well accepted. The tendency for temporal-lobe epileptics to develop schizophreniclike illness as well as changes in sexual function and emotional balance is appealing from the standpoint of functional neuroanatomy. As was noted earlier, the temporal lobe contains the primary auditory receptive area, as well as major centers for understanding languages. Auditory- and visual-association areas are also present in the temporal lobe. Deeper in the insula, and in the related mesolimbic area, are gustatory, olfactory, sexual, and autonomic centers as well as structures prominent in memory. Closely related areas such as the amygdala and septal nuclei are prominent in controlling irritability and rage. Thus, it is that acute *ictal* phenomena evoke acute *ictal* changes in these functions. Some of these changes—particularly visual and auditory hallucinations—are quite similar to schizophrenic symptoms. Thus, a chronic seizure disorder could conceivably produce chronic changes in the temporal lobe and/or mesial limbic structures and cause a permanent personality alteration. Indeed, experimental stimulation of the limbic area in human subjects produces perceptive and emotional disturbances, paranoia, and depersonalization that are reminiscent of schizophrenia (51, 52). Penfield's experiments demonstrated that temporal-lobe stimulation (including limbic stimulation) could produce *déjà vu* as well as visual and auditory hallucinations (53).

Schizophreniclike symptoms have been associated with lesions involving the temporal-limbic-lobe area (54, 55). On the other hand, the lesions described by Davidson and Bagley (55)—whose survey is the most extensive—are not all in the temporal lobe. These researchers observed that left-temporal-lobe disease correlated with delusions and catatonia, diencephalic disease correlated with auditory hallucinations, basal-ganglia disease with catatonia, and brainstem pathology with thought disorders. Since the brainstem and basal ganglia, as well as most (or all, depending on different definitions) of the diencephalon are not part of the limbic lobe—although they have connections with it—it is not clear whether these data support or refute the temporal limbic locale for schizophrenia. Encephalitis, particularly that in which the temporal and limbic areas have been predominantly affected, has been repeatedly reported to give a clinical picture similar to schizophrenia (56, 57, 58, 59).

Some contend that schizophrenics (treated or untreated) have an increased number of dopamine receptors in the nucleus accumbens (60). This nucleus is a part of the lateral septal nucleus complex and is connected with the temporal lobe and limbic system. Electrodes implanted in the brains of schizophrenics have demonstrated random spike activity in the region of the nucleus accumbens as well as in other areas of the septal nucleus complex, the head of the caudate, and the amygdala (61, 62, 63).

The symptoms displayed during a temporal-lobe seizure relate to a derangement of functions ascribed to the temporal-limbic area. Schizophrenics have similar symptoms which can also be interpreted as a functional derangement of the temporal-limbic areas. There are reports in which electrical disturbances—usually different from typical epileptiform discharges—have been recorded in temporal-limbic areas in schizophrenics, sometimes but not always correlated with severity of symptoms (63, 64, 65). Some investigators contend that patients with temporal-lobe epilepsy are at risk for developing schizophrenia, usually several years after the seizures begin (66).

These ideas are quite controversial. Many studies in which temporal-lobe epileptics were age- and background-matched to patients with generalized or centrencephalic epilepsy fail to support the correlation reported by Gibbs (67, 68, 69, 70, 71). Most of these studies, however, did note higher rates of psychopathology for both epileptic groups than would be expected in a nonepileptic population.

Stevens (72), in a survey of 100 adults attending a university seizure clinic, noted no difference in the rates of psychiatric hospitalization between patients with temporal-lobe epilepsy and those with generalized epilepsy. Psychiatric hospitalization rate was higher, however, for both those groups than for patients with only focal motor seizures. Bingely (73) reported on his wide experience with patients who had temporal-lobe gliomas. Of 253 such patients, of which 116 had partial complex seizures, there was no evidence of psychosis in any patient, although many had considerable intellectual impairment.

Mignone et al. (22) found no significant differences in aggression, impatience, sexual dysfunction, or affective disturbance between temporal-lobe epileptics and other epileptics. Likewise, in a study of nonuniversity patients at a large private neurology clinic, there was no difference in psychopathology between the temporal lobe and other epileptic patients (10, 72). Finally, a large English survey (74) concluded that the extent of psychopathology in patients with epilepsy depended more upon the socioeconomic background than on the location of the lesion.

One team of investigators (75) noted no difference in psychological test data and blind psychiatric interviews between 25 patients with temporal-lobe seizures and 25 patients with other types of epilepsy. Others (76) could find no difference on the Halstead-Reiten, WAIS, Wechsler Memory, or Ravens Matrices tests which could characterize different types of epilepsy.

The question of violence or aggressive interictal behavior has also been raised. Delgado (77) states that violence in epileptics is quite rare, but that when it occurs, it is found in relationship to temporal-lobe epilepsy. In a study of 100 temporal-lobe epileptics, Falconer and Serafetinedes (78) noted that 31 had aggressive personality disorders, 24 suffered from depression, 15 had inadequate personality, 12 were psychotic, 11 were hysteric, 10 were anxious, 7 were paranoid, 4 were mentally retarded, and 4 were normal. These patients had been referred for consideration of temporal lobectomy; thus, as Falconer himself observed, they were highly selected. Aggression, when found, seemed to be related to mesial temporal sclerosis. Psychosis appeared to correlate with hamartoma of the amygdala (79).

Taylor (80) reanalyzed the data from 100 of Falconer's patients. He found that they all had a high prevalence of family and social disturbances. He also noted that early onset, male sex, and low I.Q. most significantly related to aggression. He also contended that *ictal* behavior was not aggressive.

Roth and Ervin (81), studying 1,154 male prisoners in the Lewisberg Federal Penitentiary, noted a 2.5 percent prevalence of epilepsy within the prison population, compared to a normal prevalence of 0.5 percent. Gunn (82) studied all men admitted to prison in England and Wales in December 1966; 8.8 per thousand were epileptic, compared to 5.5 per thousand in the general population. If one restricts the analysis to the 15-to-24-year age group, there were 11.4 epileptics per thousand in prison and 6.0 epileptics per thousand in the general population. However, a later study (83) could not demonstrate a higher incidence of violence among the epileptic, compared to the nonepileptic, prisoners. Among the epileptic prisoners, temporal-lobe patients had more convictions, but other epileptics had more convictions for violent crimes. Alstrom (67) followed 345 adults with epilepsy in Sweden for a period of 25 years and found no elevated crime rate among the subjects. Similarly, others (24, 84) could find no convincing evidence that temporal-lobe epileptics have an increased tendency toward crime.

Thus, the existence of a specific constellation of findings that can be considered to be the "temporal-lobe personality" has not become clearly established. Attempts to prove that such a constellation exists have been beset by the same problems of selection bias and contravening effects of social interaction and medication. In addition, there is the problem of organic brain damage, which may give rise to both the seizure and to the psychological aberrations. Stevens (23) concludes that in psychomotor seizures, as in other types of epilepsy, if there are personality disturbances, they are more likely to be owing to the specific site and extent of the patient's primary organic lesion (if one is present), to the patient's psychological milieu, and to the patient's treatment, than to the seizures themselves. Nonetheless, as we have noted, there is also support for the contrary view, that the presence of abnormal temporal-lobe discharges can cause personality alteration (46).

Recently, new approaches have been applied to the assessment of personality structure of the psychomotor epileptic. These differ from traditional approaches in that they examine more limited and well-defined aspects of mental function and analyze them quantitatively rather than deal with larger concepts such as psychiatric diagnoses or historical life events such as arrests, convictions, or psychiatric commitments. This approach is similar to the use of the MMPI but, as has been noted, the MMPI and other standardized tests were not of great discriminative value.

Bear and Fedio (85) departed from the usual testing method, identifying 18 behavioral characteristics which they believed temporal lobe patients might possess. Each characteristic had been suggested as a possible concomitant of the temporal-lobe personality by other investigators. Bear and Fedio then devised two true-false questionnaires. In one, the patient rated himself regarding the presence or absence of each of these 18 characteristics. In the other, a rater (either a family member, spouse, friend, or health-care professional) rated the patient on these characteristics. Unlike many previous studies, care was taken to ensure that the sample was not unduly enriched with patients who had presented to a clinic seeking psychiatric care. Fifteen patients with right temporal-lobe lesions, 12 patients with left temporal-lobe lesions, 12 normals, and 9 patients with neurologic disorders other than epilepsy (neuromuscular disease) were compared. Several interesting findings were reported.

First, temporal-lobe epileptic patients could be discriminated from the nonepileptic contrast groups upon the basis of either the self-rated scores or the ratings supplied by others. All of the behavioral characteristics—emotionality, elation, euphoria, sadness, anger, aggression, altered sexual interest, circumstantiality, obsessionalism, viscosity, hypermoralism, guilt, dependence, passivity, philosophical interest, sense of personal destiny, humorlessness, sobriety, religiosity, hypergraphia, and paranoia—occurred more frequently in the temporal-lobe patients than in the control groups. From this group of traits, a discriminant behavioral profile was obtained which characterized the temporal-lobe epileptic patients as a group. This profile consisted of "circumstantial concern with details, religious and philosophical interests, and intense, sober affect." Bear and Fedio also discovered a significant difference between right- and left-temporal-lobe epileptics. The right-temporal-lobe epileptics exhibited more emotive characteristics—aggression, depression, and emotional lability. Patients with left temporal foci exhibited more introspective ideational traits—religiosity, hypergraphia, philosophical tendencies, and a strong sense of personal destiny.

These findings concur with those of Flor-Henry (66), who noted that patients with right temporal foci had a higher prevalence of affective disorders, whereas those with left temporal foci had a higher prevalence of thought disorders. It is also concordant with the general interpretation of right hemispheric processes as nonverbal and those of the left hemisphere as verbal, as long as one accepts the assumption that a seizure disorder is reflective of functional *overactivity* of the area from which the spikes arise. A priori, however, it would be just as reasonable to assume that the interictal function of the lobe from which the foci emerges should be depressed.

Bear (85, 86) theorizes that "an active epileptic process in the temporal lobe may bring about new connections through a process of physiological learning." He acknowledges that such new connections are speculative. Indeed, one may also speculate that patients with idiopathic unilateral temporal-lobe epilepsy may simply have an overactivity of one temporal lobe—without the existence of any new connections. In symptomatic temporal lobe epilepsy—i.e., in cases wherein the seizures appear to result from a structured temporal-lobe lesion—the psychological findings may well be the reverse—i.e., indicative of underactivity of the affected hemisphere.

A recent study (87) compared responses to dichotic listening in patients having idiopathic versus symptomatic complex partial seizures. Differential stimuli were simultaneously presented to each ear. Ordinarily, patients with an organic lesion in one temporal lobe perceive the stimuli less well in the contralateral ear than in the ipsilateral ear. However, patients with idiopathic temporal-lobe seizures perceived *better* with the contralateral ear, while patients with temporal lobe epilepsy secondary to demonstrable organic pathology perceived *worse* with the contralateral ear. These findings support Bear's notion that the epileptic temporal lobe (in idiopathic cases) has increased functional interictal activity.

Although controversy reigns in this area of research, some conclusions can be drawn which may help the practitioner to better understand the temporal-lobe epileptic.

(1) Many manifestations of schizophrenia may be seen during attacks of complex partial seizures. These signs and symptoms are also quite similar to those produced by stimulation of the anterior mesial temporal and limbic structures, as well as by tumors of, and trauma to, these structures. These structures are also the sites from which the abnormal neuronal discharges of complex partial seizures most commonly arise. Such data support the supposition that the anatomic locale of schizophrenia may include these temporal and limbic areas, although the data in no way prove that the areas are the anatomic locale of schizophrenia, that schizophrenia has an anatomical locale, or that schizophrenia and complex partial seizures are caused by the same process.

(2) For whatever reason, patients with complex partial seizures appear to be at risk for developing psychological problems, including schizophrenia. It may be that the risk of psychiatric illness is largely due to social and interpersonal factors such as societal discrimination, personal rejection, and/or secondary effects of anticonvulsant drugs. Alternatively, there may be a biological substrate underlining this risk. A combination of these factors may be operative.

Whatever the cause, it is important that the patient's physician be aware of the possibility of psychiatric difficulties. This awareness should not create a pejorative atmosphere, in which the patient is viewed as mentally impaired, flawed, or destined to have emotional problems. Instead, an awareness of the patient's potential problems allows the physician to practice preventive medicine and to function better as the patient's advocate and counselor. For example, one should be aware that discrimination against epileptics may make it difficult for them to get jobs. This may not only require social work intervention; it may also require psychiatric support.

(3) In addition to the risk of psychiatric illness, there is the potential independent question of whether or not there are more subtle differences in the personality structures of temporal-lobe epileptics as compared with other epileptics, patients with other neurological impairments, and normals. Differences between right- and left-temporal-lobe epileptics are also possible.

We have described several lines of evidence which indicate that such differences may exist. This information, while tentative, offers exciting prospects for future research. Can this knowledge be used prospectively to predict psychiatric morbidity? More important, can we use such knowledge of information processing and personality structures to significantly improve the life adjustment of patients with temporal-lobe epilepsy and to lower their risk of psychiatric difficulties? Finally, can this knowledge help us elucidate the link between the anatomical, electrophysiological, and biochemical structure and function of the central nervous system with the cognitive and emotive activities?

REFERENCES

1. Strudler, L.A. & Perlman, L.G. (Eds.). *Basic Statistics on the Epilepsies*. Philadelphia: Davis, 1975.
2. Gastaut, H. Clinical and electroencephalographical classification of epileptic seizures. *Epilepsia* 11: 113, 1970.
3. Brodmann, K. In Barth, J.A. (Ed.), *Vergleichende Lokalisationlehre der Grosshirnrinde in ihren Prinzipen dargestellt auf Grand des Zellenbanes*. Leipzig: 1909.
4. Krieg, V.J.S. *Connections of the Cerebral Cortex*. Evanston, Ill.: Brain Books, 1963.
5. Penfield, W. & Jasper, H. *Epilepsy and the Functional Anatomy of the Human Brain*, p. 507. Boston: Little, Brown, 1954.
6. Papez, J.W. A proposed mechanism of emotion. *Arch. Neurol. Psychiat.* 38: 725–43, 1937.
7. Scoville, W.B. & Milner, B. Loss of recent memory after bilateral hippocampal lesions. *J. Neuro. Neurosurg. Psychiat.* 20: 11–21, 1957.
8. Horel, J.A. The neuroanatomy of amnesia. *Brain* 101: 403–45, 1978.
9. Kluver, H. & Bucy, P.D. Preliminary analysis of functions of the temporal lobes in monkeys. *Arch. Neurol. Psychiat.* 42: 979–1,000, 1939.
10. Stevens, J.R. Interictal clinical manifestations of complex partial seizures. In Penry, K. & Daly, D. (Eds.), *Advances in Neurology*, vol. 11. New York: Raven, 1975.
11. Remick, R.A. & Wada, J.A. Complex partial and pseudoseizure disorders. *Am. J. Psychiat.* 136: 320–23, 1979.
12. Engel, J., Ludwig, B.I., & Fetell, M. Prolonged partial complex status epilepticus: EEG and behavioral observations. *Neurology* 28: 863–69, 1978.
13. Rodin, E.A. Psychomotor epilepsy and aggressive behavior. *Arch. Gen. Psychiat.* 28: 210–13, 1973.
14. Spitzer, R. Schizophrenic disorders. *Schizo. Bull.* 4: 495–510, 1978.
15. Stauder, K.H. *Konstitution and Wesensanderung der Epileptiker*. Lepzig: Thieme, 1938.
16. Goldkuhl, E. Rorschach tests in epilepsy. *Uppsala LaKarofarenings* 51: 284–311, 1946.

17. Kogan, K. The personality reaction patterns of children with epilepsy with special reference to the Rorschach method. *Res. Publ. Assoc. Nerv. Ment. Dis.* 26: 616–30, 1947.

18. Massignan, L. The Rorschach Test in Epilepsy. *Riv. Patol. Nerv. Ment.* 74: 17–83, 1953.

19. Harrower-Erickson, M.R. Psychological studies of patients with epileptic seizures. In Penfield, W. & Erickson, J.C. (Eds.), *Epilepsy and Cerebral Localization.* Springfield, Ill.: Thomas.

20. Okuma, F. Personality changes in epileptic patients, as examined by the Rorschach Test. *Clin. Psychiat.* 4: 245–53, 1962.

21. Matalay, K. & Pavlovkin, M. Personality traits of disabled epileptics. *Epilepsia* 13: 47–50, 1972.

22. Mignone, R.J., Donnelly, E.F., & Sadowsky, D. Psychological and neurological comparisons of psychomotor and non-psychomotor epileptic patients. *Epilepsia* 11: 345–59, 1970.

23. Stevens, H. Psychiatric aspects of epilepsy. *Med. Ann. D.C.* 16: 53–541, 1974.

24. Lennox, W.G. Seizure states. In Hunt, J.M. (Ed.), *Personality and the Behavior Disorders.* New York: Ronald Press, 1944.

25. Bridge, E.M. *Epilepsy and Convulsive Disorders in Children.* New York: McGraw-Hill, 1949.

26. Livingston, S. *Living with Epileptic Seizures.* Springfield, Ill.: Thomas, 1963.

27. Van Zijl, C.H. Influences of psychological functioning of epileptics on their social adaption. Paper presented at the third European Symposium on Epilepsy, June 1970.

28. Horowitz, M.J. *Psychosocial Function in Epilepsy.* Springfield, Ill.: Thomas, 1970.

29. Paillas, J.E. & Subirana, A. Semeiologie neuropsychique: le lobe temporal. *Rev. Otoneuroopthal.* 22: 123–92, 1950.

30. Delay, J., Pchot, P., Lemperier, R. Le test de Rorschach dans l'epilepsie. *Encephale.* 44: 45–46, 1955.

31. Mirsky, A.F., Primac, D.W., Ajmone-Marsan, C. A comparison of the psychological test performance of patients with focal and nonfocal epilepsy. *Exp. Neurol.* 2: 75–89, 1960.

32. Meier, M.J., & French, A. Changes in MMPI scale scores and an index of psychopathology following unilateral temporal lobectomy for epilepsy. *Epilepsia* 6: 263–73, 1965.

33. Jordan, E.J. MMPI profiles of epileptics: a further evaluation. *J. Consult. Psychol.* 27: 267–69, 1963.

34. Klove, H. & Doehring, D.G. MMPI in epileptic groups with differential etiology. *J. Clin. Psychol.* 28: 149–53, 1962.

35. Gibbs, F.A., Gibbs, E.L., & Lennox, W.G. Cerebral dysrhythmias of epilepsy. *Arch. Neurol. Psychiat.* 39: 298–314, 1938.

36. Gibbs, E.L., Gibbs, F.A., & Furster, B. Psychomotor epilepsy. *Arch. Neurol. Psychiat.* 60: 331–39, 1948.

37. Gibbs, F.A. & Gibbs, E.L. *Atlas of Electroencephalography,* Vol. 3. Reading, Mass.: Addison-Wesley, 1964.

38. Green, F., Duisberg, R., & McGrath, W.B. Focal epilepsy of psychomotor type. A preliminary report of observations on effects of surgical therapy. *J. Neurosurg.* 8: 157–72, 1951.

39. Luddell, D.W. Observations on epileptic automatisms in a mental hospital population. *J. Ment. Sci.* 99: 732–48, 1953.

40. Pond, D.A. Epilepsy and personality disorders. In Vinken, P.L. & Bruyn, G.W. (Eds.), *Handbook of Clinical Neurology.* Amsterdam: North Holland, 1974.

41. Rodin, E.A., DeJong, R.N., Waggoner, R.W. Relationship between certain forms of psychomotor epilepsy and schizophrenia. *Arch. Neurol. Psychiat.* 77: 449–63, 1957.

42. Gastaut, H. So-called "psychomotor" and "temporal" epilepsy—a critical study. *Epilepsia* 2: 59–76, 1953.

43. Gastaut, H. & Collomb, H. Etude de Comportement Sexuel Chez les Epileptiques Psychomoteurs. *Ann. Medicopsychol.* 112: 657–96, 1954.

44. Gastaut, H., Morin, G., & Lesevre, N. Etude de comportement des epileptiques psychomoteurs dans l'intervalle de leurs crises. *Ann. Medicopsychol.* 1: 1–27, 1955.

45. Gastaut, H., Miletto, G., & Vigouroux, R. Etude electroclinique des episodes psychotiques. *Rev. Neurol.* 95: 588–94, 1956.

46. Blumer, D. Temporal lobe epilepsy and its psychiatric significance. In Benson, D.F. & Blumer, D. (Eds.), *Psychiatric Aspects of Neurologic Diease.* New York: Grune and Stratton, 1975.

47. Geschwind, N. The borderland of neurology and psychiatry. In Benson, D.F. & Blumer, D. (Eds.), *Psychiatric Aspects of Neurologic Disease.* New York: Grune and Stratton, 1975.

48. Serafetinides, E.A. Aggressiveness in temporal lobe epileptics and its relation to cerebral dysfunction and environmental factors. *Epilepsia* 6: 33–42, 1965.

49. Landolt, H. Some clinical electroencephalographic correlations in epileptic psychoses (twilight states). *Electroenceph. Clin. Neurophysiol.* 5: 121, 1953.

50. Kristensen, O. & Sindrup, Z.H. Psychomotor epilepsy and psychosis. I. Physical aspects. *Acta Neurol. Scand.* 57: 361–69, 1978.

51. MacLean, P.D. Commentary biological functions of emotion. Edited by Celhorn, E. (Ed.), Foresna, Scott, 1968.

52. Roberts, D.R. Schizophrenia and the brain. *J. Neuropsychiat.* 5: 71–9, 1964.

53. Mullan, S. & Penfield, W. Illusions of comparative interpretation and emotion. *Arch. Neurol. Psychol.* 81: 269–94, 1959.

54. Malamud, N. Psychiatric disorders with intracranial tumors of the limbic system. *Arch. Neurol.* 17: 113–23, 1967.

55. Davidson, K. & Bagley, C.R. Schizophrenia-like psychos associated with organic disorders of the central nervous system: a review of the literature. In Herrington, R.N. (Ed.), *Current Problems in Neuropsychiatry.* Special Pub. No. 4. Ashford, Kent: Headley Brothers, 1969.

56. Drachman, D.A., Adams, R.D. Herpes simplex and acute inclusion-body encephalitis. *Arch. Neurol.* 7: 45–63, 1962.

57. Brierly, J.B., Corsellis, J.A.N., Hierons, R. Subacute encephalitis of later adult life—mainly affecting the limbic areas. *Brain* 83: 357–68, 1960.

58. Himmelhoch, J., Pincus, J., Tucker, G. Sub-acute encephalitis: behavioral and neurological aspects. *Brit. J. Psychiat.* 116: 531–38, 1970.

59. Glaser, G.H., Solitare, G.B., & Manuelidis, E.E. Acute and subacute inclusion encephalitis. *Res. Publ. Assoc. Nerv. Ment. Dis.* 44: 178–215, 1968.

60. Crow, T.J., Johnstone, E.C., Longden, A.J. Dopaminergic mechanisms in schizophrenia: the antipsychotic effect and the disease process. *Life Sci.* 23: 563–68, 1978.

61. Kendrick, J.F. & Gibbs, F.A. Origin, spread, and neurosurgical treatment of the psychomotor type of seizure discharge. *J. Neurosurg.* 14: 270–84, 1957.

62. Goldman, D. Specific electroencephalographic changes with pentothal activation in psychotic states. *EEG Clin. Neurophysiol.* 11: 657–67, 1959.

63. Hailey, J., Rickles, W.R., Crandill, P.H. Automated recognition of EEG correlates of behavior in a chronic schizophrenic patient. *Am. J. Psychiat.* 128: 1,524–28, 1972.

64. Yde, A., Lohse, E., & Faurbye, A. On the relation between schizophrenia, epilepsy and induced convulsions. *Acta Psychiat. Neurol. Scand.* 16: 325–88, 1941.

65. Hill, D. EEG in episodic psychotic and psychopathic behavior: a classification of data. *Electroenceph. Clin. Neurophysiol.* 4: 419–42, 1952.

66. Flor-Henry, P. Psychosis and temporal lobe epilepsy: a controlled investigation. *Epilepsia* 10: 363–95, 1969.

67. Alstrom, C.H. A study of epilepsy in its clinical, social, and genetic aspects. *Acta Psychiat. Neurol.* (Suppl)63: 1–284, 1950.

68. Vislie, H. & Henriksen, G.F. Psychic disturbances in epileptics. In Lorentz de Haas, A.M. (Ed.), *Lectures in Epilepsy.* Amsterdam: Elsevier, 1958.

69. Guerrant, J., Anderson, W.W., Weinstein, M.R. *Personality in Epilepsy.* Springfield, Ill.: Thomas, 1962.

70. Mirsky, A.F., Primac, D.W., Marsan, C.A. A comparison of the psychological test performance of patients with focal and non-focal epilepsy. *Exp. Neurol.* 2: 75–89, 1960.

71. Small, J.G., Milstein, V., & Stevens, J.R. Are psychomotor epileptics different? *Arch. Neurol.* 7: 187–94, 1962.

72. Stevens, J.R. Psychiatric implications of psychomotor epilepsy. *Arch. Gen. Psychiat.* 14: 461–71, 1966.

73. Bingley, T. Mental symptoms in temporal lobe epilepsy and temporal lobe gliomas. *Acta Psychiat. Neurol.* 120: 1–151, 1958.

74. Tizard, B. The personality of epileptics: A discussion of the evidence. *Psychol. Bull.* 59: 196–210, 1962.

75. Small, J.G., Small, I.F., & Hayden, M.P. Further psychiatric investigations of patients with temporal and nontemporal epilepsy. *Am. J. Psychiat.* 123: 303–10, 1966.

76. Stevens, J.R., Milstein, V., & Goldstein, S. Psychometric test performance in relation to the psychopathology of epilepsy. *Arch. Gen. Psychiat.* 26: 532–38, 1972.

77. Delgado, J.M.R. Violence within the brain. Paper presented at NINDS Symposium, New York, 1971.

78. Falconer, M.A. & Serafetinedes, A. A follow-up study of surgery in temporal lobe epilepsy. *J. Neurol. Neurosurg. Psychiat.* 26: 154–65, 1963.

79. Falconer, M.A. Reversibility by temporal-lobe resection of the behavioral abnormalities of temporal-lobe epilepsy. *New Eng. J. Med.* 289: 451–55, 1973.

80. Taylor, D.C. Aggression and epilepsy. *J. Psychosom. Res.* 13: 229–36, 1969.

81. Roth, L.H. & Ervin, F.R. Psychiatric care of federal prisoners. *Am. J. Psychiat.* 128: 56–62, 1971.

82. Gunn, J. The prevalence of epilepsy in prisoners. *Proc. R. Soc. Med.* 62: 60–63, 1969.

83. Gunn, J. & Bonn, J. Criminality and violence in epileptic prisoners. *Brit. J. Psychiat.* 118: 337–43, 1971.

84. Lennox, W.G. & Lennox, M.A. *Epilepsy and Related Disorders*. Boston: Little, Brown, 1960.

85. Bear, D. & Fedio, P. Quantitative analysis of interictal behavior in temporal lobe epilepsy. *Arch. Neurol.* 34: 454–67, 1977.

86. Bear, D. The temporal lobes: an approach to the study of organic behavioral changes. In Gazzaniga, M.S. (Ed.), *Handbook of Behavioral Neurology*. New York: Plenum, 1979.

87. Mazzuchi, A. & Parma, M. Responses to dichotic listening tasks in temporal epileptics with or without clinically evident lesions. *Cortex* 14: 381–90, 1978.

11

Childhood Aspects
of Psychophysiological Disorders

A. SCOTT DOWLING

The title of this chapter can imply that discussion will be limited to the disorders of childhood. It can also be viewed as an invitation to consider the childhood or developmental aspects of psychophysiological disorders of patients of all ages. It is my intention to take the latter course.

Although all would agree that pathways of psychophysiological stability are achieved in childhood, few writers have considered developmental lags in achieving this stability, or simple regressions from achieved stability, as explanatory models of disordered physiology. In such a conceptual organization, the adult disorders would be recognized as special cases rather than as prototypical examples of psychophysiological disturbance. Most writers have organized discussion of etiology and treatment of these disturbances by static consideration of major symptom complexes (the "Big Seven"—asthma, ulcerative colitis, regional ileitis, hypertension, duodenal ulcer, rheumatoid arthritis, thyrotoxicosis) of affected organ systems (e.g., disorders of gastrointestinal system or respiratory system) or of presumed etiological factors (e.g., specific conflicts, personality types). Invariably, adult disorders have been the prototype. Only rarely has the total psychological position of the patient been the focus of discussion, and even more rarely have the ebb and flow of psychological developmental factors been brought into discussions of etiology or treatment (1, 2).

A developmental approach places the symptoms in the context of physical, and particularly psychological, characteristics. It employs a longitudinal perspective (age and stage characteristics of cognitive and affective-motivational experience and expression) and a cross-section one (patterns of developmental stability-instability and consistency-inconsistency of cognitive and affective-motivational functions and of their interactions). This developmental perspective is sensitive to the gradations from normal to identifiably pathological functioning, and it emphasizes the variability of expression of similar disorders in individuals of the same age groups and across age groups. Two 3-year-olds with asthma may both be in an early Oedipal stage of object relations and show characteristics of preconceptual cognition; one child may, however, be far more susceptible to regression at earlier levels of object relationship, may have quite different patterns of defense and different external realities with which to contend. The expression of the asthma may correspondingly be different in each of these two children, in much the same way as differing physical characteristics may alter the manifest expression of asthma. Also, quite obviously, asthma in a 3-year-old is occurring in a different psychological setting than is asthma in a 13-year-old or in a 23-year-old. It is these developmental psychological differences which tend to be ignored. Furthermore, there is a pay-off. Useful treatment considerations flow from an approach which places a particular symptom expression in its proper developmental setting.

The term "psychosomatic" has fluctuated in meaning since its first era of popularity, some 50 years ago. Presently, the trend is toward a very general meaning, the term designating an approach to medicine as a whole, rather than a defined group of disorders (3). Terminological confusion has been relieved in recent years with George Engel's introduction of the term "biopsychosocial model" (4, 5) as a replacement for this broad meaning of "psychosomatic." The biopsychosocial model is one which does not limit the physician to a physical-biological approach to medicine but, rather, includes psychological and social dimensions as necessary considerations in evaluating a person's state of health or disease.

Even the term "psychophysiological disorder" does not have an agreed-upon definition. I set the boundaries of the term by taking a developmental viewpoint while readily acknowledging that this use of the term is in disagreement with most other clinicians. I limit the term "psychophysiological disorder" to those nonneurotic disorders in which psychological factors are intimately and critically involved in the causal chain leading to physical symptoms expressive of automatic function or dysfunction.

Three partially overlapping types of disturbance are included in my use of the term:

1) Maladaptive autonomic functioning due to developmental disturbances or interferences.
2) Affect equivalents—disorders in which the physiological component of an affect occurs without the accompanying feeling state.
3) Disorders in which an unusual autonomic manifestation occurs in connection with an unconscious (or sometimes conscious) affect or fantasy but does not directly symbolize wish and defense, as do conversion symptoms.

Specifically excluded from my use of the term are:

1) Willful or accidental damage to the body, such as suicide, accident proneness, or disorders due to disuse of body parts.
2) Psychological consequences of physical illness or injury, including the effects of functional damage to sensory, motor, or integrative structures; helplessness resulting from sensory or affective flooding; and symptoms resulting from the symbolic meaning of the illness or injury or of the diagnostic procedures or treatment.
3) Those instances in which the body is used for symbolic expression of an unconscious conflict, as in conversion disorders.

A more detailed consideration of each of the groups I have included as psychophysiological disorders will illustrate the diagnostic application of a developmental viewpoint and lay the groundwork for a consideration of the treatment implications of this approach.

The first group are those disorders secondary to developmental disturbances or interferences (6). Throughout life, each of us faces a series of stressful periods, which are inherent in the very fact of our ongoing maturation and development. The intensity of these developmental disturbances will vary within the life of the same individual, and from one individual to another. Some periods of psychological stress and readjustment are well known; e.g., early adolescence and the menopause. Others are recognized but considered "too normal" to be given much respectability as potential emotional troublemakers; e.g., learning to walk, leave-taking of older adolescents from their parents, marriage, birth of children, promotion. Still others are often unrecognized; e.g., adjustment from placental to oral feeding, the experience of affective differentiation of one person from another at six–eight months, onset of latency, with widespread repression of memories of past events. Unlike developmental disturbances, developmental interferences are intrusions into the developmental process. Sometimes, they are necessary or unavoidable; at other times, unnecessary and preventable. Some common examples would include leg casting or other immobilizing procedures during infancy and early childhood; medically advised genital manipulations during the Oedipal period; parental divorce; one's own divorce; and removal from employment and social usefulness, with advancing age. An intimate knowledge of normal developmental steps and patterns and an understanding of the development of each patient is, clearly, a prerequisite for effective recognition and evaluation of the presence and relevance of these factors.

A listing of symptomatic complaints referable to these developmental events would include disorders of physiological functioning, ranging from mild and virtually inconsequential to life-threatening or fatal conditions. These are most striking in infancy, when colic, evening fussiness, and mild and temporary disturbances of feeding and bowel function are so regular as to be medically ignored. Yet they stand as the prototypes of disturbed psychophysiological functioning, the earliest psychophysiological disorders. In more virulent forms—such as feeding disturbances, with vomiting and dehydration; psychogenic failure to thrive; and deprivation syndrome, with marasmus and infant death—we see a more sober side of developmental disorders. Disturbances of growth in latency and adolescence are referable to psychological interferences (7, 8). There are a host of other, more frequent and sometimes serious, symptoms in older children and adolescents (e.g., recurrent abdominal pains, periodic syndrome, headaches) (9, 10, 11) and in adults (headaches, backaches, wryneck, and the like).

The second group of psychophysiological disorders are affect equivalents. The patient experiences the physiological aspect of an emotional state (e.g., fast heartbeat, tearing of eyes, perspiration) without any conscious awareness of emotion. My use of the term refers to very simple, frequent occurrences seen, often as incidental findings, in many patients. The physiological phenomena involved are not unusual or particularly threatening; however, their occurrence in dissociation from awareness of emotion renders them inaccessible to understanding, modification, or resolution. They may, therefore, continue as chronic, sometimes disabling, symptoms. An example is Miss J., a 20-year-old depressed student. Several months into her analysis, she described two experiences which occurred frequently while grocery shopping. The first was a vaguely unpleasant impression of "all that food on the shelf," accompanied by lacrimation; the second was awareness of tachycardia when she stood in front of the meat counter. The former experience was traced to its original association with painful longing for care and feeding; it was an affect equivalent for emotional hunger and longing for human contact. The experience at the meat counter was an affect equivalent for sexual excitement and fear related to repeated genital seduction, from ages four–six, by her grandfather. Improvement occurred with a coherent awareness of the meaning of the childhood experiences; their meaning achieved access to adult forms of thought and emotional expression.

The third group includes those disturbances of visceral functions which are unusual accompaniments of conscious or unconscious emotion or fantasy. They are "unusual" in the sense that they are not simply dissociated, "usual" physiological events, as are the affect equivalents. They may be relatively simple, time-limited responses, such as some arrhythmias, disturbances of temperature regulation, or dermatoses (12, 13, 14, 15, 16, 17). They include complex disorders such as the Big Seven. Neither severe regressive phenomena to preverbal ego functioning nor psychoticlike functioning need be postulated in any of these conditions.

An 11-year-old boy found himself caught up in a cyclone of parental conflict in which he was an unwilling, but helpless, pawn, a keeper of secrets, and guardian of the family's honor in the community. In addition to a severe inhibition of learning, he experienced repeated elevations of temperature (101°–103°). Repeated hospitalizations for diagnostic study revealed no identifiable cause for the fevers. They receded rapidly with psychotherapy, which consisted of little more than interventions that allowed him to articulate and deal consciously and verbally with the psychological burden he had been carrying. Conflict was then expressed through behavioral and neurotic symptoms.

A 17-year-old boy, while recounting a vivid recollection of being beaten and choked by his father, threw his head back and clutched his hands over his throat but did not touch his skin. As he sobbed and spoke in an agonized way of these experiences, erythema and extensive linear wheals appeared over his neck.

The reader will realize that if he accepts the boundaries of psychophysiological disorders which I have proposed, then it will follow that neither the frequency nor the range of severity of these conditions has been appreciated. Viewed from a developmental-psychological framework, they are ubiquitous expressions of developmental stress and frequent by-products of conflict about expression and conscious awareness of affect and fantasy. These symptoms are seen frequently in psychiatric practice; a summary of their occurrence in one day's work makes the point (see Table 11-1). Note that only one patient had no psychophysiological symptoms, whereas seven made no mention of them prior to treatment.

David Graham, M.D., in his 1979 presidential address to the American Psychosomatic Society, observed:

> One reason for the general ignorance or lack of interest in these facts (many different kinds of illnesses are reactions to disturbing life events) is that it has been difficult to show—or at least has not often been shown—that paying attention to them is of any great utility in treating patients (3).

By paying attention primarily to the most severe forms of these illnesses (the Big Seven), we have blinded ourselves and others to treatment possibilities for the full range of this group of disorders; if we examined viral illness only from the perspective of the most disabling and inaccessible types, we would similarly bias our understanding and treatment approaches to the full range of viral illness. Examination of diagnostic and treatment experience with the more tractable conditions may provide assessment guidelines for therapy in the less tractable conditions.

There can be no more dramatic therapeutic experience than effective intervention in the killing types of developmental interference such as maternal

TABLE 11-1
Typical Psychophysiological Symptoms

	Age Group and Sex	Initial Reason for Therapy	Psychophysiological Symptoms	Type of Treatment and Response of Psychophysiological Symptoms to Treatment
1.	Preadolescent Male	Enuresis Learning problems	Enuresis Headaches	Psychoanalysis—4 yrs. Enuresis cleared Headaches persist
2.	Early-adolescent Male	Enuresis Learning problems	Enuresis	Psychoanalysis—1 yr. No change
3.	Early-adolescent Male	Temperature elevations to 101°–103° Learning problems	Temperature elevations Periodic syndrome	Psychotherapy—1 yr. Cessation of psychophysiological symptoms; onset of neurotic symptoms
4.	Middle-aged Male	Obsessive-compulsive neurosis	Mild asthma—31 yrs.	Psychoanalysis—3 yrs. Asthma cleared. All medication stopped
5.	Young-adult Female	Phobic neurosis	Tachycardia Abdominal pains Neurodermatitis	Psychoanalysis—2 yrs. All symptoms cleared

6.	Young-adult Male	Obsessive-compulsive symptoms, with borderline personality	Chest pains Abdominal pains	Psychotherapy—18 mos. Much improved
7.	Young-adult Male	Character neurosis	None known	Psychoanalysis
8.	Middle-aged Male	Depression, nonpsychotic	Shifting, debilitating aches and pains	Psychotherapy—1 yr. Much improved as becomes consciously aware of depressed feelings
9.	Young-adult Female	Phobic neurosis	Hyperhidrosis Tachycardia	Psychoanalysis—1 yr. No change
10.	Middle-aged Female	Depression, nonpsychotic	Headaches Abdominal pains Rectal bleeding Urinary retention	Psychoanalysis—1 yr. Much improved
11.	Elderly Female	Depression, nonpsychotic	Watery eyes Back pains Eye pains Muscle aches	Psychotherapy—3 yrs. Improved when aware of associated affect

deprivation syndrome. Psychophysiological competence in infancy requires adequate maternal care; provision of such care permits physical survival. The circumstances are entirely comparable to providing adequate nutrition to a starving child; a life is saved by providing a specific "nutrient." Far less dramatic, but for many a source of great satisfaction, are the effective guidance interventions in simple developmental disturbances, interventions which can shape the unfolding relationship of an infant or young child with his parents as well as significantly benefit his physiological status.

Apart from guidance interventions in developmental interferences or disturbances, psychological treatment is, in my view, the mutual investigation by patient and therapist of the meaning of events in the patient's life, especially of intrapsychic events, together with a reconsideration and revision of that meaning and of its place in the organization of the patient's personality. A patient's symptoms are, in effect, an ultimately maladaptive mode of organizing or integrating meaning; symptoms resolve with revision of the meaning or of the mode of integration. Neurotic symptoms integrate meaning through the distorting effect of repression, conversion, regression, and the like; psychophysiological disturbances, as I have described them, integrate meaning with other elements of the personality by removing conscious awareness of feeling while retaining usual physiological responses (affect equivalents) or by substituting physiological experience for the experience of affect or fantasy.

A few vignettes, necessarily brief, will illustrate these treatment interventions:

> Jane, age 4, was being hospitalized for the fourth time in two months with severe intractable asthma. On each occasion, the symptoms improved rapidly with entry to the hospital. She was the eldest of three girls; her mother was due to deliver a fourth child in four months. Both parents felt coerced into marriage; both felt they had given up careers for the marriage partner. Stringent religious scruples were apparent in the absolute prohibition of expression of angry feelings by adults and children and in the avoidance of contraception. Jane was a bright, alert child, very controlling of parents and sibs through teasing, cajolery, and regressive behavior; direct aggressive or competitive expression, whether in word or deed, was absent.
>
> In a series of meetings with her mother and me, Jane could join with me in drawing pictures, playing simple doll games, and talking about the hospital, her asthma, her siblings, and her mother's pregnancy. With her mother's permission, feelings of anger and bewilderment connected with these aspects of her life were permitted and given verbal form. To a modest degree, it became possible for her to both express and talk about her feelings. In separate meetings between her mother and me, these areas were explored in greater detail; the use of verbalization appealed to her. After daily meetings with me for three weeks, Jane was discharged home. She remained totally free of asthmatic symptoms for over a year; a mild attack occurred on the first birthday of her youngest

sibling, sixteen months later, and recurred, in mild form, occasionally for two years. Now, ten years later, she has no asthmatic symptoms for many years.

In this, as in all instances, treatment, as I have defined it ("mutual investigation by patient and therapist of the meaning of events in the patient's life"), required modifying the form of discussion to meet the developmental capabilities and characteristics of the patient. Drawing pictures together, depicting family circumstances through doll play, and making use of the special relationship of a mother with her preschool child were elements of the technique. A vital factor was the verbalization of feeling and experience, a necessary step to a more mature mode of integration.

Bill, a 14-year-old boy, complained of watery eyes while walking home from school. His 20-year-old brother was in the midst of a severe crisis involving suicidal depression, drugs, and psychiatric hospitalization. To Bill, an expression of sadness connoted helplessness and "turning myself over to my mother." Clarification and connection of these previously known meanings to the present experience of "watery eyes" led to the full experience of sadness with crying. Affect equivalents are often similar to Bill's—easily resolved through basic psychotherapeutic techniques. In the next case, this was not so; the result was tragic.

17-year-old Marlene, afflicted with cystic fibrosis and moderately severe pulmonary disease, was admitted to a pediatric hospital for routine examination and a course of intensive pulmonary care. Physical examination, chest films, and pulmonary-function studies indicated that her pulmonary pathology was not significantly more severe than at the time of her last admission for routine studies, nine months previously. Although underweight and chronically ill, she attended school regularly, worked as a counselor at the local cystic fibrosis camp, and was involved in a variety of social and academic interests. In the hospital, she complained of "nervousness" about her condition but was active, and frequently left the hospital to visit and eat with her family. One week after her admission, a young man, her close friend and fellow counselor at the summer camp, died, in the hospital, of advanced pulmonary disease. Unknown to hospital personnel, Marlene witnessed his death from the corridor. The next day, she complained of a sore throat and lack of appetite; there was no evidence of physical disease of her throat, but she remained severely anorexic in spite of attempts to help her eat. Six days later, she was hyperventilating, complained of weakness, and refused to leave her bed. Her psychogenic anorexia had resulted in metabolic acidosis compensated by the hyperventilation. Laboratory studies gave no indication of progression of her pulmonary disease. Neither anorexia nor weakness could be explained in terms of physical disease.

I saw her at that point. She appeared severely depressed and ill, breathing rapidly and barely able to lift her arms from the bed. She told me of her friend's death but said she felt no sadness about it. It didn't bother her. Her throat, she said, was all tightened up like a lump. She just didn't want to eat or get up. In my discussion with her then and on a subsequent visit, I attempted, with little or no success, to help her find a conscious awareness of the sadness and fear that were evident in her symptoms. Still she refused to eat. Her breathing became more variable and was no longer a direct response to metabolic condition. She hyperventilated when slower breathing would have been metabolically appropriate, and vice versa. Medical regulation of the fluctuations from acidosis to alkalosis became extremely difficult. In this unstable metabolic state, she suddenly expired.

Autopsy revealed only the moderate pulmonary disease. It was concluded that the affect equivalents of anorexia and lassitude, complicated by respiratory fluctuations, also of a psychogenic basis, were responsible for the metabolic disturbance which preceded her death.

Affect equivalents may be lifelong, forming a significant component of adult disability:

> A 40-year-old woman had had a febrile illness at age 6, with residual bilateral, sixth-nerve paralysis. Repeated hospitalizations for surgical correction of strabismus accentuated feelings of estrangement from her chronically ill mother and elderly father and were unsuccessful in correcting the strabismus. Prohibition of verbal expression of emotion, as with Jane, contributed to lifelong feelings of distrust of, and an expectation of being hurt by others, and to a complete absence of crying or verbally expressed sadness. Painful tearing of, and sensations in, the eyes were temporally correlated with actual experiences, or with the memory of experiences, in which disappointment or sadness would have been expected. These findings were incidental to this woman's reasons for seeking treatment, as is often the case with affect equivalents. Treatment is designed to assist emotions to find access to consciousness and to achieve integration with past and present determinants.

The Big Seven are all examples of unusual autonomic responses to affect or fantasy. Treatment may be uncomplicated, as we have seen with Jane, or may be difficult or impossible, as with steroid-dependent asthma. Treatment of asthma in adults, even when it is of long standing, may also be uncomplicated or of limited or no benefit, especially if secondary physical changes have occurred in respiratory epithelium, or alveoli.

> A 39-year-old man entered psychoanalysis for long-standing, severe, obsessive-compulsive neurosis. After one month of analysis, he described asthma of 32 years' duration, which required repeated hospitalizations when he was in latency and desensitization shots thereafter. As an adult, he had mild expiratory wheezing six–eight times each year, usually associated with times of angry frustration and helplessness. As a child, hospitalizations always meant a temporary lull in the otherwise constant fighting of his parents; as an adult, he

always arranged for desensitization shots to be given by older women, unconscious substitutes for his mother, a nurse. With gradual analysis of his obsessive-compulsive symptoms, and especially with analysis of the Oedipal aspects of those symptoms, his asthma simply ceased; he no longer sought desensitization shots. In his words, "I just felt they were no longer necessary."

An unstated implication of both the diagnostic scheme I have proposed and of the therapeutic possibilities I have described is that the clinician be a diagnostician capable of making psychological diagnoses on the basis of specific findings, a clinician who is thereby freed from the straitjacket of "wastebasket" approaches to psychological diagnosis, which emphasize "ruling out organic disease" (an impossibility) or which regulate psychological factors to a tenuous relevance ("overlay") or irrelevance ("not the business of medicine"). The physician must approach his patient through a biopsychosocial model or its equivalent, or consign himself to the position of a man who, asked to explain the nature of a strange book, limits himself to measuring and recording the physical characteristics of the book and the ink marks on its pages but rejects as irrelevant the possibility that the ink marks are symbolic expressions of meaning. Psychological diagnosis requires sophistication in recognizing and deciphering psychologically connected physical complaints. These determinations cannot be assigned to psychological testing or questionnaires, but require empathic interviewing techniques and, for most physicians, supervised training experience.

Of course, no claim is made that all instances of any of the symptoms mentioned in this discussion are determined by psychological factors; if so, diagnosis would be no problem. Failure to thrive, asthma, tearing eyes, headaches, backaches, and so on, often are the result of other determinants of disturbed physiological functioning. Treatment in many instances can be done by the knowledgeable nonpsychiatric practitioner; see, for example, the extraordinarily competent work described in the monographs and articles by a group of pediatricians (9, 10, 11).

The following points summarize some of the treatment considerations which I, and others (1, 2), have found relevant in easing psychological treatment, especially with children.

Direct psychological treatment is most apt to be successful:

1) If the symptom derives from a transitory conflict between mother and child; for example, a conflict based on reversible developmental interference or developmental disturbance.
2) If disease onset comes after the major developments of psychological structuring have occurred; that is, after age four–five years.
3) If exacerbation and remission of somatic symptoms can be correlated with specific psychological factors.

4) If therapy is provided soon after the onset of symptoms; that is, before extensive secondary elaboration of symptom meaning has occurred.
5) If cooperation can be obtained in developing new modes of affective expression, as in verbalization or sublimatory activities, and in undoing crippling defensive measures.
6) If irreversible physical changes in structure or function have not occurred.

These issues are more relevant to the success or failure of treatment than the type of symptom or its acute clinical severity.

REFERENCES

1. Furman, R.A. Psychosomatic disorders. In Furman, R.A. & Katan, A. (Eds.), *The Therapeutic Nursery School*. New York: International Universities Press, 1969.
2. Dowling, S. Psychosomatic disorders of childhood. In Copel, S. (Ed.), *Behavior Pathology of Childhood and Adolescence*. New York: Basic, 1973.
3. Graham, D. What place in medicine for psychosomatic medicine? *Psychosomatic Medicine* 41: 357–67, 1979.
4. Engel, G. The need for a new medical model: a challenge for biomedicine. *Science* 196: 129–36, 1977.
5. Engel, G. The clinical application of the biopsychosocial model. *Am. J. Psychiat.* 137: 535–44, 1980.
6. Nagera, G. *Early Childhood Disturbances, The Infantile Neurosis, and The Adult Disturbances*. New York: International Universities Press, 1966.
7. Fried, R. & Mayer, M. Socio-emotional factors accounting for growth failure in children living in institutions. *J. Pediat.* 33: 444–56, 1948.
8. Bettelheim, B. & Sylvester, E. Physical symptoms in emotionally disturbed children. *Psychoanalytic Study of the Child*, Vols. 3 & 4. New York: International Universities Press, 1949.
9. Apley, J. *The Child with Abdominal Pain*. Oxford: Blackwell Scientific, 1959.
10. Apley, J. & MacKeith, R. *The Child and His Symptoms*. Philadelphia: Davis, 1968.
11. Apley, J. & Naish, J. Limb pains in childhood. In O'Neill, D. (Ed.), *Modern Trends in Psychosomatic Medicine*. London: Butterworths, 1955.
12. Falstein, E. & Rosenblum, A. Juvenile paroxysmal supraventricular tachycardia: psychosomatic and psychodynamic aspects. *J. Am. Acad. Child Psychiat.* 1: 246–52, 1962.
13. Renbourne, E. Body temperature and pulse rate in boys and young men prior to sporting contests. A study of emotional hyperthermia with a review of the literature. *J. Psychosom. Res.* 4: 149–75, 1960.
14. White, K. & Long, W. The incidence of "psychogenic" fever in a university hospital. *J. Chron. Dis.* 8: 567–86, 1958.
15. Blank, H. & Brody, M. Recurrent herpes simplex. *Psychosom. Med.* 12: 254–60, 1950.
16. Ullman, M. On the psyche and warts. I. Suggestion and warts: a review and comment. *Psychosom. Med.* 21: 473–87, 1959.
17. Ullman, M. & Dudek, S. On the psyche and warts. II. Hypnotic suggestion and warts. *Psychosom. Med.* 22: 68–75, 1960.

12

Some Psychophysiological Problems of the Elderly

CHARLES M. GAITZ

The interplay of psychological and physiological disease is so widely recognized that hardly anyone believes it is possible to separate these disorders. Although we continue to discuss "functional" and "organic" problems as if these were mutually exclusive, the reality is that patients with organic disorders also experience psychological disturbances, and vice versa. The interrelationship between psychic and somatic aspects of illness is especially clear in elderly patients. They usually have multiple impairments, and a comprehensive evaluation almost always reveals that psychologic, physiologic, and social factors contribute to the clinical picture. One can assume, consequently, that nearly any social or health problem in an elderly person is likely to be psychophysiologic.

This has important implications for treatment. The needs of elderly persons will not be met when a treatment plan is limited to a unidisciplinary approach or when treatment is directed toward specific diseased organs or body systems, to the exclusion of associated social and emotional problems. Similarly, a treatment plan that focuses on social aspects alone will fall short. Although good nutrition, adequate housing, and opportunities for social activity contribute much to a patient's sense of well-being and good health in the broad sense, someone with congestive heart failure requires specific attention to that condition.

Here a disclaimer, if not an apology, is in order because I will not review many aspects and approaches that contribute significantly and specifically to understanding illness in elderly persons. I will not report on the rather extensive literature on the biology of aging (1), the physiology of aging (2), or the psychology of aging (3), nor will I review such topics as social psychology, theories of aging, life satisfaction, or life cycle (4). Studies of the many physiologic and psychologic parameters related to stress (5, 6) obviously have application to problems of the elderly. Without offering a literature survey, let me say that all these studies confirm that each approach, even if comparatively narrow, helps us understand the roots of problems faced by elderly persons. It follows that, to approach treatment rationally, one must consider the problems as psychophysiologic and to address a combination of stressors.

I want to share some of my experiences as a psychiatrist, who has worked for almost 25 years with persons who happen to be chronologically elderly. To begin, a few general observations on aging and illness.

AGING AND ILLNESS

It is obvious that, with increasing age, persons are more likely to have physical disorders (7). But the presence of a disorder, whether it is physical or mental, cannot be equated clearly with disability. Ideally, we should be able to distinguish between "normal" aging and disease or "abnormal" aging. In reality, however, there is much phenomenological overlap, and we find it difficult to make such distinctions. We continue to refer to the "aged" or the "elderly" as if they could be categorized as a group having similar characteristics and capacities. Actually, chronological age is of limited use in understanding elderly persons. Research has shown conclusively that there is much heterogeneity among the elderly. Measurements of physical and mental capacities show much diversity and do not correlate highly with chronological age.

Nevertheless, some trends should not be ignored. Elderly persons are likely to experience changes in most organ systems. Metabolic changes occur. Sensory impairment, such as hearing loss and poor vision, are noted with increasing frequency in older people. The trends noted range from superficial and easily observed changes such as wrinkling of the skin, to disturbances in neurotransmitter systems, which can be measured only with advanced technological procedures.

Because we still are unable to distinguish clearly between normal aging and illness, we face serious problems in diagnosing certain physical disorders, and especially mental illness. Although chronological age cannot be closely correlated with many physical and mental changes, the prevalence of some conditions increases with aging. Furthermore, late life constitutes a phase in the life cycle that has unique features, and it is helpful at times to use a life-stage approach to explain certain phenomena.

Even when a problem seems to be associated with aging, we may not be able to establish a cause-effect relationship. Are changes in a joint attributable to aging or to arthritis? Many psychological tests indicate that elderly persons have a delayed time response. How shall this be explained? Is it a manifestation of normal aging, changes in brain metabolism, neuromuscular changes, arthritis, or of alterations in perception or motivation? How should we diagnose somatic complaints? Should changes that are prevalent be considered "normal aging?" As the incidence of physical impairment increases, so do the somatic complaints of older people. But where does one draw the line between normal and abnormal processes?

Aged persons are part of a high-risk group likely to have episodes of depression, and depressed persons, regardless of age, are likely to have somatic complaints (8). But for elderly persons, particularly, in whom depression is often associated with demonstrable pathology, the clinician must distinguish etiologically between depression and such other conditions as dementia, advanced heart or pulmonary disease, or other chronic problems. The symptoms are quite similar, regardless of etiology, and it is often difficult to determine cause-and-effect relationships.

There are differences of opinion, of course, on the true nature of psychiatric disorders. Along with scientific advances in psychiatry, many experts have become inclined to emphasize biological aspects and to give less credence to social and psychological factors. Of all psychiatric diagnoses, the presence of organic brain syndrome unquestionably implies a strong relationship of symptomatology to structural and metabolic changes in the brain. Yet we know that many other factors affect the clinical picture of organic brain disease and that its symptomatology does not correlate closely with neurophysiologic and anatomic data. When changes in the brain are demonstrated with computerized tomography, for example, we still have no absolute assurance of a correlation with clinical observations. We cannot explain why some persons in whom we find changes in brain substance have dementia and others do not. Careful consideration of physiologic and psychologic stresses, however, sheds some light and helps us understand why the quality and severity of the symptoms may not match the neurophysiologic and anatomic findings.

A patient's having or lacking community and family supports may be quite influential; perhaps social support determines, more so than the quantity of structural changes in the brain, whether a person with such brain impairment will have mild or severe symptoms or adjustment problems. Social and sensory isolation has been implicated in explaining syndromes that suggest dementia. The similarities between signs of depression and dementia have already been mentioned. Even when changes in the brain can be demonstrated, much is unknown about the extent to which, and how, such clinical manifestations as delirium, depression, and paranoid ideation relate to the "organic" changes.

We know that many metabolic disorders can produce symptoms resembling an organic brain syndrome when they are associated with physical disorders of the heart, liver, kidney, and with infections. One could question whether the behavioral and cognitive changes seen in association with these conditions are really analogous to symptoms associated primarily with brain disorders. It seems reasonable to conclude that the physical disorders exert a significant stress on brain function and that the "aging brain" is more sensitive to stressors than the younger brain. This approach, while difficult to document, is useful to clinicians.

There is no doubt that increasing age is often accompanied by reduced capacity to cope with stress, but one cannot use chronological age per se to identify physical or emotional problems. We may agree that elderly persons tend to have less energy, and tire more easily, than younger persons. As diagnosticians and therapists, however, we are obligated to determine whether such complaints are caused by depression, by a physical disorder, or by processes we might appropriately consider normal aging.

Some therapists see normal aging as an irreversible pattern of deterioration and degeneration for which there is no treatment. Although this view is incorrect, the concept of changes in old age as related to disease may, paradoxically, give more hope to patients and therapists than attribution of these changes to normal aging. Another hopeful possibility is that normal aging processes might be altered by preventive measures. This may be so, but it hardly captures the interest of physicians who are oriented toward treatment of disease and not impressed by preventive measures whose effectiveness is difficult to prove.

Elderly patients may be slower, but they also have more time than younger persons do. Care-givers should keep this in mind when they allocate time for examinations and history-taking. An older patient may also require more time to recover from illness and surgery. It has been said that older persons continue sexual activity, but it takes longer. For many, it is time well spent.

Regardless of etiology, changes with aging are less disabling and produce less impairment when time is not an important factor. A 70-year-old woman may not swim as fast or as far as a 20-year-old one, and perhaps not as far as fast as she might have swum at 20. But qualitatively, the pleasure and satisfaction are the same. It may take an older person longer to shop for groceries or to eat, but elderly persons often have plenty of time to spend on these activities.

AGING AS A PSYCHOPHYSIOLOGIC DISORDER

The aging process is, of course, not limited to persons whom we label as chronologically old. In fact, labeling a person as old has to be done in a specific context. Depending on the sport, a professional athlete may be old at 20, 30, or 40. On the Supreme Court, a justice may be young at 65, and old in other contexts. Even a casual observer will quickly recognize the desirability, and inherent difficulty, of understanding or defining normal aging, since chronological age is not a reliable predictor. Value judgments, cultural attitudes, physiological changes, and disease processes have been implicated as factors altering the condition, or at least the evaluation of the condition, of elderly persons. Consequently, it behooves clinicians to evaluate chronologically ill middle-aged and older persons as having psychophysiologic disorders and to treat them accordingly. The approach is especially valid if we accept the concept that emotional problems often find expression in physical ailment or pain, and that chronic physical illness is often an exacerbation of psychiatric disorders.

Longitudinal studies ultimately may reveal cohort differences, but members of the current generations of middle-aged and older persons are quite apt to express emotional problems with physical symptoms. Ethnicity, sex, and possibly social class are fundamental factors that also deserve consideration (9, 10). But the occurrence of physical changes accentuates most persons' concern with bodily functions and performance. Cumulative and combined effects of physical or psychologic changes are easily observed, and it is helpful if clinicians remember that the middle and later stages of life have unique sociologic and psychologic characteristics, and that an interesting interplay with physiologic changes is likely to occur during this same period.

Categorizing disorders as psychophysiologic troubles some clinicians. Results of a broad diagnostic approach raise questions about etiology and the relative importance of some of the findings. A narrow diagnostic approach is less likely to stir up doubt and uncertainty, so some clinicians understandably rely on physical examination and test results and shy away from considering social and psychological factors that might require much time and personal investment.

Diagnosticians strive for precision and specificity, with the hope that these will lead to specific interventions and effective treatment. Multiple diagnoses have been challenged as avoiding this hoped-for precision and accuracy. We are taught to make as few diagnoses as possible and to explain as much as possible as being related to a single diagnosis. The reality is, however, that elderly people given careful examinations are often found to have several disorders. These conditions are likely to interact and produce both physical and mental symptoms; and etiologically, of course, both physical and mental factors are implicated. As a result, taking a comprehensive diagnostic and treatment approach is more likely to be helpful than insisting on precise cause-and-effect relationships. One cannot treat diabetes mellitus, for example, without giving attention to emotional and social considerations. The patient's acceptance of a diet and following a prescribed medical regimen depends on many factors.

DIAGNOSIS OF MENTAL DISORDERS

We have begun to use a new diagnostic manual for psychiatric disorders, developed by the American Psychiatric Association. The *Diagnostic and Statistical Manual* has been revised; for the sake of brevity, the current edition is called *DSM-III*. In considering appropriate diagnoses for the disorders we observe in elderly persons, we find that some of the newer terms in the nosology will be especially helpful in that they indicate an increasing awareness of the interaction of physical and mental conditions. Two designations are especially applicable.

Adjustment Disorders

These disorders are described as maladaptive reaction to identifiable life event(s) or circumstance(s). Maladaption is indicated by the presence of either impairment in social or occupational functioning, or symptoms or other behaviors that are in excess of the normal and expectable reaction to the stressor. Stressors, single or multiple, social, psychological, and physical, in various settings and possibly associated with specific developmental stages, may be implicated. The associated features also vary. A few that are mentioned in this diagnostic category are physical symptoms and behavioral manifestations, such as withdrawal, aggression, excessive drinking, depression, and anxiety (11).

Psychological Factors Affecting Physical Disorders

By itself, this is not considered to be a diagnosis, but it is a category that many psychiatrists will find useful. It will help document the certainty with which a clinician judges psychological factors to be contributing to the initiation or exacerbation of a physical disorder. *DSM-III* "accepts the tradition of referring to certain factors as 'psychological,' although it is by no means easy to define what this phrase means" (11). This category may be useful to describe conditions which in the past have been referred to as either "psychosomatic" or "psychophysiologic." To make the diagnosis, there should be the presence of a physical disorder and a temporal relationship between psychologically meaningful environmental stimuli and the initiation or exacerbation of the physical disorder. The environmental stimuli are judged to be contributory in a particular individual and to the initiation or exacerbation of a physical disorder (11).

Generally, one may assume that mental illness in elderly persons has many of the characteristics and the symptoms of illness and disorders observed in younger persons. Neuroses and psychoses may persist into old age, while some conditions may have their onset in late life. The symptomatology may vary in older persons, but .it often can be categorized descriptively, with syndromes as they are usually described. Older patients are likely to have experienced losses and may manifest affective disorders as a consequence. Paranoid conditions and problems related to personality disorder are not uncommon. Alcoholism, which may have persisted over many years and still be a problem in old age, may, on the other hand, be a response to an inability to cope effectively with life stresses.

The changes one can associate with aging are often ill-defined, with their etiology poorly understood. It is quite clear, however, that the problems of older people can be understood only when one considers many factors and assumes the influence of stressors in producing organic changes and behavioral changes. We are not able to describe precisely the changes occurring in the brain and their relationship to symptom formation, but those of us who work with elderly persons find it useful to refer to the "aging brain" and to recognize that it is not as adaptable and efficient as it was. The ultimate explanation for this phenomenon is not known, and may eventually be related to chemical and physiologic changes in the brain not demonstrable with currently available technologies. Generally, the diminished capacity of elderly persons to cope with stresses may in itself comprise a stressor. The diminished capacity to cope with stress has important implications for treatment.

The conditions labeled "organic brain syndrome" are particularly likely to occur in old age. The concept of an aging brain with diminished capacity to handle stress may be useful to clinicians in evaluating the mental state of persons with serious physical health problems, and in understanding what we term reversible dementia or pseudodementia. Unquestionably, certain anatomic and, presumably, neurochemical, changes occur in the brains of elderly persons; consequently these deserve special consideration.

DEMENTIA AS A PSYCHOPHYSIOLOGIC DISORDER

It is clear that the disorder now called organic brain syndrome becomes more prevalent in older age groups. Why this occurs is not entirely clear, but it is certain that there is an interaction of social and physical health aspects. Several theories have been advanced, but there is no universal agreement on cause and effect.

Most elderly persons who are referred to a psychiatrist because they have symptoms suggesting dementia are likely to have senile dementia of the Alzheimer's type. Others may be better diagnosed as having multi-infarct dementia. Not many years ago, we tended to diagnose "hardening of the arteries," based on a strong conviction that impaired blood circulation explained the condition we were then labeling chronic brain syndrome, or "senility." We now know that blood circulation to the brain of elderly persons may be diminished, but we doubt that diminished blood flow per se is *the* critical factor in producing symptoms. Diminished blood flow may be related more to scarring or to decreased size of the brain and not be the primary cause of dementia.

Researchers have recently reported findings of various neurophysiologic and morphologic changes in the aging brain. Changes in neurotransmitter systems, in cell membranes, in loss of cells, in types of cells, accumulation of lipofuscin, and other alterations too numerous to mention, have been implicated. As researchers cannot agree on the importance of these changes, pity the clinician responsible for rational treatment based on etiology of persons who have symptoms of dementia!

Although most of these patients probably do not have reversible conditions, careful evaluation may reveal that some have brain tumors, infections, systemic diseases, diseases of other organ systems, or head trauma producing a subdural hematoma, metabolic disorders, and other conditions that may be associated with symptoms indistinguishable from dementia.

Appropriate and specific treatment for certain conditions often dramatically reverses the mental disorder. An elderly person with uremia or coronary insufficiency may, for example, present symptoms indistinguishable from symptoms associated with primary neuronal degeneration. A brain tumor may be overlooked if the patient is chronologically aged, because of the stereotypical view that elderly persons have irreversible dementia. A history of declining cognitive functions may be quickly attributed to senile dementia, and other diagnoses may be scarcely considered. Psychiatrists should always think of the possibility that cognitive changes seen in elderly persons may be related to reversible etiologies. They must also consider the importance of social and psychological factors. Social isolation, changes in social roles, losses by death of significant persons, losses of self-esteem, income, prestige, and other stresses may be important in understanding the onset and progression of cognitive changes.

Environmental manipulation and psychotherapy to alleviate the severity of these stresses may be very helpful. The behavioral manifestations of cognitive impairment may be correlated with results of neuropsychologic testing, blood-flow studies, electroencephalography, and the more recently available computerized tomography. But there are many exceptions. Environmental stress and premorbid personality also are to be weighed carefully by the clinicians in evaluating elderly persons and their families.

Rationally, we must approach elderly persons as likely to have psychophysiologic disorders, knowing that it is impossible to treat them adequately by using only an organ system-disease approach. It also is impossible to treat elderly persons with such psychiatric disorders as depression, dementia, and psychoses, without giving attention to their physical health status. Age-related changes in metabolism, which might affect drug reactions, deserve special attention. Considerations like these become important when we must decide whether the risks in giving an elderly depressed patient a tricyclic antidepressant are greater than the risks associated with electroconvulsive therapy. Age of the patient, then, is a factor in making decisions about treatment.

IMPLICATIONS FOR TREATMENT

Timing of intervention is important. What are the critical problems? Which ones deserve immediate attention? What is the patient and his or her family ready to accept? When life is at stake, the answers are relatively clear. A patient who has recently had a stroke and is in shock must be given treatment addressed to these conditions before one worries about financial matters, health status of the spouse, or willingness of the spouse and other family members to help in a rehabilitation program. But ultimately these will be important factors. Similarly, a patient with a bleeding ulcer may need psychiatric counseling after the ulcer is treated. Persons with progressive dementia may be helped, with environmental manipulation, to relieve or minimize external stresses, and giving family members some assistance may also help, but the timing of intervention is important and will be determined by an appraisal of the patient's physical and psychological capabilities.

The following case illustrates why treatment cannot be directed exclusively to either physical or psychological disorders, and that timing of intervention is important.

> An 82-year-old widower living in a nursing home was referred for psychiatric consultation because he was depressed. However, the patient, who had only one lung, complained of shortness of breath, had edema of the feet and ankles, and his color was ashen. Obviously, it was necessary to give attention to these symptoms, although the man was clearly depressed. His children had not visited him for a long time, and he was convinced he had made a mistake in moving from another city, where he had lived for years. He felt isolated but was ambivalent about returning to his old home because of memories associated with his wife's death a year ago.

He was unable to face some of these factors contributing to his depression, until his physical condition improved. Then he made some decisions that led to an improved mental state. First, he had to know that he was well enough physically to be able to consider several options regarding matters that were important psychologically.

Rehabilitation of persons with physical impairments may be stymied unless attention is given to the patient's motivation and willingness to proceed with therapy. Psychiatrists often observe that patients who respond to treatment for depression become more hopeful and more willing to follow medical regimens and to participate in physical therapies. Socializing with other older persons helps an elderly handicapped patient to accept his or her own need for help. Sharing concerns with other old people seems to help newly admitted patients in institutions. Discussions with peers may reveal possibilities for meaningful experiences which the patients had not considered. With social contacts, elderly persons may gain the confidence to cope with their situations, and they may even be able to remain out of institutions.

The following short case study illustrates the importance of combining treatment for psychological and physical health problems. Obviously, these conditions can be treated concurrently or sequentially, depending on the circumstances.

> A 74-year-old woman was referred for psychiatric treatment when she was hospitalized because she had failed to respond to prolonged outpatient treatment for high blood pressure. Varying medications and dosages had done little more than produce side effects.
>
> Psychiatric examination clearly showed her to be depressed. She was upset about having been compelled to place her husband, who had advanced symptoms of organic brain syndrome, in a nursing home. Exhausted by the demands of nursing him at home, she could no longer be responsible for his safety and care. She was living in her home, driving a car, and she visited her husband daily. His disturbed behavior and failure to recognize her invariably upset her. She was particularly distressed when he identified a resident of the nursing home as his wife. During the two months after his admission, her depression had deepened, and the marked increase in hypertension required a brief stay in the hospital. Afterward, in supportive psychotherapy at one- and two-week intervals, she began to accept her husband's condition and his need for institutional care. Soon, she started to explore other interests and activities, joined a senior center, and grew less tense and depressed. She continued visiting her husband, but less frequently, and felt less guilt. Regretfully acknowledging his condition would not improve, she was finding pleasure in activities on her own and with her children. As the depressive symptoms cleared up, her blood pressure decreased; a relatively simple medical regimen sufficed to control it.

Elderly patients usually have multiple problems; indeed, this patient had to be treated for arthritis and allergy and several other somatic complaints during the next several months. But with reassurance that her health was fairly normal, she improved to the point of being able to take vacations out of the city, trusting her husband's care to the nursing home's personnel.

The recognition that psychological factors contributed to this patient's failure to respond to treatment for hypertension had resulted in her referral for psychiatric treatment. Brief psychotherapy helped her to improve both physically and emotionally.

Other aspects of the comprehensive care approach should be highlighted. Deciding what is important to elderly persons may constitute a value judgment. They may derive much benefit from attention to comparatively minor conditions. For example, aged individuals, if they have arthritis, cannot bend over and give adequate attention to foot care. Improving locomotion by treating their ingrown toenails has helped to improve the quality of life for many people.

Clinicians should give adequate attention to nutrition. Many elderly persons who live alone decide that preparing balanced meals is too much trouble. This may be a manifestation of depression, but whatever the reason, elderly persons may suffer the consequences of inadequate fluid and food intake.

Therapists also should determine whether or not patients understand prescriptions. It may be beyond the capacity of an elderly person to remember complex instructions, such as using different strengths of eye drops and a different number of drops in each eye. Even mildly demented patients have difficulty remembering when to take medications; the simpler a medical regimen, the better. A patient recently was advised to discontinue one tranquilizer and substitute another. Instead, he continued taking both and then had to be treated for a variety of side effects. Elderly persons are likely to be taking several medications, each of which may have been prescribed appropriately. Although a patient may decide that the doctor treating his depression does not have to know about the medicine he is taking for hypertension, arthritis, and gastrointestinal disease, it behooves the therapist to check carefully on all of the patient's medications. The cumulative effects of medications and drug-drug interactions may well affect the patient's status (12). We must know, for example, that a patient understands he should be taking 40 units of U100 insulin, not 100 units of U40 insulin, and that spouses and other family members who may be helping the patient are competent to do so. It was assumed, for example, that both members of a couple, one of whom had a hearing impairment and the other of whom was nearly blind, could help each other. It turned out that neither one understood the medication instructions, and the consequence was overmedication.

CONCLUSIONS

Elderly persons are likely to have a combination of psychological, social, and physical health problems. Rational treatment requires, therefore, that we approach their care in a manner appropriate to psychophysiologic disorders. Obviously, specific treatment should be administered when needed, but general measures based on the premise that aging processes represent stresses may be useful. Eliminating the time dimension as a pressure is important: Elderly patients need more time to think and express themselves, to formulate ideas in interviews, and to recover from illnesses. Balancing expectations with performance is easier when we accept that an elderly person's mind and body may be less resilient, creative, and productive when he or she is subjected to stress.

These general principles, rather than a specific treatment or cure approach, are helpful to therapists as well. Many conditions are treatable, and a full range of therapeutic modalities is available. Chronological age should not be the critical factor in prescribing treatment; few disorders are clearly associated with aging; and, in turn, therapeutic techniques applicable to young persons also benefit older patients.

Old people are likely to have both psychologic and somatic disorders concurrently; and treatment, to give attention to both types of illness, should not be limited to the disease or the organ system primarily involved. To be trite, the *individual* having these disorders must be treated—not the disorders. Finally, therapists should not be misled by using chronological age as a determinant for either diagnosis or treatment; to do so often leads to premature closure and therapeutic nihilism.

REFERENCES

1. Finch, C.E. & Hayflick, L. *Handbook of the Biology of Aging*. New York: Van Nostrand, 1977.
2. Reichel, W. *The Geriatric Patient*. New York: HP Publishing, 1978.
3. Birren, J.E. & Schaie, J.P. *Handbook of the Psychology of Aging*. New York: Van Nostrand, 1977.
4. Binstock, R.H. & Shanas, E. *Handbook of Aging and the Social Sciences*. New York: Van Nostrand, 1976.
5. Dohrenwend, B.P. & Dohrenwend, B.S. *Stressful Life Events: Their Nature and Effects*. New York: Wiley, 1974.
6. Gaitz, C.M. & Varner, R.V. Adjustment disorders. In Busse, E.W. & Blazer, D.G. (Eds.), *Handbook of Geriatric Psychiatry*. New York: Van Nostrand, 1980.
7. Riley, M.W. & Foner, A. *Aging and Society*. New York: Russel Sage Foundation, 1968, pp. 204–20.
8. Gaitz, C.M. Depression in the Elderly. In Fann, W.E. (Ed.), *Phenomenology and Treatment of Depression*. New York: Spectrum, 1977.
9. Scott, J.C. & Gaitz, C.M. Ethnic and age differences in mental health measurements. *Dis. Nerv. Sys.* 36: 389–93, 1975.
10. Antunes, G., Gordon, C., Gaitz, C.M., & Scott, J. Ethnicity, socioeconomic status, and the etiology of psychological distress. *Sociol. Soc. Res.* 58: 361–68, 1974.
11. DSM-III Draft. *Diagnostic and Statistical Manual of Mental Disorders*, third edition. American Psychiatric Association, 1978.
12. Hartford, J.T. How to minimize side effects of psychotropic drugs. *Geriat.* 34: 83–93, 1979.

13

Sleep Disorders and Their Psychiatric Significance

SABRI DERMAN
ROBERT L. WILLIAMS
ISMET KARACAN

The last decade witnessed a rapid growth in the number of sleep laboratories and sleep researchers. In the eighties, sleep evaluation is expected to become a routine part of patient evaluation. The abundant data collected to date will not only help physicians in their daily practice, but will also facilitate the communication between sleep researchers and a variety of other medical specialists. With additional assistance from bioengineers and computer specialists, medical experts are revealing unsolved problems in the basic mechanisms of sleep and its disorders.

DISORDERS OF SLEEP AND AROUSAL

In the past decade, clinicians and investigators have individually devised several working classification schemes which, although somewhat arbitrary, have demonstrated their practical value (1). Nevertheless, the rapidly growing sophistication of observation tools and lengthening list of sleep-associated symptoms seen by clinicians have emphasized the need for a sleep nosology that could be shared by all researchers and clinicians in the field. In response to that need, the Association for the Psychophysiological Study of Sleep (APSS) held the first formal workshop on the nosology and nomenclature of sleep disorders, in 1972. The year 1975 marked the formation of the Association of Sleep Disorders Centers (ASDC). The following year, the ASDC appointed a nosology committee which eventually became the Sleep Disorders Classification Committee. Its task was to create a diagnostic system for sleep and arousal disorders, a comprehensive collection of all conditions encountered clinically. This work culminated in late 1979, when the "Diagnostic Classification of Sleep and Arousal Disorders" first appeared in *Sleep* (2).

The new classification system is divided into four main sections. The first classifies the disorders of initiating and maintaining sleep (DIMS); the second covers the disorders of excessive somnolence (DOES); the third examines the disorders of the sleep-wake schedule; and the last describes the dysfunctions associated with sleep, sleep stages, or partial arousal, including abnormal behaviors and symptoms appearing during sleep.

DIMS: Disorders of Initiating and Maintaining Sleep

DIMS are a heterogeneous group of conditions formerly defined as insomnia. As many as 75 million people are estimated to complain about the quality or quantity of their sleep. Over 200 million hypnotic medications were prescribed in the United States between 1971 and 1976 (3). An additional large population is seeking help from over-the-counter sleeping compounds. Since 1971, there has been a gradual decline in the prescription of hypnotic drugs, which probably reflects the more cautious use of medication, rather than any decline in complaints of insomnia. Difficulty in initiating and maintaining "sufficient" nighttime sleep remains one of the most common sleep disorders. Yet, the complaint of insomnia seldoms concerns the physician enough to discover its underlying etiology, which is usually obscure because multiple causes contribute to the final symptoms. Like other nonspecific signs such as fever, complaints of insomnia should be traced to specific causes and treated directly.

With advancing age, the sleep parameters of healthy, normal individuals show certain predictable changes (4). While the average sleep latency and number of awakenings increase with age, the total sleep time and amount of slow-wave sleep (SWS) decreases. Consequently, sleep efficiency decreases from 0.95 in youth to 0.84 in the elderly. Physicians must also be cautioned against treating for insomnia the so-called short sleepers, who require less sleep than average. Short sleepers typically complain of insomnia when, in a futile attempt to get "normal" amounts of sleep, they force themselves to spend more time than necessary in bed. Prescribing hypnotics for such short sleepers leads eventually to a real DIMS problem.

DIMS can have psychophysiological causes, be associated with psychiatric disorders, or result from drug and alcohol use.

DIMS with Psychophysiological Causes

DIMS with psychophysiological causes can be either transient and situational or persistent.

Transient and situational DIMS is a brief period of sleep disturbance usually initiated by acute emotional arousal. Its main features, difficulty falling asleep, intermittent awakenings, and early-morning arousal, are occasionally experienced by everyone. Generally, the affected individual is not sleepy during the day, but complains of fatigue, pains, and tiredness. The disturbance lasts less than three weeks from the onset of the precipitating event; shortly after the resolution of the emotional reaction, sleep returns to normal. Transient DIMS requires serious medical treatment only when the sleep disorder exacerbates a preexisting medical or psychiatric condition or results from a medical (involving pain, discomfort, metabolic disturbance, physical therapy), toxic, or environmental condition. The fleeting nature of such problems makes successful short-term treatment with hypnotics possible.

Unlike transient or situational DIMS, the persistent psychophysiological DIMS generally lasts much longer than three weeks. Unrelated to recent events, the disorder is caused by long-standing tension or anxiety, internal arousal, or negative conditioning to sleep. Patients with persistent DIMS generally do not sense their chronic tension and anxiety but instead tend to somatize, complaining of restlessness, hyperactivity, tension headaches, palpitations, and cervical or lower back pain. Such patients tend to sleep better on weekends, holidays, or trips away from their original environment. Patients whose sleep disorder results from internal arousal and negative conditioning typically complain of a sleep-onset difficulty or inability to go back to sleep after awakening at night.

DIMS Associated with Psychiatric Disorders

DIMS is found in several types of psychiatric disorders; i.e., personality disorders, affective psychoses, and other functional psychoses.

DIMS associated with personality disorders is a sleep-onset and intermediary-sleep-maintenance insomnia that is clearly related to the psychological and behavioral symptoms of the clinically established and classified nonaffective and nonpsychotic psychiatric disorders. The severity and fluctuation patterns of the clinical symptoms usually closely parallel those of insomnia. Many of the symptoms appear to depict an imperfectly successful attempt to control anxiety. Numerous psychiatric problems, including anxiety, hypochondriasis, obsessive-compulsive neurosis, and various personality disorders, may be associated with DIMS. Careful psychiatric evaluation and treatment usually remedy insomnia as the patient's psychiatric condition improves.

DIMS are frequently found in patients with affective disorders. Sleeplessness has been observed for decades as one of the major components of both depression and mania. In one of the earliest clinical applications of sleep EEG, Diaz-Guerrero et al. (5) evaluated six young manic-depressive, depressed type, patients in the sleep laboratory. Although REM sleep had not yet been discovered, their findings were basically in accordance with our present knowledge. These investigators recognized that "the disturbed sleep of patients with manic-depressive psychosis, depressed type, is not only characterized by difficulty in falling asleep and/or by early or frequent awakenings, but by both a greater proportion of sleep which is light and more frequent oscillations from one level to another than normally occur" (5) (p. 404).

Sleep patterns are more or less similar in different forms and degrees of unipolar depression. However, the severity of the DIMS is closely correlated with the severity of the affective pathology. Although patients with unipolar depression have either normal or moderately increased sleep latency, the most typical characteristic of their sleep is repeated awakenings leading eventually to early-morning awakenings. Therefore, their cardinal complaint is waking up early and not being able to return to sleep. Sleep polysomnography, which reveals significantly shortened REM latency and reduced stages-3-and-4 sleep, usually confirms this complaint.

Sleep disturbance may foreshadow impending depression and can often be detected before the clinical signs of depression clearly develop. DIMS are also found in patients with less severe depressions, depressed mood reactions, and in depressed children. In patients suffering from secondary depression—depression occurring in connection with other psychiatric and/or medical syndromes—the major characteristics of DIMS persist. Although the percentage of REM sleep is usually decreased in these patients, REM latency may not be reduced, as it is in other forms of depression.

The sleep pattern of patients with hypomania or mania contrasts with that of patients in a depressive state. The former have severe sleep-onset insomnia and a short total sleep time (TST). They do not try to go back to sleep once awakened at night, and feel refreshed after two to four hours of sleep. REM latency may also be slightly shortened and percentages of stages-3-and-4 sleep decreased. The most striking feature of hypomanic or manic patients is that they seldom complain of sleep disturbance, maintaining the high arousal level until they are completely exhausted.

For more information on sleep patterns in patients with affective disorders, the reader is referred to several articles (6, 7, 8, 9).

The major psychosis associated with DIMS is schizophrenia. Growing interest in the hypothesis that there is a relationship between dreaming and psychosis led to Dement's pioneering study of sleep parameters in schizophrenia (10). Although Dement's working hypothesis—that there are consistent, early, recognizable differences between schizophrenic and normal dream content— failed to produce definitive results, such early correlational studies led to REM-deprivation studies, which played an important role in the overall evolution of sleep research. Dement's study indicated that there were no significant differences in the eye motility of schizophrenics and normals during REM sleep, but that REM latency was shorter for schizophrenic patients, who also reported less dream recall. However, difficulties in specifying particular types of schizophrenic patients, their clinical status at the point of the study, and the extent of their medication use, make comparison difficult.

In his recent review, Zarcone (11) noted that studies of sleep variables for schizophrenic patients have yielded inconsistent results. Various researchers have found REM-sleep variables such as latency to the onset of the first REM period, eye-movement activity, number of awakenings, REM-period number and duration—as well as other sleep variables such as percent of sleep stages 3 and 4 and electrodermal activity—to be either increased, decreased, or the same as in comparison populations.

Reich et al. (12) examined different sleep correlates in schizoaffective, latent, and acute schizophrenic patients, and reviewed several earlier studies. They concluded that the schizoaffective and psychotic-depressed groups had short REM latencies and increased REM density, while acute schizophrenics had more sleep disturbances and decreased amounts of NREM sleep. REM latency was shortest in patients who required antidepressant therapy. Decreases in SWS were attributed to depression in all of the schizophrenic patients. Feinberg (13) had suggested, in an earlier study, that decreased SWS is probably symptomatic of the chronic stress commonly seen in either prolonged endogenous depression or schizophrenia.

One of the most prevalent sleep disturbances in acute schizophrenic patients is the inability to fall asleep. Anxiety and increased motor activity heightened by delusions and hallucinations keep agitated patients awake for hours. Once asleep, they may spend a close-to-normal amount of time in bed (TIB), but their sleep is usually disturbed by frequent awakenings. As a result, the schizophrenic patient's arising time might gradually shift from morning to afternoon.

There have been a number of REM-deprivation studies comparing schizophrenic with nonschizophrenic patients (14, 15, 16, 17, 18). It appears that actively schizophrenic patients fail to rebound after deprivation nights, whereas nonschizophrenic controls show REM rebound both in total REM time and REM percentage. In other studies, however, REM rebound in schizophrenic patients was noted (19, 20).

Observations by Dement and coworkers (21) led to the hypothesis that REM phasic events intrude into wakefulness and cause schizophrenic symptoms. The schizophrenic patient consequently experiences "an unpredictable mixture of externally and internally generated perceptions" (11) (p. 34).

Wyatt et al. (22) postulated that the intrusion of REM phasic events into wakefulness is based on a malfunction of serotonin synthesis and a failure of REM phasic activity inhibition. Predicting a decrease in clinical symptoms, Wyatt et al. administered to nonparanoid schizophrenics a serotonin-precursor—5-HTP—combined with a peripheral decarboxylase inhibitor. The researchers' predictions were confirmed; the experimentally treated, nonparanoid schizophrenics significantly improved. Paranoid schizophrenics, however, either remained unchanged or became worse on 5-HTP. Therefore, there may be subgroups of schizophrenics with more severe REM phasic-event intrusion who will benefit from this type of treatment. Unfortunately, since Wyatt et al. failed to report sleep polysomnographic data and based their observations on nursing scales, documentation of the effect of 5-HTP on sleep parameters is unavailable.

DIMS Associated With the Use of Drugs and Alcohol

DIMS can be induced by drugs acting on the central nervous system (CNS), either with administration or withdrawal, or by the use of alcohol and its withdrawal. For a more comprehensive review of this topic, refer to books edited by Kales (23) and Williams and Karacan (24).

DIMS are often triggered by the daily use of CNS depressants, including barbiturates; nonbarbiturate sleep agents such as glutethimide, chloral hydrate, methaqualone, and ethchlorvynol; beverage ethanol; over-the-counter and prescription antihistamines; sedatives; bromides; rapid-metabolizing benzodiazepines; and slow-metabolizing benzodiazepines taken in high doses. Typically, patients are prescribed these drugs for treatment of nonspecific insomnia, without a detailed diagnostic work-up for underlying pathology. Hospitals routinely dispense hypnotics to relax the patient and promote sleep. Since the drugs lose their sleep-inducing effect within the first few weeks, the patient—or, often, the physician—increases the dosage, leading to the development of tolerance and physical and/or psychological dependence on the medication. A relatively large group of insomniacs are preoccupied, or overly concerned, with the quantity and quality of their sleep, medication effectiveness, and the relationship of their sleep disturbance to their daytime activities. Aware of the dangers of taking sleeping pills for prolonged periods, these patients often try to cut consumption or quit completely. The resulting withdrawal symptoms—nausea, muscle tension and cramps, aches, restlessness, and irritability—convince the patients that a cure for their insomnia is hopeless and that they need the medications in order to sleep. When evaluated in the sleep laboratory while taking medications, these patients usually have decreased percentages of slow-wave and REM sleep, increased stages-1-and-2 sleep, frequent stage changes, as well as reduced spindles, K-complexes, delta activity, and rapid eye movements. Patients taking high doses of barbiturates show fast EEG activity in frontal areas of the brain.

DIMS are also associated with the prolonged use of CNS stimulants. Today CNS stimulants are used extensively in everyday life, with or without medical supervision. The sustained use of analeptic agents, amphetamines, diet pills, and caffeine causes insomnia, especially if consumed later in the day and/or in excessive amounts. Patients taking high doses of CNS stimulants present with prolonged sleep latency, decreased total sleep time, and frequent awakenings.

Both SWS and REM sleep percentages are reduced. Disturbed sleep, in turn, instigates daytime tiredness and sleepiness. This leads the patient to increase the daytime stimulant dosage in order to maintain alertness, and sometimes to take hypnotics in order to restore nocturnal sleep. Individuals using stimulants for extended periods and/or in high doses are also susceptible to symptoms secondary to medication; i.e., anxiety, irritability, personality changes, inability to concentrate, and depression.

Like many other drug-related DIMS, insomnia associated with CNS stimulants usually begins with the temporary prescription of small amounts of stimulants. The stimulants soon become a routine part of the patient's daily medication. Too frequently, patients are prescribed stimulants, upon suspicion of narcolepsy, without sleep polysomnographic documentation. When the medication is decreased or abandoned completely, REM rebound is inevitable. This withdrawal is often associated with an increased incidence of nightmares, in addition to restlessness and other symptoms of drug withdrawal. When CNS stimulant consumption is the suspected cause of DIMS, it is important for the clinician to withdraw the patient from the medication under medical supervision and to evaluate him in a sleep laboratory after at least a two-week, drug-free period. Patients prescribed amphetamines or comparable drugs for narcolepsy, without polysomnographic documentation, should receive similar supervision and evaluation. For more information on this topic, refer to Kay et al. (25), Oswald (26), and Hartmann (27).

A number of studies (28, 29, 30, 31, 32, 33, 34) have revealed that caffeine, widely consumed in coffee, affects most sleep parameters. When given to the subject 30 minutes before bedtime, coffee and caffeine significantly increased sleep latency, and shifted the bulk of stage-1-REM sleep to the first half of the night, and stages-3-and-4 sleep to the second half of the night. In other words, the normal distribution of these stages throughout the night was reversed. Subjective ratings of sleep were also lower when compared to baseline values. Significantly, decaffeinated coffee failed to produce similar sleep disturbances. Although the mechanism of action of caffeine on sleep is unknown, there is circumstantial evidence that it affects serotonin and catecholamine synthesis (35, 36, 37).

The prolonged use and/or withdrawal of a large variety of drugs which are not CNS stimulants or depressants can also lead to DIMS. Thyroid preparations, anticonvulsant agents, ACTH, alpha-methyl-DOPA, and agents such as diazepam, major tranquilizers, and sedating tricyclics interfere with normal nocturnal sleep. Clinicians must keep in mind that if the action of a prescribed medication is associated with REM suppression, withdrawal from it may lead to REM rebound, often precipitating dream disturbances and nightmares.

Both research and patient management have implicated acute and chronic alcohol use as a cause of DIMS. In chronic alcoholics, the sleep structure disintegrates, total sleep time decreases, REM sleep becomes fragmented, and its percentage of total sleep time reduced. During withdrawal, SWS usually decreases or disappears, transient REM increase is observed, and sleep-onset insomnia is common. In severe cases, the patient may never regain a normal sleep structure. Patients presenting with alcohol-related DIMS should be carefully evaluated for possible underlying motivations for alcohol consumption as well as for other psychophysiological DIMS preceding or not specifically resulting from alcohol use (38, 39, 40).

DIMS may also accompany symptomatically vague, less common clinical conditions, which are described in the new classification system (2). DIMS associated with sleep apnea syndromes, alveolar hypoventilation syndrome, nocturnal myoclonus and restless legs syndrome, as well as various medical, toxic, and environmental conditions, require careful differential diagnosis and cause-oriented treatment (41, 42).

DOES: Disorders of Excessive Somnolence

The disorders of excessive somnolence are a heterogeneous group of syndromes in which sleepiness and/or sudden, uncontrollable spells of sleep (sleep attacks) are the major symptoms. Two of the more prevalent syndromes, narcolepsy and sleep apnea (sleep-induced respiratory disorders), are relatively easy to diagnose through an appropriate sleep laboratory evaluation. Others, such as DOES due to psychophysiological problems or idiopathic hypersomnolence, have more complicated and puzzling clinical pictures. In either case, prescribing a CNS stimulant to a patient who complains of excessive daytime sleepiness is generally more harmful than helpful. As previously mentioned, stimulants tend to increase sleep disturbance and create drug dependency and withdrawal problems.

DOES Associated With Psychophysiological Conditions

As in the DIMS, DOES associated with psychophysiological conditions are divided into the transient and situational type and the persistent type.

The main feature of the transient and situational type is disruption of the sleep-wake cycle, marked by unusually increased TIB and TST and frequent daytime naps. Excessive daytime sleepiness and fatigue occur in response to an identifiable, recent stressful event. Transient hypersomnolence disappears within three weeks after termination of the source of stress. During this period, neither sleep structure and cycles nor individual sleep-stage durations and proportions change significantly. Some individuals develop the habit of reacting to disappointment by seeking refuge in sleep (or in bed). In this case, excessive spells of sleepiness are episodic, lasting for a few days and reoccurring in an irregular pattern. Although these episodes might be classified as transitory depressed periods, patients who react in this manner do not necessarily appear to be depressed.

Persistent complaints of excessive daytime sleepiness are characteristic of individuals who have a chronic disposition to weariness, excessive sleepiness, bedrest, and daytime napping when unable to cope with tension and stress. No polygraphically demonstrated increase of daily total sleep time accompanies the complaints. Long naps and rests in bed compound the problem by disturbing the normal diurnal rhythm, leading to more daytime sleepiness and sleep spells. This type of hypersomnolence may be a somatically expressed form of mild depression. Taking sedatives for "nerves" not only fails to improve the condition, but tends to aggravate the symptoms. It is important to distinguish this condition from the symptoms of drug abuse and other organic conditions, especially nocturnal myoclonus, which may actually reflect nocturnal sleep disturbance.

DOES Associated With Psychiatric Disorders

Disorders of excessive somnolence can also be associated with affective disorders and other functional disorders. DOES is observed in both major affective and other depressive syndromes, but is most characteristic of the depressed phase of the bipolar affective disorder. In major bipolar depression, a nocturnal polysomnographic evaluation usually reveals short REM latency and decreased amounts of SWS. Subjectively, patients complain of not getting enough sleep and of feeling unrefreshed in the morning. However, polysomnographic recordings reveal that they typically obtain normal or prolonged amounts of sleep, without any significant increase in the number of awakenings.

Generally, patients with excessive daytime somnolence need to be as carefully evaluated as patients complaining of insomnia. The severity of depression and the presence of vegetative symptoms must be documented in order to differentiate this disorder from DOES associated with persistent psychophysiological conditions. Functional disorders associated with excessive somnolence include personality disorders, dissociative disorder, hypochondriasis, borderline states, conversion, and schizophrenia.

DOES Associated With Use of Drugs and Alcohol

The use of either CNS stimulants or depressants often results in DOES. Patients who become habituated or physiologically dependent on CNS stimulants experience daytime sleepiness, difficulty with arousal from sleep, and morning drowsiness, especially when the growth of tolerance to, and/or withdrawal from, these drugs is involved. CNS stimulant users and abusers frequently complain of irritability, rapid mood changes, automatic behaviors, and seemingly paradoxical hypersomnolence. Although increasing the dosage temporarily relieves daytime sleepiness, it reoccurs to an even greater degree when the drug wears off. Just as chronic users of sleeping pills take stimulants to improve daytime functioning, chronic users of CNS stimulants may take sleeping pills to overcome the arousal effects of high-dose stimulants on nocturnal sleep. Progressive dependence on the excessive use of caffeinated beverages such as coffee also contributes to daytime sleepiness, especially to morning drowsiness.

The sustained use of CNS depressants (opiates, barbiturates, tranquilizers, and alcohol), as well as the intake of a variety of medications for sleep-unrelated medical conditions (antihypertensive medication, antiepileptics, contraceptive pills, antihistamines, beta-adrenergic blockers, muscle relaxants) can cause excessive hypersomnolence. Once the physician is aware of possible sources of DOES associated with the use of CNS stimulants and depressants, differential diagnosis is not difficult.

A comprehensive examination of DOES associated with psychophysiological and psychiatric conditions, as well as drug use, can be found elsewhere (25, 26, 27, 43, 44).

DOES Associated With Sleep-Induced Respiratory Impairment

This group of sleep-induced respiratory impairments consists of the sleep apnea DOES syndrome and the alveolar hypoventilation DOES syndrome.

A relatively recent clinical and research interest, sleep apnea has quickly become a major diagnostic and treatment concern due to its association with cardiovascular-disease fatalities and its suspected relationship to sudden infant deaths. Furthermore, its obscure pathology has drawn the attention of researchers in the basic medical sciences who are exploring the interactions of sleep, respiration, and cardiovascular regulatory mechanisms.

A respiratory disorder is diagnosed as a sleep apnea syndrome if both nasal and oral airflow cease for longer than 10 seconds and more than 30 times during a seven-hour sleep period. The majority of apnea patients greatly exceed these criteria, exhibiting as many as 600 episodes, some of them lasting up to two minutes each. Based on the respiratory motor output of the CNS, there are three different types of sleep apnea: central, obstructive, and mixed. The patient's diaphragmatic effort reflects this output, which is determined polysomnographically via intraesophageal-pressure measurements. In central apnea, the airflow ceases due to a lack of motor output to the chest. Obstructive apnea, also known as the upper-airways or occlusive type, is due to blockage of the oropharynx, which occurs despite the continuous effort of the respiratory muscles. The mixed type starts as a central apnea episode, but is followed by an obstructive episode.

Respiratory motor output then increases gradually, and after the release of the obstruction—often accompanied by brief arousal or complete awakening— breathing resumes. Generally, respiration at the onset of the apnea episode is in the form of a brief hyperventilation characterized by increased rate and tidal volume. During an apnea episode, a progressive O_2-desaturation and $PECO_2$-increase occur. Apnea and breathing periods are usually associated with varying degrees of brady-tachycardia. Other EKG abnormalities, especially premature ventricular contractions (PVCs) are also common. Current data suggest that sleep-apnea-associated arrythmias in this patient group are not random events, but a direct result of the altered and abnormal sleep state (45). Schroeder et al. (46) reported cyclic changes in both systemic and pulmonary arterial pressure, corresponding to sleep apnea periods.

Although sleep apnea syndrome strikes predominantly middle-aged, overweight males, it occurs at all ages and in both sexes. A long-standing history of loud snoring is its most prominent symptom. Other important symptoms of sleep apnea syndrome are excessive daytime sleepiness, prolonged but unrefreshing naps, disorientation, and periods of automatic behavior accompanied by amnesia. Besides frequent arousals and awakenings, the sleep EEG reveals decreased or absent SWS in apneic patients. In some cases, early onset of REM sleep is observed, probably owing to chronic REM deprivation caused by the frequent arousals.

Sleep apnea syndrome is a chronic and progressive problem leading eventually to significant impairment due to excessive sleepiness. Secondary debilities often resulting from this disorder include reduced intellectual capacity, personality changes, sudden bursts of anger and hostility, impaired social life, and disturbed family relations. In addition, impotence, a frequent secondary complaint, aggravates marital problems. In children, poor school performance, hyperactivity with hypersomnolent episodes, and a reversion to nocturnal enuresis despite completed toilet training are common.

Until a better understanding of its pathology is obtained, the treatment of sleep apnea syndrome must remain symptomatic. So far, weight reduction and tracheostomy have been the most successful therapeutic measures for relieving daytime symptoms and decreasing nocturnal episodes. The efficacy of medical treatment using various respiratory stimulants as well as of the experimental use of various medications such as progesterone requires further substantiation. A phrenic pacemaker for central-type apnea is a promising treatment, yet its current lack of wider application as well as the need for long-term patient follow-up preclude present practicality. Two books (47, 48) and several recent papers (49, 50, 51,52) offer up-to-date information on sleep apnea syndromes.

The alveolar hypoventilation syndrome, another cause of DOES, differs from sleep apnea in that respiratory hypoventilation appears or significantly worsens during sleep, but there are few or no apneic spells. Although most frequently encountered in grossly overweight individuals, this syndrome is also found in patients with myotonic dystrophy, narcolepsy, poliomyelitis and other CNS infections, ventrolateral cervical spinal cord lesions, and CNS neoplasia (53, 54).

DOES Associated With Nocturnal Myoclonus and "Restless Legs" Syndrome

Nocturnal myoclonus and the "restless legs" syndrome disturb sleep by causing frequent arousals and brief awakenings. Patients suffering from these disorders are generally unaware of the nocturnal disturbances and complain instead of excessive daytime sleepiness. Nocturnal myoclonus presents as periodic uni- or bilateral, abrupt contractions of leg muscles (usually tibialis anterior) which can be seen in EMG recordings. Such polysomnographic recordings are essential for differentiating this disorder from the hyperactivity of sleep apnea patients and from generalized body movements. Since the daytime complaints of both nocturnal myoclonus and "restless legs" syndrome sometimes mimic those of persistent psychophysiological DOES and drug-related DOES, a careful psychological evaluation is also essential (55).

Narcolepsy

Studies of narcolepsy have been prominent in the sleep literature (56, 57, 58, 59, 60, 61). According to the new diagnostic classification of sleep disorders (2):

> Narcolepsy is a syndrome consisting of excessive daytime sleepiness and abnormal manifestations of REM sleep. The latter include frequent sleep-onset REM episodes, which may be subjectively appreciated as hypnagogic hallucinations, and the disassociated REM sleep inhibitory processes, cataplexy, and sleep paralysis. The appearance of REM sleep within ten minutes of sleep onset is considered evidence for narcolepsy (p. 72).

Cataplexy, a pathognomic feature of narcolepsy, may occur alone or in combination with sleep attacks. Cataplectic attacks consist of either (1) a brief, almost imperceptible weakness of isolated muscle groups, giving rise to jaw drop, head drop, facial sagging, weakness of the knees, or loss of grip, or (2) sudden paralysis of all skeletal muscles, with a complete postural collapse. If cataplexy occurs separately from the sleep attack, consciousness remains clear; however, it may develop into a full REM-sleep period. Cataplectic episodes are almost always triggered by intense expressions of emotions such as laughter, anger, or sexual arousal.

Although sleep attacks, cataplexy, sleep paralysis, and hypnagogic hallucinations are considered the classic tetrad of the disorder, only 11–14 percent of patients experience all four of them. The onset of narcolepsy occurs usually in the second decade of life. Sleep attacks typically precede other symptoms by several years, making prompt diagnosis and treatment difficult without polysomnographic recording. Percentage of occurrence is approximately equal in both sexes, but there is a strong heredofamilial trend (60). Narcolepsy has an estimated incidence of 0.02 percent to 0.09 percent.

Narcolepsy usually develops slowly but steadily. Once the symptoms have fully developed, the course of the disease stabilizes and remains unchanged until advanced age. Depending on the severity of the sleep attacks and cataplexy, impairment of normal functioning is mild to severe. A lasting disappearance of all the symptoms is rare.

There is no proven cure for narcolepsy at the present time. However, symptoms can usually be treated satisfactorily. Excessive sleepiness and sleep attacks are combated with methylphenidate, among other CNS stimulants. Imipramine has been proven to prevent or lessen the severity of cataplectic attacks. In cases of profound sleep disturbances, a low dose of diazepam may be prescribed. CNS-stimulant and other medication dosages should be kept at a minimal but effective level. Patients should be advised to substitute short naps for medications whenever circumstances allow, and to take "drug holidays" to minimize the development of tolerance.

Narcoleptic patients commonly experience problems in relations with their families, co-workers, and supervisors, as well as with the side effects of medications. Reactive depression is reported frequently. The sustained use of CNS stimulants may also lead to some secondary psychological problems such as personality changes and paranoid thinking.

Polysomnographically, the most prominent feature of narcolepsy is sleep-onset REM episodes, which can be observed during both nocturnal sleep and daytime naps. Multiple Daytime Sleepiness tests are also very helpful for objectively detecting hypersomnolence. For differential diagnosis, all other DOES conditions, alcoholism, and psychotic depression should be considered as possible alternatives. To a lesser degree, hypothyroidism, epilepsy, hypo-glycemia, myasthenia gravis, multiple sclerosis, and organic brain diseases may mimic some of the symptoms of narcolepsy. A carefully noted history of illness and sleep laboratory evaluation, however, make accurate differential diagnosis feasible.

Idiopathic CNS Hypersomnolence

Also called NREM-narcolepsy or idiopathic DOES, idiopathic CNS hypersomnolence is characterized by recurrent daytime sleepiness in the absence of any detectable cause. In this syndrome, unlike narcolepsy, daytime sleepiness is continuous and does not result in sudden, irresistible sleep attacks. The patient suffering from idiopathic DOES takes long but unrefreshing naps, which are preceded by long periods of drowsiness. As demonstrated in Multiple Sleep Latency tests, both daytime and nighttime sleep latencies are very short, while TST and TIB are prolonged. Although patients feel that their sleep is very deep and undisturbed, they still have difficulty waking up in the morning.

DOES Associated With Other Medical, Toxic, and Environmental Conditions

DOES is associated with a wide variety of other medical, toxic, and environmental conditions, including infections, hormonal imbalances, CNS trauma, and food allergies. The qualifying feature of this type of DOES is that the hypersomnolence is directly caused by the medical, toxic, or environmental condition, or results from sleep deprivation caused by this condition. This topic is discussed in detail by Williams (42).

DOES Associated With Other DOES Conditions

Certain relatively rare DOES conditions typically accompany any of the other DOES conditions already described. They may be intermittent, such as the Kleine-Levin and menstrual-associated syndromes, or result from chronic insufficient sleep.

Kleine-Levin syndrome, a relatively rare disease most common in adolescent males, is ascribed to intermittent organic dysfunction in limbic or hypothalamic structures. Its major symptoms are periodic hypersomnia and excessive eating (62). Emotional stress and febrile illness occasionally precipitate the episodes of hypersomnolence. Behavioral abnormalities such as excessive sexual excitement or disinhibition, preference for sweets, some degree of amnesia, depression, and insomnia following the attack occur in conjunction with Kleine-Levin syndrome.

Another periodically occurring DOES is temporally related to the menstrual cycle. No gross abnormalities in sleep structures were found in the few cases that have been polysomnographically evaluated. Some women exhibit bizarre behavior during the hypersomnolent periods, implicating a similarity with Kleine-Levin syndrome. Although there is no evidence explaining the pathology of menstrually related DOES, hypothalamic etiology has been postulated (63).

A person who chronically gets insufficient sleep yet is unaware of his or her need for more sleep may complain of DOES. Sleep loss often results from unrealistic attempts to follow an exhaustive social and work schedule. Over time, the sleep-deprived person typically develops secondary symptoms: irritability, difficulty in concentration, reduced vigilance, distractability, reduced motivation, depression, fatigue, and restlessness. A detailed interview supplemented by a sleep log carefully kept for a minimum of two weeks will help the clinician differentiate this condition from other DOES (2).

No DOES Abnormality

Some individuals regularly sleep a substantially greater number of hours per night—occasionally as many as 14—than is considered normal for their age group. Others neither sleep excessively nor sleep in the daytime yet subjectively complain of excessive somnolence that cannot be objectively verified. Neither of these conditions is considered a true DOES abnormality because polysomnographically detectable abnormalities in sleep architecture and physiology are absent and psychological functioning is within normal limits. As in cases of insufficient sleep, a detailed interview and sleep log will aid in diagnostic clarification (2).

Disorders of the Sleep-Wake Schedule

The prominent, 24-hour sleep-wake cycle of humans is kept relatively constant by a biological clock but is affected by such factors as social obligations and artificial light. Both endogenous and exogenous factors can disturb the normal sleep-wake cycle and lead to clinically important sleep disorders (2, 64). Conditions imposed by chronic DIMS and DOES, in which persistent abnormalities in maintenance of the normal, daily wake-sleep cycle affect sleep-wake rhythm, will be excluded. Disorders of the sleep-wake schedule, examined next, may be transient or persistent.

Transient Disorders of the Sleep-Wake Schedule

Transient disorders of the sleep-wake schedule include the rapid-time-zone-change syndrome and work-shift changes.

Also called "jet-lag" syndrome, the former disorder results from a single rapid change of multiple time zones and subsequent attempts to immediately continue on the new clock-hour schedule. Common ill effects of the jet-lag syndrome—daytime sleepiness and fatigue and nighttime insomnia—can be avoided by ignoring the new clock time; i.e., by keeping the original sleep-wake hours of the old time zone. Although the circadian rhythms start adapting to the new clock time within two days, symptoms may last for a week or longer and tend to be more severe after eastward flights.

A similar transient sleep-wake problem arises from work-shift changes. When the work period is scheduled during the habitual sleep phase (almost always at night), sleepiness and decline in physical and intellectual performance occur immediately. Correspondingly, sleep periods during the former awake phase are disrupted and shortened. The symptoms may last three weeks or longer, especially if one resumes the former normal sleep-wake schedule during weekends and holidays to meet familial and social demands.

Sleep-wake disorders become persistent when the sleep-wake schedule is changed frequently over a long period of time. The rotating-shift work of some industrial personnel, recurrent jet lag experienced by flight crews or other regular air travelers, and poor sleep hygiene common in college students and combat soldiers disrupt, shorten, or increase the frequency of sleep-wake episodes.

Other persistent sleep-wake schedule disorders emerge if one loses the natural synchronization of the internal, sleep-wake phase schedule (biological clock) and the clock time, or any other *Zeitgeber*. Sleep onset and wake times may intractably occur later than desired (delayed sleep-phase syndrome) or earlier than desired (advanced sleep phase syndrome). In both cases, the patient has no difficulty staying asleep once he falls asleep. However, since many people must maintain a conventional sleep-wake schedule or work-rest schedule, secondary DIMS and DOES unavoidably arise (65).

The non-24-hour sleep-wake syndrome features an incremental pattern of delays in sleep-onset and wake times to steadily later hours on successive days. The internal (biological) clock becomes progressively asynchronous with clock time by differences usually not exceeding two hours daily. Consequently, when the biological clock is "out of phase" with the socially desired sleep-wake schedule, the patient experiences sleep-onset insomnia at night and difficulties remaining awake during the day. However, as the asynchronicity advances, there is eventually a period when the patient is "in phase" with a conventional sleep-wake schedule. During this period, the affected individual does not complain of DIMS or DOES. Therefore, this disorder is also referred to as "periodic insomnia" or "periodic hypersomnia" (2, 66).

Dysfunctions Associated With Sleep, Sleep Stages, or Partial Arousals (Parasomnias)

The parasomnias are clinical conditions that are unrelated to sleep-wake mechanisms. This category includes activities considered normal during the waking state, but abnormal—and often undesirable—during sleep, as well as some medical conditions which had been formerly classified by some researchers as sleep-exacerbated and sleep-improved disorders (4). Most parasomnias are more prevalent among children than adults. Certain parasomnias— sleepwalking, sleep terror, and enuresis—are suspected to be disorders of the state of partial arousal. The remainder of the sleep-related disorders, classified together as "other dysfunctions," include dream anxiety attacks, epileptic seizures, bruxism, head-banging, familial sleep paralysis, impaired sleep-related penile tumescence, painful erections, cluster headaches and chronic paraoxysmal hemicrania, abnormal swallowing syndrome, asthma, cardiovascular symptoms, gastroesophageal reflux, hemolysis, and asymptomatic polysomnographic findings.

Sleepwalking (Somnambulism)

Sleepwalking is the automatic execution of a sequence of complex behaviors that may include dressing, eating, or bathroom visits as well as walking. This phenomenon nearly always happens in the first half of the night, during SWS, and begins with repetitive motor acts while sitting up, which do not always progress to actual walking. The somnambulant person resists attempts to communicate with or arouse him, but may awaken spontaneously, experiencing mild confusion lasting several minutes. Others return to sleep, either in bed or in an unusual place, without awakening until morning. The sleepwalker generally does not recall the episode the next morning.

Somnambulism is a fairly common occurrence in childhood and adolescence, but may signify psychological disturbance in adulthood. One to 6 percent of children, more often males, experience frequent episodes, with a typical onset being between 6 and 12 years of age. Sleepwalking typically disappears after adolescence but may reappear in the third or fourth decade. There seems to be a heredofamilial trend. This disorder has been associated with epilepsy, CNS infections and traumas, genito-urinary complaints, psychopathology, sleep-talking, nocturnal enuresis, and nightmares (67, 68).

Sleep Terror (Pavor Nocturnus, Incubus)

Like sleepwalking, sleep terror is an arousal from SWS in the first half of the night. The attack usually erupts with a piercing scream or cry accompanied by behavioral manifestations of intense anxiety. Prior to a sleep terror episode, the EEG delta waves may be higher in amplitude than usual, accompanied by slower respiration and heart rates. During the attack, however, an alpha pattern appears, and there is significant tachycardia. The individual typically sits up in bed, appears agitated and frightened, and may also exhibit automatism, mydriasis, perspiration, and tachypnea. Full consciousness is gained only after 5 or 10 minutes, and the episode is rarely remembered the next morning.

More common in males, sleep terror is experienced by at least 1 to 4 percent of all children (pavor nocturnus). Its onset is frequently between ages 4 and 12, disappearing in early adolescence. The disorder occasionally does not begin until the second or third decade of adulthood (incubus), but rarely commences after age 40.

Psychophysiological functioning in children with sleep terrors is within normal limits, and such children are not more predisposed than others to mental illness in later life. Adults with this disorder, however, are prone to emotional disturbances such as chronic anxiety (69).

Sleep terrors are often misrepresented as sleep anxiety attacks (nightmares), but are easily differentiated by the timing of the episode in the sleep cycle, a marked degree of sympathetic arousal, and lack of vivid dream recall. They also closely resemble the hypnagogic hallucinations of narcoleptics and depressed patients as well as sleep-related epileptic seizures.

Sleep-Related Enuresis (Nocturnal Enuresis)

Sleep-related enuresis is the involuntary nocturnal micturition, usually during SWS, in the first third of the night, of a person older than three years. Sphincter release usually occurs after arousal has begun, but control of micturition is never gained because the individual fails to fully awaken. Although difficult to arouse, the patient, once awakened, is usually disoriented after the episode.

Primarily, children, but also some adults, suffer from the disorder. Some individuals are enuretic because they have never successfully accomplished toilet training (primary enuresis), while others become enuretic after having completed toilet training (secondary enuresis). Both of these types of idiopathic nocturnal enuresis spontaneously disappear, usually by late childhood or early adolescence, whereas symptomatic nocturnal enuresis, which has an underlying urogenital or other disease, requires specific treatment.

Idiopathic nocturnal enuresis has long been associated with emotional problems and even significant psychophysiological disturbance. Despite a 35 percent incidence in institutionalized children, no typical personality pattern or psychophysiological features have been correlated with nocturnal enuresis. Nevertheless, the afflicted individual's feelings of shame, guilt, and obvious embarrassment are often serious enough to create problems in intrafamilial relations and to limit social interactions (4, 70, 71).

Other Dysfunctions

Dream anxiety attacks, or nightmares, are awakenings from REM sleep after a disturbing dream and are accompanied by anxiety and mild autonomic arousal. Their most obvious difference from night terror is the time of the episodes—later in the nocturnal sleep cycle—when REM sleep rather than SWS is prominent. The afflicted individual always vividly recalls a nightmarish dream, is completely oriented upon awakening, and shows fewer signs of sympathetic arousal than the night terror victim, although a moderate degree of tachycardia is common.

Another dysfunction, sleep-related epileptic seizures, are, according to the Sleep Disorders Classification Committee, "characterized by attacks of epileptic mechanism that recur in sleep. The seizures either take the form of generalized epileptic convulsions—tonic-clonic, tonic, or myoclonic in type—or are partial seizures of complex symptomatology—often 'psychomotor' type with confusion and automatisms" (2) (p. 107). They occur at any age, but most frequently in childhood. The prevalence of epilepsy is approximately 0.5 percent while "sleep epilepsy," in which seizures are almost exclusively confined to sleep, is observed in 20–25 percent of the epileptic population. Sleep, probably the most effective seizure activation procedure used in clinical EEG, has been shown to be more effective than hyperventilation and stroboscopic stimulation (72), especially in temporal-lobe epilepsy (73). Since a comprehensive discussion of sleep and epilepsy is beyond the scope of this chapter, the reader is referred to Freemon (74).

Like sleepwalking and sleep terror, sleep-related bruxism may be considered a disorder of partial arousal. Also known as nocturnal teeth grinding, this disorder consists of rhythmic masseter muscle activity in sleep, predominantly in stage 2. The firm contact of upper and lower jaws is often accompanied by a loud grating and clicking sound.

There has been no evidence of epileptic activity underlying bruxism. It is more common in children and young adults, and might involve a heredofamilial trend. Systematic studies of psychological variables have not demonstrated a predisposition of certain personality types to bruxism, nor have they shown that emotional factors contribute to the disorder (75). Although bruxism is easily diagnosed, there is no proven medical treatment. In severe cases, a special teeth-protecting prosthesis must be fitted in order to prevent extensive dental damage.

Sleep-related head-banging—*jactatio capitis nocturnus*—is another sleep behavior characterized by rhythmic muscle activity, predominantly of the head, and to a lesser degree, of the whole body. It occurs most commonly just prior to sleep onset and continues into light sleep (stage 1). This condition normally appears in childhood and seldom after adolescence (76).

Although it is one of the major symptoms of narcolepsy, sleep paralysis can occur independently in otherwise healthy individuals. Familial sleep paralysis, a form displaying a strong heredofamilial trend, typically occurs just at the onset of sleep, immediately upon awakening at night, or in the morning. Characterized by a sudden inability to execute voluntary movements, sleep paralysis episodes are usually accompanied by clear consciousness. Although capable of lasting several minutes, paralysis may be terminated by a strong external stimulus such as another person's touch. Some patients learn to break an episode by vigorously moving their eyes. Familial sleep paralysis must be differentiated from narcolepsy and familial periodic paralysis, in which paralysis is associated with periodic hypokalemic episodes (77).

Impaired sleep-related penile tumescence results from an organic dysfunction within the sequence of complex processes responsible for obtaining and maintaining an erection.

Nocturnal penile tumescence (NPT) occurs in all healthy males, mainly during stage 1-REM sleep. The number and duration of episodes vary with the age of the subject. NPT monitoring is currently used to distinguish organic from psychogenic causes of impotency (78). The most common organic cause of diminished episodes of NPT and, correspondingly, of impotence, is diabetes mellitus.

In some men, normal nocturnal penile tumescence is accompanied by painful sensations that awaken them. A rare phenomenon, sleep-related painful erections may lead to REM-sleep-related awakenings and eventually to DIMS. Although sleep-related painful erections are possible in the absence of pathology of the penis, they are often observed in anatomical defects of the penis such as Peyronie's disease and phymosis (79).

Headache complaints are common among patients suffering from various sleep disorders. Sleep-related cluster headaches and chronic paroxysmal hemicrania, while sleep-associated, may occur even in the absence of other sleep disorders. "Sleep-related cluster headaches are agonizingly severe, unilateral headaches that appear often during sleep and are marked by an on-off pattern of attacks" (80) (p. 113). They typically occur 1 to 3 times a day and may last for hours. Chronic paroxysmal hemicrania is also unilateral and severe, but lasts only a few minutes and happens more frequently than cluster headaches; there may be up to 24 episodes a day. Both types are vascular headaches clearly associated with REM sleep (81). These headaches commence after puberty and are more likely to affect women. There is an apparent heredofamilial trend.

In the sleep-related abnormal swallowing syndrome, inadequate swallowing results in aspiration of saliva, coughing, and choking. It is accompanied by intermittent brief arousals and awakenings. In contrast to sleep apnea syndrome, in which sleep is also disturbed by frequent arousals and awakenings, the patient is aware of the choking and occluded airway. Sleep polygraphy does not demonstrate prolonged apnea episodes.

Asthma, a chronic respiratory disease, is considered to be a sleep-exacerbated condition. Consequently, sleep-related asthma attacks are frequent in sleep. Absent in stage 4 sleep, attacks are more likely to occur late in the sleep period (82, 83).

Sleep-related cardiovascular symptoms originate in disorders of cardiac rhythm, myocardial incompetence, coronary artery insufficiency, and blood-pressure variability during sleep. Since cardiac disease is the number-one cause of death in developed nations, and the peak time for cardiac deaths coincides with the REM-sleep-abundant interval between 5 and 6 A.M., sleep research exploring a possible connection between cardiac failure and REM sleep is currently capturing the spotlight. Since chest pain and breathing difficulties during sleep may be present in several sleep disturbances (84) and medical conditions (42), the patient who complains of these symptoms should be referred for a complete cardio-respiratory examination, preferably before polysomnographic evaluation.

Sleep-related gastroesophageal reflux has been described as "a disorder in which the patient awakens from sleep either with burning substernal pain, a feeling of general pain or tightness in the chest, or a sour taste in the mouth" (2) (pp. 118–119). Coughing, choking, and vague respiratory discomfort are also common with this syndrome. Affecting women and men alike, this disorder occurs almost only in adults. No familial trend has been established. A progressive condition, gastroesophageal reflux worsens over time, leading to serious sleep disturbances as well as medical complications (85).

Paroxysmal nocturnal hemoglobinuria is a relatively rare, chronic, and persistent disease consisting of the intravascular hemolysis of large amounts of erythrocytes, resulting in hemoglobinemia and hemoglobinuria. The exact nature of the causal relationship between hemolysis and sleep, perhaps to sleep stages, has yet to be established. Intensification of symptoms is irregular but ongoing. Paroxysmal nocturnal hemoglobinuria is most common in young adulthood, but may begin at any age (86). This disease has a poor prognosis; it is eventually fatal in most cases.

CONCLUSIONS

Fully recognizing how little is yet known about the pathology of sleep disorders, the Sleep Disorders Classification Committee members do not present their scheme as an authoritatively rigid doctrine. Rather, they acknowledge that any classification scheme based on symptoms, not causes, must remain a transient working frame subject to continuous improvement. As the committee chairman astutely points out, "A consensus arrangement of diagnoses simply establishes a focused synchronization of viewpoints, not validity. Diagnostic boundaries must continue to be appraised as research explores the mechanisms of disorders . . . . Concepts of classification will surely change as new findings and improved conceptual frameworks evolve" (84) (p. 9). However, the new classification does provide medical practitioners with more consistent and definitive guidelines for the recognition, differential diagnosis, and treatment of disorders of sleep and arousal. As is evident from the preceding description, patients may present with a puzzling array of complaints which, without careful psychiatric and polysomnographic evaluation, could be symptomatic of several different disorders.

REFERENCES

1. Williams, R.L. & Karacan, I. Introduction, in *Sleep Disorders: Diagnosis and Treatment*. New York: Wiley, 1978.
2. Association of Sleep Disorders Centers. Diagnostic classification of sleep and arousal disorders, 1st ed, prepared by the Sleep Disorders Classification Committee, Roffwarg, H.P., Chairman. *Sleep* 2: 1–137, 1979.
3. Cooper, J.R. (Ed.). *Sedative-Hypnotic Drugs: Risks and Benefits*, pp. 1–112. Rockville, Md. National Institute on Drug Abuse, US DHEW, Publication No. 78-592, 1977.
4. Williams, R.L., Karacan, I., & Hursch, C.J. *Electroencephalography (EEG) of Human Sleep: Clinical Applications*. New York: Wiley, 1974.
5. Diaz-Guerrero, R., Gottlieb, J.S., & Knott, J.R. The sleep of patients with manic-depressive psychosis, depressive type. An electroencephalographic study. *Psychosom. Med.* 8: 399–404, 1946.
6. Hawkins, D.R. & Mendels, J. Sleep disturbances in depressive syndromes. *Am. J. Psychiat.* 123: 682–90, 1966.
7. Hawkins, D.R. Sleep and depression. *Psychiatr. Ann.* 9: 13–28, 1979.
8. Kupfer, D.J. & Foster, F.G. EEG sleep and depression. In Williams, R.L. & Karacan, I. (Eds.), *Sleep Disorders: Diagnosis and Treatment*. New York: Wiley, 1978.
9. Gillin, J.C., Mazure, C., Post, R.M., Jimerson, D., & Bunney, W.E., Jr. An EEG sleep study of bipolar (manic-depressive) patients with a nocturnal switch process. *Biol. Psychiat.* 12: 711–18, 1977.
10. Dement, W. Dream recall and eye movements during sleep in schizophrenics and normals. *J. Nerv. Ment. Dis.* 122: 263–69, 1955.
11. Zarcone, V.P., Jr. Sleep and schizophrenia. *Psychiatr. Ann.* 9: 29–40, 1979.
12. Reich, L., Weiss, B.L., Coble, P., McPartland, R., & Kupfer, D. Sleep disturbance in schizophrenia. *Arch. Gen. Psychiat.* 32: 51–5, 1975.
13. Feinberg, I. & Hiatt, J.F. Sleep patterns in schizophrenia: A selective review. In Williams, R.L. & Karacan, I. (Eds.), *Sleep Disorders: Diagnosis and Treatment*. New York: Wiley, 1978.
14. Zarcone, V., Gulevich, G., & Pivik, T. Partial REM phase deprivation and schizophrenia. *Arch. Gen. Psychiat.* 18: 194–202, 1968.
15. Zarcone, V., Azumi, K., Dement, W., Gulevich, G., Kraemer, H., & Pivik, T. REM phase deprivation and schizophrenia. II. *Arch. Gen Psychiat.* 32: 1,431–36, 1975.
16. Azumi, K. A polygraphic study of sleep in schizophrenia. *Seishin Shinkeigaku Zasshi* 68: 1,222–41, 1966.
17. Azumi, K., Takahashi, S., Takahashi, K., Maruyama, N., & Kikuti, S. The effects of dream deprivation on chronic schizophrenics and normal adults: a comparative study. *Folia Psychiat. Neurol. Jap.* 21: 205–25, 1967.
18. Gillin, J.C., Buchsbaum, M.S., Jacobs, L.S., Fram, P., Williams, R., Jr., Vaughn, T., Mellon, E., Snyder, F., & Wyatt, R. Partial REM sleep deprivation, schizophrenia and field articulation. *Arch. Gen. Psychiat.* 30: 653–61, 1974.
19. Vogel, G. & Traub, A. REM deprivation. I. The effect on schizophrenic patients. *Arch. Gen. Psychiat.* 18: 287–329, 1968.
20. de Barros-Ferreira, M., Goldsteinas, L., & Lairy, G. REM sleep deprivation in chronic schizophrenics: effects on dynamics of fast sleep. *Electroencephalogr. Clin. Neurophysiol.* 34: 561–69, 1973.
21. Dement, W., Zarcone, V., Ferguson, J., Cohen, H., Pivik, T., & Barchas, J. Some parallel findings in schizophrenic patients and serotonin-depleted cats. In Siva Sankar, D.V. (Ed.), *Schizophrenia: Current Concepts and Research*. Hicksville, NY: PJD Publications, 1969.

22. Wyatt, R., Vaughn, T., Galanter, M., Kaplan, J., & Green, R. Behavioral changes of chronic schizophrenic patients given L-5 hydroxytryptophan. *Science* 177: 1,124–26, 1972.
23. Kales, A. (Ed.) *Sleep. Physiology & Pathology*. Philadelphia: Lippincott, 1969.
24. Williams, R.L. & Karacan, I. (Eds.) *Pharmacology of Sleep*. New York: Wiley, 1976.
25. Kay, D.C., Blackburn, A.B., Buckingham, J.A., & Karacan, I. Human pharmacology of sleep. In Williams, R.L. & Karacan, I. (Eds.), *Pharmacology of Sleep*. New York: Wiley, 1976.
26. Oswald, I. Sleep and dependence on amphetamine and other drugs. In Kales, A. (Ed.), *Sleep: Physiology & Pathology*. Philadelphia: Lippincott, 1969.
27. Hartmann, E. Long-term administration of psychotropic drugs: effects on human sleep. In Williams, R.L. & Karacan, I. (Eds.), *Pharmacology of Sleep*. New York: Wiley, 1976.
28. Müller-Limmroth, W. Der Einfluss von coffeinhaltigem und coffeinfreiem Kaffee auf den Schlaf des Menschen. *Z. Ernaehrungswiss* (Suppl.) 14: 438–45, 1964.
29. Goldstein, A., Warren, R., & Kaizer, S. Psychotropic effects of caffeine in man. I. Individual differences in sensitivity to caffeine-induced wakefulness. *J. Pharmacol. Exp. Ther.* 149: 156–59, 1965.
30. Brezinova, V. Effect of caffeine on sleep: EEG study in late middle-age people. *Brit. J. Clin. Pharmacol.* 1: 203–208, 1974.
31. Karacan, I., Booth, G.H., Thornby, J.I., & Williams, R.L. The effect of caffeinated and decaffeinated coffee on nocturnal sleep in young adult males. In Chase, M.H., Stern, W.C., & Walter, P.L. (Eds.), *Sleep Research*, vol. 2, p. 64. Los Angeles: U. of California, Brain Information Service/Brain Research Institute, 1973.
32. Karacan, I., Thornby, J.I., Anch, A.M., Salis, P.J., Williams, R.L., Okawa, M., & Booth, G.H. Dose-response effects of coffee on the sleep of normal middle-aged men. In Chase, M.H., Stern, W.C., & Walter, P.L. (Eds.), *Sleep Research*, vol. 5, p. 70. Los Angeles: U. of California, Brain Information Service/Brain Research Institute, 1976.
33. Karacan, I., Thornby, J.I., Anch, A.M., Booth, G.H., Williams, R.L., & Salis, P.J. Dose-related sleep disturbances induced by coffee and caffeine. *Clin. Pharmacol. Ther.* 20: 682–89, 1976.
34. Bonnet, M.H., Webb, W.B., & Barnard, G. Effect of flurazepam, pentobarbital, and caffeine on arousal threshold. *Sleep* 1: 271–79, 1979.
35. Berkowitz, B.A., Tarver, J.H., & Spector, S. Release of norepinephrine in the central nervous system by theophylline and caffeine. *Eur. J. Pharmacol.* 10: 64–71, 1970.
36. Berkowitz, B.A. & Spector, S. The effect of caffeine and theophylline on the disposition of brain serotonin in the rat. *Eur. J. Pharmacol.* 16: 322–25, 1971.
37. Corrodi, H., Fuxe, K., & Jonsson, G. Effects of caffeine on central monoamine neurons. *J. Pharm. Pharmacol.* 24: 155–58, 1972.
38. Gross, M.M., Goodenough, D.R., & Hasten, J. Experimental study of sleep in chronic alcoholics before, during, and after four days of heavy drinking, with a non-drinking comparison. *Ann. NY Acad. Sci.* 215: 254–75, 1973.
39. Pokorny, A.D. Sleep disturbances, alcohol, and alcoholism: a review. In Williams, R.L. & Karacan, I. (Eds.), *Sleep Disorders: Diagnosis and Treatment*. New York: Wiley, 1978.
40. Williams, H.L. & Salamy, A. Alcohol and sleep. In Kissin, B. & Begleiter, H. (Eds.), *The Biology of Alcoholism*. New York: Plenum, 1972.
41. Mendelson, W.B., Gillin, J.C., & Wyatt, R.D. *Human Sleep and its Disorders*. New York: Plenum, 1977.
42. Williams, R.L. Sleep disturbances in various medical and surgical conditions. In Williams, R.L. & Karacan, I. (Eds.), *Sleep Disorders: Diagnosis and Treatment*. New York: Wiley, 1978.
43. Williams, R.L. & Karacan, I. (Eds.), *Sleep Disorders: Diagnosis and Treatment*. New York: Wiley, 1978.

44. Kupfer, D.J. & Foster, F.G. The sleep of psychotic patients: does it all look alike? In Freedman, D.X. (Ed.), *Biology of the Major Psychoses: A Comparative Analysis*. New York: Raven, 1975.

45. Tilkian, A.G., Motta, J., & Guilleminault, C. Cardiac arrythmias in sleep apnea. In Guilleminault, C. & Dement, W.C. (Eds.), *Sleep Apnea Syndromes*. New York: Liss, 1978.

46. Schroeder, J.S., Motta, J., & Guilleminault, C. Hemodynamic studies in sleep apnea. In Guilleminault, C. & Dement, W.C. (Eds.), *Sleep Apnea Syndromes*. New York: Liss, 1978.

47. Lugaresi, E., Coccagna, G., & Mantovani, M. Hypersomnia with periodic apneas. In Chase, M.H. (Ed.), *Advances in Sleep Research*, vol. 4. New York: Spectrum, 1978.

48. Guilleminault, C. & Dement, W.C. (Eds.) *Sleep Apnea Syndromes*. New York: Liss, 1978.

49. Guilleminault, C. & Dement, W.C. (Eds.) Sleep apnea syndromes and related sleep disorders. In Williams, R.L. & Karacan, I. (Eds.), *Sleep Disorders: Diagnosis and Treatment*. New York: Wiley, 1978.

50. Guilleminault, C. & Dement, W.C. 235 cases of excessive daytime sleepiness: diagnosis and tentative classification. *J. Neurol. Sci.* 31:13, 1977.

51. Remmers, J.E., Anch, A.M., & deGroot, W.J. Respiratory disturbances during sleep. *Clin. Chest Med.* 1: 57–71, 1980.

52. Derman, S. & Karacan, I. Sleep-induced respiratory disorders. *Psychiatr. Ann.* 9: 411–25, 1979.

53. Coccagna, G., Mantovani, M., Parchi, C., Miroui, F. & Lugaresi, E. Alveolar hypoventilation and hypersomnia in myotonic dystrophy. *J. Neurol. Neurosurg. Psychiat.* 38: 977–84, 1975.

54. Lugaresi, E. Snoring and its clinical implications. In Guilleminault, C. & Dement, W.C. (Eds.), *Sleep Apnea Syndromes*. New York: Liss, 1978.

55. Zorich, F., Roth, T., Salis, P., Kramer, M. & Lutz, T. Insomnia and excessive daytime sleepiness as presenting symptoms in nocturnal myoclonus. In Chase, M.H., Mitler, M., & Walter, P.L. (Eds.), *Sleep Research*, vol. 7, p. 256. Los Angeles: U. of California, Brain Information Service/Brain Research Institute, 1978.

56. Roth, B. *Narkolepsie und Hypersomnie vom Standpunkt der Physiologie des Schlafes*. Verlag Volk und Gesundheit. Berlin: 1962.

57. Dement, W.C., Carskadon, M., & Ley, R. The prevalence of narcolepsy, II. In Chase, M.H., Stern, W.C., & Walter, P.L. (Eds.), *Sleep Research*, vol. 2. Los Angeles: U. of California, Brain Information Service/Brain Research Institute, 1973.

58. Zarcone, V. Narcolepsy. *New Eng. J. Med.* 288: 1,156–66, 1973.

59. Guilleminault, C., Dement, W.C. & Passouant, P. (Eds.) Narcolepsy, in *Advances in Sleep Research*, vol. 3. New York: Spectrum, 1976.

60. Roth, B. Narcolepsy and hypersomnia. In Williams, R.L. & Karacan, I. (Eds.), *Sleep Disorders: Diagnosis and Treatment*. New York: Wiley, 1978.

61. Karacan, I., Moore, C.A., & Williams, R.L. The narcoleptic syndrome. *Psych. Ann.* 9: 69, 73–76, 1979.

62. Critchley, M. Periodic hypersomnia and megaphagia in adolescent males. *Brain* 85: 627–56, 1962.

63. Billiard, M., Guilleminault, C., & Dement, W.C. A menstruation-linked periodic hypersomnia. *Neurol.* 25: 436–43, 1975.

64. Weitzman, E. (Ed.) Periodicity in sleep and waking states. In Chase, M.H. (Ed.), *Sleeping Brain*. Los Angeles: U. of California, Brain Information Service/Brain Research Institute, 1972.

65. Czeisler, C., Richardson, G., Coleman, R., Dement, W. & Weitzman, E. Successful non-drug treatment of delayed sleep phase syndrome with chronotherapy: resetting a biological clock in man. In Chase, M.H., Stern, W.C., & Walter, P.L. *Sleep Research*, vol. 8, p. 179. Los Angeles: U. of California, Brain Information Service/Brain Research Institute, 1979.

66. Webb, W.B. & Agnew, H.W. Sleep and waking in a time-free environment. *Aerospace Med.* 45: 617–22, 1974.
67. Jacobson, A. & Kales, A. Somnambulism: all-night EEG and related studies. In Kety, S.S., Evarts, E.V., & Williams, H.L. (Eds.), *Research Publications of the Association for Research in Nervous and Mental Disease. Sleep and Altered States of Consciousness*, vol. 45. Baltimore: Williams & Wilkins, 1967.
68. Kales, A., Jacobson, A., Paulson, M.J., Kales, J.D., & Walter, R.D. Somnambulism: psychophysiological correlates. *Arch. Gen. Psychiat.* 14: 586–94, 1966.
69. Fisher, C.J., Byrne, J., Edwards, T., & Kahn, E. A psychophysiological study of nightmares. *J. Am. Psychoanal. Assoc.* 18: 747–82, 1970.
70. Broughton, R. Sleep disorders: Disorders of arousal? *Science* 159: 1,070–78, 1968.
71. Ritvo, E.R., Ornitz, E.M., Gottlieb, F., Poussaint, A.F., Maron, B.J., Ditman, K.S., & Blinn, K.A. Arousal and non-arousal enuretic events. *Am. J. Psychiat.* 126: 77–84, 1969.
72. Kooi, K.A. *Fundamentals of Electroencephalography*. New York: Harper & Row, 1971.
73. Kikuchi, S. An electroencephalographic study of nocturnal sleep in temporal lobe epilepsy. *Folia Psychiatr. Neurol. Jap.* 23: 59–81, 1969.
74. Freemon, F.R. Sleep in patients with organic diseases of the nervous system. In Williams, R.L. & Karacan, I. (Eds.), *Sleep Disorders: Diagnosis and Treatment*. New York: Wiley, 1978.
75. Reding, G., Sepelin, H., Robinson, J.E., Zimmerman, S.O., & Smith, V.H. Nocturnal teeth-grinding: all-night psychophysiology studies. *J. Dent. Res.* 47: 786–97, 1968.
76. Baldy-Moulinier, M., Levy, M., & Passouant, P. A study of jactatio capitis during night sleep. *Electroencephalogr. Clin. Neurophysiol.* 28: 87, 1970.
77. Hishikawa, Y. Sleep paralysis. In Guilleminault, C., Dement, W.C., & Passouant, P. (Eds.), *Advances in Sleep Research*, vol. 3: *Narcolepsy*. New York: Spectrum, 1976.
78. Karacan, I., Salis, P.J., & Williams, R.L. The role of the sleep laboratory in diagnosis and treatment of impotence. In Williams, R.L. & Karacan, I. (Eds.), *Sleep Disorders: Diagnosis and Treatment*. New York: Wiley, 1978.
79. Karacan, I. Painful nocturnal penile erections. *JAMA* 215: 1,831, 1971.
80. Dexter, J.D. Studies in nocturnal migraine. *Arch. Neurobiol. (Madr).* (Suppl.) 37: 281–300.
81. Kayed, K., Godtlibsen, O.B., & Sjaastad, O. Chronic paroxysmal hemicrania. IV. "REM sleep locked" nocturnal headache attacks. *Sleep* 1: 91–5, 1978.
82. Kales, A., Beall, G.N., Bajor, G.F., Jacobson, A., & Kales, J.D. Sleep studies in asthmatic adults: relationship of attacks to sleep stage and time of night. *J. Aller.* 41: 164–73, 1968.
83. Kales, A., Kales, J.D., Sly, R.M., Scharf, M.B., Tan, T.-L., & Preston, J.A. Sleep patterns of asthmatic children: all-night electroencephalographic studies. *J. Aller.* 46: 300–308, 1970.
84. Roffwarg, H.P. Introduction, in Association of Sleep Disorders Centers: Diagnostic Classification of Sleep and Arousal Disorders, 1st ed. *Sleep* 2: 1–137, 1979.
85. Orr, W.C., Robinson, M.G., & Johnson, L.F. Acid clearing during sleep in patients with esophagitis and controls. *Gastroent.* 76: 1,213, 1979.
86. Rosse, W.F. Erythrocyte disorders—paroxysmal nocturnal hemoglobinuria. In Williams, W., Beutler, E., Ersley, A., & Rundles, R.W. (Eds.), *Hematology*. New York: McGraw-Hill, 1977.

14

Stuttering

DAVID B. ROSENFIELD

This chapter will briefly address aspects of stuttering. I shall first define stuttering, discuss its prevalence and sundry characteristics, and then present some of the theories pertaining to its etiology. Finally, I shall discuss aspects of therapy.

It is important for psychiatrists to be familiar with stuttering not only because there are several million stutterers in this country, many of whom may see a psychiatrist, but because understanding stuttering permits an understanding of various aspects of speech and language, certainly an important function of the mind's realm.

Stuttering is a syndrome of repetitive speech dysfluencies. Each stutterer knows that there are certain sounds that he or she has difficulty pronouncing, that "blocks" frequently occur at the beginning of phrases and sentences (see below), and that circumlocution to permit fluency is automatic. Oftentimes a stutterer may say, "Well, I was kind of wondering how I could get to the Methodist Hospital," when what that person really wanted to say was, "H-h-h-h-how do I get to the Methodist Hospital?" Rather than stutter and stumble and thus subject oneself to the various vagaries of ridicule and loss of self-esteem, stutterers (almost subconsciously) circumlocute (1).

Stutterers frequently avoid particular speaking situations that are disconcerting to them. Consequently, many "closet stutterers" are considered to be snobs or aloof, whereas in reality they are merely hiding their fear of speaking.

There are different types of stuttering. Clonic stutterers may say "Wh-wh-wh-where is the book?" whereas tonic stutterers may say "wh . . . where is the book?" Clonic stutterers repeat and bounce on sounds; tonic stutterers hold them. Speech therapists in England used to differentiate stuttering from stammering along these lines, the stutterer being the clonic individual and the stammerer being the tonic one. In reality, these are both probably forms of the same disturbance, and, in recent times, people do not differentiate the two (1, 2).

Stuttering has been with us forever. It is mentioned in the Bible, it is mentioned in all languages (there is one Indian language in which there seems to be some question as to whether there is a word for stuttering; there probably is, but the Indians do not consider stuttering to be naturally aberrant), and it is worldwide. It is transcultural, pan-global, and found in all societies.

The American Speech and Hearing Association contend that 1.1 percent of the total population stutters (1). Many studies have attempted to ascertain the prevalence of stuttering, but many problems arise. First, there is difficulty in deciding who truly is a stutterer. Oftentimes, researchers have asked schoolteachers who stuttered in their classes and were told that a given number of students did so. Very frequently, the teachers would be incorrect in their assessment, oftentimes overlooking individuals who were "closet stutterers," those who appeared to be fluent as a result of circumlocutions but who in reality were not. (For instance, there were 4 medical students in my medical-school class of 200 who were stutterers; the school administration thought that there was 1. Three of them appeared to be relatively fluent, but when they were not permitted to circumlocute, they were very dysfluent.) Porfert and Rosenfield (3) evaluated a large college population, asking individual students whether or not they were stutterers; the prevalence was 2.1 percent. One should note that the prevalence of stuttering has not decreased over recent years despite an increase in the number of speech therapists.

Although one may argue whether the prevalence of stuttering is 1.1 percent or perhaps as high as 4 or 5 percent, no one disagrees that the prevalence is much higher among men than among women. Some studies have found that the ratio of males to females is 2:1, others, as high as 9:1. The majority have found that the ratio is 4:1. There is something about the sexes that somehow predisposes men to a higher incidence of stuttering than women. Also of note is the fact that although there is a lower prevalence of stuttering among women, their prognosis is not as good (1, 2, 3).

There are several "secondary symptoms" associated with stuttering. Many stutterers "learn" to develop facial contortions, closing their eyes, pursing their lips, taking deep breaths, and avoiding eye contact. These are usually easily controlled with the aid of good speech therapy.

Stutterers can predict particular forthcoming sounds that will cause them difficulty. Consequently, they circumlocute. This "predictive" aspect of stuttering may be nonspecific. The sounds that usually cause stutterers the greatest degree of difficulty are at the beginning of phrases and sentences. These "Jonah" sounds, the sounds on which the individual will frequently stutter, oftentimes are "h" (i.e., "hello"), "d" (i.e., "didn't"), and bilabial sounds ("b" and "p") (1, 2).

Several conditions enhance a stutterer's fluency. Stutterers are usually more fluent when they whisper (2, 4). It is extremely rare for them to stutter when they sing or when they speak in cadence with a metronome. (I have personally seen many stutterers who were unaware that this phenomenon applied to others as well as themselves.) It is also uncommon for stutterers to block when speaking while inhaling (2). This, too, may involve different speech mechanisms.

There are many theories pertaining to stuttering. Johnson (5) contended that an individual stuttered because of the way that the individual's parents focused attention on speech, and that the individual then became overly concerned about speech. Once the child "learned" that he was a stutterer, the appellation stuck and he became a stutterer. This is referred to as the listener/speaker interaction hypothesis.

There are many psychiatric theories pertaining to stuttering (1, 2). However, psychotherapy has been nonproductive in treating stutterers, and few contend that the major cause of stuttering is psychiatric. This is not to say that a psychiatrist does not have a role in treating stuttering; stutterers frequently have major problems in adjustment and difficulties pertaining to self-concept. Psychiatric intervention is often important in speech therapy, especially as the stutterer leaves the realm of stuttering and enters the realm of more fluent speech.

In the early 1900s, Orton and Travis (6) popularized a theory of several years' standing in Germany, which contended that stutterers had speech in both hemispheres of the brain. The Orton-Travis theory contended that, whereas most people had language in the left side of their brain, stutterers had language in both sides, and that somehow this caused them to stutter. Were this true, stutterers would have an increased prevalence of nonright-handedness (i.e., less left-hemisphere language dominance) (7). Bryngelson (8) analyzed many stutterers and contended that 68 percent were ambidextrous; others (3, 9) were unable to confirm this. Porfert and Rosenfield (3) also found no major differences in handedness between stutterers and controls. The thesis fell out of favor because of the many contradictory findings.

In the late 1960s, Jones (10) revived interest in this hypothesis. He had performed Wada tests on four stutterers who had subsequently developed brain tumors or aneurysms. A Wada test involves injecting a short-acting barbiturate into one of the carotid arteries during an angiogram; this is done to ascertain whether language is present in the hemisphere being examined. If the right hemisphere (in a right-handed patient) is injected with the barbiturate (sodium amytal), the individual develops a left hemiplegia, left hemisensory loss, and a left-visual-field deficit. If the left side is injected, the individual will become aphasic in addition to developing the latter symptoms on the right, since language is present in the left hemisphere.

Jones performed this study on four stutterers who required brain surgery. He performed the Wada test to ascertain whether they would become aphasic following surgery on the diseased side. To his surprise, all stutterers, three of whom were left-handed, had language in both hemispheres and they ceased stuttering, following removal of the diseased hemisphere. Subsequent Wada testing failed to reveal any language deficit on the operated side. This renewed considerable interest in the relationship between stuttering and cerebral dominance.

Dichotic listening is an experimental technique that permits evaluation of cerebral dominance. The right ear has more connections to the left hemisphere than it does to the right hemisphere; the left ear has more connections to the right hemisphere than it does to the left hemisphere. If competing messages are heard in both ears, the ear which has the strongest connection to the side of the brain where language resides scores the best. There are many ways of performing dichotic tests—looking at digits, or listening to words, melodies, and sundry other sounds.

Rosenfield and Goodglass (11) performed dichotic listening tests on right-handed adult male stutterers. They examined aspects of language (which related to the left hemisphere) and melody (which related to the right hemisphere). They noted that stutterers were different from controls. This substantiated the relationship between stuttering and altered cerebral laterality.

Other theories of stuttering pertain to the larynx. Many authors have demonstrated that muscles that abduct the vocal cords and those that adduct them fire simultaneously during many stuttering blocks, and that if a stutterer fakes a stuttering block or if a nonstutterer fakes a stuttering block, he cannot reproduce this abnormality (12, 13).

Some have queried whether stutterers are brain damaged. If anything, stutterers are probably smarter than nonstutterers (14). There is no evidence whatsoever that stutterers have suffered brain damage. However, some individuals may develop stuttering-like behavior following brain damage. This was first reported by Rosenfield in 1972 (15), when he described an individual who became a stutterer following left cerebral ischemia. Since then, other individuals have noted acquired stuttering (16, 17). "Acquired" stutterers are different from "routine" stutterers in that the former's blocks usually do not occur at the beginning of sentences or phrases but instead occur throughout; also, oftentimes, they do not show improvement with melody.

One theory contends that stutterers have abnormal laryngeal reflexes that they have carried over from childhood (18). The act of vocalization involves subglottic air-pressure changes. These changes in pressure exert force on laryngeal muscles, which initiates several muscle contractions and reflexes. Cerebral dominance probably plays a role in controlling this reflex system (19). Stutterers may sing fluently because singing initiates a marked rise in subglottic pressure, thereby adding tension to the vocal cords and, possibly, initiating different reflex mechanisms. This, then, can also explain why stutterers do not stutter while inhaling, since, again, different speech mechanisms are involved (19).

THERAPY

There are many forms of therapy for stutterers. It is not possible to cover all of them in this chapter. They are excellently reviewed by others (1, 20). Psychiatric therapy is probably good for the transition from stuttering to (one hopes) nonstuttering behavior. Other aspects of therapy relate to behavioral modification (21). These therapists contend that a major component of stuttering can be "unlearned" by focusing upon durations of sounds (21).

The Edinburgh Masker (22) is an electronic device that may better one's speech. This device takes advantage of the fact that stutterers often do not stutter if they cannot hear themselves talk (2). Part of the apparatus is strapped across the larynx; a small stethoscope apparatus is plugged into the ear. When the stutterer starts to speak, he literally cannot hear himself speak. This has had a positive effect on many stutterers. Although it is slightly cumbersome, it frequently can "decondition" many stutterers and help them attain fluency when they use it. Also, it may help to decondition various fears and uncertainties in particular situations.

Speech-therapy evaluation is a must for all stutterers. Stutterers should not be told that they will outgrow the disturbance and that they do not need to see a speech therapist. Many types of speech therapy relate to overcoming fears and anxieties of the speech problem, speaking at a slower rate, controlling air flow, and other learned mechanisms.

Research in stuttering and other areas of the voice sciences are in a period of rapidly expanding knowledge. This is largely a result of new physiological approaches to evaluating speech, such as laryngeal electromyography. It is our expectation that the coming decade will witness a further understanding of this common problem.

REFERENCES

1. Bloodstein, O. A *Handbook on Stuttering*. Chicago: National Easter Seal Society for Crippled Children and Adults, 1969.
2. Van Riper, C. *The Nature of Stuttering*. Englewood Cliffs: Prentice-Hall, 1971.
3. Porfert, A.R. & Rosenfield, D.B. Prevalence of stuttering. *J. Neurol. Neurosurg. Psychiat.* 41: 954–56, 1978.
4. Cherry, C. & Sayers, B. Experiments upon the total inhibition of stammering by external control, and some clinical results. *J. Psychsom. Res.* 1: 233–46, 1956.
5. Johnson, W. *The Onset of Stuttering*. Minneapolis: U. of Minnesota Press, 1955.
6. Orton, S.T. A physiological theory of reading disability in stuttering in children. *New Eng. J. Med.* 199: 1,045–52, 1928.
7. Benson, D.F. & Geschwind, N. Cerebral dominance and its disturbances. *Pediat. Clin. N. Am.* 15: 759–69, 1968.
8. Bryngelson, B. Sidedness as an etiological factor in stuttering. *J. Gen. Psychol.* 47: 204–17, 1935.

9. Daniels, E.N. An analysis of the relation between handedness and stuttering with special reference to the Orton-Travis theory of cerebral dominance. *J. Speech Dis.* 5: 309–26, 1940.

10. Jones, R.K. Observations in stammering after localized cerebral injury. *J. Neurol. Neurosurg. Psychiat.* 29: 192–95, 1966.

11. Rosenfield, D.B. & Goodglass, H. *Dichotic testing of cerebral dominance in stutterers. Brain & Lang.*, 1980.

12. Freeman, F.G. Phonation stuttering: a review of current research. *J. Fluency Disord.* 4: 79–89, 1979.

13. Shapiro, A.I. An electromyographic analysis of the fluent and dysfluent utterances of several types of stutterers. *J. Fluency Disord.*, 1980.

14. Sheehan, J.G. *Stuttering: Research and Therapy.* New York: Harper & Row, 1970.

15. Rosenfield, D.B. Stuttering in cerebral ischemia. *New Eng. J. Med.* 287: 991, 1972.

16. Helm, N.A., Butler, R.B., & Benson, V.F. Acquired stuttering. *Neurol.* 28: 1,159–65, 1978.

17. Rosenbek, T.C., Messert, B., Collins, M. Stuttering following brain damage. *Brain & Lang.* 6:82–96, 1978.

18. Wyke, B. The neurology of stammering. *J. Psychosom. Res.* 15: 423–32, 1971.

19. Rosenfield, D.B. Cerebral dominance in stuttering. *J. Fluency Disord.*, 1980.

20. Gregory, H.H. *Controversies About Stuttering Therapy.* Baltimore: University Park Press, 1979.

21. Webster, R.L. Evolution of a target based behavioral therapy for stuttering. *J. Fluency Disord.*, 1980.

22. Dewar, A., Dewar, A.D., & Anthony, J.F. The effect of auditory feedback masking on concomitant movements of stammering. *Brit. J. Disord. Commun.* 14: 219–30, 1979.

15

Treatment Approaches to Psychophysiological Distress

NORMAN DECKER

Modern concepts of disease include multi-causal etiologies. Psychological, social, and organic factors, in varying combinations and strengths, play etiologic roles in virtually all disease states. In that sense, setting aside a separate category of disease as psychophysiological or psychosomatic has become an increasingly archaic conceptualization. Psychiatric treatment approaches can play some role in most diseases. I will confine myself, however, to a brief overview of psychiatric treatment approaches to those diseases in which psychological etiologic factors are generally believed to play a major role.

I will focus primarily on those diseases involving demonstrable end organ pathology. I will not cover conversion disorders or somatopsychic distress; namely, those situations in which major emotional dysfunction can be seen secondary to significant organic disease.

The treatment of psychophysiological disorders almost always starts with a primary-care physician. Unfortunately, many significant pathognomonic details involving psychiatric ailments are beyond the competence of the general medical practitioner. Psychiatric intervention starts, therefore, with education of the nonpsychiatric physician. Consultation-liaison psychiatry has developed an extensive literature (1, 2, 3) on the use of the consultation model for education of primary clinicians. The next several suggestions refer to procedures that psychiatrists, in a consultative role, can utilize to help nonpsychiatric physicians improve their diagnostic abilities.

As Almy (4) and others have pointed out, the usual approach of most clinicians is first to evaluate, via medical history, physical examination, and laboratory studies, all physical parameters of disease. Evaluation of psychosocial factors is reserved for a later time if the early investigation proves insufficient. Such a sequence has several negative features, including the relegation of psychosocial factors to a lesser status. Patients often get the message that the physician has little interest in, respect for, or expertise in, these areas; and when a psychosocial evaluation is undertaken, it often implies a pejorative judgment of the patient. "We can't find anything wrong with you, so perhaps you had better see a psychiatrist." Referral to a mental-health specialist at this time has negative connotations. Patients often feel that their primary doctor is deserting them. These factors lead, in many cases, to poor compliance with psychiatric treatment. Other adverse effects of reserving psychosocial evaluation for last include a plethora of unnecessary laboratory procedures and many unnecessary invasive operations as well.

It is suggested, therefore, that the primary physician, in his initial history taking, take as much care in discovering psychosocial factors as he does somatic factors in disease. In particular, he should look for precipitating stresses which have a significant causal relationship with the onset or exacerbation of the disease process. A life chart can be constructed by the physician in order to correlate psychosocial stress and somatic illness. The resulting continuum will usually reveal one of two major patterns when psychogenic factors are significant. The first of these describes patients with relatively good ego strength who have achieved reasonably high levels of social and occupational functioning and have been relatively disease-free except during periods of major stress. The second pattern will show patients with relatively poor ego strength who have been more or less incapacitated by disease for many years and who have achieved relatively poor levels of social and occupational adaptation. Many of these patients' lives revolve around their disease states. Exacerbations of disease are less clearly related to acute stresses.

For the first group, those with good ego strength and only intermittent disease clearly related to stress, several approaches are useful. First, the connection between the stress and the illness can be brought to the patient's attention and the patient can be helped to ventilate feelings about the stress in a supportive environment. Although it is not conclusively proven, most authorities believe that there is an inverse relationship between expression of affect and psychophysiologic symptomatology. Ventilation of affect may be rendered difficult by the presence of alexithymia, as described by Nemiah (5). This refers to a relative inability to verbalize or express emotion. Nemiah feels that alexithymia is frequently present in psychophysiologic patients. It may be present in both groups of psychophysiological patients, those with good ego strength and intermittent symptoms and those with poor ego strength and ongoing symptomatology. Many feel that alexithymia impedes not only ventilation of affect, but most other forms of psychotherapy as well.

Let me now return to therapeutic approaches to the first, or healthier, group. Some stresses, such as the death of a loved one, are irreversible. Others are potentially reversible, but patients frequently feel helpless to effect this reversal. Brief counseling, direction, and supportive psychotherapy can be extremely helpful, in many cases, to attenuate acute stress. Vocational counseling and brief marital and family counseling can be effective here in mitigating the realities of financial disaster, marital disruption, delinquency, and other stress-laden situations. Brief therapy, as described by Castelnuevo-Tedesco (6), aimed toward ego strengthening and problem solving is also relevant here. All of the treatments mentioned thus far can be undertaken by the well-trained and interested primary-care doctor, or they can be undertaken by a mental-health specialist working in close conjunction with the primary-care physician. Close connections must be established between primary-care physicians, mental-health specialists, and specialists in various areas of somatic medicine.

It is worth noting that anticipation of stress and preparatory training can go a long way toward reducing the intensity of that stress, thereby reducing secondary illness. In this regard, preparation for surgery, preparation for chemotherapy, preparation for childbirth, preparation for marriage, preparation for divorce, preparation for opening a medical practice, and preparation for the rigors of medical and surgical training are all extraordinarily useful.

We now move on to the second group of patients—namely, those with poor ego strength, major incapacitation by disease, poor correlation between acute stress and disease exacerbation, and a social and vocational life which focuses around the disease. These are the kinds of patients whom one characteristically thinks of when considering psychophysiologic illness. Endocrinopathies such as diabetes mellitus, inflammatory bowel disease such as ulcerative colitis, dermatologic disorders such as neurodermatitis and psoriasis, and respiratory disorders such as bronchial asthma have all been studied by psychiatrists, from Alexander (7) to numerous current investigators.

A perennial question in psychiatry has been whether psychotherapy is helpful in the treatment of these patients. Although it has been established that psychoanalysis reduces the utilization of other medical modalities to the point where it becomes cost-effective (8), there is still controversy about whether psychoanalysis or intensive dynamic psychotherapy is of value in the treatment of psychophysiologic disorders. There is a paucity of careful studies in this area. There are some few which indicate intensive psychotherapy does benefit certain types of psychophysiologic distress, and there are some studies to the contrary. Weiner (9) has noted the heterogeneity of etiologies in psychophysiological disorders and has stated that single major conflicts, as postulated by Alexander (7), are not present in all cases of any given disorder. In this regard, type A profiles are not uniformly present in all cases of coronary thrombosis, and the typical peptic ulcer profile is not universally present in all cases of peptic ulcer. This is not to say, however, that such conflicts are not present and do not have a causal relationship with the disease process in many cases. If this be so, then psychotherapy aimed at resolving the emotional conflict can be efficacious.

To my mind, intensive, insight-oriented psychotherapy or psychoanalysis should be reserved for only a selected group of psychophysiologic patients:

(1) those who do not have alexithymia and thus are capable of discussing their emotional lives. It is true, however, that some patients with "relative alexithymia" are capable of learning this language; (2) patients who have some nodding awareness that there are inner problems which not only affect their physiologic status but also affect other areas of their adaptational life; (3) patients who are motivated to do long-term insight-oriented work; (4) patients (and therapists) who are aware at the outset that the therapeutic work may or may not significantly alter the psychophysiologic symptoms. The aim is to resolve intrapsychic conflict, and the areas in which this will be of benefit are not entirely predictable at the outset. Nevertheless, in the hands of many clinicians, such an approach does bear fruit. Let me illustrate:

> A middle-aged woman entered intensive, dynamic psychotherapy because of severe distress revolving around a failing marriage. She had a long history of passive and grudging obedience to a domineering, abusive husband, which in turn recapitulated a relationship she had had with an older brother during her formative years. She had great difficulty asserting herself and standing up for her rights. The dissolution of the marriage was unavoidable, and the patient remained in therapy with me for approximately three years. She had a lengthy history of approximately 15 years' of vasomotor rhinitis and low-level hypertension. In therapy, she worked through many of the sources of her passive obedience, resentment, and inhibitions about self-assertion. She felt she had become a very different person when she terminated her therapy. No focus was placed on her physiological symptoms, and I was surprised to learn, in the latter stages of her therapy, that, for the first time in many years, her vasomotor rhinitis had cleared and her hypertension had likewise disappeared and made further pharmacotherapy for it unnecessary.

Intensive, insight-oriented psychotherapy or psychoanalysis is not the treatment of choice for those patients with psychophysiologic disorders who have an associated psychotic condition. Likewise, some care must be exerted, if this kind of therapy is undertaken, to modulate the speed with which the therapy progresses. More specifically, defenses must be worked through gently, sensitively, and gradually, so as not to lead to an overly rapid exposure to instinctual material. If there is too quick an exposure to such material, severe exacerbations of the physiological illness frequently follow.

Twenty years ago, this form of psychotherapy for psychophysiologic disorders was the treatment of choice, and, for many, the only known form of psychiatric treatment. Since then, other forms of treatment have been found to be extremely useful. Most of these other forms of therapy have been behavioral, systems-oriented, or some combination of the two. The most direct and obvious form of behavioral treatment is biofeedback. Since many psychophysiologic disorders are mediated along autonomic pathways, many individuals have been able to develop conscious control of autonomic functioning through biofeedback training. Certain psychophysiologic symptoms can thus be reversed. Biofeedback has been found to be useful in the irritable-bowel syndrome and in control of the lower esophageal and anal sphincters. It has been found useful in the treatment of Raynaud's Disease, and is promising for migraine headaches as well. Some patients have been able to alter their blood pressure with biofeedback training, but such effects have not thus far been sustained. Patients have also learned to alter heart rate and in some cases have been able to alter cardiac arrhythmias.

From the behavioral point of view, psychophysiological symptoms can be seen as aberrant behavior in a social context. In this sense, the behavior has been seen to yield rewards which, from a psychodynamic frame of reference, have been conceptualized as secondary gain. More specifically, the psychophysiologic symptomatology has been found to appear when certain affects might appropriately be expressed but are not, or when certain interpersonal problems arise which are not faced. In this context, psychophysiologic symptoms or "behaviors" become stereotyped substitutes for a rich and varied interpersonal life. One corollary of this conception has been that it is necessary to broaden and extend areas of life performance in which a patient can successfully operate, in order for the patient to surrender the symptomatic "physiological behaviors."

Careful evaluation of the ebb and flow of symptomatology has yielded information which can be utilized to plan strategic interventions yielding striking results. For example, if one conceptualizes pain as behavior, a behavioral model can be utilized to markedly reduce pain. This has become one of the mainstays in the psychological treatment of chronic pain. This approach has perhaps received its most sophisticated application in the family-therapy format, as elucidated by Minuchin and his coworkers (10). In their model, the physiological symptomatology is seen as a form of aberrant behavior utilized by an entire family matrix for ulterior purposes. Specifically, the identified patient and that patient's symptomatology are utilized by the family when a conflict situation demanding explicit interaction and resolution of conflict is called for. Rather than face this task, the family turns to the identified patient to have an exacerbation of symptomatology and thus to abort work and resolution of the interfamilial conflict. This is to be distinguished from the intrapsychic conflict referred to by Alexander and other psychoanalysts. A panoply of strategic interventions are utilized by the therapist to bring a family to grips with avoided tasks. The family is discouraged from utilizing the identified patient as a means of avoiding these tasks.

In the language of family therapists, the psychosomatic family shows (1) excessive enmeshment; (2) excessive diffusion of roles between intrafamilial units, which should be more discrete; (3) overprotectiveness, particularly of the psychosomatic individual; (4) a rigidity of transactional patterns which are modified only slowly; and (5) participation of the identified patient in the solution of conflicts of other family members via the symptomatology. An attempt is made in therapy to alter all of these patterns. Such an approach has been found by Minuchin and his coworkers to be of significant value in alleviating psychophysiologic symptoms in 80 to 90 percent of their cases of anorexia nervosa, brittle childhood diabetes, and bronchial asthma.

Since many psychophysiologic disorders seem to be mediated along sympathomimetic pathways, attempts at reduction of circulating neurogenic amines have been found useful. Two psychotherapeutic modalities are of note here. The first is, once again, behavioral; namely, relaxation training. An alternative to relaxation training is the systematic and regular use of one or another form of either transcendental meditation or its secular counterpart, the Relaxation Response, as elucidated by Benson (11). If these techniques are practiced regularly, striking reductions in anxiety levels and statistically significant reductions in blood pressure have been found. I regularly prescribe the Relaxation Response for many of my patients. For those patients in whom anxiety and its physiological correlates play a large part in symptomatology, antianxiety medication may be of use. Neuroleptics are generally useful for those psychophysiologic patients with an associated schizophrenia, whereas the benzodiazepines are more useful for those with anxiety unrelated to psychosis. It is worth noting that chronic usage of benzodiazepines has been found to be of questionable value, in that both tolerance and addiction can develop. It is also noteworthy that in the case of diazepam, tolerance does develop to the sedative and anxiolytic effects of the drug, but not to its muscle-relaxant properties. One must guard against the temptation to use a pharmacologic agent in place of a more definitive treatment maneuver.

Many patients with a variety of physiological complaints without demonstrable pathology—most notably excessive pain—are actually suffering from unrecognized depression. Many of these patients show a striking amelioration of their symptomatology with the use of tricyclic antidepressant drugs. These drugs have been noted to have a primary analgesic effect in addition to their antidepressant properties (12).

Before closing, I would like to mention the benefit that a positive disease-fighting attitude can have in many situations. This has been dramatically demonstrated in the treatment of metastatic malignant disease. Several experimental approaches to cancer therapy, most notably the work of Simonton (13) and his associates, have carefully fostered a positive disease-fighting attitude; patients encouraged in this manner seem to live longer, and research is continuing in several centers. The intermediary mechanisms have yet to be worked out, but some feel that alterations in immune systems are caused by these alterations in attitude. You will note that I have here increased the scope of the term "psychophysiological" to include malignant disease. Not all would agree with this conceptualization, but I feel that it is relevant, and has been corroborated by those studies demonstrating increased frequency and intensity of stress immediately prior to the onset of cancer. To return to the question of a positive disease-fighting approach, this probably has applicability to a wide variety of medical conditions. Norman Cousins (14) has made note of the salutary, even curative, effect on his severe arthritic condition of a positive, cheerful attitude.

Many of the approaches briefly outlined in this chapter are largely within the realm of the mental-health professional. Some, such as the fostering of attitudinal changes, utilization of psychopharmacologic agents, and prescription of the Relaxation Response, can be done by the primary physician. In closing, I wish to reemphasize the necessity in psychophysiological cases of a close liaison between the psychiatrist and other members of the mental-health team and the primary physician. This team approach, and the utilization of many of the methods I have outlined, have led to a much brighter outlook for psychophysiological cases than was the case 20 years ago. This has the reciprocal effect of making these patients more attractive to both mental-health and primary-care practitioners than in the past. Further research in psychiatric modalities of treatment will probably further strengthen our hand in struggling with difficult psychophysiologic diseases in the future.

REFERENCES

1. Strain, J.J. *Psychological Interventions in Medical Practice*. New York: Appleton-Century-Crofts, 1978.
2. Caplan, G. *The Theory and Practice of Mental Health Consultation*. New York: Basic, 1970.
3. Vacher, C.D. & Stratas, N.E. *Consultation-Education Development and Evaluation*. New York: Human Sciences, 1976.
4. Almy, T.T. Therapeutic strategy in stress-related digestive disorders. *Clin. Gastroent.* 6(3): 709–22, 1977.
5. Nemiah, J.C. Alexithymia: theoretical considerations. *Psychother. Psychosom.* 28: 199–206, 1977.
6. Castelnuevo-Tedesco, P. *The Twenty-Minute Hour*. Boston: Little, Brown, 1965.
7. Alexander, F. *Psychosomatic Medicine: Its Principles and Applications*. New York: Norton, 1950.
8. Based on actuarial statistics from West Germany. Personal communication from member of Insurance Committee of the American Psychoanalytic Association.
9. Weiner, H. *Psychobiology and Human Disease*. New York: Elsevier, 1977.
10. Minuchin, S., Rosman, B.L., & Baker, L. *Psychosomatic Families*. Cambridge: Harvard U. Press, 1978.
11. Benson, H. *The Relaxation Response*. New York: Morrow, 1975.
12. Hackett, T.P. The pain patient: evaluation and treatment. In Hackett, T.P. & Cassem, N.H. (Eds.), *Massachusetts General Hospital Handbook of General Hospital Psychiatry*. St. Louis: Mosby, 1978.
13. Simonton, C. *Getting Well Again*. New York: Bantam, 1980.
14. Cousins, N. *Anatomy of An Illness As Perceived By The Patient: Reflection on Healing and Regeneration*. New York: Norton, 1979.

Phenomenology and Treatment of Psychophysiological Disorders

16

Personality Correlates of Keratoconus

EMILE J. FARGE
PAUL E. BAER
GEORGE L. ADAMS
DAVID PATON

There is evidence that ophthalmic disorders are often accompanied by emotional stress (1, 2, 3, 4, 5, 6, 7). Moreover, there is support in the literature for the contention that emotions are linked to visual impairment (8, 9, 10, 11, 12, 13, 14, 15). Nevertheless, the role of vision in the development of personality—or vice versa—has been neglected by behavioral scientists. In an early attempt at describing personality characteristics in farsightedness and myopia, Rice (16, 17) suggested that vision was one of the determinants in the development of a child's character and that farsightedness or myopia led to the development of certain personality types.

There have also been studies of the relationship between intelligence and refractive states which suggested that higher IQ scores associated with myopia, and lower scores with hypermetropia. The evidence, however, has never been developed convincingly, and other variables could account for the results in these studies (18, 19). Further, there have been some more recent studies (20) which support the contention that personality changes occur in persons as a result of chronic illness. One such study (21) provides evidence that (1) physical illness and disability significantly alter personality characteristics and behavior, and (2) the occurrence of illness after childhood can interfere with psychological development by retarding emotional maturity and creating devaluation in self-concept. Many studies over recent decades have shown that self-devaluation in the development of self-concept occurs in children and adolescents with disabilities. Burlingham (15) describes the psychological foundations established in children with visual impairment. Meighan (21) specifically reports the development of negative self-concept in visually handicapped adolescents. One example of a postulated link betwen visual impairment and personality is a published impression that persons with keratoconus are hyperactive, demanding, difficult to please, and often appear suspicious and untrusting (22). That author recommended a psychological sensitivity to the keratoconus patient. He questioned whether hyperkinetic, psychologically disturbed patients developed keratoconus, or whether keratoconus patients become hyperkinetic and psychologically disturbed. The body of his presentation discusses the difficulties in treating the keratoconus patient and concludes that regardless of etiological considerations, "keratoconus patients need psychotherapy as much as medical and technical expertise."

Keratoconus is a process of thinning and bulging of the cornea (23, 24), resulting in irregular astigmatism, corneal scarring, and a marked limitation of visual acuity that often reaches the point at which even contact lenses fail to provide normal acuity. In its advanced stage, the vision of the patients is markedly impaired, and when contact lenses fail to give adequate correction, the appropriate management is corneal transplantation—with an excellent prognosis for restoration of good acuity, often dependent upon the reintroduction of contact lenses. It is an important fact that keratoconus is accompanied by a mixture of seemingly overlapping entities. There is a definite but not frequent incidence of positive family history of keratoconus in these patients. Some have syndromes associated with known collagen abnormality, and others have no demonstrable disorder except for the thinness and conical deformity of their corneas. It seems that keratoconus or a variant thereof may indeed be induced by rubbing the eyes or even by malfitting contact lenses, particularly in the predisposed individual. Whether keratoconus may be induced by such modalities without congenital predisposition is unknown.

Persons with keratoconus as a group seem to share a personality structure that transcends considerations of education, family history, demonstrable syndromes, or other recognizable commonalities. It was the purpose of this study to examine these patients to determine if they truly differ psychologically from the general population and from other approximately aged-matched patients with visual impairments. We also sought to get a better definition of what ophthalmologists think about patients having keratoconus. It is rare that professional opinion is objectively assessed—too often clinicians perpetuate opinions that are popular but inexact clinical impressions based on hearsay.

METHODS

We studied a group of patients with keratoconus and used a comparison group of patients with visual impairments similar in most respects to those of the keratoconus group (having a progressive ocular disease often leading to blindness) but with other unrelated causes. The major purpose of the study was to note whether keratoconus patients are psychologically unique, differing from patients with a visual deficit of other etiology.

To document and substantiate clinical impressions of ophthalmologists regarding the personality deficits of patients with keratoconus, ophthalmologists were asked to use a standard method rating the personality characteristics of these patients. The Adjective Check List (ACL) (25) was chosen for this purpose. The ACL consists of 300 adjectives which are marked by the respondent as to whether they do or do not characterize the individual being rated. The test is used most frequently for self- and observer rating, but it has also been applied successfully for rating an average or a representative person, as in the present usage. Its reliability and validity have been satisfactorily established, and a substantial literature has evolved around this instrument. The test has 24 scales and indices, some of which reflect stylistic characteristics of the rater, but most of which describe personality dispositions from the perspective of a need system.

One panel of ophthalmologists known to treat keratoconus was asked to use the ACL to describe the typical keratoconus patient. A second panel of ophthalmologists, chosen randomly from a roster of members of a metropolitan ophthalmological society, was asked to check adjectives describing the hypothetical, typical patient with progressive eye disease starting in youth, potentially reversible, but often demanding drastic intervention to correct. Eighteen clinicians responded, nine to form the group which treats keratoconus, and nine to form the second group. These two groups of raters did not differ in years of ophthalmological experience or in professional status.

To examine the psychological profiles of keratoconus patients directly, several ophthalmologists provided us with an arbitrary selection of 50 patients who had late-stage keratoconus, some of whom had been treated with successful corneal transplantation. The mean age was 30 years (SD = 9.5). Twenty-one of these individuals were female and 29 were male. A nonkeratoconus comparison group was formed, composed of persons with severe and progressive eye disease. Of the total of 19 patients in this latter group, 12 had retinitis pigmentosa and 7 had high myopia. Their mean age was 38.8 years (SD = 9). Nine of these patients were women and 10 were men.

The Sixteen Personality Factor Questionnaire (16PF) (26) was administered to the patients because of its relatively nonthreatening content and well-established psychometric characteristics. The test contains 187 items in a three-point rating scale format, and is easily comprehended. This set of factor-based scales provides 16 scores of personality descriptors. Norms are available that are correct for age and sex.

RESULTS

The ratings of the ophthalmologists for a representative keratoconus patient and a representative patient with other progressive eye disease are shown in Table 16-1. Because of the small number of raters and the possibility of heterogeneous variance, the Mann-Whitney U test was employed to assess differences between the two groups of raters. Of the 24 ACL measures, the two groups of raters differed from each other on four scales at the p < .05 level of significance, and tended to differ on four other scales. The ACL results indicated that the raters for progressive eye disease took a more defensive and supportive stance on behalf of such a representative patient than did the raters for keratoconus. Otherwise, the representative keratoconus patient was thought to be significantly less

TABLE 16-1

Median Adjective Checklist Scale Scores for Two Groups of Ophthalmologists who Rated a "Representative Patient" with Either Keratoconus or Progressive Eye Disease

Scale	Rating Construct Keratoconus Eye Disease		Mann-Whitney U
	(N=9) Md	(N=9) Md	
Defensiveness	30	42	12**
Self-Confidence	39	46	16**
Self-Control	41	47	21*
Lability	41	35	21*
Personal Adjustment	31	38	16**
Achievement	41	50	19
Dominance	44	51	27
Endurance	46	48	35
Order	46	46	33
Intraception	34	42	19*
Nurturance	39	46	24
Affiliation	33	41	16**
Heterosexuality	40	40	40
Exhibition	48	48	36
Autonomy	43	45	38
Aggression	53	50	31
Change	42	42	31
Succorance	64	49	24
Abasement	56	49	30
Deference	49	51	29
Counseling Readiness	57	53	27
Favorable Adjectives	25	34	19*
Unfavorable Adjectives	49	47	32
Total Checked	32	34	36

*P < .10
**P < .05

self-confident, more poorly adjusted personally, and less affiliative and friendly than the patient with progressive eye disease. In addition, the raters tended to view the average keratoconus patient as less self-controlled, more emotionally labile, and less insightful.

Table 16-2 shows 16PF factor scores for two groups, keratoconus patients (n = 50) and a comparison group (n = 19) of patients with retinitis pigmentosa or severe myopia. As can be seen for both groups, a number of factor scores differed significantly from the standard mean value of 5.5. These comparisons were obtained following the procedure recommended by Cattell et al. (26).

For the group of keratoconus patients, factors A (outgoing), C (emotionally stable), and M (imaginative), were significantly lower than the standard mean, while factors L (suspicious), O (apprehensive), and Q_4 (tense), were significantly higher than the standard mean. As can be seen in several instances—i.e., for factors C, L, M, O, and Q_4—the deviation of scores for the keratoconus patients was substantial, and represents a well-established pattern. The pattern suggests a conglomerate of personality traits: concern with doing the right thing, lack of trust in interpersonal relations, poorly controlled emotionality, inadequate

TABLE 16-2
Sixteen Personality Factor Scores for Two Groups of Vision-Impaired Patients[1]

Factor	High Score Description	Group K[2] (N=50) X	SD	z	Group RM[3] (N=19) X	SD	z
A	Outgoing	4.8	2.1	−2.4*	4.4	1.9	−2.4*
B	Intelligent	5.5	1.9	0	6.2	1.8	1.4
C	Emotionally Stable	4.2	2.0	−4.5***	4.7	1.6	−1.8
E	Assertive	5.4	1.9	−0.4	5.3	1.7	0.5
F	Happy-go-lucky	5.6	2.6	0.3	5.3	2.3	0.4
G	Conscientious	5.6	2.0	0.2	6.1	2.0	1.3
H	Venturesome	5.3	2.2	−0.8	5.0	2.5	1.0
I	Tender-minded	5.7	2.0	0.8	6.4	2.1	2.0*
L	Suspicious	6.5	2.0	3.5***	6.7	1.8	3.8***
M	Imaginative	4.5	2.1	−3.6***	5.0	1.8	−1.0
N	Astute	5.5	1.9	0.1	5.8	2.0	0.6
O	Apprehensive	6.4	2.0	3.1**	6.0	2.2	1.1
Q1	Experimenting	5.3	2.0	0.6	5.0	1.4	1.0
Q2	Self-sufficient	5.5	2.0	0	5.8	2.1	0.6
Q3	Controlled	5.2	2.1	−1.1	5.7	1.8	0.5
Q4	Tense	6.8	2.1	4.6***	6.5	2.0	2.1*

[1]Tested against $\overline{X}$=5.5, SD=2.0 (Cattell et al., 1970)
[2]Keratoconus
[3]Retinitis Pigmentosa (N=12) and Severe Myopes (N=7)
*$P < .05$
**$P < .01$
***$P < .001$

coping with stress, and a high level of anxiety, frustration, and insecurity, all of which can be seen as being compatible and internally consistent.

The comparison patients also demonstrated differences from the standard mean, but only one factor, L (suspicious), was strongly statistically significant. Factors A and Q_4, as well as I (tender-minded) also differed. The pattern of significant factor scores suggests that individuals in this group lack trust in others; they are distant from others, and are tense and frustrated but self-reliant and realistic.

Direct comparisons of the factor scores between these two groups yielded no significant differences. From an indirect perspective, the keratoconus group had more significantly different factor values relative to the standard mean than the comparison group. Further, the deviant factor scores of the keratoconus group more often had a substantial degree of statistical significance. Moreover, when the deviant factor scores of the comparison group are examined, it can be seen that in only one instance, tender-mindedness (Factor I) did the comparison group manifest a deviant factor score not found for the keratoconus group. In this case, the comparison group was significantly more tender-minded than the universal mean.

CONCLUSIONS

From the adjectival descriptions by ophthalmologists of keratoconus and progressive eye disease patients, it was evident that the anecdotal clinical impressions of keratoconus patients as emotionally distinct could be substantiated by this more objective means of assessment. The view that ophthalmologists have of the keratoconus patient reflects the evident psychological distress and personal maladjustment of these patients. Interestingly, it also suggests that clinicians are disenchanted with these patients as a group.

The 16PF results clearly demonstrate that individuals with keratoconus have personality traits different from those of the average person. The traits in question identify the keratoconus patients as anxious, tense, having difficult interpersonal relations, and being somewhat blunted in the richness of thought content. This description is reminiscent of clinical impressions of these patients, and tends to support both the anecdotal opinions of clinicians about these patients and their ACL ratings. There is a distinct parallel between the two separate sources of information about keratoconus patients: the clinicians' judgment of the average patient on the one hand, and the disclosures of the patients themselves on the other. Both the patients and the raters point to emotional distress, interpersonal problems, and poor adjustment. Such correspondence represents a source of convergent validity for the findings.

An important feature of the present study was the inclusion of a comparison group of individuals with severe visual impairment other than keratoconus but similar to it in aspects of visual loss—or threat thereof. A possible alternative interpretation of the finding that keratoconus patients are psychologically different is that anyone with severe, debilitating visual impairment which is difficult to treat might manifest the sort of psychological and emotional reactions attributed here to keratoconus patients. While our results do not resolve the issue, they do tend to isolate certain elements of the question. We have no statistical evidence to indicate that keratoconus and other visually impaired patients are psychologically different from one another when considered as separate groups. Nevertheless, individuals with visual impairment other than keratoconus also differed from the standard mean and did not demonstrate traits that represent a pattern clearly different from that shown by the keratoconus patients.

These results suggest that individuals with severe visual impairment that has its origin early in life and is difficult to treat are likely to demonstrate certain traits involving anxiety and psychological impoverishment. It seems reasonable to suppose that the development of such traits occurs as part of an attempt to cope with the visual impairment. When the visual impairment is due to keratoconus, these traits are markedly exacerbated, and thereby more readily observed by the clinician. Why such exacerbation should be related to impairment from keratoconus is not made clear from the data. Despite the care we exercised in choosing a comparison group whose visual impairment matches that of keratoconus patients, it remains possible that the occurrence of keratoconus is much more distressing to the patient than impairment from other sources. Further study focusing on the patient's degree of anxiety about prospective loss of vision should be useful in clarifying this point. In any case, emotional disturbances and relatively unproductive coping traits appear to occur in the presence of visual impairment, particularly in the case of keratoconus. It seems reasonable to recommend that patients being treated for keratoconus, particularly if the treatment is to be surgical, be given the necessary time by the surgeon and staff, and substantive information, to ward off possible anxieties.

REFERENCES

1. Schulz, P.J. Reaction to loss of sight. In Pearlman, J.T., Adams, G.L., & Sloan, S.H. (Eds.), *Psychiatric Problems in Ophthalmology.* Springfield, Ill.: Thomas, 1977.
2. Adams, G.L., Pearlman, J.T., & Sloan, S.H. Guidelines for the psychiatric referral of visually handicapped patients. *Ann. Ophthalmol.* 3: 72–81, 1971.
3. Wolf, S.R. Psychiatric reaction to threatened blindness; a personal account. *Psychsom.* 12: 316–20, 1971.

4. Jackson, C.W. Clinical sensory deprivation: a review of hospitalized eye-surgery patients. In Zubek, J.P. (Ed.), *Sensory Deprivation: Fifteen Years of Research*. New York: Appleton-Century-Crofts, 1969.

5. Linn, L., Kahn, R.L., & Coles, R. Patterns of behavior disturbance following cataract extraction. *Am. J. Psychiat.* 110: 281–89, 1953.

6. Linn, L. Psychiatric reactions complicating cataract surgery. *Int. Ophthalmol. Clin.* 5: 143–64, 1965.

7. Ziskind, E. An explanation of mental symptoms found in acute sensory deprivation: researches 1958–1965. *Am. J. Psychiat.* 121: 939–46, 1965.

8. Solomon, P. Sensory Deprivation. In Freedman, A.M. & Kaplan, H.I. (Eds.), *Comprehensive Textbook of Psychiatry*. Baltimore: Williams & Wilkins, 1967.

9. Weisman, A.D. & Hackett, P.T. Psychosis after eye surgery. *New Eng. J. Med.* 258: 1,284–89, 1958.

10. Schlaegel, T.F., Jr. *Psychosomatic Ophthalmology*. Baltimore: Williams & Wilkins, 1957.

11. Schlaegel, T.F., Jr. Psychosomatics: the second face of ophthalmology. *Int. Ophthalmol. Clin.* 8: 409–85, 1968.

12. Sloan, S.H. & Wahl, C.W. The eye and "I." In Pearlman, J.T., Adams, G.L., & Sloan, S.H. (Eds.), *Psychiatric Problems in Ophthalmology*. Springfield, Ill.: Thomas, 1977.

13. Drews, R.C. Organic versus functional ocular problems. *Int. Ophthalmol. Clin.* 7: 665–96, 1967.

14. Karseras, A.G. Psychiatric aspects of ophthalmology. In Howels, J.G. (Ed.), *Modern Perspective in the Psychiatric Aspects of Surgery*. New York: Brunner/Mazel, 1976.

15. Burlingham, D. *Some Notes on the Development of the Blind in Psychoanalytic Study of the Child*. New York: International Universities Press, 1961.

16. Rice, Therman, B. Physical defects in character. I. Farsightedness. *Hygeia*. 8: 536–38, 1930.

17. Rice, Therman, B. Physical defects in character. II. Nearsightedness. *Hygeia*. 8: 644–46, 1931.

18. Nadell, C. & Hirsch, M.D. The relationship between intelligence and the reactive state in a selected high school sample. *Am. J. Optom. and Arch. Am. Acad. Optom.* 35: 321–26, 1958.

19. Stevens, A. & Wolff, H. The relationship of myopia to performance on a test of leveling sharpening. *Percep. and Mot. Skills.* 21: 399–403, 1965.

20. Meighan, T. *An Investigation of the Self-Concept of Blind and Visually Handicapped Adolescents*. New York: American Foundation for the Blind, 1971.

21. Barton, K. & Cattell, R. Personality before and after a chronic illness. *J. Clin. Psychol.* 28: 464–67, 1972.

22. Crossen, R.J. Psychological handling of contact lens wearing in keratoconus patients. *Contact and Intraoc. Lens. Med. J.* 4: 49–50, 1978.

23. Arentsen, J.J., Morgan, B., & Green, W.R. Changing indications for keratoplasty. *Am. J. Ophthalmol.* 81: 464–67, 1972.

24. Paton, D. The prognosis of penetrating keratoplasty: based upon corneal morphology. *Ophth. Surg.* 7(3): 36–45, 1976.

25. Gough, H.G. & Heilbrun, A.B. *The Adjective Checklist Manual*. Palo Alto: Consulting Psychologist, 1965.

26. Cattell, R.B., Eber, H.W. & Tatsuoka, M.M. *Handbook for the Sixteen Personality Factor Questionnaire*. Champaign, Ill.: Institute for Personality and Ability Testing, 1970.

17

Psychotherapy
of Psychophysiological Disorders

JAMES W. LOMAX

Interest in the relationship between mind and body has persisted from ancient Greek notions of the connection between bodily humors and personality types through the present times. A major change in the nature of investigations related to this interest was marked by William Beaumont's observations on the relationship of gastric secretions to emotions. Beaumont's early attempt to systematically study mind and body relationships occurred contemporaneously with very different but equally serious scientific investigations in Europe. Studies of hysterical phenomena by Charcot, Janet, Breuer, and, finally, Sigmund Freud demonstrated a far more pervasive effect of the mind on bodily functions than had ever before been appreciated. These divergent streams of thought began to merge around the developing discipline of psychosomatic medicine during the 1930s and 1940s. Studies done at the Chicago Institute for Psychoanalysis led to the development of specificity theory and a special therapeutic zeal for psychological intervention in psychosomatic disorders. Perhaps even more important than the theory of specificity itself is an underlying theme of these investigations and similar ones which have continued in many centers: Reliance on the study of phenomenologic parameters of disease processes is rarely adequate to either understand illness or plan comprehensive interventions. Since recent investigators have tended to develop one or more lines of investigations which match their theoretical and personal interests, it is now possible to describe illness processes at numerous levels of complexity and with considerable detail.

Grinker's description of the difficulty in defining the relationship of the investigator as an observer to what he or she is observing highlights the difficulties inherent in coordinating these levels of description (1). Scientific investigators often find themselves in a position analogous to the blind men and the elephant. As they describe a system with enumerable foci, they bring into being the classes of observations which determine the eventual patterns of understanding and consequent means of intervention. Grinker and others have attempted to understand the elements of an illness process in terms of transactions between systems of bodily, personal, and social function, and integrating mechanisms between the systems. The human organism is thus conceived of as many small systems which are linked by various internal transactions. Each organism relates as a functional whole or self-system which finally, in turn, relates to the family, society, and the natural environment it greets. Helpful observations can be made at levels of progressively increasing complexity ranging from enzymatic systems through organ systems, intrapsychic processes, interpersonal phenomena, family systems, and sociocultural systems. Increasingly, psychosomatic or psychophysiologic illness is seen as a "final common pathway" phenomenon indicating dysfunction in one or more levels of a system or the linkages between systems. Attention to one level of description of the illness process should never mean ignoring the multiple other levels. However, for particular purposes, one may helpfully focus on one level of understanding and intervention in psychosomatic illness while remaining mindful of the implication for the rest of the systems.

This chapter will predominantly focus on psychological factors in the initiation of, continuation of, and intervention in, psychophysiologic and psychosomatic illness. My thesis is that psychological factors do play a role in illness, and one way of intervening in illness is through psychotherapy. In planning psychotherapeutic interventions, there are several specific problems associated with psychosomatic illness which must be considered. As already noted one must consider the distinction between initiating and sustaining factors in the disease process, and one must deal with a characteristic tendency of certain individuals with psychosomatic illness to have a low level of awareness of their internal life—a particularly important obstacle to most methods of psychotherapy. This latter problem—termed alexithymia by Sifneos, Nemiah, and others—will be described first. The problem of distinguishing, initiating, and sustaining factors will be considered at several points in the chapter. In this manner, an overview of the different modes of psychotherapeutic intervention in psychophysiological disorders will be developed.

Less than a decade ago, Sifneos used the term alexithymia to describe individuals who are characterized by a marked difficulty in expressing feelings with words and a lack of fantasies appropriate to or expressive of feelings (thought content, therefore, being dominated by details of events in their external environment) (2). In a more recent article, John Nemiah speculates on a psychogenetic theory of the development of this condition (3). He raises the interesting possibility that a disturbance in the mother/infant relationship results in a failure to develop a mental representation of the mother. This partial defect in object constancy leads to defects in symbol formation and fantasy. Whether the mother/infant disturbance is due to factors involving the mother (excessive gratification of the infant's instincts or undue prohibition from normal autoerotic gratification) or in the child (hereditable defects of neuroanatomic structure or synthesis of neurotransmitters) is not important to this point. In either case, individuals develop who have difficulty in expressing feelings or forming fantasies. These individuals compose an undue proportion of those with psychosomatic illness, and are distinguishable from individuals with more neurotic symptomatology.

Psychotherapeutic intervention in psychosomatic or psychophysiological disorders has very different goals at different phases of the illness. In acute psychosomatic crises, attention to medical consequences of the illness and the precipitating factors of the acute phase should be paramount. Many psychosomatic illnesses have life-threatening consequences at times, and the psychiatrist must be willing to assume an active, directive medical role when appropriate. Thus, the facilitation of medical treatment by liaison activity with the primary-care physician and medical staff of the hospital is imperative. Some of the very personality characteristics which lead to the development of psychosomatic illness tend to make these individuals overrepresented among so-called "problem patients." Psychiatrists can facilitate the primary-care physician's and medical staff's understanding and tolerance of chronically ill individuals. This certainly does not mean that the direct involvement with the patient should be forgotten or neglected by the therapist during the acute phase. The opportunity for the patient to ventilate pragmatic and realistic concerns about his or her illness is important. Acknowledgment of the gravity of the situation to the therapist, the provision of a constant factor in an often chaotic and rapidly changing hospital environment, and the reassurance of the availability of the psychiatrist all play major roles in this treatment phase.

The evaluation of sustaining and initiating factors of the illness must be explored as the acute phase of the illness subsides. At this point, many patients with psychosomatic illness will be found to be still unsuitable for exploratory psychotherapy. In such cases, it is necessary to help the patient establish and maintain a supportive relationship with either the general physician or psychiatrist. If the formal relationship is to be with the primary-care physician, the liaison function of the psychiatrist again is the important role. Experienced family physicians are generally aware of the effectiveness of regular visits in a medical setting to provide a "safe anchorage" for psychosomatic patients. However, since more recent graduates of medical training institutions tend to be better prepared in the technical and scientific aspects of medicine, some family physicians may need considerable coaching or supervision in giving their patients emotional support. They should be advised to provide patients with regular, and initially rather frequent, appointments. Each interview should have the complementary goals of reviewing physiologic function and important emotional factors which appear to have precipitated the acute phase of the illness. Direct interventions, in terms of manipulating stressful environmental factors, are appropriate. (For example, a patient may be isolated from his family or particularly stressful family interactions, or encouraged to take a vacation.) The physician may need to meet with family members and ask them to decrease economic pressures or work collaboratively with the primary patient to reduce other environmental stresses. The patient should be informed that a component of his or her symptoms is psychogenic. Acceptance of the importance of such factors is essential, but the ease with which this step is accomplished varies tremendously. It is usually necessary for the physician to repetitively interpret certain situational or precipitating conflicts. In most of these cases, initiating psychological factors will never be addressed directly. Some of the sustaining factors of the illness and, it is hoped, a larger proportion of precipitating factors of acute crises will receive attention. Longer-term exploratory treatment of more basic initiating and sustaining conflicts and misperceptions should probably be undertaken only by a highly trained professional who can function as part of a multispecialty team. In summary, the goal of these more supportive and synthetic psychotherapeutic interventions is to decrease the effect of sustaining factors in psychosomatic illness and to quickly prevent or identify and remove precipitating factors of acute psychosomatic crises. Such physician/patient relationships are usually interminable, although many patients will remain free of overt illness as long as there are no major stresses on any of the various levels of vulnerability.

A more ambitious and exploratory psychotherapy is to be considered for certain patients when more profound change seems possible and necessary. Indications include rather low levels of situational stress which precipitate overt illness, or the presence of more profound conflicts or character traits which become evident during the evaluation phase. Objectives for such treatment have included modification of characterologic predisposition, exploration of self-concept, and treatment of specific infantile traumas (4).

Since the specific concerns and objectives of treatment have varied considerably over the past 40 years, a brief review of some of the trends might be valuable. In the 1930s and 1940s, Franz Alexander developed the specificity theory of psychosomatic illness. His theory linked certain infantile traumata to adult personality type and consequent psychosomatic illness. However, Alexander himself was well aware that it was "an error to assume that once the psychological etiology is established, then somatic medical management becomes unnecessary" (5). He saw psychotherapy rather as a long-range project which must be coordinated with the rest of medical management. He used an "anamnestic" study of the precursory systems to arrive at a careful psychosomatic diagnosis. There followed a reconstruction of adaptive qualities of behavior and response to the psychological stress and conflict. Study of these factors was believed to lead to control of the local systems requiring immediate care. Alexander was also aware that the exploratory therapy which followed these preliminary steps might exacerbate somatic symptoms. He therefore proceeded to a cautious exposure of the original conflict situations in those cases in which more than a supportive psychotherapy was to be involved. He believed, however, that the shared knowledge of conflict situations with the patient would serve as a beginning of "legitimate outlets" for repressed desires. In addition to the content of psychotherapy, Alexander heavily utilized the physician/patient relationship. He felt that it was appropriate for the physician to "order" the patient to act on desires in an authoritative manner, as well as analyze the behavioral solutions to intrapsychic conflict.

Flanders Dunbar (6) was a contemporary of Alexander's, and their psychotherapeutic recommendations share several qualities. She felt that the source of unresolved emotional conflicts should be detected, and the patient helped to remove the obstacles to the expression of drives. She was concerned, however, that the doctor could become the pathogen when his or her personality configurations stimulated conflict and regression on the part of the patient. She was aware that relief came from the identification of symptoms, but that this was not the same as a cure. Like Alexander, she noted that getting at the essential problems might require environmental manipulation, educational intervention, and alternative forms of activities.

In his text on psychophysiologic medicine, Eugene Ziskind (7) describes nonspecific and specific objectives in psychotherapy of psychophysiologic disorders. Nonspecific elements include rapport, ventilation, desensitization, suggestion, education, and rehabilitation. Graduated specific goals of psychotherapy include acceptance of the psychogenetic origin of the symptoms, treatment for situational precipitating conflicts, treatment for characterologic or predisposing conflicts, and treatment for specific infantile traumas. Ziskind describes a preliminary phase of therapy in which situational and precipitating conflicts are relatively easily discovered and fairly easily treated—provided the psychogenetic nature of the symptoms is acknowledged by the patient. At this point, either the patient would be relatively symptom-free and appropriately terminated from treatment, or the resolution of situational conflicts would have clarified a deep-seated and chronic but previously latent "neurosis."

George Curtis (8) describes his therapeutic considerations in a review of psychotherapy with patients having psychosomatic disorders. He acknowledges that a unitary therapeutic approach is inappropriate with such a diverse and multidetermined group of disorders. He recognizes two components of psychophysiologic disorders that are essential to their understanding: (1) the onset and exacerbation of psychosomatic illness tends to occur in the setting of a real or potential disruption of a key object relationship, and (2) physical illness per se tends to induce psychological regression. The fact that a threat to an important current relationship is so disruptive to ordinary mechanisms of coping with life indicates that the relationship is invested with an intense set of feelings stemming in part from an early uneasy childhood relationship. His description of "the process of falling ill" emphasizes the requirement for flexibility on the part of the therapist during the acute phase of psychosomatic illness. In this regressed state, patients tend to endow current relationships involving caretaking individuals with qualities reminiscent of very early relationships with their own parents. If these relationships were insecure or unpredictable, it will be difficult for the patient to develop a secure and trusting relationship with a medical team. The recovery phase of the illness may have analogies to the patterns of adolescent relationships, and can be just as stormy. Considerable conflict can be generated over the progressive awareness of independence, and there is often the development of a strong but unconscious dependent transference to the medical team. Curtis notes that the psychotherapy during this acute phase may have a major goal of defusing a highly charged relationship between the patient and ward or the physician in charge. He feels that the decision to undertake a more ambitious psychotherapeutic treatment rests on "ego strengths, capacity for relationships, and capacity for insight." The therapist must decide whether or not the patient can withstand the unavoidable degrees of frustration inherent in such treatment. Curtis emphasizes the importance of maintaining a relationship with the primary-care physician in order to minimize feelings of rejection and abandonment even if the more extensive psychotherapeutic treatment is undertaken. The goal of successful psychotherapy, including the more ambitious or exploratory variety, is to return the patient to normal structure and function (provided there was no irreversible tissue damage prior to therapy). The effect of therapy would be to reduce the impact of emotional stress on tissue vulnerability. The therapist must be prepared for exacerbations, and should work to prevent unrealistic illusions either in himself or in his patient. Curtis sees the "removal of organ vulnerability" as a task remaining for biological research.

In her important book on eating disorders, Hilde Bruch (9) describes the evolution of her psychotherapeutic approach to obesity and anorexia nervosa. She cautions about overreliance on early psychoanalytic ideas concerning eating disorders as expressions of oral aggressive or dependent drives. Her orientation is toward the failure in "self-experience and the defective tools and concepts for organizing and expressing the patient's own needs." Collaborating in team efforts with specialists in internal medicine, she thwarts attempts to demand that the patient change abnormal eating patterns early in treatment. Dr. Bruch cautions that an overreliance on interpretive interventions on the part of the therapist may produce a painful repetition of the significant interaction between patients and parents, in which "Mother always knew how I felt." She believes that this type of interaction carries the implication that the patient does not know how to feel, and must rely upon the therapist to obtain ideas regarding self. She advocates a step-by-step clarification of what the patient is saying, through careful reconstruction of both current life events and memories of early interpersonal interactions. This process leads the patient to experience him- or herself as an active participant in a collaborative psychotherapeutic process. Competitive struggles on the part of the therapist to "say it first" are particularly discouraged. Bruch suggests that the therapist realize and utilize his or her own "ignorance" of the patient to embark on a voyage of mutual discovery with the patient rather than explain personal difficulties to the patient. Through helping the patient to become more aware of his or her participation in other areas of function, patients' abnormal eating habits are altered through the newfound abilities to recognize and make decisions about personal needs. The eating function is thereby no longer misused as a pseudosolution for a wealth of personal difficulties.

I believe that the most important factor in the more definitive forms of psychotherapy for psychophysiologic disorders requires addressing the person's sense of self and inferences about the self made as a consequence of remote and current interactions. It is a mistake to focus on the presenting symptom itself. Avoiding this particular pitfall is facilitated by a team approach which provides the opportunity for the patient to discuss physical symptoms with the appropriate specialist. The psychiatrist focuses the orientation of his involvement with the patient toward a full understanding of current interpersonal, intrapsychic function and the relationship between problems in current function and early life experiences. This orientation inevitably leads to a rather intensive reflection on self-concept with the patient. Focusing on events and memories of events avoids some of the difficulties encountered when one tries to pursue discussion of feelings with patients who could be characterized as alexithymic. Generally, a thorough understanding of interpersonal events and the interpretations made by the patient of such events eventually does lead to a greater awareness of associated feeling states. During this process, not only the therapist, but also other significant individuals in the patient's life, become less important as potentially need-gratifying or need-frustrating individuals; therefore less of the patient's behavior is aimed at either the frustration or gratification of significant others in his or her life. Such behavior is replaced by indications that significant individuals become of value in and of themselves as opposed to what they may or may not do for the patient. A patient experiences the gentle but persistent curiosity of the therapist as indicating that he or she must have a value which perhaps was not previously recognized. Self becomes not only more valuable, but also sufficient cause for initiating behavior (as opposed to initiating behavior because of some presumed wish on the part of others). The resulting decrease and resentment in rage which are the necessary accompaniment of exclusively other-directed behavior leads to amelioration of the psychophysiologic and psychosomatic disorder.

REFERENCES

1. Grinker, R.R. *Psychosomatic Concepts*. New York: Aranson, 1973.
2. Sifneos, P.E. The prevalence of "alexithymic" characteristics in psychosomatic patients. *Psychother. Psychosom.* 22: 255–62, 1973.
3. Nemiah, J.C. Alexithymia. *Psychother. Psychsom.* 28: 199–206, 1977.
4. Gaddini, R. The pathology of the self as a basis of psychosomatic disorders. *Psychother. Psychosom.* 28: 260–71, 1977.
5. Alexander, F. *Psychosomatic Medicine*, pp. 263–71. New York: Norton, 1950.
6. Dunbar, F. *Mind and Body: Psychosomatic Medicine*, pp. 88–103, 146–62. New York: Random House, 1947.
7. Ziskind, E. *Psychotherapy of Psychophysiologic Disorders*, pp. 89–126. Lea and Feibiger, 1954.
8. Curtis, G.C. Psychotherapy with patients with psychosomatic disorders. In Hamer, M. (Ed.), *The Theory and Practice of Psychotherapy*, 1969.
9. Bruch, H. *Eating Disorders*, pp. 334–77. New York: Basic, 1973.

18

Psychopharmacology and Psychophysiological Disorders

WILLIAM E. FANN
JEANINE C. WHELESS

INTRODUCTION

Many patients who consult a primary-care care physician suffer from anxiety and/or depression to some degree, and these emotional disturbances generally play an important role in the patient's physical complaints. Based on the relationship of emotions to somatic condition, patients can be categorized into three groups. In one group of patients, anxiety/depression contributes entirely to the presenting complaints (1). When anxiety is prominent, the patient may complain of such symptoms as palpitations, breathlessness, vocal tremors, tremors of the extremities, gastrointestinal hyperactivity, excessive sweating, diarrhea, muscular tension, urinary frequency. The depressed patient may present with symptoms of excessive fatigue, lack of energy, loss of appetite, loss of libido, insomnia, chronic headache or backache, constipation, or other vegetative signs. Symptoms of anxiety and depression may also occur simultaneously. "Masked depression" is very common; hypochondriacal complaints, psychosomatic disorders, and acting-out behavior frequently are depressive equivalents and may be precursors of true depressive reactions (2, 3). Supportive psychotherapy, with or without the use of psychotropic drugs, usually alleviates the anxiety and/or depression, along with their physical concomitants.

A second group of patients presents with physical complaints of organic or complex etiology in which anxiety and/or depression appear to have contributed to the onset of the condition (1). These are the psychosomatic or psychophysiological illnesses such as asthma, ulcerative colitis, peptic ulcer, essential hypertension, and neurodermatitis. These disorders involve overactivity or underactivity of organs and viscera innervated by the autonomic nervous system; if the exaggerated responses continue for prolonged periods of time, structural changes in the affected organs may occur. Anxiety plays a role in the development of peptic ulcer, for example, by contributing to hypersecretion, hypervascularization, and gastrointestinal hyperactivity. When confronted with a diagnosis, patients with psychosomatic conditions generally react with increasing anxiety or depression, thus exacerbating the illness. Goldberg (1) refers to this cycle as "anxiety-disease."

The final category of patients includes those with physical complaints that derive from sources other than anxiety or depression; that is, patients with purely medical or physical conditions. These patients frequently become anxious and/or depressed about the fact of their illness, and emotional concomitants contribute to symptomatology and complicate medical management of the underlying disorder. Ramos (4) states that psychosomatic stress, characterized by anxiety, anguish, and restlessness, occurs to some degree in all somatic illnesses.

Thus, it is extremely rare for a patient to present with a physical disorder without concurrent anxiety or depression. Uhlenhuth and coworkers (5) conducted a survey in which health problems were classified as physical, psychologic, situational, or psychosomatic. In the total sample of 735 respondents, three quarters reported more than one category of health problems. Almost one quarter of the respondents reported psychosomatic disorders coupled with situational, physical, or psychologic disturbances.

In 1972, 144 million prescriptions for daytime psychotropic drugs (excluding hypnotics) were written in the United States. Most of these prescriptions were for anxiolytic sedatives for the treatment of patients with anxiety and/or depression resulting from, or associated with, a wide variety of somatic complaints. The most commonly prescribed drug of any class is diazepam. Chlordiazepoxide ranks third (6, 7). These two drugs are used by one in every 10 adults each year (8). Between July 1974 and June 1975, approximately 44,180,000 prescriptions were written for benzodiazepines. Only 15 percent of these prescriptions were written by psychiatrists and neurologists, and almost 85 percent of them were ordered by general practitioners, internists, surgeons, obstetricians/gynecologists, osteopaths, and other categories of physicians (9). A survey by Parry and associates (10) confirms that most of the psychotropic prescribing is done by general practitioners and internists, and reports that 85 percent of the survey's respondents who had used psychotropic drugs had never seen a psychiatrist. A survey conducted in Finland (11) reports that general practitioners prescribe psychotropics largely for somatic disease and for "nonmedical" problems of everyday life. Thus, it appears, as Blackwell (6) suggests, that emotional distress has replaced pain as the most common reason for prescribing a medication.

The surveys reviewed here indicate that psychotropics are most frequently prescribed as adjuvant treatment in patients with nonpsychiatric conditions. Patients with a primary diagnosis of mental disorder account for only 37 percent of anxiolytic prescriptions, 52 percent of the prescriptions for neuroleptics, and

53 percent of the prescriptions for antidepressants (12). Otherwise, the psychotropics are administered to patients who carry primary diagnoses of physical disorders. For example, Waldron (8) reports that diazepam and chlordiazepoxide are frequently prescribed for angina, hypertension, asthma, peptic ulcer, and other psychosomatic conditions, though their primary indication is for anxious and psychoneurotic patients; furthermore, only one fourth of new prescriptions for the benzodiazepines are for primarily anxious and psychoneurotic patients. Nevertheless, regardless of primary diagnosis, the therapeutic intent of physicians prescribing psychoactive medications is the amelioration of symptoms of emotional distress (12).

A particularly important principle in the use of psychotropic drugs is to withhold administration of any of these agents until a thorough psychological evaluation has been conducted. Frequently, the emotional support provided during four to six brief interviews will obviate the need for medication (13). Ban (14) adds that most of the conditions for which anxiolytics are commonly prescribed are mild and have a high rate of spontaneous remission; these ailments respond to placebo about 50 percent of the time. About 75 percent of them respond to active medication.

The most common approach to the treatment of psychosomatic illnesses has been the use of supportive psychotherapy. Comprehensive management of patients with such disorders, however, often includes the adjunctive use of psychotropic drugs which may be prescribed concurrently with other drugs. The choice of a particular psychotropic among those with similar activity may depend entirely upon the autonomic side effects which may occur or the possible interactions which may result (15). In the following sections we will discuss the pharmacological management of a variety of psychophysiological disorders including anorexia nervosa, asthma, dermatological disorders, psychogenic pain, headache, cardiovascular disorders, and psychophysiological gastrointestinal disorders (peptic ulcer and functional bowel syndromes).

ANOREXIA NERVOSA

Anorexia nervosa (discussed at length in Chapter 9) is classified as a psychophysiological gastrointestinal disorder, considered to be "psychogenic malnutrition." About two thirds of patients with anorexia nervosa emerge improved or recovered, while one third remain unchanged or die. Some patients fully recover, but others relapse shortly after apparent recovery. Malnutrition can usually be ignored unless weight loss is excessive and becomes life-threatening, at which time hospitalization and voluntary or forced feeding may become necessary (16). At present, no single treatment is generally accepted, and a combined therapeutic approach, including psychotherapy, behavior modification, and medication, where appropriate, is the most effective intervention (16, 17).

Some of the neuroleptics have been useful in treating anorexia nervosa by reducing activity and decreasing anxiety about eating and weight gain (17, 18). The diagnosis of schizophrenia is given to about 20 percent of patients with anorexia nervosa (19), making a positive response to neuroleptics not surprising. The dosage of a major tranquilizer should be low enough to bring about positive effects without eliminating motivation; thus, Crisp (20) has employed 400–600mg/day of chlorpromazine in the treatment of anorexia nervosa. Dally (18), however, initiates treatment with 150mg/day of chlorpromazine, steadily increased to 1,000mg/day or more, if necessary. Although favorable responses to the phenothiazines have been reported, How and Davidson (21) recently presented two case studies of patients with anorexia nervosa who developed progressive hemolytic anemia during chlorpromazine therapy; withdrawal of the drug alone led to prompt hematological response. Clinicians should be aware of the possibility of this adverse reaction.

The use of antidepressants is appropriate when depression is a significant part of the clinical picture. Needleman and Waber (22) had noted that some patients with anorexia nervosa display signs of motor and speech retardation and express feelings of sadness. They hypothesized that tricyclic antidepressants might be an efficacious treatment for these patients. Six consecutive patients admitted for anorexia nervosa (five adolescent females and one adolescent male), all of whom exhibited depressive signs and symptoms, were treated with amitriptyline as the sole therapeutic intervention. All six patients began to gain weight between 6 and 12 days after the drug was instituted, and weight gain was preceded by a striking improvement in mood and social relationships and by increased warmth of the extremities. Three patients discontinued medication after discharge, and three patients were maintained on the drugs, but all six continued gaining weight to an appropriate level (22, 23). Mills (24) concurs that tricyclics are useful in treating anorexia nervosa but feels that Needleman and Waber's results were exaggerated. A group of anorectics who exhibited depression was prescribed nortriptyline or amitriptyline, and although many of the patients showed improvement, some still required hospitalization; 100 percent response did not occur.

White and Schnaultz (25) present case histories of two adolescents who were successfully treated with psychotherapy and imipramine. In one patient, discontinuation of the drug resulted in a return of induced vomiting and reduced caloric intake, which cleared with resumption of medication. These authors speculate that disinterest in the environment due to depression may contribute to noneating. O'Flanagan (26) reports beneficial results in anorexia from intravenous chlorimipramine combined with glucagon and adenosine triphosphate (ATP). Moore (27) describes a patient who had not responded to a three-month trial of imipramine but who improved within one week after amitriptyline was instituted. When amitriptyline was discontinued, the patient began an episode of bulimia and induced vomiting, but these behaviors subsided when amitriptyline was resumed. In this patient, amitriptyline was prescribed after two and a half years of bulimia and induced vomiting (27), and Solomon (28) questions why there was such a prolonged delay in administering this agent. He suggests that urinary MHPG levels be obtained in depressed anorectic patients to aid in the selection of appropriate drugs; those patients with low MHPG levels should be prescribed imipramine, while those with normal or high MHPG levels generally respond to amitriptyline.

Coppen and colleagues have measured free plasma tryptophan levels in patients with either depression (29) or anorexia nervosa (30). In both conditions, tryptophan levels are significantly low. In recovered depressed patients, however, tryptophan returns to control levels, while remaining low in anorectics after a return to near normal weight. The failure of plasma levels to return to control levels suggests that induced weight gain *alone* does not attack the basic causes and leaves the patient at risk for frequent relapses.

Barcai (31) reports on a subgroup of anorexia nervosa patients who may respond to lithium. He presents case studies of two adult anorectics with clinical manifestations similar to a combination of hypomania and depression, accompanied by vacillation in weight. Within six weeks of lithium administration, one patient gained 9kg and the other gained 12kg, and weight gains were maintained for a year of follow-up with lithium maintenance. The author cautions, however, that lithium is a potentially dangerous drug and patients prescribed lithium should be carefully selected and conscientiously monitored. The drug is appropriate only in adults who manifest lithium-responding clinical symptoms—manic mood, physical hyperactivity, and pressure and rapidity of thought and/or speech. One side effect of lithium is weight gain due to fluid retention, and this additional weight gain might erroneously be attributed to increased body tissue. Furthermore, if patients on lithium do not eat properly, the danger of lithium toxicity becomes imminent.

Some investigators have postulated that increased activity of dopamine at central dopamine receptor sites plays an important role in the pathophysiology of anorexia nervosa (32, 33). Needleman and Waber (22) noted that four of six patients in their study displayed slow speech, immobility of the lower face, rigidity of the shoulders, and small gait, suggesting a parkinsonian-like movement disorder. Johanson and Knorr (34) also remarked on the similarity between anorexia nervosa and Parkinson's disease, pointing out that some anorectic patients exhibit rigid, obsessive-compulsive, often stereotyped, behavior. Based on the hypothesis that dopaminergic hyperactivity could be a factor in anorexia nervosa, they prescribed levodopa to six anorectic patients and reported improvement in appetite with weight gain in four of the patients (34). In a subsequent uncontrolled study, Johanson and Knorr (35) reported that five of nine anorectics treated with low-dose levodopa had significant weight gain; one patient later relapsed. Of the four nonresponders, two patients subsequently responded to other treatment and two remained unchanged. Barry and Klawans (32) suggest treating anorexia nervosa with pimozide, a selective dopamine-blocking drug. Plantey (36) reports a dramatic improvement with weight gain and reduction in obsession with weight in a 17-year-old male treated with pimozide for four weeks.

Since cyproheptadine is an antiserotonergic drug which has been reported to promote weight gain in underweight patients (37, 38, 39), Vigersky and Loriaux (40) conducted a double-blind trial of the drug in 24 patients with anorexia nervosa. The drug was not superior to placebo. Only 4 of the 13 cyproheptadine patients (31 percent) and 2 of 11 placebo patients (18 percent) increased in weight over the two-month trial. The remaining 18 patients neither gained nor lost weight. No side effects or adverse reactions occurred.

Anorexia nervosa continues to present a therapeutic challenge to the physician. At present, the indicated therapies are eclectic. Neuroleptics, antidepressants, or other psychotropics may be used to reduce anxiety or to treat depression, and a wide variety of other types of treatments, ranging from supportive strategies through hypnosis and behavior modification, may also be applied (16).

ASTHMA

Pulmonary disorders have been discussed in detail in Chapter 2. In almost half of asthmatics investigated with a full range of allergic examinations, predominant extrinsic allergens cannot be incriminated with any certainty. Because etiology is equivocal, this group of asthma sufferers is called "cryptogenic" (41). For centuries, however, clinical wisdom has implicated emotional factors in the initiation of changes in bronchial asthma. Hippocrates is alleged to have stated, "The asthmatic patient must guard against anger." Since emotions frequently play a major role in asthma, psychotropic drugs have been used therapeutically.

Tricyclic antidepressants have been successful in ameliorating some of the symptoms of asthma. These drugs have been shown to exert a bronchodilatory effect (42). The mechanism of action of antidepressants may be pluralistic, since anticholinergic and antihistaminic properties are combined with catecholamine-receptor blocking effects. Conceivably, tricyclics act not only in a nonspecific way on depressed mood, but also their specific therapeutic action of augmentation of catecholamine activity and their anticholinergic effects may be beneficial centrally as well as peripherally (43, 44). Ananth (45) presents a case study which exemplifies the specific and nonspecific therapeutic actions of tricyclics. A 45-year-old asthmatic patient was referred for manic-depressive illness, and psychiatric condition and asthma were both controlled by the administration of 75mg/day of amitriptyline. Sugihara and associates (46) report that 37 of 60 asthmatics were clinically improved on amitriptyline. Meares et al. (47) report that in guinea pigs, amitriptyline counteracted the bronchoconstrictor actions of histamine, serotonin, and acetylcholine, and that the drug was more potent than imipramine or desmethylimipramine. These investigators subsequently administered amitriptyline to eight asthmatics, and clinical improvement and reduction in the use of other antiasthmatic medications occurred in all eight. The authors suggest that the therapeutic effects of amitriptyline may be due to antagonism of bronchoconstrictor substances rather than to antidepressant action. Other investigators have reported similar results on the beneficial effects of amitriptyline (48) and imipramine (49, 50).

Although psychotropics are generally used as adjuncts in the treatment of asthma, Sanger (49) conducted double-blind trials of a variety of medications as the sole treatment in a number of psychosomatic disorders. Of 51 patients with asthma, he reports that 32 (63 percent) demonstrated a good to excellent response, and 10 (20 percent) a fair response, to treatment with antidepressants alone. Of 43 asthmatics, 28 (65 percent) had a good to excellent response, and 7 (16 percent) had a fair response, to tranquilizers as the sole therapeutic agent.

Hydroxyzine, a minor tranquilizer with antiemetic and antihistaminic properties, has also been useful in the management of asthma (51, 52, 53). Shah and associates (52) administered hydroxyzine daily for one month to 84 asthmatics. The medication provided complete symptomatic relief in 58 patients (69 percent), partial relief in 25 (30 percent), and only one patient failed to improve. In another study (53), asthmatic patients receiving hydroxyzine reported increased calmness and improved sleep, but only partial relief of asthmatic symptoms. Although less antiasthmatic medication was required by these patients, no patient could be managed with hydroxyzine alone.

A number of investigators have reported that lithium may have favorable results in asthmatic patients. Nasr and Adkins (54) present two case studies of patients who exhibited unexpected improvement in asthma, following the administration of lithium carbonate for recurrent manic-depressive illness. Putnam (55) reports a remarkable remission of asthma in two patients treated with lithium carbonate. Winig (56) presents a case study of a patient with severe asthma who required pharmacotherapy and occasional hospitalization. When the patient was hospitalized for his first psychotic break, all antiasthmatic and steroid medications were withdrawn, and lithium and trifluoperazine were prescribed. The patient had no asthmatic symptoms during his three-week hospitalization. Three days following discharge, he discontinued lithium and trifluoperazine, and three days later was admitted to intensive care for a severe asthmatic attack. During a second psychiatric hospitalization, the patient was again prescribed lithium, and again responded favorably, with improvement in both psychiatric condition and asthmatic symptoms.

Although the mechanism of lithium's beneficial effect on asthma is uncertain, Nasr and Adkins (54) suggest that lithium "modulates the balance between PCE_1 and PGF_{2d} and cAMP and cyclic guanosine 5'-monophosphate, thus abating the clinical manifestations of asthma." Furthermore, Bracha et al. (57) had observed in their laboratory that lithium appears to have a biphasic effect, activating adenylate cyclase when the enzyme is active, and inhibiting the enzyme's full activation. This biphasic effect would reconcile the B-adrenergic theory of asthma and the increasing evidence that lithium affects B-adrenergic adenylate cyclase. Bracha and coworkers "predict that chronic lithium therapy would prevent recurrent asthma but would reduce the effectiveness of epinephrine treatment in the acute asthmatic attack."

Because both medical and psychological factors are involved in the development and precipitation of bronchial asthma, treatment of this condition should be collaborative (58). The adjunctive use of psychotropic medications and, occasionally, the use of psychotropics as sole treatment have been reported to have favorable effects in patients with asthma. However, all sedatives produce some degree of respiratory depression, and thus, in acute respiratory conditions, especially during acute exacerbations of chronic asthma, negative therapeutic effects may occur (59). Psychotropics should be cautiously employed in the asthmatic.

DERMATOLOGICAL DISORDERS

The role of emotional factors in the etiology of urticaria, eczema, angioedema, and other dermatologic disorders is controversial. Sanger (49) reports that allergic patients frequently exhibit both physiological and psychological stress and that anxiety and/or depression can aggravate allergic symptoms. Lockey (60) states that emotional factors are implicated and can tend to exacerbate symptoms in some patients, but that emotions are doubtful as the primary or sole cause of dermatological disorders. Turner and Gale (61), on the other hand, propose that psychological trauma is most often responsible for causing chronic cases of urticaria. Medansky (62) states that about 80 percent of dermatologic patients have a psychogenic overlay. Keegan (63) categorizes the majority of cases of both chronic and acute urticaria as "idiopathic," a label suggesting the occurrence of a multifactorial, rather than a single specific, etiology. Lockey (60) agrees that most cases of chronic urticaria are idiopathic in origin but he feels that allergy in these cases tends to disappear spontaneously with time. Spontaneous remission does occur, and a placebo response has been reported in about one quarter to one third of dermatologic patients (62, 64).

There is also debate concerning the most appropriate treatment for dermatological disorders, with some investigators favoring purely somatic treatment, others recommending a combination of psychotherapy and other behavioral treatments and still others proposing the concurrent use of somatic and psychological treatments. The first step in treating dermatological conditions should be a complete history and physical examination, including an assessment of the patient's psychological status. Once this information has been gathered, as Freedman et al. (65) state, "the therapeutic approach may be directed from the allergic angle if evidence of existing allergy can be elicited, or from the psychological angle if evidence of existing allergy can be elicited, or from the psychological angle if evidence of emotional maladjustment can be elicited."

The most widely used medications for dermatological diseases are the sedative antihistamines, such as hydroxyzine (12, 66). Hydroxyzine is especially useful since, in addition to antihistamine action, it blocks serotonin and acetylcholine and has anxiolytic effects. Nurse (66) reports that the addition of low doses of diazepam or imipramine potentiates the positive effects of antihistamines without increasing side effects. Other psychotropics have been found to be helpful in treating dermatological disorders, but since many of these compounds have anticholinergic effects, it is uncertain whether beneficial responses are due to anticholinergic action or to psychotropic action (61). However, there is general agreement that tranquilizers and antidepressants are most efficacious in relief of cutaneous symptoms when disturbances of affect and behavior are prominent, but are of minor benefit when psychopathology is negligible (67).

A variety of psychotropics have been effective in dermatological conditions. Putnam (55) reports that two patients with severe eczemotoid dermatitis showed remarkable remission of dermatological symptoms following the administration of lithium. Sanger (68) conducted an 18-month double-blind trial comparing the effectiveness of doxepin and amitriptyline in dermatological disorders. Twelve of 16 doxepin patients, compared to 5 of 16 amitriptyline patients, demonstrated a moderate to marked improvement, a highly significant difference favoring doxepin. Green and Green (69) report that nortriptyline produced moderate to marked improvement, indicated by relief of anxiety, depression, tension, and allergic symptoms, in over half of their sample of patients. Sanger (49) reports that of 60 patients with eczema or urticaria, 34 (57 percent) showed good to excellent response, and 9 (15 percent) showed fair response to tranquilizers alone. Of 51 patients with eczema or urticaria, 25 (49 percent) exhibited good to excellent response, and 8 (16 percent) had fair response to antidepressants as the sole therapeutic agent.

Lester and associates (64) conducted a study of the relationship of psychiatric symptomatology and diagnosis, somatic manifestations, and drug response in 71 patients with a variety of "psychosomatic" dermatologic reactions (atopic dermatitis, hyperhidrosis, psoriasis, seborrheic dermatosis). Four drugs—imipramine, meprobamate, chlordiazepoxide, and chlorpromazine—as the sole therapeutic agent in the treatment of cutaneous disorders were assessed in a double-blind placebo-controlled trial. Overall, about 50 percent of the patients showed improvement in skin disorder with drug treatment, while the improvement rate with placebo did not exceed 30 percent. The drugs, especially imipramine and chlorpromazine, were more effective than placebo in ameliorating both skin disorders and emotional disturbances.

Chlorpromazine had the best antipruritic effect, while imipramine was most helpful in itching when depression was prominent. An interesting finding was that the effectiveness of the drugs for cutaneous pathology was relative to the degree of initial psychiatric symptomatology; thus, patients with severe anxiety or tension displayed the most favorable dermatologic response to the psychotropics, whereas patients with negligible psychopathology showed minimal dermatologic improvement. In other words, psychotropics afforded relief of both skin and psychiatric conditions in patients with the greatest psychiatric disturbances, and improvement in dermatologic status paralleled degree of relief of psychiatric symptoms. Greenblatt and Shader (70) have also reported that cutaneous improvement following the administration of benzodiazepines corresponded to improvement in relief of emotional distress.

In the study by Lester et al. (64), a differential response to psychotropics was noted among subgroups of dermatologic patients. Those with depressive symptoms showed marked dermatologic improvement with the drugs. Patients with personality disorders, such as passive-aggressive and aggressive-dependent personality, and prepsychotic patients also responded favorably to psychotropics, but nondepressed neurotic patients did not have a beneficial response to the drugs. Based on clinical experience, Musaph (71) suggests that the treatment of choice for patients whose itching represents "repressed anxiety" is the use of sedative benzodiazepines such as diazepam; for patients who itch with "repressed anger," the best treatment is narco-analysis and short-acting barbiturates such as sodium pentothal or sodium methohexital; for patients with "delusions of parasitosis," the neuroleptics, particularly thioxanthenes, are most efficacious.

Although a number of studies have demonstrated the effectiveness of psychotropic compounds in the treatment of dermatological conditions, most investigators agree that these agents should be used as adjunctive therapy, not as a substitute for other methods (49, 63, 69). The treatment of choice generally combines drugs, either somatic or psychological or a combination of the two, and some form of supportive psychotherapy or behavioral treatment.

PSYCHOGENIC PAIN

Pain of psychogenic origin is commonly associated with functional motor weakness, hyperalgesia, changes in autonomic function, and localized tenderness. When the patient describes an extremely variable and inconsistent pain, a chronic, diffuse pain, or a continuous dull ache with intermittent excruciating episodes, the physician should suspect that the pain might be psychogenic (72, 73, 74). DeVaul and coworkers (75) have classified patients with psychogenic pain into five groups. First, pain most frequently is a depressive equivalent; careful history-taking usually reveals depression preceding the onset of pain, or the patient presents with other depressive symptoms (76). The remaining categories include pain as a delusional symptom of psychosis; as a conversion symptom of hysterical neurosis; as unresolved grief, and as a need to suffer. Other characteristics of psychogenic pain patients include excessive rigidity, irritability, anxiety, depression, compulsiveness, and feelings of isolation and loneliness. These patients are generally difficult to treat, and many physicians avoid dealing with them. However, Harris (73), speaking about psychogenic oral-facial pain, suggests that pain symptoms disguise deeper disturbances which require treatment. He states:

> Emotional disturbances such as anxiety neurosis, depression or hysteria create oro-facial symptoms which may vary from severe pain to an altered sense of taste. An awareness of these conditions enables the underlying problem to be recognized and treated by specific measures. To dismiss these problems as hypochondriasis is as detrimental to the patient as unnecessary surgery. Psychogenic disturbances are best considered to be an appeal for help.

Tyber (77) conducted a study to investigate the prevalence of depression in the Painful Shoulder Syndrome (PSS) and to evaluate the effectiveness of antidepressant medication as the sole treatment for this disorder. In the first phase of the study, a significantly greater incidence of depression was found in PSS patients, of whom 76 percent were depressed, as compared to a control group with other musculoskeletal conditions. In another part of the study, 56 PSS patients were treated for four months with only amitriptyline and lithium. Forty-four of the patients (79 percent) showed marked clinical improvement, with a dramatic disappearance of, or reduction in, dystrophic calcification. Eleven other patients with PSS were treated with physiotherapy for 1–24 months and then switched to amitriptyline-lithium for 4 months. Comparing improvement during each phase of treatment, the drug combination was far superior to physiotherapy. The author concludes:

> The high prevalence of depression in PSS (76%) and the dramatic improvement achieved by combined lithium and amitriptyline therapy would indicate that PSS is a psychogenic disorder, in spite of objective clinical and radiologic evidence of physical pathology . . . . Until more information is available about the biochemical aberrations in PSS, it would be best . . . to treat it with antidepressant medications rather than with local therapy directed to the shoulder (77).

Raft et al. (78) prescribed relaxation therapy and low doses of haloperidol (4–6mg/day) to 12 patients with psychogenic pain. Pain of these patients was generalized, disabling, and out of proportion to objective physical findings, and all of these patients had failed to respond to other forms of therapy, including behavior modification, hypnosis, and biofeedback. Two to four weeks after haloperidol was initiated, notable decreases in anxiety occurred. All of the patients responded favorably, 11 of the 12 reporting an 85 percent improvement over baseline, and one patient improving 65 percent over baseline. Subsequent to improvement with haloperidol, behavior modification was effective in inducing additional improvement.

Gilbert and Koepke (79) conducted a double-blind placebo-controlled trial of aspirin (325mg), meprobamate (200mg), and a combination of both drugs in the treatment of 188 outpatients suffering from musculoskeletal symptoms associated with anxiety, tension, and apprehension. A 2×2 factorial analysis, testing for main drug effects and drug interactions, was employed. Aspirin significantly reduced emotional distress, and reduced pain to a lesser extent. The combination of the two compounds resulted in greater improvement in both musculoskeletal and emotional symptoms than occurred with either drug alone. Interaction tests indicated that the action of each drug was produced independently and that the clinical response to the combination treatment appeared to result from additive effects.

The treatment of choice for psychogenic pain is generally supportive psychotherapy with or without drugs. Analgesics probably owe part of their effectiveness in alleviating pain to their role as placebos. Minor tranquilizers, such as diazepam, 2mg twice daily and 4mg at night, may be helpful in relieving symptoms of anxiety (73). Tricyclics are especially important in the treatment of patients with psychogenic pain. Not only do these drugs reduce the intensity of depression in many patients, but they also increase pain tolerance and thus may improve sleep. Additionally, by using antidepressants, the addictive potential of narcotic analgesics is avoided (13). If drugs prove ineffective in patients whose pain is a symptom of depression, ECT is a viable alternative. Neuroleptics are effective in ameliorating pain that represents somatic delusions (75, 80).

Sternbach (81) has pointed out the similarities in behavioral, affective, and physiological manifestations between acute pain and anxiety, and between chronic pain and depression. Thus, he recommends the use of anxiolytics for acute (short-term) pain but feels that antidepressants are more appropriate for patients with chronic pain (82). The use of antianxiety agents past the acute stage tends to potentiate depression. Pace (83) concurs that minor tranquilizers are of no value in alleviating chronic pain and states that these drugs may actually have a negative influence when disinhibition and increased hostility and depression result from their use. For chronic pain patients with anxiety, he recommends the administration of neuroleptics such as trifluoperazine, chlorpromazine, or thiothixene. For chronic pain patients with depression, tricyclics are the treatment of choice. If insomnia is a problem, the use of 75mg amitriptyline at bedtime, increased in dose by 25mg/week as needed, up to a total of 200mg/day, is recommended (76). If insomnia is not a problem or amitriptyline proves to be overly sedative, imipramine can be prescribed instead. Frequently, the concurrent administration of amitriptyline and trifluoperazine or thioridazine may be beneficial in allaying both anxiety and depression. Because the onset of therapeutic action of tricyclic antidepressants does not occur rapidly, an initial course of sedation and analgesia for about 10 days may be helpful (73).

There is no agreement as to whether antidepressants should be prescribed only to patients manifesting concurrent pain and depression or whether these drugs exert an analgesic effect independent of antidepressant action. Sternbach (84) favors administering antidepressants only to patients with concomitant pain and depression, but Mersky and Hester (85) suggest that both phenothiazines and antidepressants may have analgesic effects independent of their mood-altering effects. The question remains unsettled, but it is clear that most patients experiencing severe, chronic organic or psychogenic pain are also anxious and/or depressed, and for many of these patients the addition of an antidepressant or antipsychotic drug to the treatment regimen will not only alleviate emotional distress but will also provide substantial relief from pain (86).

HEADACHE

A number of investigators have suggested that there is a relationship between headache and depression (see Chapter 4 for a detailed discussion of headache). Diamond (87) surveyed 423 depressed patients and found that 84 percent of them complained of headache. In fact, headache was the third most common complaint among depressed individuals, following sleep disturbance and early awakening. Cassidy and coworkers (88) reported a significantly greater incidence of headache among manic-depressive patients (49 percent) than among medically sick controls (36 percent) or healthy controls (25 percent). The incidence of headache among manic-depressive patients was almost double the incidence among healthy subjects. Of 100 patients who were assessed by neurologists as having "functional headache," 68 were diagnosed as having some type of psychiatric disorder (89). Fifty percent of all patients had depressive syndrome and 15 percent had hysteria. These studies indicate that patients with chronic headache are frequently depressed, using pain as a symptomatic manifestation of depression. The associated symptoms of disturbances of sleep, appetite, and sexual activity assist in the diagnosis of depressive syndrome.

Antidepressants have been reported to be effective in the treatment of chronic headache occurring in anxious/depressed patients (89, 90, 91, 92). Lance and Curran (91) evaluated various medications in the treatment of 280 patients suffering from chronic tension headaches. In a controlled trial of 27 patients, 3 patients improved with both amitriptyline and placebo, 12 improved with amitriptyline but not placebo, and 12 did not improve with either compound; no patient responded only to placebo. Results indicated that amitriptyline was significantly effective in reducing headache. Comparative assessments of other preparations demonstrated that diazepam, chlor-diazepoxide, imipramine, and Bellergel were also efficacious, while amylobarbitone, methysergide, orphenadrine, and vasodilators were not superior to placebo.

Kashiwagi et al. (89) assessed the effectiveness of amitriptyline on both headache and depression in 29 patients who had been prescribed the drug sometime during treatment. Data were obtained from medical charts and from telephone conversations with the subjects. Favorable responses in both headache and depression were reported by 65.5 percent of the sample; 17.2 percent reported that neither headache nor depression improved; 13.8 percent showed favorable response in terms of depression only, and 3.5 percent improved in terms of headache only.

In a double-blind, placebo-controlled trial, Diamond and Baltes (90) divided 90 patients with anxiety and/or depression who complained of headache into three treatment groups. Five patients dropped out of the study, leaving 28 patients in the amitriptyline 25mg group, 28 patients in the amitriptyline 10mg group, and 29 patients in the placebo group. Eight target symptoms, one of which was headache, and global evaluations were assessed. Amitriptyline 10mg resulted in statistically significant decreases in symptom scores for all eight symptoms, and the patients' global responses were significantly better with amitriptyline 10mg than with the other two compounds. The 25mg dose did not produce a superior response than the lower dose. Based on these results, Diamond (87, 90) recommends small doses of amitriptyline (10mg at night) for patients suffering from headache with anxiety and/or depression. Aring (93), however, supports the use of 75–100mg/day, to be prescribed at bedtime when insomnia is a problem, and Kashiwagi (89) administers 100mg/day.

Okasha and associates (94) compared the efficacy of three drugs and placebo in the treatment of 80 patients with psychogenic headache. Doxepin, 10mg tid, provided the greatest relief of both headache and anxiety and/or depression, followed by amitriptyline, 10mg tid. Diazepam, 2mg tid, produced less improvement but was superior to placebo. An interesting finding was that patients prescribed doxepin continued to improve between the fourth and eighth weeks, while those prescribed the other drugs demonstrated no further improvement. The authors conclude, "This means that headaches secondary to anxiety/depression which do not improve on amitriptyline and diazepam after 4 weeks will show no significant change on continuation of therapy, whereas with doxepin there is the possibility that further improvement will occur after the fourth week to a maximum by the eighth week" (94).

The first step in the treatment of the chronic headache sufferer is a detailed physical and neurological examination. A combined therapeutic approach, including psychotherapy, relaxation exercises, and drugs such as aspirin, other mild analgesics, and psychotropics, is generally helpful. For migraine sufferers, minor and major tranquilizers and barbiturates may be temporarily beneficial in migraine prophylaxis by reducing anxiety and by modifying the patient's reaction to stress. For treatment of muscle-contraction headaches, antidepressants, muscle relaxants with tranquilizing actions, analgesics, and sedatives play a useful but limited role (93, 95). Aring (93) has also suggested the use of fluphenazine HCl (Prolixin) in the smallest dose that will produce results, stating that 1 mg tid will frequently suffice. There is general agreement that the use of psychotropics for chronic behavior should be adjunctive only, and that these agents should be discontinued when the patient can get along without them. Aring (93) states that for headache patients, there is a "tendency to use psychotropic drugs much too liberally and far too long."

CARDIOVASCULAR DISORDERS

Psychological factors, particularly emotional stress, have long been implicated in the etiology of mild or serious arrhythmias, coronary occlusion, and sudden death (97, 98, 99). Changes in cardiovascular function are an integral part of emotional arousal, and fear, anxiety, anger, elation, and excitement are all accompanied by changes in heart rate and arterial blood pressure. Strong emotions can exert powerful cardiovascular effects; these effects are usually magnified in patients with preexisting cardiac disease (13, 100). It has been hypothesized that intense or sustained arousal can cause cardiovascular dysfunction or disease, and, alternatively, cardiovascular dysfunction and disease have been shown to produce anxiety and/or depression.

More than half of patients·hospitalized for the treatment of ischemic heart disease exhibit symptoms of moderate or severe anxiety and/or depression. The more severe the physical disease, the more chronic the emotional disturbance is likely to be (100). In 400 patients evaluated following heart attack, 55 percent were found to be suffering from moderate to severe anxiety; 40 percent displayed substantial depression which contributed to disability; and 26 percent were judged in need of antidepressant medication (101).

A number of studies investigating the effectiveness of various psychotropics in patients with cardiac disorders have been conducted. Samet and Richards (102) treated 66 cardiac outpatients with lorazepam and reported that the drug produced significant improvement over placebo in both psychological and somatic dysfunction. Finkel (103) conducted a double-blind randomized four-week study of lorazepam in patients with moderate to severe anxiety associated with cardiovascular symptomatology of equivocal organic etiology. Hypertensive disease was the primary diagnosis of 75.3 percent of the sample. Thirty-eight patients received lorazepam and 35 were prescribed placebo. The average dose of lorazepam was 3mg/day, 1mg in the morning and 2mg in the evening. Global responses, Hamilton Anxiety Rating Scale scores, and the 35-Item Self-rating Scale scores indicated that lorazepam was significantly more effective than placebo (both clinically and statistically) in relieving anxiety. Adverse reactions were rare and transient, and occurred in only 2 lorazepam patients; sedation was reported in 4 placebo patients. The author concludes, "From the findings of this study there is little doubt that lorazepam can be used to advantage as an adjunct in the treatment of anxiety associated with cardiovascular disorders. These results should not be construed as indicating that lorazepam is effective in the treatment of cardiovascular symptoms arising from cardiovascular disorder" (103).

Patients who had suffered from their first myocardial infarction participated in a three-month double-blind trial of clorazepate or placebo (104). A single nightly dose of 15mg clorazepate or an identical placebo was administered. Overall, 79 percent of the clorazepate patients improved, while 33 percent of the placebo patients improved. Both treatment groups displayed a significant decrease in anxiety symptoms. Mean anginal rate and mean nitroglycerin requirement were less in the clorazepate patients, the nitroglycerin rate being significantly less. By the end of the trial, there was also a significant decrease in systolic blood pressure in the patients treated with clorazepate.

The frequent need for psychotropic medication among cardiovascular patients presents the clinician with a difficult management decision because most of the psychotropics exert clinically significant cardiovascular side effects. Reported side effects of neuroleptics and tricyclic antidepressants include hypotension, EKG changes, arrhythmias, myocardial degeneration, myocardial infarction, congestive heart disease, and cardiac failure (105, 106, 107, 108, 109, 110). These effects are more likely to occur in patients with preexisting cardiovascular disease (108, 109, 111, 112). Since the advent of the tranquilizer era, there has been an increase in the number of deaths, unexplainable at autopsy, among psychiatric patients treated with neuroleptics (113, 114, 115, 116, 117, 118, 119). Although there is general agreement that cardiac arrest is the immediate cause of death among these patients, the exact mechanism is unknown. Deaths have also been reported among patients prescribed tricyclic antidepressants. Moir and associates (120) report a significant increase in the incidence of sudden, unexpected death among cardiac patients treated with amitriptyline as compared to a control group, but another survey (121), of 80 cardiac patients, failed to find any cardiotoxic effects of tricyclics.

Psychotropics interact with a variety of compounds. The neuroleptics, particularly the butyrophenones, and the sedative barbiturates enhance the degradation of phenindione by enzyme induction, reduce prothrombin time, and increase the dose requirement for coumarin-type anticoagulants (105). Barbiturates, benzodiazepines, and propanediols accelerate the metabolism of numerous drugs, including phenothiazines, Digitoxin, and Warfarin (122, 123), through enzyme induction.

Discontinuation of barbiturates during treatment with anticoagulants may lead to severe bleeding episodes (124, 125, 126 ,127).

Although the antidepressant and neuroleptic drugs may produce deleterious side effects, the fear and anxiety that commonly accompany myocardial infarction can lead to fibrillation and ventricular arrhythmia that cannot be reversed by psychotropic drugs. In the immediate postinfarct phase, benzodiazepines, which do not produce significant autonomic side effects, are recommended for the alleviation of anxiety and depression (59). Treatment with benzodiazepines should always be short-term, however, because withdrawal of such agents can lead to a recrudescence of symptoms. For long-term administration, the benzodiazepines have been increasingly replaced by propranolol (128). The major tranquilizers should be reserved for use with more severe cases of arrhythmias, agitation, hyperarousal, and psychotic symptoms. Although the various neuroleptics are very similar in their clinical effects, they differ considerably in major side effects. Adverse cardiac effects occur more frequently with aliphatic and piperidine phenothiazines. Thus, thioridazine and chlorpromazine produce more autonomic effects, and a patient who shows a drop in blood pressure with these compounds may show little or no hypotension when switched to piperazine phenothiazines or a butyrophenone (129). In addition to its hypotension-inducing effects, thioridazine is also more likely to cause EKG changes (130, 131). On the other hand, the prolongation of the Q-T interval produced by thioridazine (132) in low doses may be similar to the antiarrhythmic effect of quinidine (13). Haloperidol appears less likely to produce cardiac complications, including hypotension, when administered within the therapeutic range (105, 133, 134, 135). The virtual absence of EKG changes with haloperidol (136) makes this neuroleptic preferable for use during the immediate postinfarct period.

Tricyclics should be avoided during the acute recovery phase and should be used cautiously during the months following myocardial infarction. When tricyclics are required in cardiac patients, initial dose should be lower than usual—for example, 25mg bid imipramine—with slower increases to the lowest effective dose. In some cardiac patients, the use of ECT with cardiac monitoring may prove safer than prolonged administration of antidepressant medication.

Psychotropic medications are not efficacious in the treatment of cardiovascular symptoms arising from cardiovascular disease. They are useful, however, as adjuncts in the treatment of anxiety and depression which so commonly are associated with cardiovascular disorders. By ameliorating psychological disturbances, positive responses in cardiovascular functions often follow. As Lasagna (9) states, "The allaying of anxiety and autonomic hyperactivity in patients with ischemic heart disease might well result in protection of some patients from disordered cardiac rhythm or sudden death, either during acute periods of special risk or in long-term administration."

ESSENTIAL HYPERTENSION

The adjunctive use of psychotropics in patients with essential hypertension is appropriate when there is a concomitant psychiatric condition (see Chapter 3 for a detailed discussion of hypertension). Additionally, these drugs may be prescribed for their tranquilizing, sedative, or antidepressant properties when it is felt that sustained emotional tension, such as anxiety and/or depression, may be aggravating the physiological disorder (137). For example, Bant (138) surveyed patients followed for one year in a hypertension clinic and found depression in a third of them. A number of studies have described high levels of anxiety, hostility, and tension among hypertensives (139, 140, 141). Esler et al. (139) reported that patients with high-renin essential hypertension differed from normotensive individuals on behavioral indices which measured suppressed hostility, a behavioral pattern associated with increased sympathetic activity. Patients with high-renin essential hypertension also scored high on measures of control, guilt-proneness, submission, and level of unexpressed anger. These are characteristics which might be modified by psychotropic medications.

Heine and coworkers (140) tested the hypothesis that prolonged emotional disturbance leads to an irreversible increase in blood pressure. They related the duration of illness to blood pressure in 25 severely depressed patients when they had recovered following ECT. Allowing for age and sex, these investigators found a significant correlation between both duration and number of spells of illness and blood pressure on recovery, findings strongly supporting the hypothesis. Likewise, on recovery, a hypertensive and normotensive group were significantly differentiated on the two measures of amount of illness, but not on genetic factors or differing treatment. Ratings of anxiety and agitation, but not depression ratings, were correlated with blood-pressure levels when ill. Patients who demonstrated a reduction in diastolic pressure on recovery were significantly more anxious and agitated when referred than those who did not display a change in blood pressure. These authors concluded that the physiological effects of prolonged or repeated episodes of emotional disturbance may indeed lead to structural changes that result in hypertension.

Whitehead and associates (142) compared the charts of hypertensive patients prescribed benzodiazepines with matched hypertensive controls who were not prescribed these drugs. The results suggested that psychological complaints reliably led to the prescription of an anxiolytic, and that such prescribing was followed by reduction in psychiatric complaints. Secondly, physicians prescribed benzodiazepines because they believed that these agents reduce blood pressure; and, indeed, in 62 percent of the patients, the administration of benzodiazepines was followed by a decrease in blood pressure. The average reduction in blood pressure, 6.69mm Hg diastolic, was clinically significant. No significant changes in systolic pressure resulted.

In addition to diazepam, other benzodiazepines have been tested. Carabello et al. (143) treated 57 hypertensive patients with lorazepam and reported reduction in both anxiety and hypertension. Satisfactory blood-pressure control was maintained in these patients, despite the discontinuation of diuretic therapy. In a double-blind study, 62 adults with significant hypertension and concomitant moderate-to-severe anxiety were randomly assigned to treatment with lorazepam or placebo for four weeks (144). Patients were assessed by seven cardiologists under double-blind conditions, and results were pooled. Symptoms of anxiety were measured by the Global Physician Rating Scale, Hamilton Anxiety Scale, and Patient Self-rating Scale. As compared to placebo, anxiety symptoms improved significantly with lorazepam. On patient self-rating scales, those in the drug group rated themselves significantly less angry and hostile during the fourth week and at the final evaluation. The beneficial effects of lorazepam on anger and hostility may provide additional improvement in hypertensive patients, since suppressed hostility, a behavioral pattern linked to increased sympathetic activity, has been shown to be characteristic of high-renin essential hypertension patients (139).

In most cases, the combination of neuroleptics and antihypertensive agents produce additive hypotension (108, 127). However, neuroleptics, tricyclics, and sympathomimetic amines block activity of the adrenergic-membrane transport system, which transports, in addition to norepinephrine, guanethidine and its congeners (145). By preventing accumulation of guanethidine at its site of action, the hypotensive effect of the drug is antagonized (105, 109, 122, 123, 124, 127, 146, 147, 148). For a hypertensive patient whose blood pressure is well controlled on the combination of guanethidine and tricyclics or neuroleptics, withdrawal of the psychotropic drugs during the course of treatment may result in hypotensive shock (122). Molindone has almost no effect on norepinephrine uptake by sympathetic nerves and thus would not block the antihypertensive action of guanethidine; this neuroleptic can be administered safely and effectively in combination with guanethidine (149). Tricyclics have been reported to antagonize the hypotensive effects of clonidine. These interactions could prove hazardous to hypertensive patients (150).

Benzodiazepines are the psychotropics used most frequently among hypertensive patients. However, the benefit of anxiolytics in the treatment of hypertension is controversial. Although some of the psychotropics exert effects on autonomic functions, including a degree of inhibition of, or interference with, adrenergic sympathetic activity, such effects do not in themselves constitute indications for use in patients with essential hypertension. Some investigators propose that these compounds be used as adjuncts only if anxiety appears to contribute to elevated blood pressure, while others suggest that these drugs may have a direct cardiovascular effect (151). Whitehead et al. (142) report that a clinically significant reduction in diastolic blood pressure followed the administration of benzodiazepines. Greenblatt and colleagues (152), however, report that anxiolytics have no specific hypertensive effects and that any reduction in blood pressure is due to central-nervous-system depression; they feel the practice of prescribing antianxiety agents rather than specific antihypertensives for patients with hypertension is "unfortunate" and "usually results in a drowsy but still hypertensive patient." A recent article (153) states: "Diazepam is not an antihypertensive drug and it has not been shown to be useful in the long-term treatment of hypertension. Furthermore, there is no evidence that diazepam enhances the antihypertensive effect of any blood pressure-reducing drug." Thus, the controversy concerning the efficacy of anxiolytics in hypertension continues.

PSYCHOPHYSIOLOGICAL GASTROINTESTINAL DISORDERS

Emotional factors, particularly anxiety, are viewed as playing a significant role in the genesis and maintenance of various organic and functional gastrointestinal disorders, such as duodenal ulcer, dyspepsia, dysphagia, aerophagia, heartburn, diarrhea, constipation, and irritable bowel syndrome (154) (see Chapter 1 for a more detailed discussion of gastrointestinal disorders). It is therefore not surprising that anxiolytics have been extensively employed in the treatment of these conditions. Such compounds frequently contribute to a reduction in the self-perpetuating cycle of pain-anxiety-pain, and thereby are beneficial (59). Diazepam has been shown to reduce resting gastric secretion and acid production in peptic ulcer patients (155), and also appears to slow gastric emptying and small-bowel transit time in patients with hypermotility (156). These effects are presumably due to the central anxiolytic action of the drug, not to action on the gastrointestinal tract (12).

A number of studies have investigated the efficacy of benzodiazepines in the treatment of functional gastrointestinal disorders. Fifty-two subjects with psychophysiological GI disorders with significant anxiety overlay participated in a double-blind study of the adjunctive administration of either diazepam or placebo with propantheline bromide (157). Mean global ratings showed progressive improvement in all patients, but after one week, the diazepam group displayed significantly superior improvement, with greater reduction in anxiety and related symptoms. Although improvement in gastrointestinal complaints did not occur following use of diazepam, the addition of diazepam surpassed the benefits from propantheline bromide alone. Twenty-eight patients with symptoms of functional gastrointestinal distress (aerophagy, irritable colon, nervous dyspepsia) participated in a double-blind, placebo-controlled crossover trial of diazepam and lorazepam (158). Both drugs were significantly superior to placebo, but there was no difference in efficacy between the two benzodiazepines. Diazepam and lorazepam were also significantly effective in patients whose major complaint was aerophagy. Kaisch and colleagues (159) studied 120 patients with chronic gastrointestinal distress and found that diazepam and lorazepam not only decreased anxiety and tension, but also relieved somatic symptoms referrable to the GI tract. These effects also occurred to a lesser extent with placebo.

Chaplan and Vanov (160) conducted a double-blind study of 60 moderately or highly anxious individuals who had gastrointestinal disorders, 82 percent of which were "functional." The patients were randomly divided into two groups and prescribed either lorazepam (3 patients) or placebo (29 patients) for four weeks. Ratings, using the Hamilton Anxiety Rating Scale, Global Psychopathology Rating Scale, 35-Item Lipman-Rickels Self-rating Scale, and the GI Target Symptom Checklist, were collected at two and four weeks. The lorazepam group exhibited significantly greater decreases in anxiety and associated somatic symptoms as well as improvement in specific gastrointestinal complaints. Furtado (161), in a double-blind crossover study, demonstrated that lorazepam was beneficial in the treatment of gastrointestinal neurosis. A double-blind study of lorazepam and placebo in the treatment of 70 patients with anxiety-associated gastrointestinal symptoms was conducted by Berkowitz (162). Forty-three percent of the lorazepam patients and 49 percent of the placebo patients had "functional" GI disorders. During the four week study, the usual daily dose of lorazepam was 3mg, 1mg in the morning and 2mg in the evening. As indicated by Kruskal-Wallis analyses of Global, Hamilton, and 35-Item ratings, the active medication, as compared to placebo, produced statistically and clinically significant reduction in symptoms associated with anxiety. Placebo effects did occur, but lorazepam was nonetheless statistically superior. Side effects were few and were generally controlled by adjustment of dose.

All of these studies suggest that lorazepam (3–4mg/day) is a safe, well-accepted, and useful adjunct in patients with gastrointestinal disorders when anxiety plays an important role. On the other hand, Ramos (163) reports that 8 of 38 patients (21 percent) who were prescribed lorazepam for treatment of anxiety and restlessness associated with somatic illnesses developed moderate gastrointestinal disturbances. Therefore, clinicians need to be alert to the possibility that lorazepam may aggravate GI symptoms.

It appears that the antisecretory effects of many of the psychotropics coupled with their sedative, anxiolytic, and/or antidepressant effects make these compounds useful in the treatment of gastrointestinal disorders. As Deutsch (157) states:

> It can be concluded that addition of a psychoactive drug provides more rapid comfort to the patient because it alleviates anxiety and related burdens. . . . Data from the controlled study support the rationale that a two-pronged approach should be considered in managing patients with functional gastrointestinal complaints. One treatment should be aimed toward abating gastrointestinal dysfunctions, and the other toward promptly alleviating emotional overtones that contribute to the patient's discomfort.

Peptic Ulcer

Peptic ulcer includes duodenal and gastric ulcers. These conditions are generally assumed to be psychosomatic. Ten percent of individuals who attempt suicide and 3 percent of those who commit suicide have peptic ulcer disease (164). As a general rule, the less psychic energy that is bound by symptoms and their treatment, such as diet and medication, the better the prognosis. When a great deal of the patient's energy is bound with his peptic ulcer, the possibility that surgery will be beneficial becomes more remote. Furthermore, surgery for removal of intractable peptic ulcer symptoms may result in the formation of new symptoms (165). Thoroughman and colleagues (166) compared a group of patients with intractable symptoms of duodenal ulcer requiring surgery with a group of patients requiring surgery for hemorrhage, obstruction, or perforation. While 90 percent of the former group obtained favorable results, only 60 percent of the intractable symptoms were relieved by surgery. These authors reported that the most important prognostic factor in the intractable group was the degree to which the patient had been able to satisfy basic social needs prior to surgery. In an earlier study, Browning and Houseworth (167) studied two groups of patients with intractable duodenal ulcers. One group was treated with gastrectomy and the other control group received the usual medical treatment. After gastrectomy, only 43 percent of the surgery group retained ulcer symptoms, whereas all of the medical group retained symptoms. In the gastrectomy group, however, although only 13 percent had presented with other psychosomatic symptoms prior to surgery, 37 percent manifested such symptoms after surgery. Furthermore, the incidence of neurotic symptoms rose from 50 percent to 100 percent in the gastrectomy group, while no new neurotic symptoms occurred in the medical group. On the basis of these findings, the authors concluded that surgical removal of ulcer symptoms appears to result in replacement by new symptoms in a significant number of patients.

Anticholinergic drugs are most widely used in the treatment of peptic ulcer patients for reducing gastric secretion. H_2 blockers also reduce gastric secretion but have serious side effects, so these compounds are rarely prescribed. A number of psychotropic compounds reduce gastric secretion and acid output. Benzodiazepines have been found to slow gastric emptying and small-bowel transit time (155, 156) in peptic ulcer patients. These effects are presumably due to the central anxiolytic action of the drugs, not to action on the gastrointestinal tract. Trimipramine has been reported to reduce gastric secretion and acid output significantly, without affecting pepsin output (168). Although some investigators feel these effects are due to anticholinergic properties of the tricyclics, Bohman and associates (168) report that the effects appear to result from a noncholinergic action of trimipramine. At any rate, owing to their psychoactive and anticholinergic properties, psychotropics have been successful in ameliorating the anxiety and/or depression which frequently play a role in the origin and maintenance of peptic ulcers.

In conducting a preliminary study of eight duodenal ulcer patients, Guldahl (169) found symptoms of depression as measured by psychiatric interview and Beck Test in all eight. In a double-blind placebo-controlled trial, half of these patients were prescribed trimipramine, and the other half received placebo. After treatment with trimipramine, neither depression nor somatic symptoms remained, and three of the four patients showed healing of the duodenal ulcer. In the placebo group, on the other hand, there was no improvement in depressive symptoms, no evidence of improvement in somatic complaints, and no healing of the ulcer. One patient in the placebo group had to terminate participation in the study because of deterioration of his condition. Guldahl (170) also reports that trimipramine appears to be superior to treatment with antacids and anticholinergics.

Wetterhus et al. (171) conducted a double-blind study comparing the efficacy of trimipramine on symptoms and healing of peptic ulcer. Eighteen of 24 trimipramine patients (75 percent), as compared to 13 of 28 placebo patients (46 percent), had healed ulcers after four weeks, a significant difference favoring the antidepressant. Fourteen of 21 drug patients (67 percent), as compared to 5 of 24 placebo patients (21 percent), displayed improvement in gastroduodenitis—again, a significant difference. Thus, significantly more trimipramine patients than placebo patients were symptom-free at the end of the four-week trial. During the first two weeks of treatment, however, a higher frequency of minor side effects, such as drowsiness and dry mouth, occurred in the drug group. The authors reported a number of conclusions: trimipramine (50mg/day), as compared to placebo, produces a more rapid improvement of dyspeptic complaints in peptic ulcer patients, a marked improvement in gastroduodenitis, and a more rapid healing of peptic ulcer.

Nitter and colleagues (172) reported on a double-blind study comparing 50mg trimipramine and placebo administered in the evening. In all seven patients given the antidepressant, healing of the ulcer had occurred after four weeks of treatment; 3 of 11 placebo patients (27 percent) had a healed ulcer after four weeks. The superiority of trimipramine over placebo was statistically significant.

Forty patients with gastric ulcers completed a double-blind study comparing trimipramine and placebo during four weeks of treatment (173). Daily dose of the drug was 50mg or an identical placebo administered at bedtime. Twenty patients participated in each group. Healing of the ulcer occurred in 12 trimipramine patients (60 percent) and only 4 placebo patients (20 percent), a statistically significant difference in favor of trimipramine. Furthermore, there was also a significant improvement in "complaints" in patients in the active drug group; 16 patients with trimipramine, as compared to 9 placebo patients, "felt better." Thus, it appears that trimipramine both promotes healing of ulcer and decreases patients' complaints.

PSYCHOPHYSIOLOGICAL INTESTINAL DISORDERS

Ulcerative colitis, ulcerative ileitis, malabsorption syndrome, regional enteritis, and irritable bowel syndrome are generally considered to be "psychosomatic intestinal disorders" (174). These functional bowel syndromes consist of a group of symptoms which are not related to any detectable organic disease and which exhibit a component of anxiety or nervous stress in their genesis and perpetuation. McKechnie and coworkers (175) surveyed 50 cases of ulcerative proctitis to ascertain if emotional tension or life stress precipitated an exacerbation of symptoms. Rectal bleeding occurred during emotional stress "definitely" in 17 cases, "possibly" in 14 cases, and "not" in 19 cases. In other words, 62 percent of the cases were associated with emotional upset. Other investigators claim, however, that abnormal behavior patterns might be an effect rather than a precipitating factor. Gruner et al. (176) report that among 178 Norwegian patients who underwent colectomy for ulcerative colitis, the frequency of psychological disturbance did not differ significantly from the general population. Psychotropic drugs had been used by 18.5 percent of the patients prior to colectomy and by only 10.1 percent of the patients following surgery. The authors propose that, judging by the very low use of psychotropics both pre- and postoperatively, psychological factors were not prominent in the development of ulcerative colitis.

Psychotropic drugs have been used successfully as adjunctive treatment in patients with ulcerative colitis. Krisner (177) reports that imipramine is useful for improving depressed mood in these patients, and Raft (178) recommends the use of imipramine or amitriptyline or combinations (Etrafon, Triavil). In addition to improving mood, the tricyclics may alleviate some of the bowel symptoms because these compounds have antispasmodic activity. Amitriptyline has sedative properties and may be more useful in patients who exhibit substantial anxiety and in those who complain of insomnia. The usual daily dose for adults is about 150mg, though 50–75mg at night may suffice for the relief of insomnia. In the elderly patient, however, individual response is extremely variable, and low doses of the phenothiazines may be more effective against agitation and depression. Thioridazine (50–150mg/day) may be administered, but again, individual tolerance must be determined. The most disturbing side effect of the phenothiazines is hypotension (178).

Benzodiazepines are also beneficial in the treatment of functional bowel diseases. Three clinical trials confirm the value of chlordiazepoxide-clidinium bromide (Librax) and diazepam in the treatment of such patients (157, 179, 180). Kaisch and coworkers (181) commented on the efficacy of meprobamate and of phenaglycodol in treating psychophysiological bowel disorders. Forty-eight patients with moderate-to-severe anxiety associated with chronic enteritis and ulcerative colitis participated in a double-blind trial comparing lorazepam and placebo (182). The patients involved in the study were from nine outpatient centers, and assessments were made by physician-rated Global and Hamilton scales and by patient-rated 35-Item Rating scales. By all three measurements and at virtually all assessment periods, lorazepam was significantly more effective than placebo in reducing anxiety-related symptoms. Undesirable side effects were minimal, and 79 percent of the patients responded adequately to 3mg/day or less lorazepam. Baume and colleagues (158) report that lorazepam was also useful in relieving symptoms of aerophagy, irritable colon, and nervous dyspepsia.

Zisook (183) presents a case of a 67-year-old patient with severe and chronic ulcerative colitis who was administered lithium for concomitant manic-depressive illness. Both conditions improved markedly, and all symptoms have been alleviated during the 16-month follow-up. Symptoms of colitis began to improve substantially before affect responded. The author is unable to explain the favorable response to lithium. Rask-Madsen and associates (184) reported that transmucosal potential difference across the rectal mucosa was greater in lithium-treated patients, and they propose that this effect may prove beneficial for ulcerative colitis patients.

Although psychotropics have been shown to be useful in the management of the patient with functional bowel disorders, these compounds should be regarded as adjuncts to therapy, not the major effort.

CONCLUSIONS

Psychophysiological disorders tend to occur in different organs for different patients. For example, under similar emotional stress, one individual reacts with a peptic ulcer, another develops neurodermatitis, a third complains of chronic headache, and another becomes hypertensive. However, it is possible for a patient to present with more than one psychosomatic illness. Steiner et al. (185) present a case study of a patient hospitalized for severe depression who had continuous asthmatic attacks, marked indigestion and peptic ulcer, and an acute exacerbation of seborrhea of the head. The patient was prescribed a number of drugs for his somatic condition plus amitriptyline with supportive psychotherapy for his psychiatric condition. During the next three weeks, the depression gradually subsided, the seborrhea cleared, and the patient had no asthmatic attacks or indigestion. When the patient was symptom-free, he disappeared from the clinic for one week and was returned in a hypomanic state, with severe asthma, indigestion, and seborrhea. Following two weeks of psychotropic treatment, both mood and somatic symptoms had improved. At one-year follow-up, the patient was continuing to do well on nortriptyline and thioridazine. This patient demonstrates the possibility that psychotropic drugs alone can ameliorate a variety of symptoms.

In summary, five points should be noted by clinicians who treat patients with psychophysiological disorders. First of all, the need for a psychotropic drug should be carefully assessed; many of these patients respond to supportive psychotherapy and placebos. Second, when psychotropics are required, short-term use is preferable. For some patients, psychotropics should only be used as adjunct; that is, these compounds may facilitate patient management and improve "well-being" without being curative (59); in other patients, the administration of a psychotropic may obviate the need for other medication. The choice of a particular agent among those with similar properties depends primarily upon the side effects which may result. Finally, in the patients treated with psychotropic and medical drugs in combination, the clinician needs to be aware of possible interactions.

REFERENCES

1. Goldberg, M. Answers to questions about anxiety and your practice. *Behav. Med.* 7: 36–40, 1980.
2. Lesse, S. Psychotherapy in combination with antidepressant drugs in patients with severe masked depression. *Am. J. Psychother.* 31: 185–203, 1977.
3. Harari, E. & Fail, L. "Masked" depression or missed depression? *Med. J. Aust.* 1: 92–3, 1976.
4. Ramos, F.H. Anxiety and anguish in somatic illness: clinical experience with lorazepam. *Cur. Med. Res. Opin.* 1: 528–34, 1973.
5. Uhlenhuth, E.H., Balter, M.B., & Lipman, R.S. Minor tranquilizers. Clinical correlates of use in an urban population. *Arch. Gen. Psychiat.* 35: 658–665, 1978.
6. Blackwell, G. Psychotropic drugs in use today: the role of diazepam in medical practice. *JAMA* 225: 1,637–41, 1973.
7. Blackwell, B. Minor tranquilizers: use, misuse or overuse? *Psychosom.* 16: 28–31, 1975.
8. Waldron, I. Increased prescribing of Valium, Librium, and other drugs—an example of the influence of economic and social factors on the practice of medicine. *Int. J. Health Ser.* 7: 37–62, 1977.
9. Lasagna, L. The role of benzodiazepines in nonpsychiatric medical practice. *Am. J. Psychiat.* 134: 656–58, 1977.
10. Parry, H.J., Balter, M.B., Mellinger, G.D. National patterns of psychotherapeutic drug use. *Arch. Gen. Psychiat.* 28: 769–83, 1973.
11. Hemminki, E. General practioners' indications for psychotropic drugs. *Scand. J. Soc. Med.* 2: 79–85, 1974.
12. Solow, C. Psychotropic drugs in somatic disorders. *Int. J. Psychiat. Med.* 6(1/2): 267–82, 1975.
13. DiGiacomo, J.N. & Rosen, H. Psychosomatic disorders: psychotropic medications. *Psychosom.* 20: 95–107, 1979.
14. Ban, T.A. Psychopharmacology and psychosomatic disorders. *Psychosom.* 19: 757–60, 1978.
15. Ananth, J. Psychopharmacology and psychosomatic illness. *Psychosom.* 16: 124–28, 1975.
16. Freedman, A.M., Kaplan, H.I., & Sadock, B.J. *Modern Synopsis of Comprehensive Textbook of Psychiatry*, 2nd ed. Baltimore: Williams & Wilkins, 1976.
17. Parker, J.B., Blazer, D., & Wyrick, L. Anorexia nervosa: a combined therapeutic approach. *South. Med. J.* 70: 448–52, 1977.
18. Dally, P. Anorexia nervosa. *Brit. J. Clin. Prac.* 26: 509–12, 1972.
19. Silverman, J.A. Anorexia nervosa: clinical observations in a successful treatment plan. *J. Pediat.* 84: 68–73, 1974.
20. Crisp, A.H. A treatment regime for anorexia nervosa. *Brit. J. Psychiat.* 112: 505–12, 1965.
21. How, J. & Davidson R.J.L. Chlorpromazine-induced haemolytic anaemia in anorexia nervosa. *Postgrad. Med. J.* 53: 278–79, 1977.
22. Needleman, H.L. & Waber, D. Amitriptyline therapy in patients with anorexia nervosa (letter to the editor). *Lancet* 2: 580, 1976.

23. Needleman, H.L. & Waber, D. The use of amitriptyline in anorexia nervosa. In Vigersky, R.A. (Ed.), *Anorexia Nervosa*. New York: Raven, 1977.

24. Mills, I.H. Amitriptyline therapy in anorexia nervosa (letter to the editor). *Lancet* 2: 687, 1976.

25. White, J.H. & Schnaultz, N.L. Successful treatment of anorexia nervosa with imipramine. *Dis. Nerv. Sys.* 38: 567–68, 1977.

26. O'Flanagan, P.M. A possible new treatment of weight loss in affective disorders and anorexia nervosa (letter to the editor). *Brit. J. Psychiat.* 128: 102–103, 1976.

27. Moore, D.C. Amitriptyline therapy in anorexia nervosa. *Am. J. Psychiat.* 134: 1,303–04, 1977.

28. Solomon, J.G. Treatment in anorexia nervosa (letter to the editor). *Am. J. Psychiat.* 135: 998, 1978.

29. Coppen, A., Eccleston, E.G., & Peet, M. Total and free tryptophan concentration in the plasma of depressive patients. *Lancet* 2: 60–68, 1973.

30. Coppen, A.J., Gupta, R.K., Eccleston, E.G., Wood, K.M., Wakeling, A., & DeSousa, V.F.A. Plasma-tryptophan in anorexia nervosa (letter to the editor). *Lancet* 1: 961, 1976.

31. Barcai, A. Lithium in adult anorexia nervosa. A pilot report in two patients. *Acta Psychiat. Scand.* 55: 97–101, 1977.

32. Barry, V.C. & Klawans, H.L. On the role of dopamine in the pathophysiology of anorexia nervosa. *J. Neural. Transm.* 38: 107–22, 1976.

33. Lupton, M., Simon, L., Barry, V., & Klawans, H.L. Biological aspects of anorexia nervosa. *Life Sci.* 18: 1,341–48, 1976.

34. Johanson, A.J. & Knorr, N.J. Treatment of anorexia nervosa by levodopa (letter to the editor). *Lancet* 2: 591, 1974.

35. Johanson, A.J. & Knorr, N.J. L-dopa as treatment for anorexia nervosa. In Vigersky, R.A. (Ed.), *Anorexia Nervosa*. New York, Raven, 1977.

36. Plantey, F. Pimozide in treatment of anorexia nervosa (leter to the editor). *Lancet* 1: 1,105, 1977.

37. Noble, R.E. Effect of cyproheptadine on appetite and weight gain in adults. *JAMA* 209: 2,054–55, 1969.

38. Mainguet, P. Effect of cyproheptadine on anorexia and loss of weight in adults. *Practitioner* 208: 797–800, 1972.

39. Pawlowski, G.T. Cyproheptadine: weight gain and appetite stimulation in essential anorexia patients. *Cur. Ther. Res.* 18: 673–678, 1975.

40. Vigersky, R.A. & Loriaux, D.L. The effect of cyproheptadine in anorexia nervosa: a double-blind trial. In Vigersky, R.A. (Ed.), *Anorexia Nervosa*. New York: Raven, 1977.

41. Ford, R.M. Asthma: some basic methods of prevention. *Ann. Allergy* 42: 92–4, 1979.

42. Avn, J. & Bruderman, I. The effect of antidepressants on pulmonary ventilation and the mechanics of breathing. *Psychopharmacologia* (Berl.) 14: 184–92, 1969.

43. Knapp, P.H., Mathe, A.A., & Vachon, L. Psychosomatic aspects of bronchial asthma. In Weiss, E.B. & Segal, M.S. (Eds.), *Bronchial Asthma: Mechanisms and Therapeutics*. Boston: Little, Brown, 1976.

44. Knapp, P.H. Psychotherapeutic management of bronchial asthma. In Wittkower, E.D. & Warnes, H. (Eds.), *Psychosomatic Medicine. Its Clinical Applications*. New York: Harper & Row, 1977.

45. Ananth, J. Antiasthmatic effect of amitriptyline (letter to the editor). *Can. Med. Assoc. J.* 110: 1,131–33, 1974.

46. Sugihara, H., Ishihara, K., & Noguchi, H. Clinical experience with amitriptyline (Tryptanol) in the treatment of bronchial asthma. *Ann. Allergy* 23: 422–29, 1965.

47. Meares, R.A., Mills, J.E., Atkinson, J.M., Pun, L.-Q., & Ran, M.J. Amitriptyline and asthma. *Med. J. Aust.* 2: 25–8, 1971.

48. Wilson, R.C.D. Antiasthmatic effect of amitriptyline (letter to the editor). *Can. Med. Assoc. J.* 111: 212, 1974.

49. Sanger, M.D. The use of tranquilizers and antidepressants in allergy. *Ann. Allergy* 20: 705–709, 1962.

50. Goldfarb, A.A. & Venutolu, F. The use of an antidepressant drug in chronically allergic individuals. *Ann. Allergy* 21: 667–76, 1963.

51. Kessler, F. Hydroxyzine hydrochloride in the management of allergic conditions. *Clin. Med.* 74(9): 37–45, 1967.

52. Shah, J.R., Talivalkar, C.V., & Karkanis, V. Observations on the study of an antiasthmatic preparation containing hydroxyzine. *Ind. J. Chest. Dis.* 12: 116–20, 1970.

53. Santos, I.M.H. & Unger, L. Hydroxyzine (Atarax) in allergic diseases. *Ann. Allergy* 18: 172–78, 1960.

54. Nasr, S.J. & Adkins, R.W. Coincidental improvement in asthma during lithium treatment. *Am. J. Psychiat.* 134: 1,042–43, 1977.

55. Putnam, P.L. Possible positive "side effects" of lithium (letter to the editor). *Am. J. Psychiat.* 135: 388, 1978.

56. Winig, H.R. More on lithium and asthma (letter to the editor). *Am. J. Psychiat.* 135: 998, 1978.

57. Bracha, H., Ebstein, R., & Belmaker, R.H. Possible mechanism of lithium's effect on bronchial asthma (letter to the editor). *Am. J. Psychiat.* 136: 734, 1979.

58. Stein, M. & Schiavi, R. Respiratory disorders. In Freedman, A.M. & Kaplan, H.I. (Eds.), *Comprehensive Textbook of Psychiatry.* Baltimore: Williams & Wilkins, 1967.

59. Krogh, C., McLean, W.M., & LaPierre, Y.D. Minor tranquilizers in somatic disorders. *Can. Med. Assoc. J.* 118: 1,097–1,108, 1978.

60. Lockey, R.F. Urticaria of unknown origin. *Hosp. Pract.* 14: 49–54, 1979.

61. Turner, T.W. & Gale, A.E. Urticaria. *Aust. Fam. Physician* 7: 1,497–1,501, 1978.

62. Medansky, R.S. Emotion and skin—a double-blind evaluation of psychotropic agents. *Psychosom.* 12: 326–29, 1971.

63. Keegan, D.L. Chronic urticaria: clinical, psychophysiological and therapeutic aspects. *Psychosom.* 17: 160–63, 1976.

64. Lester, E.P., Wittkower, E.D., Kalz, F., & Azima, H. Phrenotropic drugs in psychosomatic disorders (skin). *Am. J. Psychiat.* 119: 136–43, 1962.

65. Freedman, A.M., Kaplan, H.I., & Sadock, B.J. Psychophysiological allergic and skin disorders. In *Modern Synopsis of Comprehensive Textbook of Psychiatry*, 2nd ed. Baltimore: Williams & Wilkins, 1976.

66. Nurse, D.S. Urticaria: diagnosis and management. *Drugs* 9: 292–98, 1975.

67. Engels, W.D. & Wittkower, E.D. Allergic and skin disorders. In Freedman, A.M. & Kaplan, H.I. (Eds.), *Comprehensive Textbook of Psychiatry*, 2nd ed. Baltimore: Williams & Wilkins, 1976.

68. Sanger, M.D. Psychosomatic allergy. *Psychosom.* 11: 473–76, 1970.

69. Green, M.A. & Green, R.L. Psychotropic adjuvants in allergic disorders. Report of experiences with nortriptyline hydrochloride. *Psychosom.* 8: 29–32, 1967.

70. Greenblatt, D.J. & Shader, R.I. *Benzodiazepines in Clinical Practice.* New York: Raven, 1974.

71. Musaph, H. Itching and other dermatoses. In Wittkower, E.D. & Warnes, H. (Eds), *Psychosomatic Medicine. Its Clinical Applications.* New York: Harper & Row.

72. Freedman, A.M., Kaplan, H.I., & Sadock, B.J. Psychogenic Pain. In *Modern Synopsis of Comprehensive Textbook of Psychiatry*, 2nd ed. Baltimore: Williams & Wilkins, 1976.

73. Harris, M. Psychosomatic disorders of the mouth and face. *Practitioner* 214: 372–79, 1975

74. Dykeh, P.R. Headaches in children. *Am. Fam. Physician* 11: 105–11, 1975.

75. DeVaul, R.A., Zisook, S., & Stuart, H.J. Patients with psychogenic pain. *J. Fam. Prac.* 4: 53–5, 1977.
76. Sternbach, R.A., Murphy, R.W., Akeson, W.H., & Wolf, S.R. Chronic low-back pain. The "low-back loser." *Postgrad. Med.* 53: 135–38, 1973.
77. Tyber, M.A. Treatment of the painful shoulder syndrome with amitriptyline and lithium carbonate. *Can. Med. Assoc. J.* 111: 137–40, 1974.
78. Raft, D., Toomey, T., & Gregg, J.M. Behavior modification and haloperidol in chronic facial pain. *Southern Med. J.* 72: 155–59, 1979.
79. Gilbert, N.N. & Koepke, H.H. Relief of musculoskeletal and associated psychopathologic symptoms with meprobamate and aspirin: a controlled study. *Cur. Ther. Res.* 15: 820–32, 1973.
80. Kapp, F.T. Psychogenic pain. In Freedman, A.M. & Kaplan, H.I. (Eds.), *Comprehensive Textbook of Psychiatry.* Baltimore: Williams & Wilkins, 1967.
81. Sternbach, R.A. *Pain: A Psychophysiological Analysis.* New York: Academic, 1968.
82. Sternbach, R.S. Psychological aspects of chronic pain. *Clin. Orthoped. Rel. Res.* 129: 150–55, 1977.
83. Pace, J.B. Psychophysiology of pain: diagnostic and therapeutic implications. *J. Fam. Prac.* 5: 553–57, 1977.
84. Sternbach, R.A. Pain and depression, In Kiev, A. (Ed.), *Somatic Manifestations of Depressive Disorders.* Amsterdam: Excerpta Medica, 1974.
85. Mersky, H. & Hester, R.A. The treatment of chronic pain with psychotropic drugs. *Postgrad. Med. J.* 48: 594–98, 1972.
86. Webb, H.E. & Lascelles, R.G. Treatment of facial and head pain associated with depression. *Lancet* 282: 355–56, 1962.
87. Diamond, S. Depressive headache. *Headache* 4: 255–58, 1964.
88. Cassidy, W.L., Flanagan, N.B., Spellman, M., & Cohen, M.E. Clinical observations in manic-depressive disease. A quantitative study of one hundred manic-depressive patients and fifty medically sick controls. *JAMA* 164: 1,535–46, 1957.
89. Kashiwagi, T., McClure, J.N., & Wetzel, R.D. Headache and psychiatric disorders. *Dis. Nerv. Sys.* 33: 659–63, 1972.
90. Diamond, S. & Baltes, B.J. Chronic tension headache—treated with amitriptyline—a double-blind study. *Headache* 11: 110–16, 1971.
91. Lance, J.W. & Curran, D.A. Treatment of chronic tension headache. *Lancet* 286: 1,236–39, 1964.
92. Dalessio, D.J. Some reflections on the etiologic role of depression in head pain. *Headache* 8: 28–31, 1968.
93. Aring, C.D. Emotion-induced headache. *Postgrad. Med.* 56: 757–60, 1974.
94. Okasha, A., Ghaleb, H.A., & Sadek, A. A double-blind trial for the clinical management of psychogenic headache. *Brit. J. Psychiat.* 122: 181–83, 1973.
95. Freedman, A.M., Kaplan, H.I., & Sadock, B.J. Headaches. In *Modern Synopsis of Comprehensive Textbook of Psychiatry II*, 2nd ed. Baltimore: Williams & Wilkins, 1976.
96. Eliot, R.S. *Stress and the Major Cardiovascular Disorders.* Kisco: Futura, 1979.
97. Engel, G.L. Psychologic factors in instantaneous cardiac death. *New Eng. J. Med.* 294: 664–65, 1976.
98. Weiss, E., Dlin, B., Rollin, H.R., Fischer, H.K., & Depler, C.R. Emotional factors in coronary occlusion. *Arch. Intern. Med.* 99: 628–41, 1957.
99. Russek, H.I. & Russek, L.G. Behavior patterns and emotional stress in the etiology of coronary heart disease: sociological and occupations aspect. In Wheatley, D. (Ed.), *Stress and the Heart.* New York: Raven, 1977.

100. Freedman, A.M., Kaplan, H.I., & Sadock, B.J. Psychophysiological cardiovascular disorders. In *Modern Synopsis of Comprehensive Textbook of Psychiatry II*, 2nd ed. Baltimore: Williams & Wilkins, 1976.

101. Wynn, A. Unwarranted emotional distress in men with ischemic heart disease (IHD). *Med. J. Aust.* 2: 847–51, 1967.

102. Samet, C. & Richards, D.J. Lorazepam in the treatment of anxiety associated with cardiovascular symptomatology: a double-blind study, pp. 27–30. In *Lorazepam Symposium: Third Congress, International College of Psychosomatic Medicine*. Tenafly, NJ: Therapeutic Research, 1976.

103. Finkel, S. Antianxiety effects of lorazepam in patients with cardiovascular symptomatology. *J. Clin. Psychiat.* 39(Suppl. 10, sec. 2): 35–40, 1978.

104. Wheatley, D. Clorazepate in the management of coronary disease. *Psychosom.* 20: 195–205, 1979.

105. Ebert, M.H. & Shader, R.I. Cardiovascular effects. In Shader, R.I. & DiMascio, A. (Eds.), *Psychotropic Drug Side Effects*. Baltimore: Williams & Wilkins, 1970.

106. Crane, G.E. Cardiac toxicity and psychotropic drugs. *Dis. Nerv. Syst.* 31: 534–39, 1970.

107. Raisfield, I.H. Cardiovascular complications of antidepressant therapy. *Am. Heart. J.* 83: 129–33, 1972.

108. Charalampous, K.D. Pharmacotherapy of schizophrenia. In Fann, W.E., Karacan, I., Pokorny, A.D., & Williams, R.L. (Eds.), *Phenomenology and Treatment of Schizophrenia*. New York: Spectrum, 1978.

109. Davis, J.M. Tricyclic antidepressants. In Simpson, L.L. (Ed.), *Drug Treatment of Mental Disorders*. New York: Raven, 1976.

110. Editorial. Cardiovascular complications from psychotropics. *Brit. Med. J.* 1: 3, 1971.

111. Moir, D.C., Crooks, J., Sawyer, P., Turnbull, M.J., & Weir, R.D. Cardiotoxicity of tricyclic antidepressants. *Brit. J. Pharmacol.* 44: 371–72, 1972.

112. Schoolar, J.C. Mood-active agents in depression. In Fann, W.E., Karacan, I., Pokorny, A.D., & Williams, R.L. (Eds.), *Phenomenology and Treatment of Depression*. New York: Spectrum, 1977.

113. Hollister, C.E. & Kosek, J.C. Sudden death during treatment with phenothiazine derivatives. *JAMA* 192: 1,038, 1965.

114. Richardson, H.L., Graupner, K.I., & Richardson, M.E. Intramyocardial lesions in patients dying suddenly and unexpectedly. *JAMA* 195: 254–60, 1966.

115. Leetsma, J.E. & Koenig, K.L. Sudden death and phenothiazines: a current controversy. *Arch. Gen. Psychiat.* 18: 137–48, 1968.

116. Giles, T.D. & Modlin, R.K. Death associated with ventricular arrhythmia and thioridazine hydrochloride. *JAMA* 205: 108–10, 1968.

117. Alexander, C.S. & Nino, A. Cardiovascular complication in young patients taking psychotropic drugs. *Am. Heart J.* 78: 757–69, 1969.

118. Moore, M.T. & Book, M.H. Sudden death in phenothiazine therapy. *Psychiat. Quart.* 44: 389–402, 1970.

119. Fann, W.E., Gyorkey, F., Raizner, A.E., & Richman, B.W. Cardiovascular side effects of neuroleptics. In Fann, W.E., Karacan, I., Pokorny, A.D., & Williams, R.L. (Eds.), *Phenomenology and Treatment of Schizophrenia*. New York: Spectrum, 1978.

120. Moir, D.C., Cornwall, W.B., & Crooks, J. Cardiotoxicity of amitriptyline. *Lancet* 2: 561–64, 1972.

121. Boston Collaborative Drug Surveillance Program. Adverse reactions to the tricyclic antidepressant drugs. *Lancet* 1: 529–31, 1972.

122. Ban, T.A. Drug interactions with psychoactive drugs. *Dis. Nerv. Sys.* 36: 164–66, 1975.

123. Fann, W.E. Some clinically important interactions of psychotropic drugs. *Southern Med. J.* 66: 661–665, 1973.

124. Hussar, D.A. Review of some significant drug interactions. *Pa. Med.* 79: 37–41, 1976.

125. MacDonald, M.G. & Robinson, D.S. Clinical observations of possible barbiturate interference with anticoagulation. *JAMA* 204: 97–100, 1968.

126. Levy, G., O'Reilly, R.A., Aggeler, P.M., & Keech, G.M. Pharmacokinetic analysis of the effect of barbiturates on the anticoagulant action of warfarin in man. *Clin. Pharmacol. Ther.* 11: 372–77, 1970.

127. Kaufmann, J.S. Drug interactions involving psychotherapeutic agents. In Simpson, L.L. (Ed.), *Drug Treatment of Mental Disorders*. New York: Raven, 1976.

128. Wolf, S. Cardiovascular disease. In Wittkower, E.D. & Warnes, H. (Ed.), *Psychosomatic Medicine. Its Clinical Applications*. New York: Harper & Row, 1977.

129. Cole, J.O. Phenothiazines. In Simpson, L.L. (Ed.), *Drug Treatment of Mental Disorders*. New York: Raven, 1976.

130. Ayd, F.A. Cardiovascular effects of phenothiazines. *Int. Drug Ther. Newsl.* 5: 1–8, 1970.

131. Ban, T.A. & St. Jean, A. The effect of phenothiazines on the electrocardiogram. *Can. Med. Assoc. J.* 91: 537–40, 1964.

132. Huston, J.R. & Bell, G.E. Thioridazine, chlorpromazine, and ECG. *JAMA* 198: 134–38, 1966.

133. Ayd, F.J. Haloperidol: fifteen years of experience. *Dis. Nerv. Syst.* 33: 459–69, 1972.

134. Gerle, B. Clinical observations of the side effects of haloperidol. *Acta Psychiat. Scand.* 40: 65–76, 1964.

135. Ban, T.A. & Pecknold, J.C. Haloperidol and the butyrophenones. In Simpson, L.L. (Ed.), *Drug Treatment of Mental Disorders*. New York: Raven, 1976.

136. Pratt, I.T. Twilight sleep after infarction. *Brit. Med. J.* 3: 457–76, 1971.

137. Reiser, M.F. Cardiovascular disorders. In Freedman, A.M. & Kaplan, H.I. (Eds.), *Comprehensive Textbook of Psychiatry*. Baltimore: Williams & Wilkins, 1967.

138. Bant, W. Do antihypertensive drugs really cause depression? *Proc. Roy. Soc. Med.* 67: 919–21, 1974.

139. Esler, M., Julius, S., Zweifler, A., Randall, O., Harburg, E., Gardiner, H., & Dequattro, V. Mild high-renin essential hypertension: neurogenic human hypertension? *New Eng. J. Med.* 296: 405–11, 1977.

140. Heine, B.E., Sainsbury, P., & Chynoweth, R.C. Hypertension and emotional disturbance. *J. Psychiat. Res.* 7: 119–30, 1969.

141. Davies, M.H. Is high blood pressure a psychosomatic disease? *J. Chron. Dis.* 24: 239–58, 1971.

142. Whitehead, W.E., Blackwell, B., & Robinson, A. Why physicians prescribe benzodiazepines in essential hypertension: a phase IV study. *Biol. Psychiat.* 12: 597–601, 1977.

143. Carabello, R., Conde, L., & Nahas, L. Investigacion clinica con un nuovo ansiolitico WY-4036 (lorazepam). *Prensa Med. Argentina* 59: 1,076–80, 1972.

144. Hart, W.L. & Parmley, L.F. The effect of lorazepam of hypertension-associated anxiety: a double-blind study. *J. Clin. Psychiat.* 39 (Suppl. 10, sec. 2): 41–5, 1978.

145. Janowsky, D.S., El-Yousef, M.K., Davis, J.M., & Fann, W.E. Antagonism of guanethidine by chlorpromazine. *Am. J. Psychiat.* 130: 808–10, 1973.

146. Fann, W.E., Janowsky, D.S., & Davis, J.M. Antagonism of the antihypertensive effect of guanethidine by chlorpromazine. *Lancet* 2: 436–37, 1971.

147. Ayd, F.J. Psychotropic drug combinations: good and bad. In Greenblatt, M. (Ed.), *Drugs in Combination with other Therapies*. New York: Grune & Stratton, 1975.

148. Janowsky, D.S., El-Yousef, M.K., Davis, J.M., Fann, W.E., & Oates, J.A. Guanethidine antagonism by antipsychotic drugs. *J. Tenn. Med. Assoc.* 65: 620–22, 1972.

149. Simpson, L.L. Combined use of molindone and guanethidine in patients with schizophrenia and hypertension. *Am. J. Psychiat.* 136: 1,410–14, 1979.
150. Briant, R.H., Reid, J.L., & Dollery, C.T. Interaction between clonidine and desimipramine in man. *Brit. Med. J.* 1: 522–23, 1973.
151. Daniell, H.B. Cardiovascular effects of diazepam and chlordiazepoxide. *Eur. J. Pharmacol.* 32: 58–65, 1975.
152. Greenblatt, D.J., Shader, R.I., & Lofgren, S. Rational psycho-pharmacology for patients with medical diseases. *Ann. Rev. Med.* 27: 407–20, 1976.
153. Diazepam (Valium) in hypertension. *Med. Lett. Drugs Ther.* 16: 96, 1974.
154. McCawley, A. Managing psychosomatic abdominal pain. *Psychosom.* 20: 163–71, 1979.
155. Birnbaum, D., Karmel, F., & Tefera, M. The effect of diazepam on human gastric secretion. *Gut* 12: 616–18, 1971.
156. Birnbaum, D., Ben-Menachem, J., & Schwartz, A. The influence of oral diazepam on gastrointestinal motility. *Am. J. Proctol.* 21: 263–66, 1970.
157. Deutsch, E. Relief of anxiety and related emotions in patients with gastrointestinal disorders. *Am. J. Dig. Dis.* 16: 1,091–94, 1971.
158. Baume, P., Tracey, M., & Dawson, L. Efficacy of two minor tranquilizers in relieving symptoms of functional gastrointestinal distress. *Aust. NZ J. Med.* 5: 503–06, 1975.
159. Kaisch, A.M., Richards, D.J., & Vanov, S.K. Lorazepam in the management of anxiety associated with chronic gastrointestinal disease: a double-blind study. *Cur. Ther. Res.* 19: 292–306, 1976.
160. Chaplan, A. & Vanov, S.K. Gastrointestinal illness: treatment of the anxiety component. *Psychosom.* 18: 49–54, 1977.
161. Furtado, J.D. Lorazepam in gastrointestinal disorders with anxiety overlay. *Psychosom.* 17: 32–4, 1976.
162. Berkowitz, J.M. A clinical assessment of lorazepam in the treatment of anxiety associated with gastrointestinal symptomatology. *J. Clin. Psychiat.* 39 (Suppl. 10, sec. 2): 46–52, 1978.
163. Ramos, F.H. Anxiety and anguish in somatic illness: clinical experience with lorazepam. *Cur. Med. Res. Opin.* 1: 528–34, 1973.
164. Viskum, K. Ulcer, attempted suicide and suicide. *Act Psychiat. Scand.* 51: 221–27, 1975.
165. Rosenbaum, M. Peptic ulcer. In Freedman, A.M. & Kaplan, H.I. (Eds.), *Comprehensive Textbook of Psychiatry.* Baltimore: Williams & Wilkins, 1967.
166. Thoroughman, J.C., Pascal, G.R., Jenkins, W.P., Crutcher, J.C., & Peoples, L.C. Psychological factors predictive of surgical success in patients with intractable duodenal ulcer: a study of male veterans. *Psychosom. Med.* 26: 618–24, 1964.
167. Browning, J.S. & Houseworth, J.H. Development of new symptoms following medical and surgical treatment for duodenal ulcer. *Psychosom. Med.* 15: 328–36, 1953.
168. Bohmann, T., Schrumpf, E., & Myren, J. The effect of trimipramine (Surmontil) on gastric secretion and the serum gastrin release in healthy young students. *Scand. J. Gastroent.* 12 (Suppl. 43): 7–17, 1977.
169. Guldahl, M. The effect of trimipramine (Surmontil) on masked depression in patients with duodenal ulcer: a double-blind study. *Scand. J. Gastroent.* 12 (Suppl. 43): 27–31, 1977.
170. Guldahl, M. Masked depression and peptic ulcer. *Scand. J. Gastroent.* (Suppl. 34): 17, 1975.
171. Wetterhus, S., Aubert, E., Berg, C.E., Bjerkeset, T., Halvorsen, L., Hovdenak, N., Myren, J., Roland, M., Sigstad, H., Guldahl, M. The effect of trimipramine (Surmontil) on symptoms and healing of peptic ulcer. A double-blind study. *Scand. J. Gastroent.* 12 (Suppl. 43): 33–8, 1977.
172. Nitter, L., Haraldsson, A., Holck, P., Hoy C., Munthe-Kaas, J., Myrhol, K., & Paulsen, W. The effect of trimipramine on the healing of peptic ulcer. A double-blind study. Multicentre investigation. *Scand. J. Gastroent.* 12 (Suppl. 43): 39–41, 1977.

173. Valnes, K., Myren, J., & Ovistat, T. Trimipramine in the treatment of gastric ulcer. *Scand. J. Gastroent.* 13: 497–500, 1978.
174. Engel, G.L. Intestinal disorders. In Freedman, A.M. & Kaplan, H.I. (Eds.), *Comprehensive Textbook of Psychiatry.* Baltimore: Williams & Wilkins, 1967.
175. McKechnie, J.C., Bynum, T.E., Bentlif, P.S., & Lanza, F.L. Ulcerative proctitis. *South. Med. J.* 67: 1,052–56, 1974.
176. Gruner, O.P.N., Naas, R., Gjone, E., Flatmark, A., & Fretheim, B. Mental disorders in ulcerative colitis: suicide, divorce, psychosis, hospitalization for mental disease, alcoholism, and consumption of psychotropic drugs in 178 patients subjected to colectomy. *Dis. Colon Rectum* 21: 37–9, 1978.
177. Krisner, J.B. Drug therapy in ulcerative colitis. *Mod. Med.* (Minn.) 34: 115, 1966.
178. Raft, D. Psychologic management of patients with bowel disorders. *Am. Fam. Phys.* 8: 124–28, 1973.
179. McHardy, G., Sekinger, D., Balart, L., & Cradic, H.E. Chlordiazepoxide-clidinium bromide in gastrointestinal disorders: controlled clinical studies. *Gastroent.* 54: 508–13, 1968.
180. Wayne, H.H. A tranquilizer-anticholinergic preparation in functional gastrointestinal disorders: a double-blind evaluation. *Cal. Med.* 111: 79–83, 1969.
181. Kaisch, A.M., Fein, H.D., & Miller, J.W. Comparative effect of phenaglycodol, meprobamate and a placebo on the irritable colon. *Am. J. Dig. Dis.* 4: 229–34, 1959.
182. Stokes, D.K. Lorazepam in anxiety associated with chronic enteritis and ulcerative colitis. *J. Clin. Psychiat.* 39 (Suppl. 10, sec. 2): 53–57, 1978.
183. Zisook, S. Ulcerative colitis: case responding to treatment with lithium carbonate. *JAMA* 219: 755, 1972.
184. Rask-Madsen, J., Baastrup, P.C., Schwartz, P. Lithium-induced hyperpolarization of the human rectum in vitro. *Brit. Med. J.* 2: 496–98, 1972.
185. Steiner, M., Elizur, A., & Davidson, S. A psychosomatic triad in a bipolar patient. *J. Nerv. Ment. Dis.* 164: 359–61, 1977.

Index

abdominal bloating, 132
abnormal swallowing syndrome, 222
abuse, substance, 18
accident proneness, 181
acetylcholine, 122
achalasia, 1, 4
ACTH, 37
adipose depot, 60
adrenalectomy, 95
adrenaline, 44
adrenal steroids, 114
aerophagia, 278
affective disorders, 170, 172
aggression, 113, 117, 167, 170, 172, 176
aging, 191, 197
agitation, 111, 277
airflow, 212
alcoholic excess, 108
alcoholism, 196
aldosterone, 37, 117
alexithymia, 133, 236, 238, 252
alkalosis, 18
alveolar hyperventilation, 210, 212
ambivalence, 139, 165
amenorrhea, 4, 143, 144
amnesia, 216
amobarbitol, 117
amygdala, 162, 168
anaclitic dependence, 133
anemia, hemolytic, 262
anger, 6, 172
angioedema, 266
angiotensin, 44, 117
anorexia, 3, 4, 135, 143, 144, 261
antibody titer, 98
anticonvulsant drugs, 173
anxiety, 3, 11, 111, 117, 135, 162, 205, 248,
    259, 260, 269, 270, 276
appendicitis, 134
appetite, aberrations of, 131, 259
arousal, internal, 205
arrhythmias, 182, 273, 275
arthritis, rheumatoid, 179

aspirin, 48
asthma, 22, 25, 179, 186, 218, 259, 264
    biogenic, 23, 26, 28, 237
asymptomatic polysomnographic findings, 218
atropine, 117
"attractiveness," 114
attrition, 72
autistic thinking, 165
automatism, 162, 219
autonomic changes, 162
autonomic nervous system, 24

backache, 131, 259
basal ganglia disease, 169
basal metabolism, 58
behavior, 161, 163
behavior modification, 270
bemegride, 164
bewilderment, 162
biofeedback, 238, 270
bisexuality, 139
bloating, 108, 124
blood-flow studies, 198
body image, 53
body weight, 54
borderline states, 211
bradykinin, 44
brain damage, organic, 171, 197
brain diseases, organic, 215
brainstem pathology, 169
brain tumors, 198
breast tenderness, 132
breathing, 15, 30, 259
bromocriptine, 118, 122
bronchoconstriction, 29
bruxism, 218, 221

calcification, dystrophis, 269
calorie intake, 56
cardiac output, 35
cardiospasm, 5
cardiovascular regulatory mechanisms, 212
cardiovascular symptoms, 218

castration, 113, 114
cataplexy, 214
catatonia, 111, 169
catecholamines, 44
cathexes, 139
central nervous system (CNS), 208
cerebral ischemia, 232
childbearing, 140
chloasma gravidarum, 132
chronic obstructive pulmonary disease (COPD), 20
circadian fluctuations, 125
circumstantiality, 172
clomiphene citrate, 147
CNS hypersomnolence, idiopathic, 215
CNS infections, 214, 219
CNS neoplasia, 214
colectomy, 9
colic, 108, 181
colitis, 8
collagen abnormality, 244
compulsiveness, 269
confusion, 111
constipation, 10, 108, 131, 259, 278
conversion, 41, 186, 211
coronary insufficiency, 198
coronary occlusion, 273
coronary thrombosis, 237
corticosterone, 100
cortisol, 116
couvade, 129, 130, 134, 137
cravings, 131
criminality, 108, 167
cyclic heat response, 114

death, sudden, 273
dehydration, 131, 182
deja vu, 169
delirium, 193
delusions, 41, 111, 169, 207
dementia, 193, 197, 198, 199
dependence, 172
depersonalization, 169
depressed mood reactions, 206
depression, 4, 11, 108, 110, 111, 122, 134, 135, 170, 172, 193, 198, 199, 200, 201, 206, 211, 216, 259, 269, 271
dermatitis, atopic, 268
dermatoses, 182
dexamethazone, 113

diabetes, 52, 237
diarrhea, 8, 9, 131, 259, 278
digestive bite, 6
DIMS, 204, 205, 208
disinhibition, 216, 271
displeasure, 6
distractability, 216
dopamine, 47, 119
dream anxiety attacks, 218
dreaming, 206
drug reactions, 198
duodenal ulcer, 278
dyspepsia, 278
dysphagia, 4, 278
dyspnea, 16, 20, 29
dystrophy, myotonic, 214

eczema, 266, 267
edema, 108
EEG, 164, 198
EKG abnormalities, 213
elation, 172
emaciation, 4
emotion, 3, 111, 160, 162, 172
emphysema, 15
encephalitis, 169
endorphins, 47
enteritis, regional, 282
enuresis, 108, 218, 220
envy, parturition, 134
epigastric discomfort, 132
epilepsy, 108, 157, 215, 219
erections, painful, 218
erotism, respiratory, 16
erythema, 183
estrogen, 113
etiocholanolone, 150
euphoria, 172
evening fussiness, 181
excessive somnolence, disorders of (DOES), 204, 210, 215
externality, 63

fatherhood, 129
fatigue, 216, 259
fear, 3, 8, 162
feminine identifications, 130, 133
follicle stimulating hormone (FDH), 147
frustration, 248